ISLAM IN INTER-WAR EUROPE

NATHALIE CLAYER
ERIC GERMAIN
editors

Islam in Inter-War Europe

Columbia University Press
New York

Columbia University Press
Publishers Since 1893
New York

Library of Congress Cataloging-in-Publication Data

Islam in inter-war Europe / Nathalie Clayer, Eric Germain, editors.
p. cm.
Papers from the Islam in Europe in the Inter-war Period: Networks, Status, Challenges conference, held Dec. 10-11, 2004 in Paris.
Includes bibliographical references and index.
ISBN 978-0-231-70100-6 (hbk. : alk. paper)
1. Muslims—Europe—History—20th century—Congresses. 2. Muslims--Europe—Social life and customs--20th century--Congresses. 3. Muslims--Europe—Social conditions—20th century—Congresses. I. Clayer, Nathalie. II. Germain, Eric, 1970- III. Title: Islam in interwar Europe.

D726.72.M87I85 2008
305.6'9709409041—dc22

2008018222

∞

Columbia University Press books are printed on permanent and durable acid-free paper.
This book is printed on paper with recycled content.
Printed in India

c 10 9 8 7 6 5 4 3 2 1

CONTENTS

THE CONTRIBUTORS

Raja ADAL is a doctoral candidate at the Department of History, Harvard University working on the modern history of the Middle East and Japan. His publications on Shakib Arslan include "Constructing Transnational Islam: The East-West Network of Shakib Arslan" and an index of Arslan's journal *La Nation Arabe.*

Humayun ANSARI is Professor of the History of Islam and Cultural Diversity at Royal Holloway, University of London. His particular research interests are Islam, migration, ethnicity, identity and multiculturalism in Western societies. He has advised and addressed a wide spectrum of organisations in the public, private and voluntary sectors, and has contributed extensively to local, national and international print and broadcast media. He is the author, among other publications, of *The Emergence of Socialist Thought among North Indian Muslims (1917-1947)* (Lahore 1990) and *'The Infidel Within', Muslims in Britain Since 1800* (London 2004).

Muhammed ARUÇI is a researcher at the Centre for Islamic Studies in Istanbul, where he is the head of the Balkan research units. Since 2001, he has also been a lecturer at St. Kliment Ohridski University, in Sofia, in the Department of Arabic Language and Islamology, and since 2005 he has been teaching in the Faculty of Islamic Sciences in Sarajevo University and in The Faculty of Philology (Department of Turkology) in Prishtina (Kosova). His particular research interests are Islamic sciences (especially *kalam*), Islam in The Balkans, history of Balkan Muslims' migration, ethnicity, identity and multiculturalism. His main publications are *Kemal Efendi Aruçi, Şiirlerim* (Skopje 1999), *Vjershat e Mia* (Skopje 2000) and *Abu Mansour al-Maturidi, Kitab al-Tawhid* (Ankara 2003; Beirut 2006). He also wrote many entries concerning Balkans in *Islam Ansiklopedisi* (Istanbul, HYPERLINK "http://www.isam.org.tr/" www.isam.org.tr).

Yannis BONOS has studied history and anthropology at the Department of History and Ethnology of the Democritus University of Thrace (Komotini). He is interested in both Greek and Turkish history and is preparing a doctoral thesis on the Turkish language press of Greek Thrace during the inter-war period at the Ecole des Hautes Etudes en Sciences Sociales (Paris). His publications include two entries, "Inkilab" and "Osman Nuri Fettahoglu", for the database of the project "Encyclopedia of the Greek Press, 1784-1996" under the direction of L. Droulia and P. Koutsopanagou.

Xavier BOUGAREL is a researcher at the research unit "Turkish and Ottoman Studies" of the Centre National de la Recherche Scientifique (CNRS, Paris). He has been a consultant to the World Bank, in charge of the research *Local Level Institutions and Social Capital in Bosnia-Herzegovina* (2002), and a visiting scholar at the Centre for Russian and East European Studies of the University of Pittsburgh (2003). His main publications are *Bosnie. Anatomie d'un conflit,* Paris: La Découverte (1996, translated into Serbo-Croatian in 2004), *Le nouvel Islam balkanique. Les musulmans, acteurs du post-communisme (1990-2000)* (Paris 2001), co-edited with Nathalie Clayer, and *The New Bosnian Mosaic. Identities, Memories and Moral Claims in a Post-War Society* (Aldershot 2007), co-edited with Elissa Helms and Ger Duijzings.

Nathalie CLAYER is a senior fellow researcher at the National Centre for Scientific Research (CNRS, Paris), in the department of "Etudes turques et Ottomanes" (EHESS). A specialist on Islam, religious questions and nationalism in the Balkans, especially among the Albanians, her main publications are *Mystiques, Etat et société. Les Halvetis dans l'aire balkanique de la fin du XVe siècle à nos jours* (Leiden-New York-Köln 1994), *Le nouvel Islam balkanique. Les musulmans, acteurs du post-communisme (1990-2000)* (Paris 2001), co-edited with Xavier Bougarel, *Religion et nation chez les Albanais, XIX-XX siècles* (Istanbul 2003), and *Aux origines du nationalisme albanais. La naissance d'une nation majoritairement musulmane en Europe* (Paris 2007).

Sebastian CWIKLINSKI studied Turkic studies and history at Freie Universität Berlin (Germany), where he is currently completing his PhD. From 2004 to 2007 he was scientific researcher at the same university and since 1999 he has been teaching at Freie Universität and several academies in Berlin (Tatar, Bashkir languages; Tatar, late Ottoman history and Turkish language). His main research interests include the history of the Turkic Muslims in the Russian Empire, the history of the late Ottoman Empire and of contemporary Turkey, Muslim migrants in Germany. He is the author of more than 60 publications, among others: *Die Wolga an der Spree. Tataren und Baschkiren in Berlin* (Berlin 2000); *Wolgatataren im Deutschland des Zweiten Weltkriegs. Deutsche Ostpolitik und tatarischer Nationalismus* (Berlin 2002); "Tatars and Bashkirs in Berlin from the End of the 19th Century to the Beginning of World War II", *The Turks,* Bd. 5 (Ankara 2002), pp. 1004-1014; "Tatarismus versus Bulgarismus: Der „erste Streit" in der postsowjetischen tatarischen Historiographie", *FORUM für osteuropäische Ideen- und Zeitgeschichte,* 9 (2005) 1, pp. 167-202.

Eric GERMAIN is a research fellow at the Institut d'Etudes de l'Islam et des Sociétés du Monde Musulman (IISMM) in Paris. His current work focuses on pioneering Muslim Missionary organizations and Islam-Christian relations from the last decades of the nineteenth century to the first half of the twentieth century. His latest publications are *L'Afrique du Sud musulmane. Histoire des relations entre Indiens et Malais du Cap* (Paris 2006) and "Southern Hemisphere Diasporic Communities in the Building of an International Muslim Public Opinion at the Turn of the Twentieth Century", *Comparative Studies of South Asia, Africa and the Middle East,* vol. 27, no.1, 2007, Duke University Press, pp. 126-138.

Fikret KARČIĆ is professor of comparative legal history at the Faculty of Law, University of Sarajevo. A graduate of the Madrasa Gazi Husrevbeg in Sarajevo, he has obtained LLB at the Faculty of Law in Sarajevo and MA and PhD in legal studies at the Faculty of Law,

University of Belgrade. As a legal historian by training, his main academic interests are the history of Islamic law and institutions, modern developments in Islamic legal thought and practice in post-Ottoman Bosnia, and comparative legal history and modern codifications. His publications include *Šerijatski sudovi u Jugoslaviji 1918-1941* (The Sharia Courts in Yugoslavia 1918-1941) (Sarajevo 1986); *Društveno-pravni aspekt islamskog reformizma* (Social and Legal Aspect of Islamic Reformism) (Sarajevo 1990); *The Bosniak and the Challenges of Modernity—Late Ottoman and Habsburg Times* (Sarajevo 1999) among others.

Richard LAWLESS is Emeritus Reader in Middle Eastern Studies, University of Durham, UK and a former Research Associate, Queen Elizabeth House, University of Oxford, UK. He is a geographer and migration specialist particularly interested in an historical perspective of transnationalism, especially transnational networks among migrants during the late nineteenth and early twentieth centuries. He is engaged in a long-term study of emigration from Yemen during this period and the transnational networks of Yemeni communities in both Europe and the USA. Recent publications include (joint editor) *Middle East and North African Immigrants in Europe: Islam, citizenship and transnational links* (London 2005).

Wolfgang G. SCHWANITZ, Middle East historian, researches American and European relations to Islamic regions. Born in Germany and son of diplomats, he was raised in Egypt and lives near Princeton. He taught Middle East history and politics at universities in Berlin and Potsdam and teaches at Burlington County College, New Jersey. Educated at Leipzig University as Arabist, he received his PhD there on Egypt's *infitah* in 1985. He headed the research group "Middle Eastern History" at the Academy of Science, was researcher at the Centre of Modern Orient in Berlin, and visiting fellow in Cairo, Princeton, and Washington. He has edited ten and authored four books on the Middle East (http://www.trafoberlin.de/Autoren/schwanitz_wolfgang.htm). Forthcoming: *German Islam Policy*.

Mark SEDGWICK is an Associate Professor of Arab studies at Aarhus University, Denmark. He previously taught Middle Eastern history for many years at the American University in Cairo. His publications include *Against the Modern World: Traditionalism and the Secret Intellectual History of the Twentieth Century* (New York 2004), *Saints and Sons: The Making and Remaking of the Rashidi Ahmadi Sufi Order, 1799-2000* (Leiden 2005), *Sufism: The Essentials* (Cairo 2000) and *Islam & Muslims: A Guide to Diverse Experience in a Modern World* (Boston 2006).

INTRODUCTION

THE STATE OF THE ART: A LIMITATION IN SPACE AND TIME

Any search on library catalogues under the key-words "Islam/ Muslim/Europe/West" will show how interest in Muslim communities living in Europe has increased greatly over the past two decades.[1] A closer look at this bibliography reveals that these publications often share limitations of two kinds. The first one is spatial, arising directly from a mentality conditioned by the Cold War, leading several scholars simply to forget the Balkans and Eastern Europe when studying the Muslim communities of Europe. The second limitation, possibly linked with the previous one, is to regard Islam in (Western) Europe as a very recent phenomenon, an outcome of the waves of immigration during the 1950s and 1960s. Many global approaches to Islam in Europe have shown such limitations, but even works that mention the inter-war years such as Jørgen Nielsen's *Towards a European Islam* (EUP, 1992) or *Islam in Europe: The Politics of Religion and Community* (Macmillan, 1997) edited by Stephen Vertovec and Ceri Peach, reveal the rather scarce information available for the period. When such information is available, it is found in publications dealing either with migration studies[2] or with political analysis of the anti-colonial struggle

[1] For bibliographies see: Sossie Andezian *et al.*, "Bibliographie : l'islam contemporain en Europe occidentale", *Archives de Sciences Sociales des Religions*, II, 68, (October-December 1989), pp. 151–65; Dasseto, Felice and Yves Conrad (eds), *Musulmans en Europe occidentale—Bibliographie commentée*, Paris: L'Harmattan, 1996; Franck J. Buijs and Jan Rath, *Muslims in Europe: The State of Research*, October 2002, pp. 31–53, available on http://users.fmg.uva.nl/jrath.

[2] As Gérard Noiriel, *Le creuset français*, Paris: Seuil, 1998; Benjamin Stora, *Ils venaient d'Algérie, l'immigration algérienne en France, 1912–1992*, Paris: Fayard, 1992; David Assouline et Mehdi Lallaoui, *Un siècle d'immigration en France*, 3 vols., Paris: Syros,

organised from Europe,[3] and Islam is not the main focus of the work/study. As for the studies made in Communist Eastern Europe, they rarely tackled religious issues concerning the Muslim minorities. Furthermore, they were often conducted with an ideological bias, and it was difficult for foreign scholars to carry out research on this subject. Thus, the interest in a religious community *per se* is quite recent.

In recent years the subject has begun to attract a new type of interest within Muslim communities themselves, a concern that has been welcomed, even sponsored, by governmental bodies within the framework of their integration policies. In Germany, one might cite the example of the serial publications issued by the Commissioner for Foreigners of the Senate.[4] In France, this trend is a little more recent, as illustrated by a book on the Bobigny Muslim cemetery in the suburbs of Paris,[5] a publication that forms part of the collection sponsored by the "FASILD Fund" of the Ministry of Social Affairs. In a dialectical relationship, this "rediscovered history" is used pragmatically to support the demands of the community,[6] even if at the very same time it illustrates the genuine interest currently expressed by local Muslim populations anxious to stress their European roots.

In the Balkans, the political transformations that occurred with the collapse of the Socialist regimes also led to a re-reading of the recent past of the local Muslim communities. However, as in

---

1996; Ralph Schor, *L'opinion française et les étrangers en France (1919–1939)*, Paris: Publications de la Sorbonne, 1985; Neil MacMaster, *Colonial Migrants and Racism: Algerians in France, 1900–62*, Basingstoke: Macmillan, 1997.

3 Such as Claude Liauzu, *Aux origines des tiersmondismes. Colonisés et anti-colonialisme en France entre les deux guerres*, Paris: L'Harmattan, 1982; Benjamin Stora, *Aux sources du nationalisme algérien*, Paris: L'Harmattan, 1989.

4 Such as Joachim Oesterheld and Lothar Günther, *Inder in Berlin*, Berlin: Ausländerbeauftragte des Senats (AS), December 1997; Marin Greve and Tülay Çınar, *Das Türkische Berlin*, Berlin: AS, November 1998; Sebastian Cwiklinski, *Die Wolga an der Spree. Tataren und Baschkiren in Berlin*, Berlin: AS, July 2000.

5 Marie-Ange d'Adler, *Le cimetière musulman de Bobigny—Lieu de mémoire d'un siècle d'immigration*, Paris: Autrement, 2005.

6 One example can be found in Hakim El-Ghissassi, "Le projet de mosquée de Bobigny", 17 November 2004, www.sezame.info.

Western Europe, this also relates to identity claims linked to processes of social and political restructuring taking place in the former Yugoslavia, Albania and Bulgaria.

These local monographs produced all over Europe have significantly increased our knowledge of the inter-war period. Nevertheless, the Muslim communities of the inter-war period should still be considered as largely understudied, especially if we consider how the amount of academic research available varies from one place to another. Many countries lack the pioneering works that have been provided by Richard Lawless and Humayun Ansari for Britain,[7] by the late Gerhard Höpp for Germany[8] and by Alexandre Popovic for the Balkans.[9]

INTER-WAR EUROPE: A "GLOBALISED" SPACE TO REDISCOVER

Until today, no work had conducted a study of Islam in the interwar year for the whole of Europe. In particular, the networks that connected the Muslim communities in Europe at that time have been largely ignored. This very aspect appeared to us as the most salient one and led to the idea of convening a workshop on Islam in Europe in the inter-war period. Indeed, it was while discussing our respective works on the reform of Islam in Albania and on the Ahmadi-Lahori missions of Berlin and Woking that we discovered the correspondence that passed between several Albanian religious

[7] Richard I. Lawless, *From Ta'izz to Tyneside: an Arab Community in the North-East of England during the Early Twentieth Century*, University of Exeter Press, 1995 and Humayun Ansari, *'The Infidel Within'—Muslims in Britain since 1800*, London: Hurst, 2004.

[8] Among the works published by the Zentrum Moderner Orient (ZMO) of Berlin one might quote: *Arabische und Islamische Periodika in Berlin und Brandenburg 1915–45. Geschichtlicher Abriß und Bibliographie*, Berlin: Verlag Das Arabische Buch, 1994 ; *In fremder Erde. Zur Geschichte und Gegenwart der islamischen Bestattung in Deutschland* (edited with Gerdien Jonker), Berlin: Verlag das Arabische Buch, 1996; *Wessen Geschichte? Muslimische Erfahrungen historischer Zäsuren im 20. Jahrhundert* (edited with Henner Fürtig), Berlin: Verlag das Arabische Buch, 1998; *Texte aus der Fremde. Arabische politische Publizistik in Deutschland 1896–1945. Eine Bibliographie*, Berlin: Verlag das Arabische Buch, 2000.

[9] Alexandre Popovic, *L'islam balkanique—Les musulmans du Sud-Est européen dans la période post-ottomane*, Berlin-Wiesbaden: Otto Harrassowitz, 1986.

leaders and the Lahori missionaries.[10] This led us to exchange views and information, and later on it provided a strong incentive to undertake a more ambitious project that would bring together scholars from all over Europe, especially those from the Western, Eastern and Balkan parts of Europe.

The workshop "Islam in Europe in the Inter-war Period: Networks, Status, Challenges" took place in Paris on 10–11 December 2004, and was co-organised by the Institut d'Etudes de l'Islam et des Sociétés du Monde Musulman (IISMM), the Association Française d'Etudes sur les Balkans (AFEBALK), and the Etudes Turques et Ottomanes Department (UMR 8032-CNRS).[11] The two-day roundtable and the correspondence that followed provided an opportunity for scholars to cross-nurture their nationally-based works and, by offering a general view, to highlight linkages and stimulate research on new fields.

The chapters presented in this book are the direct result of this fruitful exchange and are intended to be a first step towards a global approach to Islam in Europe that will later be expanded to include the decades before 1918. As for the post-Second World War period, the historical perspective given by this book might improve the understanding of contemporary dynamics of Muslim communities. In this way, a long-term perspective should also help to encourage a reassessment of the issues concerning the building of a European Islam, the status of Muslim minorities, and the use of Islam by political authorities, as well as the *modus operandi* of transnational networks.

The period of time covered is justified by the fact that the two world wars constitute turning-points for the presence of Muslims in Europe, as we shall see below. Only the contribution by Wolfgang Schwanitz will extend beyond the inter-war period because

[10] Nathalie Clayer, "La Ahmadiyya Lahori et la réforme de l'islam albanais dans l'entre-deux-guerres", in V. Bouillier and C. Servan-Schreiber (eds), *De l'Arabie à l'Himalaya, chemins croisés*, Paris: Maisonneuve et Larose, 2004, pp. 211–28.

[11] The workshop "Islam in Europe in the Inter-war Period: Networks, Status, Challenges" took place in Paris on 10–11 December 2004; we thank the three institutions and the kind support of the Bibliothèque de Documentation Internationale Contemporaine and the Ministère délégué à la Recherche.

of its focus on the use of *jihad* by the German authorities as part of their military strategy. Concerning the geographical scope, the decision not to include Turkey and the Western parts of the USSR in our field of research is not meant to deny their European character, but is rather motivated by the specificity of their respective state religious policies. It should be noted that the very same reasons led to the absence of Kemalist Turkey and the Communist USSR from the European Muslim Congress of 1935 in Geneva. But it certainly does not mean that those countries were not influential on the European Islamic scene as the chapters by Raja Adal, Muhammed Aruçi, Yannis Bonos and Sebastian Cwiklinski will show.

Four main issues are addressed in this book. The first one, which arises from our discovery of the activities of a transnational Muslim Mission in Albania, is the existence of networks through which Islam was diffused, social activities led, ideas exchanged, and literature and money circulated. The second issue is the question of the building of a "European Islam", often seen today as a new phenomenon. In the third part, we focus on the relations between Islam and politics, examining the "Muslim agenda" of European governments. Finally, we try to look in depth at the strategies and debates existing within these European Muslim societies.

Of course, all these questions are linked together, and some contributions address a great variety of issues. For that reason, as well as to consider the cases that were not covered by the contributions, we will present some reflections on the subject at the beginning of each of the four parts, drawing upon the different chapters, as well as upon other relevant studies. But before addressing each of these themes, it is necessary to present a profile of these European Muslim communities.

AN OVERVIEW OF MUSLIM COMMUNITIES IN EUROPE AT THE TURN OF THE CENTURY

The Historical Roots

The presence of Islam and Muslims in Europe is not a phenomenon restricted to the twentieth century. Muslim rule in Spain (from the eighth century till the fall of Granada in 1492) and in Sicily (from the ninth to the eleventh century) is well known, even if often romanticised in the myth of an Andalusian Golden Age. In Spain, the last Muslims or secret Muslims, the "Moriscos", were expelled at the beginning of the seventeenth century, but at that time there was already another massive presence of Islam on the European continent, as a result of the Ottoman conquest which took place from the mid-fourteenth century, long before the fall of Constantinople (1453). During two centuries, Ottoman control gradually expanded over South-Eastern Europe, even if the troops of the Sultan twice failed to conquer Vienna (in 1529 and 1683). Consequently, a Muslim population appeared across the Balkans, as a result of different processes: the establishment of administrative, military and religious power structures, a colonisation policy in some areas, and conversion to Islam of a part of the local inhabitants. Nevertheless, those people who professed the religion of the Ottoman power remained on the whole less numerous than the non-Muslims. In addition, Tatar soldiers from the Golden Horde migrating westward settled in Eastern Europe from the late fourteenth century; this led to the establishment of small Muslim communities in Poland and Lithuania.

In Western Europe, contacts with Muslims occurred mainly on the occasion of visiting missions by diplomats from Turkey, Persia and India.[12] If those were the most visible "Mohammedans", they were not the only ones. One might note some Ottoman prisoners of war such as those in Vienna after the siege of 1683 and other soldiers such as the Muslim unit and later even a regiment in the eighteenth-century Prussian army.[13] But, more generally, it was in the main cosmopolitan ports and trading centres that Muslims were to be found. They were merchants and seamen (lascars), found in

[12] The most notable examples would be the Persian embassy of Mehemed Raza-Bey to Versailles in 1715, the Ottoman Resmi el-Hadsch Ahmet Effendi's stay in Berlin in 1763 or Mirza Abu Taleb Khan's visit to London and Paris at the very end of the eighteenth century.

[13] Jørgen S. Nielsen, "Muslimūn. II. Les musulmans immigrés en Europe occidentale", *Encyclopédie de l'islam*, 2nd édition, VII, Leiden: Brill, 1992, p. 699. Muhammad Salim Abdullah, . . . *und gab ihnen sein Königswort: Berlin, Preussen, Bundesrepublik: Ein Abriss der Geschichte der islamischen Minderheit in Deutschland*, Altenberge: CIS-Verlag, 1987, pp. 18–23.

continuously increasing numbers from the seventeenth century. Some of them played on their "exotic image", launching small businesses such as the "Hindostanee Coffee House" opened in London in 1807.[14] In Marseilles, a "Turkish cemetery" already existed before 1723, where Muslim slaves used on galleys were buried, and where there was also a small mosque.[15]

The age of nation-states

The nineteenth century saw many changes in the situation of Islam in Europe. In South-Eastern Europe, this century witnessed the gradual decline of the Ottoman Empire. Its Hungarian territories had already been lost at the end of the seventeenth century, but the major territorial losses began after 1800. After diverse episodes, the autonomy of Serbia (1829), the independence of Greece and the autonomy of Moldavia and Wallachia (1830) were recognised. At the Congress of Berlin in 1878, the independence of Serbia (which acquired the regions of Niš, Pirot and Vranje), Montenegro and Romania was confirmed, and a small Bulgarian principality was created North of the Balkan range, while Bosnia-Herzegovina was placed under Austro-Hungarian control. In 1881, Greece received Thessaly and Arta, and four years later, the autonomous province of Eastern Rumelia was united with Bulgaria. As a result the Ottoman Empire retained only Macedonia, Kosovo, Thrace and Epirus.

Although international treaties generally guaranteed some rights for the Muslims in the new autonomous or independent (Christian) states, many of them were killed during, or just after, the conflicts which led to the end of Ottoman rule; others were expelled or fled to the remaining Ottoman territories, refusing to live under Christian rule, while others were forcibly converted. Before 1878, only a few of them remained in Greece or Serbia. Nevertheless, from 1878 onwards, although the new treaties did not totally

14 On Dean Mahomed's life in Cork, London and Brighton, see Michael H. Fisher, *The First Indian Author in English–Dean Mahomed (1759–1851) in India, Ireland and England*, Oxford India Paperbacks: OUP, 1996.

15 Michel Renard, "Aperçu sur l'histoire de l'islam à Marseille, 1813–1962. Pratiques religieuses et encadrement des Nord-Africains", *Outre-Mers*, XC, 340–41 (2003), pp. 269–94 (see pp. 270–71).

prevent the states from implementing negative policies towards the Muslims and the latter from emigrating, sizeable groups of Muslims remained under Bulgarian, Romanian, Serbian, Montenegrin, Greek, Cretan or Austro-Hungarian rule. On the other side, in those Balkan regions still under Ottoman rule, the proportion of Muslims increased because of the arrival of refugees, even if some were also settled in Istanbul or across Anatolia.

In contrast to the precarious position of Muslims in the Balkans, the nineteenth century saw "the Crescent rising in the West" with the formation of visible, if not permanent, Muslim communities in Western Europe. They were made up of students, traders and a significant number of Muslim seamen on shore in the main European ports.[16] In Marseilles, a second Muslim presence consisted of pilgrims from the French colonies in transit to or from Mecca.[17] There were also an increasing number of converts including some flamboyant characters such as Dr Philippe Grenier, elected to the French parliament in 1896, and the Liverpool solicitor W.H. Quilliam, the self-styled "*Shaikh al-Islam* of the British Isles", who founded the Liverpool Moslem Institute and later Mosque in 1887. In 1897, a German scholar of Oriental languages published a statistical handbook of the Muslim population around the world. This compilation based on official census data, missionary sources, and a fairly large variety of more or less scientific publications gives the following estimates of Muslims in Western Europe:[18] 2,700 in the United Kingdom with one hundred for Gibraltar, 2,600 in France, 800 in Italy, 750 in Spain, and 150 in Portugal. Germany is not mentioned, but we know of the existence of the nucleus of a Muslim community made up of students, merchants, diplomats, and even two German converts who started some proselytisation.[19] Despite

[16] Rosina Visram, *Ayah, Lascars and Princes, Indians in Britain 1700–1947*, London: Pluto, 1986, and Fred Halliday, *Arabs in Exile, Yemeni Migrants in Urban Britain*, London: IB Tauris, 1992.

[17] M. Renard, "Aperçu sur l'histoire de l'islam à Marseille", p. 273.

[18] Dr. Hubert Jansen, *Verbreitung des Islâms mit Angabe der verschiedenen Riten, Sekten und religiösen Bruderschaften in den verschiedenen Ländern der Erde 1890 bis 1897*, Friedrichshagen, 1897, pp. 9–11.

[19] "Europe", *Revue du Monde Musulman*, X, 1 (January 1910), p. 103.

the fact that Jansen's figures are often estimates, they give some idea of the presence of Muslims in the Western part of Europe before 1914.[20]

The Great War milestone

The First World War, preceded by the Balkan Wars (1912–13), was a turning point for the Muslim presence in the whole European continent. In the Balkans, the political map was reshaped several times during the conflicts, to which we must add the Greek-Turkish war of 1919–22, as well as the aftermath of the fall of the Habsburg and Ottoman Empires. The new Republic of Turkey retained control of only a small piece of land in Europe, Eastern Thrace, while the rest of the former Ottoman territories in the Balkans was shared out between the existing states and a principality of Albania created in 1913, which was unique because it had a Muslim majority. Many Muslims had to leave the Balkans for Istanbul or Anatolia during this period, the most important exodus being organised by the League of Nations in 1923, with the massive exchange of population between Greece and Turkey.

In Western Europe, the presence of colonial troops and the practice of importing indentured foreign labour brought large numbers of Muslims to serve in France on the war front or in factories. The number of foreign Muslim workers recruited by the French government alone included some 120,000 Algerians, 35,000 Moroccans and 20,000 Tunisians, official figures that clearly underestimated the real numbers.[21] A similar appeal was made by the army and, according to figures of the Ministry of War for the Tunisian contingent alone, some 16,509 soldiers died for France

[20] Some years later, 4,000 to 5,000 North-Africans were registered in France, among them 2,000 were working in Marseilles in oil factories, refineries, smelting works, mainly as unskilled workers. The other Muslim migrants were mainly working in Paris or in the coal mines of Northern France (M. Renard, "Aperçu sur l'histoire de l'islam à Marseille", p. 275 ; M.-A. d'Adler, *Le cimetière musulman de Bobigny*, p. 64).

[21] Gilbert Meynier, *L'Algérie révélée*, Genève: Droz, 1981. Claude Carlier and Guy Pedroncini (eds), *Les Troupes Coloniales dans la Grande Guerre*, Paris: Economica, 1997.

out of a total of 62,461.[22] But the largest number of Muslim soldiers was found among the 200,000 West African soldiers, collectively known as *tirailleurs sénégalais*.[23] In Germany, which had no colonial troops in Europe, Muslims were mainly found among its prisoners of war: Russian Tatars, British Indians, and French North and West Africans. They were interned at the Wünsdorf camp, near Berlin, where the German propaganda department decided to build an impressive wooden mosque and to appoint an imam.[24] In France, the state authorities set aside a hospital in the colonial park of Nogent-sur-Marne (East of Paris) for wounded Muslims and, in 1916, a wooden mosque was built there in order to challenge the lavish wooden mosque erected by the Germans for the Muslim prisoners held in the Wünsdorf camp.[25]

After the war, streams of immigration and emigration of Muslim populations continued affecting many countries, but this was particularly obvious in the Balkans. In order to get a better picture of this Muslim presence in Europe between the two wars, it is helpful to divide the continent into three main areas: Western Europe, where the Muslims were mainly immigrants from colonial territories; Central and Northern Europe (including Germany, deprived of all its colonies after 1918), where they were mainly local Tatars, refugees from Russia or people from the former Austro-Hungarian Empire; and South-Eastern Europe, where numerically important Muslim populations were to be found as a result of Ottoman domination.

[22] Eric Derro and Pascal Le Pautremat, *Héros de Tunisie*, Tunis: Cérès, 2006; as for the Algerian troops, about 25,000 Muslim soldiers lost their lives on French soil according to Alain Boyer, *L'Institut Musulman de la Mosquée de Paris*, Paris: CHEAM, 1992, p. 2. For the British Army, see Rosina Visram, "The First World War and the Indian soldiers", *Indo-British Review*, 16, 2 (June 1989), pp. 17–26.

[23] Marc Michel, 'Le concours de l'A.O.F. à la France pendant la première guerre mondiale', unpublished PhD thesis, Paris I, 1979, p. 886 ; Joe Lunn, *Memoirs of the Maelstrom—A Senegalese Oral History of the First World War*, Portsmouth, NH: Heinemann, 1999. Senegal only witnessed the forced recruitment of some 30,000 men, of which 7,000 died on the front line.

[24] Sebastian Cwiklinski, *Die Wolga an der Spree. Tataren*, p. 22; Margot Kahleyss, *Muslime in Brandenburg—Kriegsgefangene im 1. Weltkrieg. Ansichten und Absichten*, Berlin: Museum für Völkerkunde, 1998.

[25] Pascal Le Pautremat, *La politique musulmane de la France au XXe siècle*, Paris: Maisonneuve et Larose, 2003, pp. 328–33.

CONTRASTS IN THE SITUATION OF MUSLIMS IN EUROPE AFTER THE WAR

Muslims in the colonial metropoles of Western Europe

In Western Europe, the most significant Muslim communities were to be found in France and Britain even though, from the 1930s, they also developed in other countries having Muslim colonies such as the Netherlands, Spain and Italy.[26] In most of these countries, the Muslim population belonged to one or more of the categories of workers, colonial troops,[27] students, traders, diplomats, and local converts.

With its considerable colonial Muslim population, the French metropolis contained the most numerous Muslim community in Western Europe. After 1918, the country's industry continued to rely on an important immigrant workforce, mostly recruited in other European countries but also in North Africa, and especially from the Kabylia region of Algeria. Officially, North African workers numbered 59,088 in 1919, 36,300 in 1921, 69,800 in 1926, and 102,000 in 1931, making the highest concentration of labour migrants from Muslim countries in Western Europe.[28] Their presence in the major industrial suburbs of Paris and Lyons was closely watched by the French authorities. So were the Sufi brotherhoods and political associations such as the *Étoile Nord-Africaine* founded by the Algerian activist Messali Hadj, who represented France at the Geneva Congress of 1935.[29] Apart from the immigrants working in the industrial sector, there were also hundreds, if not

[26] A significant number of Muslims lived in the colonial territories under the domination of those countries. According to Arthur Pellegrin (*L'Islam dans le Monde*, Paris: Payot, 1937, pp. 178–9) they were for the Netherlands: 54,000,000 in the Dutch East Indies and around 4,000 in Dutch Guyana and the neighbouring islands; for Italy: 15,000 in Rhodes and surrounding islands, 670,000 in Libya and 4,500,000 in East Africa; Spain: 600,000 in the Spanish zone of Morocco, 32,000 in the Rio de Oro and 34,000 in Spanish Guinea. (In fact the figure for Spanish Guinea was more probably 340 or 3,400.)

[27] Belkacem Recham, *Les Musulmans algériens dans l'armée française (1919–1945)*, Paris: L'Harmattan, 1996.

[28] P. Le Pautremat, *La politique musulmane de la France,* pp. 288–9.

[29] Benjamin Stora, *Messali Hadj (1898–1974) Pionnier du nationalisme algérien*, Paris: L'Harmattan, 1986.

thousands, of Muslim seamen from France's West African colonies[30] but also, as in other European merchant shipping fleets, from Yemen and Somalia. Some of those Muslim temporary sojourners decided to settle permanently finding employment on the docks and became part of the cosmopolitan population of Marseilles, Bordeaux or Le Havre. In the 1920s and 1930s, the Muslim population was mainly to be found in Paris and its suburbs, in the North (Nord and Pas-de-Calais departments), and more generally in the main industrial cities of Central France (such as Lyons, Saint-Etienne and Clermont-Ferrand) and in the Mediterranean region.[31] The visibility of Islam in France was strengthened by the opening in the heart of Paris of a Muslim Institute and a Grand Mosque in 1926, an institution dedicated to Muslim soldiers who lost their lives for France during the First World War.

In Britain, there were several hundred British converts scattered across the country, and between 10,000 and 20,000 Muslims from overseas.[32] The largest group was made up of several thousand Muslim seamen who had established themselves at British ports such as Cardiff, Barry, Newport, South Shields, Hull, Liverpool, and London. They were mostly Yemenis, but there were also Somalis and a few Malay and Indian seamen since, at the beginning of the twentieth century, Britain owned half of the world's shipping. If the majority of the Muslim population in Britain was found among the industrial working class of its major ports, British Islam's spiritual and intellectual centre remained in the London area. Most of the associations founded in the inter-war period reveal an Indian predominance relying on professionals such as lawyers, the important student community and the financial strength of the mercantile community. These Indian Muslims played a pioneering role in the

[30] Fatou Gassama, 'L'immigration sénégalaise en France, de 1914 a 1993: étude de l'implantation et du rôle des confréries musulmanes sénégalaises', PhD thesis, Université Lille3, 2005, published on www.univ-lille3.fr/theses/gassama-fatou/html/these_front.html.

[31] P. Le Pautremat, *La politique musulmane de la Fran*ç*e,* p. 291.

[32] In the Mediterranean region, there were also a handful of Muslims in the British possessions: in Gibraltar and Malta, and a much more significant population of some 63,000 in Cyprus, according to the Census of 1931.

organisation of Muslim missionary movements whose publications made a strong impact throughout Europe.

In Italy, the control after 1912 of Rhodes and the surrounding islands, which had been part of the Ottoman Empire, gave the country a population of some 15,000 Muslims. In the metropolis, there were some Muslim students, notably coming from Albania. But in both Italy and Spain, it was the colonial ambitions of the fascist regimes that further developed official interest in Muslims living in the metropolis. Spain's Andalusian past attracted Muslim visitors and also students who studied mainly in universities in Madrid and Granada. During the Spanish Civil War, General Franco recruited by conscription and enlistment some 78,500 Moroccan mercenaries.[33] Later, it was a white turbaned Moorish Horse-Guard that accompanied the *Caudillo* as his personal bodyguard on official visits to Spanish cities and on other ceremonial occasions. We do not know whether any special facilities were provided for these soldiers to practise their religion. The Nationalist government opened mosques in Seville and Cordoba and seems to have benefited from the resentment of Moroccan workers against the discriminatory policy of the Spanish republican government and trade unions.[34]

In the Netherlands there were some Muslims from the colonial territories of the Dutch East Indies (present-day Indonesia), and also from the Dutch West Indies and Dutch Guyana (present-day Suriname), but the history of this tiny community made up essentially of students has been mostly studied by political scientists in the context of research on the Indonesian independence movement.[35] In addition to students, there may have been some North African labour migrants, and the Alawiyya *tariqa* is reported to have

[33] Sebastian Balfour, *Deadly Embrace—Morocco and the Road to the Spanish Civil War*, New York: OUP, 2002, p. 312, who regards this figure as the most reliable for the total number of Moroccan troops deployed in Spain during the Civil War. Other sources, less thoroughly documented, suggest figures from 90,000 to 130,000. We are grateful to Richard Lawless for these references.

[34] Ibid., pp. 273–4.

[35] The Indonesische Vereeniging (Indonesian Association) was founded in 1922 by students in Holland, with leaders such as Muhammad Hatta who resided in Rotterdam from 1923 to 1932.

established a *zawiya* at The Hague in the 1920s.[36] A few hundred North Africans workers were employed in Belgium during the inter-war period, mainly in the coal mines. Most were Algerians who appear to have crossed the border from France in order to avoid being repatriated to Algeria at the end of the First World War. During the inter-war period, their number declined as local people objected to them on racial grounds and the mine owners therefore preferred to import Polish and Italian labour.[37] The Alawiyya *tariqa* is reported to have been present in Belgium during this period. No information is available for Portugal despite the fact that some 150,000 Muslims were living in its colonies.[38]

Muslims in Central and Northern Europe

In Central and Northern Europe, Muslims were to be found mainly in Poland, Germany, Hungary and Czechoslovakia. The most important group was that of the Muslims of Poland—including Vilnius at that time –, estimated at between 5,000 to 6,000 people in the 1930s.[39] They were mainly descendants of the Tatar groups established in Poland for more than five centuries, but there was also a group of Muslim Tatar immigrants from Russia, mainly settled in Vilnius and Warsaw. In addition, there were also small Tatar groups in Lithuania, Byelorussia and Finland.[40] In the latter country, Tatars

[36] See Karima Stauch's thesis quoted in Mark Sedgwick's chapter, footnote no. 52. Rheinische Friedrich-Wilhelms-Universitaet Bonn, available http://www.abc.se/~m9783/alawi.html. Shaikh Abdullah Ali al-Hakimi worked in Holland before going to Britain in 1936.

[37] On North Africans in Belgium see Franck Caestecker, *Alien Policy in Belgium, 1840–1940. The Creation of Guest Workers, Refugees and Illegal Aliens*, Oxford-New York: Berghahn Books, 2000.

[38] There were 60,000 Muslims in Portuguese Guinea, 80,000 in Mozambique and 10,000 in Angola; see A. Pellegrin, *L'Islam dans le Monde,* pp. 178–9.

[39] André Bonamy, "Les musulmans de Pologne, Roumanie et Bulgarie", *Revue des Etudes Islamiques* (1932), pp. 81–94, and the contribution of Sebastian Cwiklinski in the present volume.

[40] Alexandre Popovic, "Muslimūn. 1. Les musulmans d'Europe. A. Les communautés musulmanes de l'Europe septentrionale", *Encyclopédie de l'islam*, 2nd édition, VII, Leiden: Brill, 1992, p. 696). On Islam in Lithuania, see György Lederer, "Islam in Lithuania", *Central Asian Survey*, XIV, 3 (1995), pp. 425–48.

were mainly fur merchants, who settled there from the mid-nineteenth century. In 1925 a Muslim community, made up of some 600 people, was given official recognition.[41] In the rest of Scandinavia, alongside some foreign Muslim diplomats and traders, there were a handful of converts such as the Danish journalist Ali Ahmad Knud Holmboe (1902–31).[42] There were also Somali and Yemeni seamen to be found in the port of Copenhagen.[43]

In Germany, students formed the largest group among a Muslim community which was estimated to number over a thousand, including some three hundred converts, at the beginning of the 1930s. They were former Tatar prisoners of war, students, diplomats, merchants, etc. Despite their rather small number, they managed to get some visibility in public space with the building of a mosque in Berlin and the creation of various organisations.[44] Berlin was also a refuge for activists involved in the anti-colonial struggle in India and in the Middle East; this political and intellectual activity is attested by the several newspapers in Arabic and Persian published and distributed in Germany and the establishment of several flourishing clubs and associations. Berlin was also the heart of important Muslim missionary activity operating throughout Central Europe.

In Hungary, Islam dates back to the Ottoman domination that ended at the end of the seventeenth century, but after that time its presence totally disappeared for two centuries. However the occupation of Bosnia-Herzegovina by the Austro-Hungarian authorities in 1878, as well as the strengthening of the relations between Hungary and the Ottoman Empire, led to the formation of a new but small Islamic community. In 1916, two years before the collapse of the Austro-Hungarian Empire, Islam was even officially recognised

[41] Bichr Farès, "Notice sur la communauté musulmane de Finlande", *Revue des Etudes Islamiques* (1934), pp. 1–8; Harry Halèn, "Islaminuskoisista Suomessa", *Eripainos* (Helsinki), 5 (1984), pp. 341–53. The figure is from A. Pellegrin, *L'Islam dans le Monde,* p. 177.

[42] See his book translated by Helga Holbek, *Desert Encounter: an Adventurous Journey through Italian Africa*, London/Bombay/Sydney: George Harrap, 1936.

[43] Leigh Douglas, *The Free Yemen Movement: 1935 - 1962* in *Contemporary Yemen: Politics and Historical Background*, Beirut: American University, 1987.

[44] See the contributions of Wolfgang Schwanitz and Sebastian Cwiklinski in the present volume, and also the various works of Gerhard Höpp already mentioned.

in Hungary. In the inter-war period, there were two small groups of Hungarian Muslims: approximately three hundred former soldiers from Bosnia-Herzegovina conducting small businesses in Budapest, and about the same number of Turks who continued to work in all parts of the country as confectioners, gardeners and craftsmen. The Orientalist Julius Abdulkerim Germanus was one of the rare local converts.[45]

The situation in Bohemia-Moravia was close to that experienced in Hungary. The presence of Islam goes back to the end of the nineteenth century when some craftsmen, confectioners, ice cream manufacturers, grocers and students from Bosnia-Herzegovina went to Prague and Brno. In the new Republic of Czechoslovakia, some seven hundred Muslims formed a rather heterogeneous community: the main group seems to have been Muslims from Bosnia-Herzegovina, others were Circassians and Tatars who had fled from the Soviet Union; there were also Arab and other Muslim diplomats, a few Albanian students (from Yugoslavia or Albania), and a few local converts among whom the most active was the journalist Alois Bohdan Mohammed Abdullah Brikcius.[46]

In the inter-war Austrian Republic, there were a few hundred Muslims coming essentially from the Balkans. In Vienna Muslims were organised in an *Orientbund* and a "Union for Islamic Culture", which was dissolved by the Nazis in 1939.[47] There also existed a short-lived Muslim mission founded by Omar von Ehrenfels (1901–80) who led important networking activity in the early thirties. The Muslim presence was also noticeable in Switzerland, which hosted a few hundred students, diplomats and also political

[45] On Islam in Hungary, see A. Popovic, *L'islam balkanique*, pp. 188–94; György Lederer, "Sur l'islam à Budapest", *La transmission du savoir dans le monde musulman périphérique,* Paris, 6 (November 1986), pp. 23–37; György Lederer, "Islam in Hungary", *Central Asian Survey*, XI, 1 (1992), pp. 1–23.

[46] On Islam in Bohemia and Moravia in the inter-war period, see Miloš Mendel, "The Islamic religious Community in Bohemia and Moravia (1934–1945)", *Archiv Orientalni*, 66 (1998), pp. 127–41.

[47] Sabine Kroissenbrunner, "Islam and Muslim Immigrants in Austria: Socio-political Networks and Muslim Leadership of Turkish Immigrants", in Ahmed Al-Shahi and Richard Lawless (eds), *Middle East and North African Immigrants in Europe*, London: Routledge, 2005, pp. 90–109.

activists such as the Indian anti-colonial leader Muhammad Barakatullah Bhopali and the well-known Shakib Arslan who published his journal *La Nation Arabe* from Geneva.

Muslims in South-Eastern Europe

The most massive presence of Muslims in Europe in the inter-war period was to be found in its South-Eastern part. This was mainly due to the long Ottoman domination of this region, already mentioned. This population was greatly affected by the frequent changes of boundaries and constant migration flows, but, despite mass emigration to Turkey, the Balkan area remained the stronghold of the presence of Islam in Europe and contained the only country with a Muslim majority, Albania.

In Albania, a state created in 1913 by the Great Powers along the Eastern Adriatic shore, but only really established after the First World War, Muslims formed the majority of the population, making this country an exception in Europe. In 1937, there were around 700,000 Muslims in the Kingdom of Albania (representing 69 per cent of the population) who were mainly Albanian-speaking people and whose ancestors converted to Islam during the Ottoman period. Only a minority spoke Slavic languages or Turkish and some of them were Gypsies, but it is difficult to estimate their numbers. Muslims were represented in all socio-economic groups.[48] They were present throughout the country, but, whereas Catholic and Orthodox Christian minorities were mainly found in the North and the South of the country, Central Albania was predominantly Muslim.

Although in a minority, Yugoslav Muslims made up the most important group of Muslims in the Balkans. In the Kingdom of Serbs, Croats and Slovenes formed in 1918 and renamed the Kingdom of Yugoslavia later, they were approximately 1.5 million, but represented only 11–12 per cent of the total population. One may distinguish several groups among them. On the one hand, there were the Muslims of Bosnia-Herzegovina, mainly descendants from local converts, who had been under Austro-Hungarian administration

[48] See A. Popovic, *L'islam balkanique*, pp. 1–36, as well as the chapter by Nathalie Clayer in the present volume.

between 1878 and 1918. In 1931, some 700,000 Slavic-speaking Muslims formed 31 per cent of the population of the province, while the Orthodox Serbs were 44 per cent and the Catholic Croats 23 per cent.[49] On the other hand, there were the Muslims of so-called "Southern Serbia" (today Southern Serbia, Kosovo and Macedonia), most of which was under Ottoman rule until 1912. After the Balkan Wars, this territory was incorporated into Serbia, but it was occupied during the First World War by Austro-Hungarian and Bulgarian troops.[50] After the turmoil of the war, the Muslims who remained in these regions did not form a homogeneous group as in Bosnia-Herzegovina. They spoke Albanian, Turkish, Slavic, Roma or Circassian and multi-linguism was quite common in a place that had witnessed colonisation, conversions and continuous population movements, the most recent being the arrival of diverse groups of Muslim refugees from territories conquered by Russia and from parts of the new Balkan states. In the inter-war period statistical data varied considerably, because of constant waves of emigration to Turkey. Whereas there were more than 700,000 Muslims (making up to 48 per cent of the population of Southern Serbia, Kosovo and Macedonia) in 1921, they were estimated at only 520,000 a decade later. There were also several thousand Muslims in Montenegro,[51] who were Albanian-speaking in the regions of Bar and Ulcinj and Slavic-speaking in the Sanjak of Novi Pazar.[52]

[49] Here, it must be noted that these proportions changed after the Second World War, and in 1991, just before the recent wars in the former Yugoslavia, the Muslims had become the most important group with 43.7 per cent of the population, the Serbs being 31.4 per cent and the Croats 17.3 per cent (see Xavier Bougarel, "Bosnie: anatomie d'une poudrière", *Hérodote,* Paris, 67 (1992), pp. 84–147).

[50] Small groups of Muslims had remained in Serbia after it became autonomous from the Ottoman Empire. In 1901, their number was estimated around 15,000. Most of them were living in the Southern part of the country, around Niš, Leskovac and Vranje. They spoke different languages: Turkish, Albanian or Slavic languages. Some Muslims were working seasonally in Belgrade (A. Popovic, *L'islam balkanique*, pp. 300–2).

[51] Many Muslims left the new territories allocated to Montenegro in 1878 for the Ottoman Empire, but several thousands of them remained in the country (see A. Popovic, *L'islam balkanique*, pp. 294–98).

[52] A. Popovic, *L'islam balkanique*, pp. 311–36, as well as the chapters by Fikret Karčić, Muhammed Aruçi and Xavier Bougarel in the present volume.

In Bulgaria, the Muslim presence resulted from a process of colonisation by Turkish speaking people that had been carried out on a large scale in the first centuries of Ottoman rule. Thereafter, there were also some conversions among the local population (Pomaks) and the more recent arrival of Russian Tatars and Circassian refugees. In the mid-nineteenth century Muslims represented around one third of the total population, but many of them fled to Istanbul or Anatolia as a consequence of the Russian-Turkish War of 1877 and the creation of the principality of Bulgaria the following year. After 1918, the Bulgarian Muslim population (around 800,000) was roughly the same size as that in Albania, but it formed a minority whose proportion of the total population was about the same as that of Muslims in Yugoslavia. The inter-war figures are not quite reliable, because of emigration to and returns from Turkey and the arrival of Muslim refugees from the province of Quadrilater under Romanian rule between 1919 and 1940.[53] Officially, the 1926 census enumerated 570,000 Turks (i.e. 11 per cent of the total population), some 100,000 Bulgarian-speaking Pomaks (2 per cent of the population), and there were also Muslim Gypsies. More of them than of the Christians lived in rural communities, and they were mainly established in the Southern regions, along the Greek and Turkish borders, and in the North-Eastern areas of Ruse, Shumen and Varna.

In Romania there was also a considerable Muslim population established along the Black Sea—in the Quadrilater, the Dobrudja and the Bujak in Southern Bessarabia—where successive migration waves of Turkish and Tatar groups had settled. In this buffer zone between the Ottoman Empire and Russia, emigration to the South was common, and again the redrawing of borders following the Russian-Turkish War in 1876–78 led many Muslims to emigrate further South. While the

[53] On Islam in Bulgaria, see A. Popovic, *L'islam balkanique*, pp. 81–7 and 90–5; *Bulgaristan'da Türk-Islam Eğitim ve Kültür Müesseseleri ve Medresetü'n nüvvab*, Istanbul: IRCICA, 1993; "Image and Policy: the Case of Turks and Pomaks in Inter-war Bulgaria, 1918–1944 (with Special Reference to Education)", *Islam and Christian-Muslim Relations*, XII, 3 (July 2001), pp. 355–74; Ibrahim Hatiboğlu, "XX. Yüzyılın ilk yarısında Bulgaristan Müslümanları arasında dinî ıslâhat çabaları", *Balkanlar'da islâm medeniyeti milletlerarası sempozyumu tebliğleri*, Istanbul: Ircica, 2002, pp. 347–62.

territorial acquisitions following the First World War[54] resulted in a notable increase in the number of Muslims in the early 1920s, emigration to Bulgaria and Turkey continued. It was further encouraged by the policy of colonisation by non-Muslims implemented by the authorities in the Romanian Dobrudja. In 1930, between 170,000 and 290,000 Muslims remained in the country.[55]

The smallest Muslim community in the inter-war Balkans was to be found in Greece, essentially in territories conquered between 1912 and 1923. After the independence of the "old Greece" in 1830, only a few Muslims remained. In 1881, following the annexation of Thessaly and the region of Arta, some 45,000 Muslims obtained Greek citizenship, but less than 3,000 were still living in the country in 1911. However the Balkan Wars (1912–13) led to the incorporation of more than 450,000 Muslims in Macedonia, around 60,000 in Epirus, less than 25,000 in Crete,[56] and some 20,000 in the islands of Chio and Mytilene. At the end of the Greek-Turkish war (1919–23), the Treaty of Lausanne compelled about 360,000 Muslims of Greece (except those of Western Thrace) to leave for Turkey,[57] and the Greek Orthodox population of Turkey (excluding those of Istanbul) to emigrate to Greece. According to the 1928 official census, the 135,000 Muslims of Greece made up less than 2 per cent of the population, concentrated mainly in Thrace (100,000 speaking Turkish, Bulgarian and Roma) and Epirus (20,000 along the Albanian border, speaking

[54] They included Bessarabia with possibly some 67,000 Muslims (other sources give much lower numbers), the Quadrilater with around 130,000 to 150,000 Muslims, as well as a few hundred Muslims on the small island of Ada Kale on the Danube (close to the Iron Gates, it was submerged in 1968).

[55] On Romania see Frédérick de Jong, "The Turks and Tatars in Romania. Materials Relative to their History and Notes on their Present-day Condition", *Turcica*, XVIII (1986), pp. 165–89; A. Popovic, *L'islam balkanique*, pp. 221–48; György Lederer, "Islam in Romania", *Central Asian Survey*, XV, 3–4 (1996), pp. 349–68; Hüsseyn Ağuiçenoğlu, *Die Turko-Tatarische Presse der Dobrudscha 1897–1940. Annotierte Katalog*, Frankfurt/Main: Peter Lang, 2004.

[56] The autonomy of Crete from the Ottoman Empire implemented in 1898, although it provided special rights for Muslims, had already led many Muslims to emigrate.

[57] Some 325,000 Muslims from Macedonia, 25,000 from Crete, 3,000 from Thessaly and a limited number from the Aegean islands and Epirus left Greece.

Albanian). The latter, called Chams (or Tsamides in Greek), were probably more numerous than the official figures indicated (23,000 to 25,000).[58]

For those Muslims of South-Eastern Europe, the inter-war period was the beginning of a new era that opened with the end of the Ottoman Empire and the abolition of the Caliphate. Those who had not emigrated to Turkey had now to consider themselves as Muslims of Europe, if not as "European Muslims". Some intellectual and religious leaders then started to look for a dialogue with the small but dynamic communities established in the Western parts of the continent. Individuals such as Shakib Arslan or missionary societies such as the Ahmadi missions responded to this interest, viewing the establishment of such a fraternal network as a way to assert the preservation of Islam in Europe.

[58] A. Popovic, *L'islam balkanique*, pp. 109–64; Konstantinos Tsitselikis, *Old and New Islam in Greece. Legal and Political Aspects* (forthcoming); Georgia Kretsi, "Austauschbar- nicht austauschbar. Albanophone Muslime (Çamen) und andere Grenzbevölkerungen des Epirus der zwischenkriegszeit im Kräftefeld zwischen ethnischer Identitätskonstruktion und Entmischungspolitik", *Jahrbücher für Geschichte und Kultur Südosteuropas*, 4 (2002), pp. 205–31. These Chams were killed or expelled to Albania at the end of the Second World War.

Part I. MUSLIM NETWORKS IN CHRISTIAN LANDS

Before the twentieth century, several "transnational" networks already existed in the Muslim world (networks shaped by the pilgrimage to Mecca, Sufi orders, religious learning, etc.).[1] The end of the nineteenth century saw the development and expansion of communication networks resulting from the revolution in maritime and land transport, for example the introduction of the steamship and telegraph. It continued with a much larger diffusion of literature and newspapers. Consequently the old-established "transnational" networks that existed throughout the Muslim world were transformed to a certain extent. They were primarily of a religious nature with an increasing number of pilgrims going to Mecca, students travelling from one institution of religious learning to another and the constant development of Sufi orders. In a context of European colonial expansion and the development of secular thought, new socio-political transnational networks began to promote reformist or pan-Islamic ideologies. Such religious and intellectual networks gained a foothold in Christian lands through the Muslim minorities which remained in the new nation-states created in South-Eastern Europe following the decline and demise of the Ottoman Empire. After the First World War, they expanded significantly into Western Europe, because of the increasing presence of Muslims there. This transnational dimension, a phenomenon established long before the end of the twentieth century,

[1] Miriam Cook and Bruce B. Lawrence (eds), *Muslim Networks from Hajj to Hip Hop*, Chapel Hill-London: University of North Carolina Press, 2005.

superimposed national and regional linkages that emerged from the local communities.[2]

SOCIAL AND POLITICAL NETWORKS

Firstly, there were the networks linked to migration and diaspora. The nascent Western European Muslim communities made up of the first waves of migrants facilitated further immigration of workers, students, and political refugees. In France, the new North African Muslim migrant was found a job by one of his friends, generally someone from the same village of origin, or by the restaurant owner/boarding house keeper ("*restaurateur-logeur*") with whom he was living.[3] In a later part of this work, Richard Lawless describes the Yemeni seamen's organisations and the way they were interacting with other Muslims from Britain and overseas. In the present part, Humayun Ansari also addresses the question of occupation-based networks linking Muslims in Britain in the inter-war period. A second chapter by Sebastian Cwiklinski analyses how the activities of Russian Tatar refugees in Germany were linked to the rest of the Tatar diaspora and other anti-Bolshevik exiles through political and social organisations and newspapers. Just after the First World War, Tatars established networks to help students from Russia and Turkistan come to Berlin. Foreign students were particularly keen to mobilise politically and, as shown by Wolfgang Schwanitz and Raja Adal in this book, such Muslim student associations in Germany and France were specifically targeted in the 1930s by activists such as Shakib Arslan and the Mufti of Jerusalem, Amin al-Husaini.

The migration process and the growth of Muslim diasporic communities, which spread across the colonial empires of the European powers, facilitated the circulation of information. In this

[2] On the combination of "traditional" and "non traditional" types of links in the making of networks among the European Muslims, see Jørgen Nielsen, "Transnational Islam and the integration of Islam in Europe", in S. Allievi and J. Nielsen (eds), *Muslim Networks and Transnational Communities in and across Europe*, Leiden: Brill, 2003, pp. 28–51.

[3] L.M. [Louis Milliot], "Carte de répartition des Kabyles dans la région parisienne", *Revue des Etudes Islamiques,* Paris, IV (1930), p. 167.

context, networks developed between colonies and metropolis reflecting various types of political activism, as Humayun Ansari shows in the case of Indian Muslims, woven through the double transnational framework of the British Empire and the *umma* (the worldwide Muslim community). Such networks connected Muslims loyal to the Empire, more radical pan-Islamic militants who fought against colonial subordination and promoters of communalism favouring a struggle to promote the exclusive interests of Muslims. In the colonial metropolis, students were at the forefront of political activity promoting the idea of international Islamic solidarity. In France, one should mention the activities of the *Fraternité Musulmane*, an association founded in 1907 with the aim of creating fraternal links between young Muslims from various countries who were studying in Paris. Newspapers from several Muslim countries were available at the headquarters of the association in the Latin Quarter.[4] One of its main protagonists was the Egyptian jurist and journalist Mahmud Salim, who, after attending the 1931 Jerusalem Muslim Congress, proposed the organisation of the "European Muslim congress" in Geneva.[5]

The creation of official Muslim organisations, correspondence, travel, the organisation of international congresses and above all the diffusion of newspapers were the main tools used to build these networks. The initiators of such activities were men of diverse educational, social, and political backgrounds. One could find converts such as Khalid Sheldrake in London, anti-colonial activists such as Messali Hadj in Paris, or scholars such as Jakup Szynkiewicz in Vilnius. The latter was the only delegate representing "European Muslims" at the 1926 Caliphate Congress in Cairo.[6] But the most outstanding example of network-builders was Shakib Arslan whose attitude towards Europe is analysed by Raja Adal in the next part.

4 Louis Bouvat, "Fraternité musulmane", *Revue du Monde Musulman,* Paris, III, 1 (August-September 1907), pp. 159–60.

5 Mahmoud Salem, *Le Congrès Islamo-européen de Genève*, Paris, 1933; quoted in Martin Kramer, *Islam Assembled*, New York: Columbia University Press, 1986, p. 223.

6 "Le Congrès du Khalifat—Le Caire 13–19 mai 1926", *Revue du Monde Musulman*, LXIV (2nd trimester 1926), pp. 46–8.

Through his role as editor of *La Nation Arabe*, his abundant correspondence and his participation in various meetings and organisations all over Europe and the Middle East, this Druze refugee was at the centre of an impressive personal network directed from his Swiss exile. Arslan's motivations could be labelled as pan-Arab, anti-colonial and Islamic revivalist all at the same time. His discourse was not unknown to Muslims of Central and Eastern Europe, and it had an influence for example on the development of "traditionalism" (or "revivalism") in Bosnia-Herzegovina, as Xavier Bougarel points out.

Muslims from these parts of Europe also attempted to use the transnational dimension of the *umma* to strengthen the position of their communities. Indeed, in the 1930s, religious leaders from Hungary and Poland undertook journeys to many parts of the Middle East and India in order to make the Muslim public aware of their problems and to collect funds for the building of mosques in the capital cities of their countries. In 1934 and 1935–36, two Hungarian delegates from the small Bosnian community of Budapest, Huszein Hilmi Durics and Mehmed Reszulovics, went to Cairo, Jerusalem, Damascus, Baghdad, and Hyderabad in India.[7] Durics also corresponded on a regular basis with King Zog of Albania.[8] Similarly, the Mufti of Poland Jakup Szynkiewicz embarked upon several journeys around the Muslim world, from Turkey to the Arab countries, India, and even Yugoslavia and Albania.[9] As Sebastian Cwiklinski explains, those travels led to several Polish Tatar students being sent to study at Al-Azhar in Cairo and in Sarajevo, thus helping to strengthen the coherence of the Polish Tatar community through a deeper knowledge of Islam.

RELIGIOUS NETWORKS

Besides the socio-political fraternal links, there were networks of a more specifically religious nature which also expanded in Europe

[7] See Alexandre Popovic, *L'islam balkanique*, Berlin-Wiesbaden: Otto Harrassowitz, 1986, pp. 191–2; and Gyorgy Lederer, "Islam in Hungary", *Central Asian Survey*, XI, 1 (1992), pp. 1–23 (see p. 15).

[8] Ibid., p. 14.

[9] He went to Tirana in 1937, where he visited the *madrasa* (Imam Vehbi Ismaili, *Kujtime të rinisë*, Harper Woods: Albanian Islamic Centre, 1993, p. 31).

at that time. As far as South-Eastern Europe is concerned, several religious networks already existed binding the Balkan Muslims to Istanbul, and more generally to Anatolia in Turkey, and to a lesser extent to the Arab world. Even though the new Balkan states had established national religious structures for their Muslim inhabitants, the links to the Sultan-Caliph, the *Shaikh al-Islam* and various Turkish *madrasas* were not totally cut, nor were the connections with some Sufi orders. Nevertheless, the abolition of all these institutions by Mustafa Kemal at the beginning of the 1920s was fraught with consequences. Some of these religious networks withdrew to the Balkans, after religious leaders opposed to the Kemalist reforms fled to South-Eastern Europe. Muhamed Aruçi mentions the case of Ataullah Kurtish who went to Macedonia, and Yannis Bonos refers to a former *Shaikh al-Islam*, Mustafa Sabri, who settled in Greece for a while before going to Egypt. In addition several members of the Bektashi Sufi order migrated from Turkey to Albania. But the main consequence was that religious networks linking the Balkans and the Arab World were reinforced, notably through sending students to Al-Azhar University. Henceforth, Cairo became the centre of religious learning networking for Muslims from Europe, even if other contacts were also established with India, as we shall see below.

As for Western Europe, new religious networks spread, such as those of some Sufi orders (*tariqa*, plural *turuq*). The most widespread was the Alawiyya mentioned by Mark Sedgwick in the second part and Richard Lawless in the third part of the book.[10] From the 1920s, this Algerian mystical brotherhood gained followers first among Algerian workers in Paris, then among Muslim seamen in key port cities in France, Belgium, the Netherlands and Britain. Guided by Alawi *shaikhs*, Arab seamen settled in British ports looked towards North Africa and the Near East for spiritual guidance, in contrast to the other Muslims in Britain whose organisations were dominated by Indians, as Richard Lawless points out.

[10] Louis Milliot asserts that in 1930, Algerian migrants from the Haut Sébaou (Kabylia) resident in the Parisian region were affiliated to the Rahmaniyya. He also mentions the presence of the Alawiyya, the Ammariyya and the Tijaniyya Sufi orders (L. Milliot, "Carte de répartition des Kabyles", p. 167).

Concerning other Sufi networks introduced into Europe by migrants, the information is rather scarce and further research has to be carried out.

Beside the networks of "classical" Sufi groups which emerged in Western Europe, some "neo-Sufi" movements appeared whose doctrinal specificity is discussed by Mark Sedgwick in the second part. One of them was Inayat Khan's "Sufi" order, also mentioned by Humayun Ansari, which also had adepts in the United States and Brazil, and spread in England, Switzerland, France, the Netherlands, Belgium, Germany and Norway among the upper-middle class, with a large membership of women. As for the smaller networks, one might mention the Alawiyya branch initiated by a Swiss, Frithjof Schuon, that expanded after the Second World War, linking together converts from Switzerland, France, Italy and Romania.

Another type of religious network, which developed in inter-war Europe, was the one created by a brand new type of Muslim mission which reproduced to a large extend the organisation and methods of propaganda of the Protestant missions. They promoted a discourse of *da'wa* (propagation of the faith) aiming at both the intensification of religious feeling among Muslim communities and the conversion of non-Muslims. Missions of the two branches (Qadiani and Lahori) of the Ahmadiyya movement represent forerunners of today's Islamic transnational nongovernmental organisations. It is not by chance that these two missionary organisations originated from India, a country where Muslims experienced decades of active proselytising by Christians, then by Hindu revivalists, resulting in a feeling of insecurity intensified by their minority position. In a globalised colonial context, the defence of Islam in South Asia had to start at the very heart of the European metropolis.

The first organisation was the Lahore-based *Ahmadiyya Anjuman-i Isha'at-i Islam* (Ahmadiyya Society for the Propagation of Islam), which is analysed by Eric Germain in this first part. In financing a permanent presence in Europe, its members wanted to challenge the "evangelical Orientalism" that propagated a backward and aggressive image of Islam. For that purpose, they were very active in the field of the Islamic-Christian polemic and regularly participated in inter-faith congresses in Europe. In fact, more than converting people, they aimed at improving the self-esteem of Muslims in and outside Europe. In order to achieve that aim, their leaders set up a solid organisation, used European languages, mainly English and German, and employed the most modern communication tools of that time (press, radio, Pathé-films), just as Ahmadis would later be pioneers in the use of satellite TV and the Internet. In Europe, they relied on the support of Muslim students and European converts, whereas in India they were helped by merchants and Muslim women.

The Lahori Ahmadi network was Europe-wide. After it took control of the only proper mosque in England, built some years earlier in Woking near London, another mission was launched in Berlin. Germany was also intended to act as the headquarters for missionaries working in Central, Eastern and South-Eastern Europe, i.e. the Balkans. Indeed, from Berlin, contacts were established with Tatars from Poland and Finland. In Prague, it was thanks to the help of the Berlin mission, along with contacts with Muslims from Bosnia and the Arab World, that Qur'ans and other Islamic literature (especially from Bosnia) were acquired and the Islamic journal *Hlas* (The Voice) was published from 1937 onwards. Some Ahmadi missionaries from Berlin, as well as Muslims from Bosnia-Herzegovina, were among those who gave lectures on Islam to the local Muslim community.[11] In the 1930s, a short-lived Lahori mission was also launched in Vienna. In the Balkans, very close contacts were established with Muslims of Bosnia-Herzegovina (see Xavier Bougarel's chapter) and with Albanian religious leaders, who were also in touch with the central mission in Lahore. The missionaries did not set up a mission in Albania, because they thought that the Albanian Muslim Community itself could act as a bridgehead to other Balkan countries. The cooperation with Lahore was so close that a couple of Albanian Muslim students were sent to Lahore to study.[12] In the 1930s, the Lahore headquarters also considered sending missionaries

[11] Miloš Mendel, "The Islamic Religious Community in Bohemia and Moravia (1934–1945)", *Archív Orientální*, Praha, 66 (1998), p. 141.

[12] Nathalie Clayer, "La Ahmadiyya Lahori et la réforme de l'islam albanais dans l'entre-deux-guerres", in V. Bouillier and C. Servan-Schreiber (eds), *De l'Arabie à l'Himalaya, chemins croisés*, Paris: Maisonneuve et Larose, 2004, pp. 211–28.

to countries with growing Muslim communities such as Spain and also the Netherlands, where Mirza Wali Ahmad Beg arrived in 1938 to start a missionary work that was short-lived because of the war.

The second network of the Qadiani Ahmadiyya, originating from the same Ahmadi movement born in India, was already condemned as heretical in the inter-war period by several Sunni religious authorities. This organisation, which was also active in the USA, laid the foundation stone of London's first mosque, in Southfields, in October 1934. Just like the Lahoris, it launched another mission in Berlin, while a project to send missionaries to Greece was under study. A short-lived mission was opened in Budapest in 1936–37, when Haji Ayaz Khan and his collaborator were welcomed in the Hungarian capital by Andor Medriczky, a fervent supporter of the local Islamic community. The Hungarian press published many reports about the activity of the missionaries. Booklets were translated into Hungarian, lectures were organised and a dozen people are said to have been converted. However, in 1937, the Qadiani missionaries left Hungary for Poland.[13] During the same period, the Qadianis sent a missionary to Spain, Muhammad Sharif Gujrati, who started working in Madrid in February 1936 and went in January of the next year to Italy where he remained until the war.[14]

In the late 1930s, another missionary organisation, the Muslim Missionary Society of Singapore, tried to counter and replace the influence of the Ahmadis in Europe, accusing both Qadianis and Lahoris of heterodoxy. The new organisation, led by Maulana Muhammad Abdul Aleem Siddiqui, established contacts with Muslims in Britain, Poland and Czechoslovakia. In Western Europe, this initiative was welcomed by individuals who wanted to challenge the dominant position of the Ahmadi missions and the financial support they received from Muslim communities throughout the British Empire. Among them were Khalid Sheldrake and his Western Islamic Association which, after collaborating with the Woking Mission, became its fierce opponent. Such a context would explain

[13] Gyorgy Lederer, "Sur l'islam à Budapest", *La transmission du savoir dans le monde musulman périphérique*, Paris, 6 (November 1986), pp. 30, 36 (note 57).

[14] Dost Muhammad Shahid, *Tarikh-i-Ahmadiyyat*, vol. VIII, Rabwah, p. 293, 299.

Sheldrake's eagerness to establish links between his Association and the Parisian *Fraternité Musulmane*. For this English convert, initiating Franco-British cooperation was a way of challenging the Germano-British Ahmadi connection; but this does not mean that members of the *Fraternité* had any contact with Woking.[15] As a matter of fact, while one acknowledges the competition and the personal, ideological, ethnic, and theological rivalries that existed, the overlapping nature of these various networks should also be recognised.

N.C. - E.G.

[15] In the 1930s the *Fraternité* gathered students coming mostly from Egypt and Iraq, and that would explain the link with other UK Muslim associations.

MAKING TRANSNATIONAL CONNECTIONS: MUSLIM NETWORKS IN EARLY TWENTIETH-CENTURY BRITAIN

Humayun Ansari

Networks, whether social, political or cultural, encompass the general structure of informal relationships as well as those operating within defined associational structures, and their analysis proves helpful when exploring ways of interpreting the action and behaviour of the persons involved. Networks are characterised by the nature of the links among those within them, whose action and behaviour are likely to be considerably affected by shared beliefs, wishes, and expectations. Networks may be structured around economic assistance, kinship obligations, religious co-operation or simply friendship. They may be shaped by forms of patronage and patterns of communication, and can be mobilised on the basis of issues, norms and values arising during the course of events. Central to any understanding of a network, however, is how its various parts interact and communicate with each other and how its operations cohere.

British Muslims, like Muslims in other parts of the world, have long been involved in constructing a wide variety of networks with diverse objectives and purposes, which can offer important insights into and understandings of how they have engaged with the society in which they live. This chapter takes as its focus developments in the period leading up to the Second World War, focusing on those networks among Muslims in Britain that were established and held together by a sense of identity (in part, implicitly or explicitly, religious) and by shared ideas and responses to the broader environment, rather than those networks based solely on common ethnic, linguistic or national identities.

Britain possessed a diverse and, to some extent, expanding Muslim population during the inter-war period. Overall numbers, however, remained small compared with what they would become after the Second World War, and hence all the Muslim networks examined here were relatively small (though they did vary in terms of size). Their significance, therefore, lies in the fact that it was during these years that patterns of interaction and community formation were put in place, which provided foundations on which later British Muslim communities would be constructed. There is, however, a tendency to generalise about the Muslim experience of living and operating in Britain. By looking at the networks that functioned at this time—political, religious and work-based—it is possible both to challenge this over-generalisation and to develop a more nuanced appreciation of the differences among Muslims as well as the kinds of experiences in which they shared.

Networks in any context exist to defend and promote particular interests and concerns. For some of the networks under consideration here, their main priority was to pursue political or religious goals within a transnational context, whether it was empire or the *umma*. Britain's domination of much of the so-called Muslim world was a factor that frequently accounted for the specific networking that took place, with the result that a transnational consciousness did play a role in the lives of many Muslims in inter-war Britain. At the same time, for others, the main driving force was the need to sustain cultural and ethnic identities and community life in Britain itself. For some of these networks, the question of religious identity was a key element in their thinking, but for others religion remained a private matter, not something on which their activities and interactions hinged.

POLITICAL NETWORKS

The first major set of networks considered here were political in nature, and drew their members from Muslims from elite backgrounds who were in Britain largely as a result of empire connections. Some, the empire-loyalists, admired the British unequivocally and networked with the objective of sustaining the idea of the Empire. Others, radical pan-Islamists, deeply troubled by the

Ottoman Empire's decline and then its defeat in the First World War, sought to develop interactions that would unify the *umma* and enable Muslims to overcome their subordination to European imperial rule. With the abolition of the Ottoman caliphate, however, many pan-Islamists turned to communalism or other political ideologies.

Empire-loyalists and pan-Islamists

Many empire-loyalists belonged to Indian Muslim professional families who were concerned with rank and status and aspired to influence under the British. Incorrigibly "Anglophile", they made enormous efforts to ingratiate, and integrate with, the establishment. Key players such as Ameer Ali, Abdullah Yusuf Ali and Sir Abbas Ali Baig married Englishwomen, became members of the Reform Club and the National Liberal Club, joined lobbying bodies such as the Anglo-Ottoman Society (a group with good connections in the British establishment), and gave dinners in honour of public figures. One such dinner was held at the Savoy Hotel in December 1919 in honour of the Secretary of State for India, at which the Aga Khan (an empire-loyalist par excellence who often extolled the many liberties and even-handed justice that the British Empire bestowed on its subjects of different creeds and classes[1]) made a speech requesting sympathetic consideration for Turkey at the post-war peace conferences.[2]

With the entry of Turkey into the war against Britain, however, these empire-loyalists found themselves in a quandary. Forced to choose between the Empire and the *umma*, as symbolised by the Ottoman caliphate, and no doubt after some soul-searching, they veered towards the former. But even leading individuals, such as Ameer Ali and the Aga Khan, found their loyalties to Britain stretched following the Turkish defeat, and petitioned the government to sustain the caliphate in some way. The Aga Khan, for instance, offered cautious support to pro-caliphate activities, donating

[1] Anne Edwards, *Throne of Gold: The Lives of the Aga Khans*, London: HarperCollins, 1996, p. 84.

[2] *Muslim Outlook* (25 December 1919), p. 1. The London-based merchant M.H. Ispahani also attended this dinner.

"one hundred pounds to keep the 'Muslim Outlook' going", though stressing to its London-based editor, Mushir Husain Kidwai, that this pan-Islamist news-sheet should not be allowed to offer too radical or tendentious propaganda, for "if useful work [was] to be done in London, it [had to] be from every point of view, and not be a monopoly of any one group".[3] Mirza Hashim Ispahani, who belonged to a wealthy Calcutta commercial and financial family, likewise became actively involved in pro-caliphate activities, for instance, financing meetings of the Anglo-Ottoman Society on "Turkey's right to live".[4]

Ameer Ali epitomised this empire-loyalist response. From his time as a student in England in the late 1860s, he had wanted to become an accepted member of British society. Its values and institutions were of supreme importance to him, even if the adoption of English (as "the language of culture and civilised progress"[5]) and an English lifestyle meant that he was considered a "renegade" by other Indian Muslims.[6] Ameer Ali's genuine belief in the superiority of British values and institutions underpinned his loyalty to the Crown. This did not, however, prevent him from combining his empire-loyalism with a degree of pan-Islamic effort—for instance, warning the British government in 1919 about the "intensity of Muslim feeling" in his exchanges with Lord Sydenham in *The Times*,[7] though he was careful to argue that his main concern "is with our own Empire" and "the dangers that lurk".[8] That there could be suspicions regarding Ameer Ali's political allegiances on account of his pan-Islamic "sympathies" may be inferred from the Crown's reluctance to consent to his proposed elevation to the Privy Council. In some eyes, his criticisms of the peace terms

[3] Letter from Aga Khan to Mushir Kidwai, 25 October 1920 (copy of original with author).

[4] Letter from M.H. Ispahani to the Aga Khan, 24 March 1920 (copy of original with author).

[5] Martin Forward, "Syed Ameer Ali: a bridge-builder?", *Islam And Christian-Muslim Relations* (ICMR), VI, 1 (June 1995), p. 49.

[6] See also Martin Forward, 'Syed Ameer Ali's Interpretation of Islam as a Religion', MLitt thesis, Lancaster University, 1982, p. 115.

[7] See *Muslim Outlook* (6 November 1919), pp. 6–7 and the same (13 November 1919), pp. 7–8.

[8] *Muslim Outlook* (13 November 1919), p. 7.

offered to Turkey brought his commitment to the British Empire into question, and he was accused of stirring up "sentiments of hostility and hatred among his co-religionists".[9] In a similar vein, the India Office dismissed as a "ludicrous failure" the mission of the Aga Khan to Egypt, alongside Sir A.A. Baig, "to preach loyalty to Indian Muslim troops". Indeed, such was the extent of official paranoia about pan-Islamic activities that the Aga Khan's relations with so-called "Oriental riff-raff" were kept under surveillance during the war.[10] Even Muslims such as Abdul Majid (president of the "Islamic Society of the British Isles" in 1919), who provided intelligence on some of the more militant pan-Islamists such as Dusé Mohamed Ali, were cast as "fanatics" in some contemporary official assessments.[11]

Perhaps the most unequivocal empire-loyalist was Abdullah Yusuf Ali. Having won a scholarship to Cambridge, he was called to the Bar in the 1890s, and was selected to serve in the elite Indian Civil Service. Yusuf Ali regarded the British Empire as a blessing for mankind, and actively supported the war effort between 1914 and 1918. Unlike Ameer Ali, his empire-loyalism drove him to use all his intellectual powers to attack pan-Islamism as a political movement and he relentlessly pursued arguments that emphasised the apolitical nature of religion. Yusuf Ali's services, especially as a publicist, were much appreciated by the British government and he was duly made a Commander of the Order of the British Empire (CBE) in 1917. Yusuf Ali was appointed as one of the advisers to the Indian delegation at the Paris Peace Conference in 1919. In 1928, he represented India at the assembly of the League of Nations in Geneva, and in 1929, he reinforced his membership of the British establishment when he was elected a Fellow of the Royal Empire Society. Throughout the inter-war period, he remained keen to present what he considered were the interests of the Muslim elite in a form that would appeal to the British, and vice versa. His marriage to an Englishwoman according to the rites of the Church of England, together with his membership of the National Liberal Club, represented

[9] M. Forward, *Syed Ameer Ali*, p. 51.
[10] A. Edwards, *Throne of Gold*, pp. 101–2.
[11] FO 371 3419, 1918, National Archives.

genuine attempts to assimilate. His good contacts among some of the leading politicians of the Liberal Party, such as Lord Morley, formerly Secretary of State for India, meant that he enjoyed access to policy-makers, and he made use of his membership of the British Empire League to promote the causes in which he believed.

Empire-loyalists from the colonies were joined in their networking by a small but steady stream of white British Muslim converts. Having Unitarian tendencies and disillusioned by the failure of Christianity to prevent the wartime slaughter, these converts included well-known individuals such as Lord Headley, Marmaduke Pickthall, Sir Archibal Hamilton, Sir Lauder Brunton and Lady Evelyn Cobbold. Abdullah Quilliam, for instance, who had converted to Islam in 1887 and built up a substantial community of Muslims in Liverpool, struggled to overcome the apparent duality between his loyalty to Queen/King and country and, increasingly, his allegiance to a foreign power. Eventually in 1914 with Britain at war with Turkey, Quilliam proclaimed: "Our Holy Faith enjoins upon us to be loyal to whatever country under whose protection we reside".[12] To convey the genuineness of this loyalty, he resigned as Vice-President of the Anglo-Ottoman Society (under suspicion for "undesirable activities" in relation to Turkey) and offered to help the government to instil a greater sense of loyalty among the Empire's Muslims.[13] The case of Marmaduke Pickthall, who converted to Islam in 1917 and later wrote *The Meaning of the Glorious Quran*, reveals similar dilemmas. He was an ardent monarchist, and by his own admission "a patriotic English Tory", and, while he could be critical of British imperialism in India, he supported the Empire in Egypt. At the same time, though not a pacifist, he opposed the war between Britain and the Ottoman Empire, and he ran the Anglo-Ottoman Society almost single-handedly: for this, he was portrayed as "England's most loyal enemy".[14] A third prominent convert, Lord Headley, was less ambiguous in his pronouncements of loyalty to

[12] "Mussalmans and the War", FO 371 2173, 1914, National Archives.

[13] "Activity of Ottoman Association and Anglo-Ottoman Society", FO 371 2488, 1915; "Moslems in Turkey", FO 371 2146, 1914, National Archives.

[14] Peter Clark, *Marmaduke Pickthall: British Muslim*, London: Quartet Books, 1986, p. 2; Anne Freemantle, *Loyal Enemy*, London: Hutchinson & Co, 1938, p. 7.

the British Empire. While uneasy about the conflict with Turkey, he was happy to propose a resolution in support of the British troops, seconded by the imam of the Woking Mosque, Maulvi Sadr-ud-Din, at a meeting of the British Muslim Society, which stated: "We desire to offer our wholehearted congratulations to our Eastern brethren now at the front, and to express our delight to find that our co-religionists in Islam are fighting on the side of honour, truth, and justice, and are carrying into effect the principles of Islam as inculcated by the Holy Prophet Muhammed".[15]

Radical pan-Islamists

By the early years of the twentieth century, alongside the supporters of empire, there was also a significant cluster of activists who constituted a network that was primarily pan-Islamic in terms of its religio-political stance. Unlike their empire-loyalist co-religionists, they proclaimed their support for the Ottoman caliphate in more vociferous terms, and consequently were questioned by the police about their Turkish sympathies.[16]

In the period leading up to the First World War, while the older generation of empire-loyalists had sought to influence British policy on Muslim issues through constitutional means, attacks against the Ottomans had increased unease among Muslims. Influenced by Jamal-al-din al-Afghani's proto-nationalist ideas, many younger Muslims favoured a more openly anti-British pan-Islamic struggle to secure the freedom of the Muslim world from Western dominance.

Among the most energetic proponents of radical pan-Islamism was Maulana Barakatullah Bhopali, who pursued Afghani's vision with intense passion, and spent some time in Britain. Having left India in 1887, he joined Quilliam's congregation in 1895, attended meetings of the Muslim Patriotic League and had his movements restricted as a result of his anti-British speeches. He travelled widely, making pan-Islamic contacts in Paris, Lausanne, Berlin, Constantinople, St Petersburg, New York and San Francisco, before bringing out a militant pan-Islamic and anti-British journal, *The Islamic*

15 *Islamic Review & Modern India* [*IRMI* – Woking] (May 1914), p. 421
16 *IRMI* (January 1915), p. 36.

Fraternity, from Tokyo in 1909. After the Russian Revolution and the Ottoman defeat, he met Lenin and advocated through his publications (for example, *Bolshevism and Islamic Body Politic*) an alliance with the Bolsheviks to fight for the freedom of the Muslim world. In November 1924 he published *The Khilafat* in English and French, outlining its relevance for the modern age, and an Arabic newspaper *al-Islah* (Reform) first from Berlin in July and then from Paris. He died on his way to San Francisco from where he had planned to organise a revolutionary campaign for India's freedom, his mission unfinished.[17]

By 1919, with the future of the caliphate coming into question, the incentive to continue the pan-Islamic cause remained. Among those who were active within this network in Britain were Rafi-ud-din Ahmed, Mushir Husain Kidwai, Syed Mahmud and Nasir-ud-din from India, and Bedr-ud-din from Egypt. These were all men who were convinced that the true interests of Muslims could only be secured through total political independence from Britain and forging of greater unity among Muslim nations, and not entirely or necessarily by constitutional means. Moreover, Kidwai, together with a small group of Indian radicals, was particularly influenced by Bolshevik ideas. Like Barakatullah, he believed that revolutionary socialism was wholly compatible with the achievement of Muslim aims and published *Islam and Socialism* in London in 1913 setting out his argument. Consequently, similarly to Barakatullah, he worked hard to bring about a closer relationship between the Bolsheviks and the Ottoman caliphate, Afghanistan and Persia, the only independent Muslim states left with some hope of withstanding the power of the West.

This network of pan-Islamist activists established a range of political pressure groups centred on London, which shared the broad aim of stemming the decline of the *umma*. Rebutting accusations that the movement was in any way either fanatical or secretive, these activists asserted the need to defend Islam against Christian misrepresentations and to clear up anti-Muslim feelings in public. The Islamic Society, for instance, represented in its

[17] Khizar Humayun Ansari, *The Emergence of Socialist Thought Among North Indian Muslims (1917–1947)*, Lahore: Book Traders, 1990, pp. 239–41.

president, vice-presidents, members of its managing committee and other officials an impressive array of Muslim activists in London from different parts of the Muslim world, whose numbers also included a number of leading white British converts.[18]

The most high profile initiative in this regard, in which radical pan-Islamists joined forces with more moderate pan-Islamic empire-loyalist networks, was the visit of the Mohammed Ali-led Khilafat deputation to Europe from India in 1920. The two groups not only became involved in the financial and logistical arrangements in Britain and Paris but also arranged public meetings chaired by some of the leading lights of Britain's political elite; handled the delegates' correspondence and interviews (including one with the Prime Minister, Lloyd George, as well as two with Edwin Montagu, the Secretary of State for India); organised the deputation's publicity; and articulated and disseminated its views and demands through various media channels. However, for empire-loyalists, the "delegation was a bitter disappointment": in their view, it was a vehicle for "professional agitators" and, judging from reports in the press, it "alienated sympathy", failing to make "a good impression".[19]

More generally, Kidwai, through the Islamic Information Bureau and the London weekly *Muslim Outlook* (later continued as *Islamic News* and *Muslim Standard*), strove to sway the British government in favour of Turkey, despite a strong wave of anti-Turkish public opinion. A spate of memorials, resolutions, newspaper articles, petitions, and manifestos, produced by these activists, poured out of London.[20] The stream of telegrams from India regarding the caliphate, disseminated through *Muslim Outlook*, as well as news from different parts of the Muslim world highlighted the transnational reach of this pan-Islamic network, as well as the breadth of its connections and its capacity to mobilise international opinion and action around Islamic issues.

18 Central Islamic Society, *Rules and Regulations*, London, 1916.

19 Letter from M.H. Ispahani to the Aga Khan, 24 March 1920 (copy of original with author).

20 See, for example, *Muslim Outlook* (13 November 1919), p. 7; Kidwai's letter to Lord Curzon, *Muslim Outlook* (12 February 1920).

Dusé Mohamed Ali, an Egyptian, was another key activist who pursued his pan-Islamic objectives through a range of channels. One of his pre-war activities that survived into the post-war period was the publication of *The African Times and Orient Review* (*ATOR*) founded in 1912. Dusé used the *ATOR* as an instrument for raising political awareness and mobilisation. Under his editorship, with a circulation mainly "among Mohammedans", it proved a powerful vehicle for the dissemination of his views. Until its final closure in 1920, the publication addressed a bewildering array of issues and supported a wide range of causes. Nevertheless, all were underpinned by a coherent principle that opposition to imperialism and domination of the African and Asian people, the struggle for freedom, required solidarity with the remaining few non-European independent powers. Among these, the Ottoman empire was the most prominent, but its defence, Dusé felt, could only be mounted under the guise of pan-Islamism, and so his efforts were geared to sharpening this solidarity. Perhaps more important than editorials and articles in support of the Ottoman Empire was the active role that Dusé played in fostering pan-Islamic and pro-Ottoman pressure groups, aimed at influencing government policy in Britain, using his magazine to give these organisations and their meetings publicity.[21] Viewed as an "agitator" by the authorities, Dusé was kept under constant surveillance. Ultimately, it was his political skill and influential friends that kept him and these kinds of radical pan-Islamic Muslims out of trouble.

Communalist networking

All the efforts of the pan-Islamists, however, proved to be of no avail. With the abolition first of the Ottoman sultanate in 1922 and then of the caliphate in 1924, many of the Indian pan-Islamists in Britain turned their attention to the narrower issue of the

[21] Ian Duffield, "Duse Mohamed Ali, Afro-Asian Solidarity and Pan-Africanism in early twentieth century London", in J.S. Gundara and I. Duffield (eds), *Essays on the History of Blacks in Britain: From Roman Times to Mid-twentieth century*, Aldershot: Avebury, 1992, pp. 130–31 and 141; see also Ian Duffield, 'Duse Mohamed Ali and the Development of Pan-Africanism', PhD thesis, Edinburgh University, 1971, p. 385.

communal welfare of the subcontinent's Muslims within the context of the movements for national self-determination that were gaining ground there.

Separatist tendencies had started to emerge among certain sections of Indian Muslims during the late nineteenth century in response to their diminishing power under British rule. Sir Sayyid Ahmad Khan, for instance, had warned of declining Muslim fortunes at the time of the formation of the Indian National Congress in 1885. His cautionary message attracted noticeable support in Northern India, and led, in time, to political mobilisation in the form of the self-professedly "communal" All-India Muslim League in 1906, set up with the aim of protecting and advancing Indian Muslim political rights and interests. Thus, the defence of specifically Muslim interests was already in the minds of Indian Muslim elites prior to the emergence of any threat to the caliphate.[22]

As early as May 1908, a group of Indian Muslims resident in England launched a branch of the party in London, with Ameer Ali as president. Its members comprised primarily Muslim students either at English universities or studying for the Bar. Its aims included bringing "the Mahommedans so far as possible into touch with leaders of thought in England".[23] Muhammad Iqbal, who later in 1930 mooted the idea of some kind of separate Muslim state in India, joined the branch when he was in England in 1908. Abdullah Yusuf Ali delivered lectures to the branch between 1915 and 1917, but refrained from becoming too closely involved with its communal approach. While the London branch, as a pressure group based at the heart of the empire, helped to secure the separate communal representation conceded in the 1909 Morley-Minto reforms, it came to be overshadowed by the Khilafat movement and the Indian National Congress after the war, and was reduced merely to passing memoranda asserting the depth of feelings for the Ottoman caliph and his empire.

[22] Ayesha Jalal, "Exploding Communalism: The Politics of Muslim Identity in South Asia", in S. Bose and A. Jalal (eds), *Nationalism, Democracy and Development: State and Politics in India*, Oxford University Press, 1997, p. 83.

[23] *Report of the Inaugural Meeting of the London Branch of the All India Moslem League with the President's Address Wednesday*, 6 May 1908, p. 6.

For many of those who were involved in Khilafat agitation, the collapse of the movement in India in the early 1920s, amid heightened social conflict along communitarian lines, led to the resumption of secular Muslim politics, which meant striving for Indian freedom at the same time as strongly advocating the "Muslim case" for separate representation and safeguards. Many Indian Muslims in Britain, though conscious of their distinct religious and cultural identities, became increasingly more concerned about their subjugation by the British and the daily indignities that they suffered in Britain in common with their Hindu counterparts. Nevertheless, while alliances developed, Muslim communal consciousness continued to grow in response to a combination of British political manipulation and the incapacity of their, and Hindu, leaders to reach a mutually satisfactory agreement. By the 1930s, although ideas regarding a separate homeland for Muslims in India had begun to be put forward, they tended to be mooted within the context of a federal structure, and the grip of "Indianism" remained strong. Abdullah Yusuf Ali, when answering a question regarding the proposal for an independent Muslim homeland at the Joint Select Committee on Indian Constitutional Reform in 1933, dismissed it as a "chimerical and impracticable" students' scheme.[24]

Many Muslim politicians by this time, notably Muhammad Ali Jinnah, together with others in England, while paying homage to their Muslim identities, adopted an ostensibly Western and secular approach to life. Among those who fell into this category and were active in London was Nawab Umar Hayat Khan Tiwana, a distinguished aristocrat from Punjab. Though not himself especially politically motivated, he hosted meetings and social gatherings at his opulent house opposite Regent's Park where political conversations took place in an informal social setting.[25] The wealthy Ispahani family was part of this Westernised Muslim network. Jinnah too lived sumptuously when he practiced as a barrister-at-law in London in the early 1930s. That he socialised in elite circles of the

[24] Minutes of Evidence given before the Joint Committee on Indian Constitutional Reform, vol. II, HMSO, 1934, p. 1496.

[25] Kursheed Kamal Aziz, *Rahmat Ali: A Biography*, Wiesbaden: Steiner Verlag, 1987, pp. 46–7.

British Indian set can be gauged from his presence at, for instance, a "grand dinner" given by Mirza Hashim Ispahani's uncle, where a jazz band performed and most guests "cut capers".[26]

But the man who initiated and, through the 1930s, relentlessly spearheaded the demand for a sovereign Muslim state in South Asia, a demand for which he was ridiculed as a fantasist, was Rahmat Ali. Rahmat Ali came from a reasonably well-off landholding family in the Punjab. After graduating in 1918 he tutored several sons of the rulers and chiefs at Aitchison College, a public school in Lahore. Thanks to his tutorial assignments and his subsequent service with the Mazaris (a very large land-holding family of the Punjab), over the next ten years he cultivated contacts with men of substantial public standing (including Zafarullah Khan[27]), who wrote letters of recommendation to influential scholars and administrators when Rahmat Ali left India in November 1930 to study in England.[28] In London he encountered Tiwana, who had known him for a long time and wrote a further testimonial that helped to secure Rahmat Ali's admission to Cambridge University. Rahmat Ali became part of Tiwana's social circle and was invited to parties given in honour of Iqbal and other delegates at the Round Table Conference

However, few of the prominent communally-minded Muslims in England at the time (including Jinnah, Zafarullah Khan, Iqbal, the Aga Khan) were persuaded by Rahmat Ali's political ideas at this time, and certainly many young Muslim intellectuals at British universities were critical of them. Indeed, it took Rahmat Ali more than a month to find three students who were prepared to support and sign his declaration contained in the pamphlet, *Now or Never*, calling for the establishment of Pakistan as the homeland of the "Muslim nation" in the North-West of India.[29] To pursue his objectives,

[26] Stanley Wolpert, *Jinnah of Pakistan*, Oxford: OUP, 1984, p. 143.

[27] Zafarullah Khan was a prominent member of the Ahmadi community (Qadian branch), and one of the Muslim delegates at the Round Table Conference, who later became president of the All-India Muslim League and Pakistan's foreign minister.

[28] K. K. Aziz, *Rahmat Ali*, pp. 43–5.

[29] Ibid., p. 81.

Rahmat Ali set up the Pakistan National Movement with its purpose set out in an eight-page document. While he was able to gather some support from fellow Cambridge students, given that there were more students in London Rahmat Ali spent much time in the capital. Living in Edgware, he ran a kind of "political school" to propagate the idea of Pakistan among Muslim students. By 1938 he led a committed and motivated (albeit small) network of activists prepared to help him personally and through the provision of resources in his "campaign" for Pakistan—distributing the literature nationally by hand or by post, and even broadcasting their message at the famous Hyde Park Speakers' Corner.[30] Rahmat Ali was also in touch with Muslims in India, supplying them with written material and building a network of supporters there. These efforts did bear some fruit. Towards the end of the 1930s the British press reported that the idea of Pakistan was "spreading rapidly" and began increasingly to see it as a possible solution to the "Hindu-Muslim conflict".[31] There is little doubt that, without the resilience and determination of Rahmat Ali's network and its work in both India and Britain in keeping the Pakistan campaign alive in the "wilderness years" between 1933 and 1937, it would not have been possible to establish the organisational structures that generated the level of mobilisation which helped to persuade Muslim League leaders to issue their demand for Pakistan in 1940.

Students' associations and socialist circles

At the same time, not all Indian Muslims from elite backgrounds in Britain during the inter-war years necessarily operated within a communal framework. A number of Indian Muslim students in Britain developed close contacts with other secular nationalists of varying degrees of radicalism, and involved themselves actively in campaigns for Indian Home Rule. Organised in clubs at British universities, which afforded useful forums for the testing and refining of radical ideas and practices, they discussed India's problems and wider social issues in passionate debates between "moderates"

[30] Ibid., pp. 171–2
[31] Ibid., pp. 180–1.

and "extremists". The Indian Majlis (Indian Students' Association) founded at Oxford by Mohammed Ali and his friends at the turn of the century and the one in Cambridge set up by Indian students in 1907 developed during the 1920s and 1930s into hubs of intellectual, social and cultural activity—debating arenas, study circles, dinner parties, literary and musical evenings—and provided networking opportunities for politically-inclined Indians. It was at the Cambridge Majlis, for instance, that Ispahani and Jinnah were first introduced (a meeting that began a long personal and political friendship between the two) when the latter was invited to address its members in 1920.[32]

Politically, Majlis members remained a diverse group. In 1925, a British intelligence document provided the following analysis of the political persuasion of the 66 members of the Oxford Majlis: 18 moderates (in favour of Dominion status for India), 11 Swarajists (seeking full independence), five socialists, 20 Indian Civil Service probationers, and 12 unclassified.[33] Communalism was dormant and even declined while these students were in Britain. Majlis meetings at Oxford began with the singing of the Congress anthem *Bande Mataram* and ended with a hymn by the Muslim poet Iqbal.[34] Most participants clearly identified with the concept of an undivided "India". As one member put it, the Majlis was "a body where we feel our corporate and united existence. A living sense of oneness steals into our hearts as we meet Sunday after Sunday for debates or discussion . . . Religion and racial feelings are dissolved and forgotten for the common good . . . It keeps a vigilant watch of the interests of Indian students as a whole".[35]

A proportion of these Indian Muslim students came under the influence of the British Communist Party, which offered them revolutionary social and cultural alternatives. By the end of the 1920s, a small group—M.D. Tasir from Cambridge, Mian Iftikharuddin,

[32] S. Wolpert, *Jinnah*, pp. 142–3.

[33] Shompa Lahiri, *Indians in Britain, Anglo-Indian Encounters, Race and Identity, 1880–1930*, London: Frank Cass, 2000, p. 179.

[34] Richard Symonds, *Oxford and Empire: the Last Lost Cause?*, Basingstoke: Macmillan, 1986, p. 262.

[35] S. Lahiri, *Indians in Britain*, p. 207.

Sajjad Zaheer and Mahmuduzzafar from Oxford, Dr Z.A. Ahmad, Hajra Begum and K.M. Ashraf from London—had gathered together in a study circle based in London. Regular meetings were held at someone's residence or in the back rooms of London restaurants. Most of them came from elite families of Northern India with a tradition of serving the British *raj*. In England, however, they were influenced by the broader events of the 1920s and early 1930s: world-wide economic depression, the rise of fascism in Germany, and the imminent danger of war made an impact on their consciousness and politicised them, as did the racial prejudices that they experienced in Britain: as Sajjad Zaheer later wrote, "We were witnessing all around us a period of great conflicts and struggles".[36]

In 1934, a handful of these Muslims along with other Indians met in Sajjad Zaheer's flat and formed a committee to organise a Progressive Writers' Association. A manifesto was approved and mimeographed copies were sent to India for distribution and further discussion among writers there. The first formal meeting of the PWA, held in November 1934, attracted 30 to 35 people, mainly students from London, Oxford and Cambridge. This group of "exiles" maintained close contacts with like-minded friends and colleagues in India as well as in Europe, and, thus, developed their thought and activity through communication and circulation of ideas transnationally. Most, transformed by their experiences in Britain, in time returned to India to join those already engaged there in radical literary and political work. Their focus was the liberation of India, but with Muslims as their main constituency and audience.

RELIGIOUS NETWORKS

In late nineteenth-century Britain, negative views of Islam and Muslims came to influence a wide cross-section of society. Gladstone, four times Prime Minister, referred to the Qur'an as "that accursed book", declaring that Islam was "radically incapable of establishing a good and tolerable government over civilised and Christian races".[37] In

[36] Sajjad Zaheer, 'Yaden', *Naya Adab Kya Hai?*, Lucknow, 1941, pp. 66–86.

[37] Humayun Ansari, *'The Infidel Within': Muslims in Britain Since 1800*, London: Hurst, 2004, p. 80.

order to defend Islam against misrepresentations, scholarly and popular efforts in an organised form began to be made, albeit embryonically, by men such as Quilliam. In time, some went further: convinced that Islam was a relevant faith for people living in Britain, they became engaged in its positive propagation as a progressive moral force.

Early pioneering efforts

One of the earliest efforts to raise the profile of Islam in Britain was the establishment of the *Anjuman-i-Islam* in 1886 under the leadership of Abdullah Suhrawardy to carry out *da'wa* (missionary) work. It disseminated its ideas through a monthly called *The Light of the World*, pamphlets and letters to the press, and "mass meetings" held in Leicester Square Gardens and Peckham Rye: as Khalid Sheldrake, who converted to Islam in 1904, later recalled, "The principal events of our faith continued to be celebrated and a splendid library of Islamic literature was collected".[38] The *Anjuman*'s efforts were followed by those of Abdullah Quilliam who, also in the late nineteenth century, founded the Liverpool Mosque and Institute (LMI) that acted as the centre for his Muslim network nationally as well as abroad. Between 1891 and his departure in 1908, the LMI came to embrace a mosque, a *madrasa*, a library and reading room, a museum, schools, a hostel for Muslims, a printing press and an office for a literary society. Weekly meetings and lectures were held and two journals (one a weekly, *The Crescent*, the other, a monthly, *The Islamic World*) circulated internationally.[39]

The Woking Mission

The network centred on the LMI, however, contracted rapidly as British relations with Turkey deteriorated in the period before the First World War. But with its demise another mission took shape, this time centred on the Muslim population based in London and the Home Counties. Its objective was to construct an intellectual space

[38] For more information about Sheldrake's involvement, see Max Everest-Phillips, "The Suburban King of Tartary", *Asian Affairs* (October 1990), pp. 324–33. Also see *IRMI* (January 1914), p. 31.

[39] H. Ansari, *The Infidel Within*, pp. 122–3.

for Islam in Britain by establishing a degree of consonance between it and the "native" religion, Christianity. The Woking Mosque, built in 1889, became its institutional base. Its strategy was broadly assimilationist: if Islam was to prosper in Britain, it needed to be made indigenous, as it had been elsewhere. Very early on, Muslim "missionaries" such as Khwaja Kamaluddin realised that, if they were to make any headway in conversion, they would have to adopt a rationalist, modernist approach. The Mission's relatively liberal and tolerant approach was also reflected in its rigorously non-sectarian practice, epitomised by the rotation of imams to lead the prayers. Weekly lectures on different topics were conducted at the mosque and later at the "Prayer House" established in London. "At homes" and garden parties, increasingly popular, were arranged with a similar purpose in mind but in a more relaxed and informal setting.

Through its journal, the *Islamic Review* (distributed widely and free of charge[40]), the Mission's main figures elaborated their views on polygamy and the position of women in Islam, drinking alcohol and eating pork, usury and gambling, as well as issues of circumcision, fasting, *sadaqa* and prayer, and many other topics which aroused controversy or seemed at variance with Christian practice. The propaganda work that was pursued at Woking and London attracted some interest and was "favourably noticed by the English press".[41]

These religious networks, however, were not solely engaged in *da'wa* activities. They were also required to arrange for all-important rites of passage. Weddings were celebrated at the Woking Mosque according to the Islamic tradition, and by 1915 its imam had secured for the mosque the status of officiator at marriage, something generally reserved for the churches.[42] With casualties in the war rising, burial services had to be performed according to Muslim rites, with full military honours, for Muslim soldiers. The Woking Mosque imam played an active role in having a section of the nearby Brookwood Cemetery reserved for the use of

[40] The journal was "primarily founded for the purpose of expounding Islam and putting it before the British public", see *Islamic Review* [*IR* – Woking] (January 1916), p. 13.

[41] *IRMI* (April 1915), p. 164.

[42] *IRMI* (December 1915).

Muslims—especially those Muslim soldiers who had died while at the Victoria Royal Hospital in Netley.[43]

The British Muslim Society

A sister organisation, the British Muslim Society (BMS), had been set up in December 1914 under the leadership of Lord Headley, the most influential convert associated with the Woking Mission, and it continued to operate in the years following the end of the war. Its primary object was to bring together Muslims and interested non-Muslims. Many of the converts who joined the Society had direct experience of the "Muslim world": while the vast majority of its members remained Indian Muslim students, it also included white converts such as Marmaduke Pickthall.

The Society met regularly for Friday prayers and Sunday services. Islamic literature was disseminated at its public meetings. By the early 1920s it was attracting considerable numbers at its weekly meetings at the Muslim Prayer House in London, partly because of the opportunity that these afforded for mixing and chatting.[44] Especially popular was its annual celebration of the Prophet Muhammad's birthday at one of London's reputable hotels and restaurants.[45] These were all, in effect, multi-faith and international occasions attended by well-known Muslims as well as guests representing other religions, literature and the press.[46] Culture mingled with religious solemnity. Formal speeches on Muhammad's life were followed by odes in Urdu sung to a harmonium accompaniment, renditions of Indian classical music on the sitar, and selections of Western music on the piano and violin.[47]

Other initiatives included the establishment of a Muslim Literary Society (MLS),[48] as well as a trust for the encouragement and circulation of Muslim religious literature with Lord Headley and Sir Abbas Ali Baig, a member of the India Council, as its

[43] *IRMI* (December 1914).
[44] "At times they were packed like sardines", *IR* (March 1923), p. 83.
[45] For instance, see *IR* (January 1916), pp. 77–8.
[46] Those who attended included Princess Ola Hassan from Turkey, the Aga Khan, Begum Shah Nawaz and Prince Aly Khan. See *IR* (December 1931), pp. 425–6.
[47] *IR* (February 1916), p. 78.
[48] *IR* (September 1917), p. 398.

trustees.[49] Included in the MLS's diverse activities was a lecture series on Islamic topics; one on "modernism and Islam" by Marmaduke Pickthall a few days after his acceptance of Islam; another some time later looking at sectarianism by Lord Headley, with Mian Sir Muhammad Shafi overseeing the discussion.[50] The Prayer House was reportedly packed for Sir Iqbal Ali Shah's lecture on "The truth about Muslim modernisation".[51]

Much of the work undertaken by these religious networks was conducted with a light touch, and British cultural forms were adopted to avoid an impression of "strangeness". For instance, the Qur'an was referred to as the "Muslim bible", and the mosque, the "Muslim Church", welcomed non-Muslims to its Sunday services.[52] The success of this approach was confirmed by a steady stream of conversions regularly announced in the Woking Mission's journal in the inter-war years.[53] Less success, however, was forthcoming during this period in efforts to establish a central mosque in London that could stand as a national symbol of the Muslim presence in Britain as well as a memorial to those Muslims who had died in defence of the Empire. Despite generous donations (£60,000) from the Nizam of Hyderabad, these efforts came to nothing.[54] In 1940, in the face of disappointment at the government's refusal to support the project, three houses were bought in the East End of London with money that had been accumulating in the London Mosque Fund under the trusteeship of Sir Hussain Suhrawardy, the Aga Khan, Abdullah Yusuf Ali and Marmaduke Pickthall. After conversion work, these properties were finally inaugurated as a mosque in 1941.[55]

49 *IR* (January 1926), p. 3.
50 Lord Headley, "Is Our House In Order?", *IR* (September 1928), p. 322.
51 *IR* (January 1929), p. 7.
52 *IR* (March 1916), p.1.
53 "Roughly speaking in the last two years 80 ladies have converted to Islam", *IR* (January 1916), p. 108; again, in January 1918, *IR* reported 100 conversions in the previous year.
54 *IR* (September 1929), pp. 340–41.
55 India Office Record, L/P&J/12/468, The East London Mosque and Islamic Cultural Centre, Opening Ceremony, 1 August 1941; Scotland Yard Report, 6 August 1941; Suhrawardy to Amery, 27 July 1942.

The mission of the Qadian branch of the Ahmadiyya

Other *da'wa*-based Muslim networks, albeit in an embryonic form, also surfaced in the early decades of the twentieth century. Around the same time that Khwaja Kamaluddin, belonging to the "Lahori" wing of the Ahmadiyya movement, was establishing the Woking Mission in a strictly non-sectarian fashion, missionaries of the "Qadiani" persuasion began putting down roots in London—Fateh Sayal, for instance, arrived in 1913. They strove to convert people to the Ahmadi version of Islam, which claimed the founder of the sect as the promised Messiah. In contrast to mainstream pan-Islamists, Qadianis did not recognise the Sultan in Istanbul as their Caliph, declaring that there was nothing in the Qur'an which showed that the Sultan of Turkey was "a true Khalifa of God"; instead they urged acceptance of Mirza Ghulam Ahmad, the founder of their movement, as the true Khalifa. After the war, their view was that Islam would prevail spiritually but not temporally "as Indian Muslims had aspired to see".[56]

In the inter-war period, even with their heterodox beliefs, they were not cast outside the fold of Islam, though tensions were developing between the Woking Mission and the Qadianis by the late 1920s (as can be gleaned from the pages of the *Islamic Review*).[57] Muslim converts such as Khalid Sheldrake and Abdullah Quilliam celebrated the festival of *'Id* at the Ahmadi Mosque from time to time, and Abdullah Yusuf Ali gave speeches on such occasions.[58] Indeed, both Fateh Sayal and Abdul Rahim Dard, the two most prominent Ahmadi missionaries after the First World War, were very much part of the mainstream Indian Muslim network in London: they were included, for instance, in the elite deputation that was received by the Shah of Persia on his visit to England in November 1919.[59]

The Ahmadi Mission grew steadily in the 1920s and 1930s, though the number of its adherents remained relatively small. In

56 *Review of Religions* (*RoR*—published from 1902 to 1925 from Qadian in India and from 1925 from London), October-November 1919, p. 351.

57 *IR* (September 1928), pp. 328–9.

58 *RoR* (August 1925), p. 1.

59 *Muslim Outlook* (November 1919), p. 5.

1924 the leader of the Ahmadi community arrived in London to take part in the Wembley Conference of World Religions. He laid the foundation stone of the first mosque in the capital and, in the two years while it was being constructed in South-West London, Ahmadis deployed all their resources into developing facilities for the study and propagation of Islam, focusing on theological lectures, debates and discussions. Indeed, they were quick to challenge any views or comments that they considered denigrated Islam or the Prophet Muhammad: when *The Star* published a cartoon with Jack Hobbs, the cricketer, as a colossal figure with Adam and Muhammad among those at his feet, a letter of protest was immediately sent, which led to an expression of regret by both the newspaper and Hobbs.[60] The Fazl Mosque in Southfields was inaugurated in 1926 by Sir Shaikh Abdul Qadir, a member of the India Council, and it became the centre of Ahmadiyya activity as well as a meeting place for prominent Muslims based in London. In effect, a community grew up around it.

While the Ahmadi mosque did not achieve the same high profile enjoyed by the Woking Mosque during the inter-war period, in part because of its association with a "heretical" sect, the Ahmadi movement was not yet considered "deviant" enough to deter prominent mainstream Muslim activists, converts or otherwise, from accepting invitations to attend and participate in its religious activities. A prominent Indian Muslim, Sir Feroze Khan Noon, attended the Mosque when in London, and most notably the Saudi Crown Prince Faisal bin Abdul Aziz visited it in July 1935.

Inayat Khan's followers

Alongside the mainstream religious networks operating in Britain by the inter-war period, a tradition of Islam that stressed personal devotion and piety also made its appearance. This strand of Muslim practice and belief was established by Inayat Khan, a charismatic musician initiated in the Chishti tradition who came to England in 1912, with the instruction from his *murshid* (teacher) to "spread the

[60] For the correspondence between the journal, the Home Secretary and Jack Hobbs, see *RoR* (November 1925), pp. 28–30.

wisdom of Sufism abroad".[61] His approach to religious and theological matters was largely contemplative and spiritual, and he regarded Sufism as a path to self-illumination and the realisation of God.

Initially Inayat Khan generated interest through his music: concerts, lessons and lectures. His audience comprised artists, intellectuals, people of social standing and members of the aristocracy. He was invited to tea and dinner parties where he met literary figures and intellectuals who listened to him with much understanding, including the poets Sir Henry Newbolt and Robert Bridges, Lord Lamington and Sir Edwin Lutyens, the architect of New Delhi. During the war, he performed at charity concerts in aid of the widows and orphans of Indians killed in action,[62] and entertained wounded Indian soldiers by playing and singing to them.[63] In February 1915, assisted by his first *murid* (disciple) Mary Williams, he set up a Sufi Publishing Society, which brought out many of his philosophical and poetical works and his *Sufi Magazine*.[64]

In time, Inayat Khan collected a nucleus of devotees and disciples around him who gave his Order an organised shape. They publicised his thoughts through letters to the press, encouraged interviews, organised lectures on Indian music and his Sufi philosophy, and publicised his Universal Worship service. Inayat Khan was in demand and his lecture tours stretched as far as Scotland. Branches of the Order were founded not only in Brighton, Harrogate and Southampton; his ideas also began to attract followers in France, Switzerland, Holland and even the United States.[65] Khwaja Ismail, Yusuf Ali and Marmaduke Pickthall were good friends and honorary members of the Society, whose headquarters, Inayat's home (first in Ladbroke Road and then in Gordon Square), operated along the lines of a *khanqah*—a sort of monastery with living-quarters, guest accommodation and office—where guests were invited to "dervish dinners".

[61] *Biography of Pir-o-Murshid Inayat Khan*, London/The Hague: East-West Publications, 1979, p. 111.

[62] Elizabeth de Jong-Kessing, *Inayat Khan: a Biography*, London: Luzac, 1974, p. 144.

[63] *Biography of Pir-o-Murshid Inayat Khan*, p. 139.

[64] Ibid., p. 141.

[65] See E. de Jong-Kessing, *Inayat Khan* for details.

In 1919 Inayat was still operating within an Islamic framework. He remained involved in other Muslim networks such as the Islamic Society and the British Muslim Society, though it appears from his writings that Inayat viewed both the Woking Mission and the Qadianis with disdain and had little good to say about their activities.[66] To maintain his distinctiveness from other strands of religious activism at the time, his fortnightly lectures were organised by his own *Anjuman-i-Islam* with the objective of bringing Muslims and non-Muslims together. Among the lecturers was that old stalwart of Islam, Quilliam, or Henry Mustapha Leon as he called himself at the time.[67]

OCCUPATION-BASED NETWORKS

While many of the networks linking Muslims in Britain in the inter-war period were based on common origins or religious affiliation, there were other kinds of networks in existence that were linked to particular kinds of shared occupation. For instance, in Manchester there were still Moroccan and other Arab merchants, lured by the city's reputation as the textile manufacturing capital of the world, who had trading houses there from the middle of the nineteenth century in order to export cotton goods back to their "home" countries. As a community, these Middle Eastern and North African Muslims retained links with their homelands, helping their families and kinfolk, bringing over newly-acquired wives and taking political initiatives to accelerate their countries' independence from Ottoman rule. Engagement with British society was selective and primarily in the context of the working environment, with little mixing. Adaptations to English life were minimal, partly as a result of suspicion towards Arabs that surfaced from time to time and partly because they themselves found some features of

[66] See *Biography of Pir-o-Murshid Inayat Khan*.

[67] That Quilliam had changed his name to Leon, apparently while he was in Turkey, was confirmed by his wife after his death in 1932: see the *Daily Telegraph*, 26 April 1932, p. 14. That he used it as his "pen name" can be seen from the publicity of his lectures, for instance, in *Muslim Outlook* (27 November 1919), p. 7.

British society morally undesirable. On the whole, they wanted to retain Muslim values and secure their transmission to future generations. With increased competition from France and Japan, Manchester's domination of Middle Eastern markets declined and, with that, Arab merchant communities began to wane, finally disappearing almost completely by the end of the 1930s.[68]

The First World War, however, acted as a catalyst in stimulating migration to meet the demands of the war effort. Arab and black seamen replaced indigenous workers who were mobilised for war service. The end of the war subsequently ushered in a period of considerable social crisis. The post-war boom, which largely bypassed port industries, ended quickly, with the loss of many jobs. Muslim lascars, who were living in small communities by the early 1920s, bore the brunt of the resentment; demands for their exclusion from jobs and homes grew quickly. In 1919 they became the targets of racist violence in Liverpool, Glasgow, Cardiff, London and South Shields. These Muslim communities, largely unsupported and outnumbered, desperately defended themselves by banding together to resist mob violence. As the economic crisis deepened, and unemployment rose, especially in the older export industries where many had found work, they began to move inland in search of employment in the new industries such as car manufacturing, chemicals, electrical and consumer goods that were expanding in the 1920s.

However, on the whole, the British economic situation continued to deteriorate, especially between 1925 and 1932, and so they had to find alternative means for survival. Young men originating from rural localities in the Punjab, Kashmir, the North West Frontier Province and Sylhet in Bengal initially eked out a living by labouring and hawking. The more enterprising among the unemployed from middling Indian rural backgrounds tried their hands at petty trading and other entrepreneurial activities, in particular peddling. From 1927, as the news got around of how comparatively well many of these migrants were doing, the number of Indian Muslims from East Punjab began to multiply. Some such as

[68] Fred Halliday, 'The *Millet* of Manchester: Arab Merchants and Cotton Trade', *British Journal of Middle Eastern Studies*, XIX, 2 (1992), pp. 159–76.

Naththo Mohammed, an ex-lascar in Glasgow, pioneered one process of chain migration and the construction of kin-based networks. These networks were regularly replenished throughout the inter-war period by the regular arrival of relatives, kinsmen, friends, acquaintances and contacts. By 1940 in Glasgow alone the community had around 400 members.[69] However, as their numbers grew, tensions arose because of competition within the peddling fraternity, compelling some members, encouraged by contacts elsewhere, to disperse and try their hand at similar work in other parts of Britain. In this way the networks became nationally connected. During the late 1930s, a number of them gravitated to the Midlands, the North of England, and even Scotland, encouraged by the many stories that circulated regarding the economic success of earlier "pioneers". While the Depression years of the early 1930s made survival difficult, they were sufficiently resilient to lay the foundations of the thriving clothing and garment trade that was subsequently developed by those who followed them into wholesaling and manufacturing from the 1960s.[70]

Others, from Bengal, renewed the tradition of setting up lodging-houses to cater for lascars in London's East End. Here men were boarded and maintained free of charge when out of a job, for months at a time; in these lodging houses Muslim seamen found friends and compatriots who helped them to negotiate their way round the bureaucracy. They were initiated into the language and the craft of peddling by old hands, and given moral support. Ayub Ali, Tofusil Ali and Abdul Mannan with their lodging houses and cafes became the centres of support networks and acted as "clearing houses", meeting a variety of migrant needs. Abdul Mannan's Basement Café in Percy Road in London's East End, for instance, became the favourite haunt of Sylheti men who would gather there to exchange news of ships, factories, jobs, the war, politics and most of all "home", over tea or a homely meal. Here those without education would have their letters read for them, and replies written

[69] Bashir Maan, *The New Scots: The Story of Asians in Scotland*, Edinburgh: John Donald Publishers, 1992, pp. 98–152.

[70] Pnina Werbner, *The Migration Process; Capital, Gifts and Offerings among British Pakistanis*, Oxford: Berg, 1990, pp. 11–56.

sending all their news to the family. A few went on to set up coffee shops, after having worked as kitchen hands in hotels and restaurants in the West End. The more enterprising among them felt confident enough to try Indian cuisine, which for years they had prepared for their fellow seamen on ships and in ports, on a wider clientele. The first two restaurants were established in the late 1920s. Their success attracted others to the catering trade, and by 1946 the number of Indian, mainly Sylheti-owned, restaurants in London had risen to twenty.[71]

What made these networks of pioneering settlers all the more important was the groundwork which they carried out, forging links in the chain which would connect earlier and later generations of Muslims migrating to Britain. The common feature of all these pioneers was that they came from petty farming backgrounds and from villages situated within a few miles of each other. As they themselves became established in Britain, they called their kin over and helped to set them up. In this way Muslim workers created social networks based on their concentrations in segregated localities in Britain's port cities and industrial centres. With communications and social networks in place, these various economic activities drew an increasing stream of migrants to the employment opportunities generated by them.

The residential clustering of the vast majority of Muslim workers in Britain during the inter-war decades took place partly in response to the refusal of the white population to have any kind of close physical or social contact with them—their view was that Muslim workers residing in areas associated with crime, violence and commercial vice were men of low status. The by-product of this segregation was the emergence of Muslim communities with a distinct sense of identity. These Muslims also adopted voluntary segregation in order to avoid conflict and humiliation, preferring to congregate in cafes and boarding houses established in their own localities. Through their local networks, Muslim workers displayed considerable tenacity in their efforts to preserve certain traditions that they perceived were central to the maintenance of the Muslim character of their communities.

[71] Kathleen Hunter, *History of Pakistanis in Britain*, London: Page Bros., 1963, p. 17.

Relations between Muslim seamen and white workers, throughout this period, were strained. Language difficulties, and differences in cultures and knowledge and understanding of the role and function of trades unions, hampered communication and generated negative feelings towards each other. Misplaced sexual jealousies and competition were transferred to the workplace, adversely affecting relationships. Contacts with employers and white fellow workers did result in a degree of familiarity but the scope was limited and the relationships were unequal. Much of this inequality took institutionalised forms and was organised through the institutions of the state or by white workers themselves through their trade unions.[72]

Muslims' responses to their social circumstances and discriminatory treatment by the wider society varied according to the different purposes for which they chose to strive. The level of organisation among Muslims increased throughout the inter-war period and they became a little more effective as they learned from past mistakes and gained in terms of experience. For instance, in 1924 Yemeni boarding house masters set up the Cardiff Adenese Club and Association to defend themselves against charges of "crimping" and bribery.[73] In the aftermath of the British Shipping (Assistance) Act of 1935 the "Islamia Allawia Friendly Society" was formed in order to mobilise resistance to it. This Society provided "a meeting place for Moslem seamen. . .[and aimed] at uniting all members of the Moslem community in the port".[74] Sometimes they came together in social and self-help groups, often retaining ethnic and religious boundaries, in order to enhance their pride and give their lives a semblance of dignity. The *Jamiat-ul-Muslimin*, founded in 1934, was based in East London. A charitable society for the promotion of Islam, it gave aid to needy Muslims, and served as

[72] Marika Sherwood, "Racism and Resistance: Cardiff in the 1930s and 1940s", *LLafur*, V, 4 (1991), p. 56; Neil Evans, "Regulating the Reserve Army: Arabs, Blacks and the Local State in Cardiff, 1919–1945", *Immigrants and Minorities*, IV, 2 (July 1985), p. 83; Laura Tabili, *"We Ask For Justice": Workers and Racial Difference in Late Imperial Britain*, Ithaca/New York: Cornell University Press, 1994, pp. 104–33.

[73] N. Evans, "Regulating", p. 99.

[74] L. Tabili, *We Ask for Justice*, p. 147.

a social organisation, bringing resident Muslims and visitors together. A similar body was established in Glasgow.[75]

In the 1930s some Muslim workers joined more radical and sympathetic labour organisations to assert their rights, claim their entitlements and struggle more effectively against discrimination and prejudice directed against them. For many of these Muslims, however, religion remained a key organising principle in the late 1930s. They were persuaded to join pressure groups with specifically Muslim identities in part because they were led to believe that, since these had been initiated by Muslim professionals whose education and social class gave them access to higher levels of national government, they stood a better chance of having the Muslims' demands met. However, this analysis seemed to have been flawed. Abdul Majid and Khalid Sheldrake, who led some of these Islamic organisations (the Islamic Society and the Western Islamic Association), were unable to squeeze any concessions out of the authorities. Indeed new restrictions in the mid-1930s resulted in further bouts of prolonged unemployment, leaving many Arabs indigent and homeless.[76]

Some Muslims in Britain, therefore, found themselves forming part of broader multicultural networks, which co-existed with and sometimes transcended religion. As workers, they were drawn into setting up separate trade unions and other pressure groups in response to trade union discrimination in order to strengthen their negotiating position. In 1937, Akbar Khan, for instance, founded the Indian Workers Association (IWA) together with two Sikhs, as a mutual welfare society to protect the interests of its members, predominantly Punjabi peddlers and factory workers in Coventry. A bi-monthly bulletin in English and Hindustani, *The Indian Worker*, edited by Mohammed Fazal Hussein, was brought out. Branches were set up in many cities and those in Coventry, Birmingham, Bradford, Liverpool, Dundee, Wolverhampton flourished. As a social/welfare organisation, the IWA helped its members with

[75] Rozina Visram, *Asians in Britain: 400 Years of History*, London: Pluto Press, 2002, p. 298.

[76] Richard I. Lawless, *From Ta'izz To Tyneside: an Arab Community in the North-East of England in the Early Twentieth Century*, University of Exeter Press, 1995, p. 170.

registration and National Service papers during the Second World War; investigated cases of injury and accidents at work, taking up claims for compensation with appropriate authorities; and provided a platform for grievances concerning work and housing. It ran classes in English and Hindi and remitted funds to India. It enabled its members to participate in the British labour movement as well as campaigning for the freedom of India. Surat Ally, a skilful Indian labour organiser, founded the Colonial Seamen's Association in the mid-1930s and became its first Secretary.[77]

Through these networks Muslim workers challenged and resisted the mechanisms of exclusion that were being applied by the institutions of the state and white-centred trade unions. However, given the huge odds against them, it is no surprise that their achievements were relatively modest. It would be more accurate to say that Muslim organisation probably delivered as much in the purely religious domain and in building self-esteem and confidence as it did in the resolution of practical concerns, if not more.

CONCLUSION: OVERLAPPING NETWORKS AND TRANSNATIONAL IDENTITIES

Clearly inter-war Britain contained a range of networks of active Muslims whose backgrounds and interests drew them to common causes. All the same, it is important to point out that these networks were not necessarily mutually exclusive. Overlaps could, and frequently, did take place, some more obvious than others. For instance, Indian Muslims belonging to elite groups, whether empire-loyalist or pan-Islamic radical, were often drawn to the networks that were constructed for faith reasons. Hence Yusuf Ali (as well as British converts such as Lord Headley) participated in empire-loyalist as well as faith-centred circles, passionately opposing the Ottoman caliphate and Indian independence, while scrupulously adhering to religious ritual and taking a keen and leading interest in the activities organised under the auspices of the Woking Mission and British Muslim Society. His ecumenism prompted him to take part in events at the Ahmadiyya Mosque in Southfields and

[77] L. Tabili, *We Ask For Justice*, pp. 162–6.

even more so in Inayat Khan's Sufi Order. Yusuf Ali desperately wanted to bring about a marriage of what in his view was best in the East and the West, and, like Inayat Khan, he argued that the religion of all thinking men was essentially the same. That in 1936 he preached a sermon at the Unitarian Church to a packed congregation is testimony to his conviction of the basic unity underlying all religions.

Ameer Ali and Marmaduke Pickthall similarly straddled the empire-loyalist, pan-Islamic and faith networks. Ameer Ali, as an empire-loyalist, worked tirelessly to build bridges between Muslim interests and the British establishment, pursuing causes of Indian Muslims and elsewhere through constitutional means within the framework of empire. But as a pan-Islamist he set up funds to help Turkey and vigorously campaigned to save the Ottoman Caliphate. Yet again as a man of faith, he played a central role in organising and disseminating Islam individually through his writing and through collective mobilisation of resources, for instance, the London Mosque Fund that financed the establishment of the East London Mosque in 1941. On the other hand, the logic of radical pan-Islamism led Mushir Husain Kidwai and Dusé Mohamed Ali not only to defend and support the few independent Muslim states but also to urge common cause with colonial people in their struggle for national freedom and against racial subordination, if necessary, by revolutionary means. But, interestingly, they were also happy on occasion to work with the *da'wa* networks. In a similar fashion, prominent activists within the empire-loyalist and pan-Islamic networks of this period extended their activities to other fields where they believed that community ties based on religious identity underpinned shared concerns. For example, Khalid Sheldrake and Abdul Majid sought to link their commitment to their faith with work intended to bring improvement in the day-to-day lives of some of Britain's working-class Muslim communities in places such as South Shields and Cardiff. This pattern of overlapping networks reinforced ties and links within and between different groups of Muslims operating in inter-war Britain, and makes it hard as well as futile to disengage them from one another. It served instead to help construct a multi-faceted complex reality, which highlighted the rich texture of British Muslim experience at this time. Indeed, the existence of distinct yet interconnected networks reinforces the need to avoid oversimplification when it comes to making sense of this reality, and highlights the diversity that underpinned it.

Muslims in Britain before 1945 thus sought to sustain at least the core features of their identities, whether religious, political, social or cultural, through the construction of networks. Developments in Liverpool, Manchester, London, Cardiff and South Shields illustrate the range of ways in which various Muslims sought to organise themselves during this period. As the networks expanded, individuals identified what they perceived to be the requirements inherent in, and necessary for, their survival. In turn, more formal institutionalisation took place. In all these British cities and towns, institutions were established through which to organise Muslims according to recognised religious, political and material needs, as well as to formalise and develop Islam in the British context. In contrast to the indigenous Islam forged by British converts, Muslim networks that consisted primarily of migrants from overseas sought to reproduce expressions of Islamic practices and requirements that were somewhat more rooted in their homelands. This is not to ignore the fact that a significant degree of acculturation took place within these communities.

The evolution of Muslim networks in Britain was thus a complex process, reflecting the diversity present within its Muslim communities. A heterogeneous range of organisations emerged, representing different memberships, client groups and administrative structures. Their functions and activities reveal converging as well as conflicting concerns, depending on their particular cultural, religious and political orientations. British Muslim networks, in effect, were multi-layered and multi-purpose—they possessed multiple contents, crossing over national, physical and political boundaries, involving social, symbolic and imaginary inter-connections. Processes of transnational circulation brought Muslims into contact with one another, and also brought the countries and communities from which they came into relations with one another. Muslim participants from different parts of the *umma* contributed to these networks and found shared meanings, memories and symbols through them. All this contributed to building up forms of identity and of loyalty that were simultaneously internal and transnational.

At the same time, both the structures of Britain's Muslim population and the institutional framework of the British environment largely shaped the networks. Intellectual and organisational forms were discovered that allowed these Muslims and wider society to discuss issues within a mutually comprehensible discourse as well as effectively operating within the political-cum-legal parameters set by the host society. Thus the networks were able to achieve a measure of public status; they were able to deliver a range of required services as well as making some impact on the political, social and cultural agendas at the time. Some even provided an environment conducive to the development of an indigenised non-sectarian, depoliticised faith.

Thus, what we learn from the early twentieth century is that contemporary transnational Muslim networks in Britain are not a new phenomenon. In the past, as now, they revealed the complex nature of allegiances, allegiances that called the national sense of belonging into question. Indeed, just after the First World War, by agitating through a range of channels and pressure groups in support of Ottoman integrity, Muslims in Britain caused their patriotism and loyalties to be questioned. Then, as now, their ambivalence was predicated on what was happening in the wider world, connected to Western dominance especially of the Muslim world and the immediate position of Muslims in Britain. However, what has transformed these networks today is, in many ways, the changed global socio-economic, cultural and political context as well as the mass movement of Muslims linked by new forms of instantaneous technologically-advanced communications and media. The modes and processes of adaptation necessitated by more recent transnational flows and connections have presented Muslims with both new opportunities and new predicaments, challenging their identities as Muslims and their ways of enacting them.

BETWEEN NATIONAL AND RELIGIOUS SOLIDARITIES: THE TATARS IN GERMANY AND POLAND IN THE INTER-WAR PERIOD

Sebastian Cwiklinski

This chapter will focus on the history of the Tatar communities in Germany and Poland in the inter-war period. Special emphasis will be put on the networking activities of both communities as this might help to reveal similarities and differences in their structure. Although this is not the place to discuss all the different meanings of the designation "Tatar" during the course of history,[1] it might be helpful to recall the usages in the inter-war context. From the beginning of the nineteenth century, with the establishment of scientific discourses on Turkic peoples in the Russian Empire, the designation "Tatar" was used by Russians to include all peoples speaking a Turkic dialect/language.[2] Moreover, from the end of the nineteenth century onwards the majority of Turkic-speaking Muslims in the Russian Empire themselves used "Tatar" or "Turko-Tatar" as a collective denomination. "Tatar" served as an alternative to

[1] For a detailed analysis see Gotthard Jäschke, "Zur Geschichte des Namens 'Tatar' [On the history of the name 'Tatar']", in *Reşid Rahmeti Arat için*, Ankara: Türk Kültürünü Araştırma Enstitüsü, 1966, pp. 278–85; W. Barthold, "Tatar", in E.J. Brill's *First Encyclopedia of Islam* 1913–1936, VIII, reprint Leiden/New York/Köln: Brill, 1993, pp. 700–2.

[2] See for instance the title of Lazar Budagov's famous dictionary which used "*turetsko-tatarskii*" as the collective denomination for all Turkic peoples: Lazar Z. Budagov, *Sravnitelnyi slovar turetsko-tatarskikh narechii* [A comparative dictionary of Turkish-Tatar dialects], 2 vols, St Petersburg, 1869–1871.

"Muslim", "Turk" or the so-called tribal names such as "Kazakh", "Sart", and "Bashkir". However, "Tatar" came to designate not only the Turkic peoples as a whole, but also that part of the Turkic Muslim population inhabiting the Volga-Ural region. Therefore, at the beginning of the twentieth century "Tatar" could be used as a narrow tribal designation for Volga Tatars in the Volga-Ural region and as a collective term for all Turkic Muslims in the Russian Empire.[3] It will be the task here to determine to what extent Polish Tatars fitted into this scheme.

Any research on "German" and "Polish" Tatars has to take into account the different meanings of the word "Tatar". It has to clarify whether the term really designated identity-based groups and if so whether this usage corresponded to reality. In order to achieve this task the two communities will be analysed separately. Special attention will be paid to their networking activities as this might help to shed light on the identities of the two groups: similar identities should imply similar networking activities.

TATARS IN GERMANY

A Muslim community between Germany, Russia and Turkey

The Tatar community in Germany came into existence as a result of the First World War. The German authorities interned Muslim prisoners of war from the Russian army separately in order to persuade them to join the *jihad* or "Holy War" declared by the Ottoman Sultan. About 12,000 "Turko-Tatar" prisoners of war were grouped together in a camp in the small provincial town of Wünsdorf near Berlin, and the German Ministry of Foreign Affairs established an entire propaganda system in order to indoctrinate them with pan-Islamic ideas. This system led the Germans to construct another "propaganda camp" in the nearby town of Zossen for Muslim prisoners of war from the British and French armies, and

[3] A thorough history of the use of "Tatar" remains to be written. For a first attempt see G. Jäschke, "Zur Geschichte"; elements of an explanation can be found in Galina M. Yémelianova, "The National Identity of the Volga Tatars at the Turn of the 19th Century: Tatarism, Turkism and Islam", *Central Asian Survey*, 16 (1997), pp. 543–72.

also the first mosque built for this purpose in Germany. The Tatar staff within the German-inspired propaganda apparatus can be regarded as the core of the emerging Tatar community.[4]

The number of Tatars in Germany declined in several phases. In 1915 some 1,000 Tatars agreed to join the Ottoman army in the "Holy War" proclaimed against Russia. However, instead of using them for military purposes, the Ottomans preferred to settle these Tatars in depopulated regions in Eastern Anatolia.[5] Throughout the years of the first World War some 400 Tatars died as a result of the harsh conditions in the prisoner of war camps and were buried in the prisoner of war cemetery in the small village of Zehrensdorf near the two camps.[6] When Germany and Soviet Russia finally agreed on the repatriation of the prisoners of war in 1920, only a few dozen prisoners decided to remain in Germany. Some of them continued to live in the former prisoner of war camp until its closure in 1924, others settled down in Berlin to study at university or to find work. According to the limited information available on the structure of the community, there was almost no organised community life. The former prisoners of war quickly integrated into

[4] As there is a lot of literature on the history of the Tatar community in Germany, I will confine myself to giving a short outline of its history, focusing on their networking activities. For a more thorough review see Iskander Gilyazov, "Die Wolgatataren und Deutschland im ersten Drittel des 20. Jahrhunderts [The Volga Tatars and Germany in the first third of the 20th century]", in A. v. Kügelgen, A. Frank and M. Kemper (eds), *Muslim Culture in Russia and Central Asia from the 18th to the early 20th Centuries*, vol. 2 (*Islamkundliche Untersuchungen* 216), Berlin: Klaus Schwarz Verlag, 1998, pp. 335–55; Sebastian Cwiklinski, "Tataren und Baschkiren in Berlin: Geschichte und Gegenwart [Tatars and Bashkirs in Berlin: past and present]", *Berliner Blätter. Ethnographische und ethnologische Beiträge*, 33 (2004), pp. 86–99; S. Cwiklinski, "Tatars and Bashkirs in Berlin from the End of the 19th Century to the Beginning of World War II", *The Turks*, V, Ankara: Yeni Türkiye Publications, 2002, pp. 1004–14.

[5] On the Ottoman involvement see Nedim İpek, "Rus Ordusundaki Türk Askerlerinin Osmanlı Tâbiiyetine Geçmesi [Turkish soldiers from the Russian Army becoming Ottoman citizens]", *Tarih ve Toplum*, 145 (1996), pp. 14–19.

[6] On the cemetery see Gerhard Höpp, *Muslime in der Mark. Als Kriegsgefangene und Internierte in Wünsdorf and Zossen 1914–1924* [Muslims in the Brandenburg province of Germany. Prisoners of war in Wünsdorf and Zossen], Berlin: Verlag Das Arabische Buch, 1997, pp. 131–7.

German society, some of them even married German women. Most of the "integrated Tatars" had practical professions; we know of printers, tailors, laundry workers, but also one engineer.

The few activities within the Tatar community were carried out mainly by students both from Germany and other exile countries (such as Finland and Manchuria) and from the Soviet Union, who started to come to Germany in the early 1920s. It should be noted that the students included some women and we have further information on a few of them. For example, Saadet İshaki-Çağatay (1906–89), the daughter of the political émigré leader Ayaz İshaki, studied Oriental Studies at Berlin University and later supported her father in his networking activities. However, as Iskander Gilyazov has rightly pointed out, most of the female students, like their male counterparts, chose to study mainly practical subjects such as medicine.[7] We know of at least two female Tatar medical students in Berlin in the 1920s and 1930s. Orientalists like Saadet İshaki-Çağatay or her male counterpart Reşid Rahmeti Arat are to be regarded as an exception within the Tatar student community in Germany.

Organised community activities consisted mainly of meetings commemorating events in Tatar history which were regarded as central to the national consciousness. Berlin Tatars met to commemorate the establishment of the "National Administration" of the Volga-Ural region in 1917–18, the birthday of the Tatar national poet Gabdulla Tuqay, and to mourn the seizure of the town of Kazan by the Russian army in 1552. Sometimes the Tatars were joined by some Uzbeks and Kazakhs as their languages were mutually intelligible and all of them shared a similar history. However, these Tataro-Uzbek and Tataro-Kazakh contacts should not be regarded as relations between Muslims, because they were perceived by the participants themselves primarily as an expression of national solidarity.

However, one cannot say that the Muslims from the Volga-Ural region resident in Germany formed a coherent community. From the autobiography of the Tatar scholar Ahmet Temir (1912–2003), who studied in Berlin from 1936 onwards, it becomes clear that

[7] I. Gilyazov, "Die Wolgatataren und Deutschland", *passim*.

many of the Berlin Tatars had no contact with their compatriots.[8] The information at our disposal suggests that Tatars joined Muslim associations only at a personal level. Some of them attended the Friday services at the Berlin mosque, but they were not willing to engage in an organised form of Muslim community activities.

The history of the networking activities of the Tatar community in Germany can be divided into two phases, each of them marked not only by the inner structure of the community itself, but also by political developments in Germany, Russia, and Turkey.

The first phase of Tatar networking in Germany (1918–1922)

The first phase, lasting from the First World War until 1922, was framed by Germany's political aspirations and the Tatars' attitude towards them. During the First World War Germany actively propagated pan-Islamism among Muslim prisoners of war, and in order to carry out this propaganda it needed Tatar collaborators, two of whom were immediately sent to Berlin from the Ottoman capital, Istanbul. Abdurrashid Ibrahim (1857–1944) and, to a lesser extent, Alimjan Idris (1887–1954), both Tatar émigrés from Russia, had been actively involved in the Tatar community in Istanbul in the early 1910s.[9] After their arrival in Germany both propagandists held the official post of *Lagerimam* ("camp imam"), giving them the right to hold sermons and speeches at Friday prayers and other official meetings.

A third Tatar, Kemaleddin Bedri (1896-?) who would later gain a certain prominence among the Tatar community in Germany, came from Istanbul to study at Berlin University. He later became famous as the first lecturer in the Tatar language in Germany.

[8] Ahmet Temir, *60 Yıl Almanya (1936–1996). Bir yabancının gözü ile Geziler—Araştırmalar—Hatıralar. Sechzig Jahre Deutschland (1936–1996). Reisen—Forschungen—Erinnerungen mit den Augen eines Fremden* [60 years Germany (1936–1996). Journeys, research and memories of a stranger], Ankara: T.C. Kültür Bakanlığı, 1998, pp. 131–62. Ahmet Temir gives a short list of Tatars resident in Berlin, many of whom were married to German women; one of the Tatars he mentioned had even converted to Catholicism.

[9] On the arrival of Ibrahim and Idris in Berlin see Sebastian Cwiklinski, "Ein an tatarische Kriegsgefangene gerichtetes Propagandaflugblatt aus dem Ersten Weltkrieg [A Tatar propaganda leaflet directed at Tatar prisoners of war in the First World War]", *Bertugan*, 3 (2003), pp. 20–25.

These propagandists had not only a German, but also an Ottoman task to fulfil, and they regularly delivered reports to the newly established secret service, *Teşkilat-ı Mahsusa* (The Special Organisation), set up after the Young Turk Revolution in 1908/9.[10] In addition Ibrahim continued to keep up his ties with the Ottoman capital, writing more or less regularly in the Turkish press. In at least one article Ibrahim reported about his impressions of Germany and tried to put forward his pro-German point of view. His links to Istanbul continued to be important and in the following years Ibrahim often returned there, obviously renewing his relationships with high-ranking Ottoman officials. As a result of his efforts in 1917 his daughter Fevziye was invited to Berlin to join the staff of the *Nachrichtenstelle für den Orient* (Oriental News Service), the propaganda headquarters at the German Foreign Office, as a translator.

The younger propagandist Idris maintained his own personal contacts. As late as autumn 1917, more than three years after Germany had declared war on Russia, he published two small brochures containing texts by Tatars from Russia and others living in exile in Turkey. As well as texts by prominent "Russian" Tatars like Musa Bigiev, Sheher Sheref and Fatikh Amirhan they also included the text of a speech by the exile politician Yusuf Akçura given in Istanbul in 1915. Idris also included a lengthy analysis of German foreign policy by the renowned political analyst Ayaz İshaki, originally published in Moscow in June 1917.[11] The fact that both brochures were published in Istanbul again confirms the close links between Tatar activists in Germany and the Ottoman Empire.

Idris and some other Tatars also showed their great commitment to the development of Muslims in Russia. At the beginning of 1918

[10] On the involvement of the *Teşkilat-ı Mahsusa* with the Tatar propagandists see two publications by Vahdet Keleşyılmaz, "Tatars in Austro-German Prisoner Camps", *The Turks*, vol. IV, Ankara: Yeni Türkiye Publications, 2002, pp. 449–56; the same, "I. Dünya Savaşı'nda Esir Askerler Üzerinde Panislamizm Propagandası Teşebbüsü [An attempt to spread pan-Islamism among the prisoners of war in the First World War]", *Kebikeç*, 10 (2000), pp. 31–7.

[11] On Idris' publications see Sebastian Cwiklinski, "Po sledam dvukh tatarskikh publikatsii v Germanii [Tracing two Tatar publications in Germany]", in *Gasyrlar Avazy/Ekho vekov,* Kazan, I (2005), pp. 89–91.

they founded the "Association for the Support of Russian-Muhammedan Students" with the aim of "spreading German culture and industry among the Russian Muslims". The activists wanted to achieve this goal by bringing as many Muslim pupils and students as possible "from Tatary and Turkistan" to Germany.[12] In fact, because of Idris' activities in the early 1920s many Muslim students from Russia and Turkistan came to Germany to study at universities and secondary schools or to receive a professional training. In order to advertise Germany, Idris himself published a number of articles on Germany in several Turkistani journals and newspapers. His close links to Central Asia led him to become the cultural representative of the Bukharan Republic in Germany from 1924 onwards.[13]

However, Idris' wide-ranging contacts should not be regarded as evidence of the networking activities of the Tatar community as a whole, as he mostly acted on his own. His contacts with the Soviet Embassy in the late 1920s raised suspicions within the exile community that he was a Soviet agent, which led to his growing isolation among the Muslims in Germany.[14]

Political networking under the leadership of refugees

A second phase in networking activities by Muslims from Russia in Germany began with the arrival of a number of Tatar and Bashkir political leaders in Berlin in the period from 1922 to 1925. The networking activities of Tatars such as Ayaz İshaki, Sadri Maksudi and Fuad Tuktar and the Bashkir Zeki Velidi Togan (Validov) had a twofold focus. On the one hand they were trying to organise the exile communities of their nationalities spread all over the world, and on the other hand they cooperated with representatives of

[12] On the association see Iskander Gilyazov, "Obshchestvo podderzhki rossiisko-musul'manskikh studentov 1918–1925", in *Gasyrlar Avazy/Ekho vekov*, Kazan, 3–4 (1996), pp. 193–9.

[13] On Idris' connections to Central Asia and the arrival of Central Asian students in Germany see Dov Yaroshevski, "Bukharan Students in Germany, 1922–1925", in Ingeborg Baldauf and Michael Friederich (eds), *Bamberger Zentralasienstudien*, Berlin: Klaus Schwartz Verlag, 1994, pp. 271–8.

[14] See for instance an article in the journal of the Turkistani exiles *Yash Türkistan* of November 1930 (pp. 25–6), where the allegations are put forward openly.

exiles from other non-Russian nationalities in order to establish an anti-Bolshevik alliance. Some of them joined the Promethean League (*Ligue Prométhée*), a political union which was firmly supported by Poland and had its headquarters in Warsaw and Paris. It was in Warsaw that İshaki founded the "Committee for the Independence of Volga-Ural" (*Idel-Ural Istiqlal Komitasy*) in 1928.[15] In the same year İshaki began to edit the monthly *Yaña Milli Yul* (The New National Way) in Berlin with the help of his daughter, Saadet İshaki-Çağatay, who was continuing her studies at Berlin University. The journal was edited right up to the beginning of the Second World War in September 1939 and was printed in Tatar with Arabic letters.

The journal clearly reflected its origins among Tatar exiles. It dealt primarily with issues in the Soviet Union, Tatarstan and Bashkiria on the one hand and the development of the exile communities on the other. Apart from this, the journal had a special interest in political developments in Turkey as İshaki had always underlined the importance of pan-Turkic solidarity. Consequently, in the 1939 issues, for instance, one can find articles on the forced Russification of Tatars in the Soviet Union,[16] short news about cultural and political developments in Tatarstan and Bashkiria,[17] reports on the life of the exile communities in Germany, Finland, Poland, Japan, and Manchuria, and research on political life in Turkey after Atatürk's death.

The Tatar communities in Manchuria and Japan played a major role in İshaki's political strategy, and in the early 1930s he travelled for more than a year throughout Eastern Asia to organise them. During his absence from Europe his daughter assumed the role of his representative. However, as İshaki's leadership was not undisputed among exiled Tatars there were also alternative attempts to network. The above-mentioned Alimjan Idris, still resident in Berlin and hostile to İshaki and his activities, cooperated with another Tatar-Bashkir exile group in Japan by contributing to its

[15] For further information on the Promethean movement see below.

[16] *Yaña Milli Yul* (March 1939), pp. 11–16.

[17] See for instance the short articles about the development of opera in both republics in *Yaña Milli Yul* (January 1939), pp. 30–1.

journal *Yaña Yapon Muhbiri*. Each of the two journals (*Yaña Milli Yul* and *Yaña Yapon Muhbiri*) was active denouncing the other, accusing it of treachery and collaboration with the Soviets.

The complex structure of relationships between Muslims from Russia based in Germany and those in rest of the world came to an abrupt end in 1939 when the Germans invaded Poland and destroyed the framework for the Promethean League's activities. All the exile leaders of the non-Russian nationalities including İshaki fled Poland and found refuge in Turkey and other countries. Tatar activities in Germany in the following years have to be seen in the context of collaboration with the Nazi regime and cannot simply be reduced to internal factors such as ethnicity or culture.[18]

TATARS IN POLAND

The historical background

The Tatar community in Poland came into existence as early as the late fourteenth and early fifteenth centuries. Turkic groupings in the Golden Horde opposed to the ruling khan sought and found refuge in Lithuania (which was unified with Poland in a Commonwealth after 1569) and founded several villages. In the course of the following centuries the little community saw the rise of a tiny Tatar elite which quickly became assimilated linguistically. As religious freedom had been guaranteed in Poland since 1573 there was no interference by the state in the religious affairs of the Tatar community. In the course of time first the upper classes, then the rank and file were assimilated culturally and linguistically. In the early seventeenth century the adoption of Polish (and to a lesser extent of Byelorussian) was completed, and since that time the Polish Tatar community has communicated exclusively in these Slavonic languages.

[18] On the history of the Volga Tatars in Germany during the Second World War see Iskander Gilyazov, *Legion 'Idel-Ural'. Predstaviteli narodov Povolzhya i Priuralya pod znamenami 'Tretyego Reikha'* ["The 'Volga-Ural' legion. Representatives of the peoples of the Volga-Ural region under the flags of the 'Third Reich'], Kazan: Tatarskoe knizhnoe izdatelstvo, 2005; Sebastian Cwiklinski, *Wolgatataren im Deutschland des Zweiten Weltkriegs. Deutsche Ostpolitik und tatarischer Nationalismus* ["Volga Tatars in Second World War Germany. German *Ostpolitik* and Tatar Nationalism"], Berlin: Klaus Schwartz Verlag, 2002.

Yet assimilation was clearly limited to those spheres of life that were not linked to religion. The social integration of Polish Tatars was facilitated by the fact that a small group of them quickly rose to the upper classes of Polish society. Some families were even ennobled and played an important role in the Polish army. After the partition of Poland at the end of the eighteenth century, those parts of the country inhabited by the Tatars came under Russian rule, and the Tatars were also subjected to Russian influence. According to a Russian census in 1853, about 5,500 Muslims lived within the borders of former Poland-Lithuania—religion being the only possible way of distinguishing the Tatars from the rest of the population. By 1897 this number had risen to 23,000 because there were also many Muslims among the staff of the Russian administrative and military establishment.[19]

By the beginning of the twentieth century, not only had Russian structures been imposed on the Polish Tatars' homeland, but Polish Tatars also began slowly infiltrating into the higher echelons of Russian society. Many Polish Tatars served in the Russian army, some of them even represented Russia in Central Asia and the Caucasus as colonial representatives,[20] while others studied in the capital St Petersburg in order to rise to the upper classes of Russian society.

In the years before the first World War the Muslim community in Poland slowly acquired a double structure. In Warsaw "Russian"

[19] The literature on Polish Tatars is almost exclusively in Polish and Russian. The only detailed survey in English concentrates on the period prior to the twentieth century, see Leon Bohdanowicz, "Muslims in Poland", *Islamic Review*, XXIII (1936), pp. 94–105, 125–41, 164–70; for surveys in Polish and Russian see Piotr Borawski and Aleksander Dubiński, *Tatarzy polscy. Dzieje, obrzędy, legendy, tradycje* [Polish Tatars. History, customs, legends, traditions], Warsaw: ISKRY, 1986; Piotr Borawski, *Tatarzy w dawnej Rzeczypospolitej* [Tatars in the ancient Republic], Warsaw: Ludowa Spółdzielnia Wydawnicza, 1986; Yakov Grishin, *Polsko-litovskie tatary. Nasledniki zolotoi ordy* [Polish-Lithuanian Tatars. Heirs of the Golden Horde], Kazan: Tatarskoe knizhnoe izdatelstvo, 1995; Yakov Grishin, *Polsko-litovskie tatary. Vzglyad cherez veka* [Polish-Lithuanian Tatars. A look throughout the centuries], Kazan: Tatarskoe knizhnoe izdatelstvo, 2000.

[20] For more information on Polish Tatars serving in the Russian army see Yakov Grishin and Damir Sharafutdinov, *Otchizny vernye syny* [Faithful sons of their native country], Kazan: Gasyr, 2001.

Muslims—meaning Muslims from the Caucasus, the Crimea and the Volga region—continued to dominate the scene, whereas in Vilnius Polish Tatars were the driving force in Muslim organisations. Consequently, Russian Muslims initiated and dominated the "Warsaw Muslim Welfare Association", which was founded in 1913—out of 113 members, 85 were of "Russian" origin and there was only one Polish Tatar among the prominent founders of the association. In Vilnius, however, the brothers Kryczyński, who were Polish Tatar, were the main initiators of a similar association founded in 1909.[21]

The First World War was a turning point for the Polish Tatars. In the early years of the war they served in regular Russian units, but in the later years important changes could be observed. In 1917, when the first Muslim corps within the Russian army was organised, Polish Tatars were appointed to the leading ranks, and a Polish Tatar general, Maciej Sulkiewicz, played a prominent military role in the independence movements in the Crimea and the Caucasus. In June 1918 when the Crimean Tatars revolted against the German occupation, General Sulkiewicz led their military campaign, and one year later he was appointed Chief of the General Staff of the newly established Republic of Azerbaijan.[22] One of the Kryczyński brothers mentioned above played an important role both in the Crimea and in Azerbaijan: Olgierd Kryczyński became deputy State Minister in the Crimea in 1919 and State Minister in Azerbaijan in 1920, before returning to Poland and becoming once again a prominent figure in the Tatar community.[23]

In the two years following the end of the First World War Polish military units fought successfully for the independence of Poland. General Józef Piłsudski, the leader of the military campaign, was well aware of the importance of Polish Tatar support for the independence movement and set up a Tatar military unit which took part in all the major campaigns. The Polish-Russian war led to the

[21] Ali Miśkiewicz, *Tatarzy polscy 1918–1939. Życie społeczno-kulturalne i religijne* [Polish Tatars from 1918 to 1939. Social-cultural and religious life], Warsaw: PWN, 1990, pp. 23–4.

[22] Ibid., pp. 26–7.

[23] Jan Tyszkiewicz, *Z historii Tatarów polskich 1794–1944* [From the history of Polish Tatars from 1794 to 1944], Pułtusk: Wyższa Szkoła Humanistyczna, 1998, p. 143.

establishment of an independent Polish state, but at the same time to the partition of the "Polish-Lithuanian" Tatar community as the territory in which they lived was divided between Poland, Lithuania and Byelorussia. The enmity or at least rivalry between these states led to the development of three independent Polish, Lithuanian and Byelorussian Tatar communities with almost no contacts with one another. There is almost no information available on the communities in Lithuania and Byelorussia for the period before the Second World War, and the following pages will concentrate on developments among the Tatars in Poland.[24]

The organisation of the Tatar community in the inter-war period

In the early years after Poland gained its independence, the Tatars started to set up social and religious organisations, an activity which had not been possible to this extent in previous years. The number of Polish Tatars in the newly independent Republic of Poland is not that easy to determine as the first statistics established by the Polish Muftiate in 1925–26 refer to 5,805 "Muslims" in Poland, while a later statistic from 1936 mentions 5,425 "Polish Tatars". Quite obviously the designation "Muslims" encompassed not only the Polish Tatar population, but also the Muslim population originating from Russia. As the Polish Tatar scholar Ali Miśkiewicz has indicated, it is however possible to differentiate between the two communities as the "Russian Muslims" settled down mainly in Warsaw and, to a lesser extent, in Vilnius. It might be assumed that the Warsaw community with some 300 members consisted mainly of Muslims of "Russian" descent.[25] In contrast the Polish Tatar population lived in the Eastern provinces of Vilnius, Nowogródek and Białystok, mainly in small villages where they constituted a significant or at least visible part of the population. The "rural" character of the Tatar community also becomes clear when one looks at the

[24] One of the few articles on the community in Lithuania is by György Lederer, "Tatars in Post-Socialist Lithuania", in T. Gemil (ed.), *Tătarii în istorie şi în lume*, Bucharest: Kriterion, 2003, pp. 299–304.

[25] A. Miśkiewicz, *Tatarzy polscy*, pp. 58–65. As Ali Miśkiewicz indicates (p. 64), the statistics on the Warsaw community are hardly reliable as the number of Muslims in the Polish capital shows significant variations.

distribution of professions among the population; 43 per cent of Polish Muslims were farmers, 6 per cent gardeners and 20 per cent tanners, whereas only 14 per cent worked as civil servants or were employed in the professions.[26] In total, the Muslim population of Poland was distributed across nineteen parishes which were located mainly in rural areas in the Eastern part of the country.

The first organisation to be registered was the Warsaw Muslim Association in 1923, with Muslims from the Caucasus, the Volga-Ural region and the Crimea continuing to occupy prominent positions. At the same time the communities in Vilnius and other towns started to demand the establishment of a Polish Muftiate and its recognition by the state. The first organisational effort on a national level took place in 1925. On the initiative of the Vilnius community the first All-Polish Muslim Congress assembled in Vilnius and appointed Dr Jakup Szynkiewicz as the chairman of the Muftiate of Poland with his seat in Vilnius. Among the reasons that contributed to his election was the fact that he was the only candidate to speak Arabic and Turkish. At the time of his election he was still resident in Berlin where he was completing his doctorate in Oriental studies.[27] It might be noted that he had an Orientalist but not a theological background.

In addition to the religious organisation the Tatars also founded a national one, the "Cultural-Educational Association of the Tatars of the Polish Republic" (*Związek Kulturalno-Oświatowy Tatarów Rzeczypospolitej Polskiej*—hereafter ZKOTRP), which was supposed to meet the cultural needs of the Polish Tatars. ZKOTRP quickly set up local branches, and the case of Warsaw shows the almost total correspondence between religious and national identities. The local branch of ZKOTRP was the direct successor of the Warsaw Muslim Association.[28]

[26] Ibid., p. 66.

[27] Before studying in Berlin (1919–25), Szynkiewicz had studied Oriental studies at St Petersburg University. According to archival material from Berlin [files of the Oriental Seminar of Berlin University, Geheimes Staatsarchiv Preußischer Kulturbesitz], Dr Szynkiewicz used his studies in Berlin to join Tatar language courses at Berlin University. It is not known, however, to what extent he succeeded in learning the language.

[28] A. Miśkiewicz, *Tatarzy polscy*, p. 46.

The division of responsibilities between the two organisations (the Muftiate and ZKOTRP) was not as clear as their names might suggest. The Muftiate had the clearly defined task of dealing with all matters of faith linked to Islam. Mufti Szynkiewicz was supposed to deal with questions of religious education and of Islamic law, to revise the religious scripture of the Tatar community, to represent the interests of the Muslim community with the state authorities and to select and educate new imams.[29] With the Muftiate being responsible for religious matters, one might assume that ZKOTRP would have confined itself to secular issues such as the preservation of the Polish Tatars' cultural heritage. Indeed, the organisation first developed activities in this field. The foundation of the yearbook *Rocznik Tatarski* was one of the first ZKOTRP activities, and the composition of the editorial board of this journal was entirely determined by the organisation. Other projects of ZKOTRP included the opening of a "Tatar Museum-Archive" in Vilnius in 1929, which exhibited Qur'an manuscripts and Tatar and Turkish Qur'an translations from the eighteenth century, a collection of newspaper articles about Polish Tatar life and Arab coins found at archaeological sites in Poland. In the small library section of the museum one could find the entire Polish-language literature on Tatars in Poland, and in the archive section documents on the acquisition of land by Tatars in the sixteenth century. The museum-archive ceased to exist when its manager, the community activist Leon Kryczyński, moved from Vilnius to Zamość in 1934.[30]

ZKOTRP had more than twenty local branches, mainly in the province of Vilnius, which tried to develop cultural activities, and on a more or less regular basis it organised lectures on different subjects by known community activists. The subjects covered by these lectures can be easily identified as most of them were later published in the two Tatar journals. For example Leon Kryczyński spoke about the history of the Muslim community of Vilnius, Mufti Jakub Szynkiewicz presented impressions from his journeys to the Near East, and Olgierd Kryczyński gave some insights into the Prophet Muhammad's relationship to women. However, these

[29] Ibid., pp. 78–104.
[30] Ibid., pp. 107–15.

activists attracted only a very small audience consisting mainly of the educated members of the community who already had some knowledge of the subjects dealt with in the lectures.[31] Another activity of the local branches is worth mentioning. Some of them established folklore groups, but they had problems choosing an appropriate programme as the Tatars in Poland did not have their own folk culture. The literature written by young Polish Tatar writers was too unfamiliar to be used for song lyrics, and so the young folklore ensembles tended to use poems by Polish writers such as Adam Mickiewicz and Juliusz Słowacki. The idea of using (Crimean or Volga) Tatar songs was soon abandoned as they were unintelligible to both the singers and the public. Even though the performers made an effort to learn the songs by heart, their efforts met with little response as the Polish Tatar audience was not interested in listening to lyrics that they could not understand and melodies that were unfamiliar to them. Warsaw was the only place where folklore evenings proved more successful because Volga Tatars formed a large enough group within the city's Muslim community to support cultural activities.[32]

In the late 1920s and early 1930s a conflict emerged between the Muftiate and ZKOTRP as some ZKOTRP activists challenged the Mufti's competence to decide on all religious matters and maintained that the local parishes should keep a certain autonomy in these affairs. They also criticised the fact that Szynkiewicz had been elected Mufti for life and demanded that the office should be held for a limited period only. These criticisms, however, provoked objections among local ZKOTRP activists who declared that the critics did not have the right to speak for all the local branches of the organisation. In the end the criticism had little impact as Jakub Szykiewicz continued to serve as Mufti until the end of the Second World War.

Contacts with the Muslim world

As early as the mid-1920s the Polish Tatars tried to establish contacts with the Muslim world. In 1925 the Polish government sent Olgierd Kryczyński, one of the leading activists of the Tatar

[31] Ibid., p. 107.
[32] Ibid., pp. 108–9.

community, to the International Geographic Congress in Cairo, where he was met enthusiastically by the Egyptian intelligentsia. They were intrigued by the fact that Muslims in Poland had adopted European culture while at the same time faithfully preserving their commitment to Islam, and they approved of the positive attitude of the Polish state towards Islam. In a speech at the farewell dinner of the congress, Kryczyński underlined his role as a representative of both the Polish Muslim community and the country as a whole. The fact that the leading newspaper, *al-Ahram*, published Kryczyński's speech unabridged and the Egyptian (Arabic- and French-language) press covered his story extensively shows the great interest and importance Egyptian intellectuals attributed to this representative of European Islam.[33] Kryczyński was even received by the Egyptian king who awarded him a high decoration.[34] Kryczyński's return to Poland took almost two months as he used the opportunity to develop further contacts with the Muslim world. He went first to Palestine where he met Amin al-Husaini, the Grand Mufti of Jerusalem, who promised to support the Muslims in Poland. After visiting Jerusalem Kryczyński went to Damascus where he gave a speech on the situation of the Muslims in Poland and met a number of intellectuals. Again Kryczyński's stay in Damascus was covered by all the important newspapers of the Arab world. At the end of his journey Kryczyński held a series of talks in Turkey with the Prime Minister, other leading politicians and the Mufti of Ankara, who promised to arrange for the education of two Polish Tatar children in Turkey. At the end of his stay in Istanbul he met friends from the Crimean Tatar and the Azerbaijani diaspora and some Polish Tatar friends who had emigrated to Turkey.[35]

In the late 1920s and throughout the 1930s the most eminent representative of the Polish Tatars to make contacts with the Muslim world was Mufti Jakup Szynkiewicz. From 1926 onwards he undertook a number of journeys which took him not only to Yugoslavia and several countries in the Near East, but also to India. One of the striking features of his journeys was their official

[33] P. Borawski and A. Dubiński, *Tatarzy polscy*, pp. 155–6.
[34] A. Miśkiewicz, *Tatarzy polscy*, p. 140.
[35] P. Borawski and A. Dubiński, *Tatarzy polscy*, p. 157.

character. In 1926 he represented Poland at the World Muslim Congress in Cairo, and as he was the only European representative present his appearance had a certain impact on the Arab public. On his second journey in 1930 he was a member of an official mission by the Polish Foreign Ministry to establish relations with Saudi Arabia, and once again he used the opportunity to visit Cairo, where he was received—like Kryczyński five years before—as an official representative of Poland. Szynkiewicz travelled home via Beirut, Damascus, Haifa and Jerusalem, where he met Amin al-Husaini, with whom he had political talks.[36]

In the same year Szynkiewicz represented Poland at the celebrations for the official recognition of the Muslim Religious Association in Yugoslavia, which took place in Belgrade in October. Once again the journey had an official character, and the Polish embassy in Belgrade organised a reception for the Polish Mufti and his Yugoslavian counterpart; Szynkiewicz was awarded a high Yugoslavian state medal. Apart from two further journeys (which took him once again to the Near East in 1932[37] and to India in 1937) his attendance at the All-European Muslim Congress in Geneva in 1935 is worth mentioning. Szynkiewicz went to Geneva together with H.A. Churamowicz, the chairman of the Warsaw branch of ZKOTRP. While Churamowicz talked about both the religious and the secular organisations (the latter meaning the "national", i.e. Tatar association) of the Polish Muslims, Szynkiewicz compared the situation of Polish Muslims before 1914 and at the present time, painting a very positive picture of the policy of the Polish state. The presentations by Churamowicz and Szynkiewicz were so impressive and convincing that the congress decided to pass a motion expressing gratitude to the Polish government for its just and benevolent policy towards the Muslim minority. At the same time the congress appealed to all Muslims in Europe to aid the construction of a mosque in Warsaw.[38]

[36] A. Miśkiewicz, *Tatarzy polscy*, pp. 141–2.

[37] Szynkiewicz's report on the 1932 journey was published in 1977: "Sprawozdanie Muftiego Jakuba Szynkiewicza z podróży do Turcji, Syrii, Palestyny i Egiptu w roku 1932 (9.IV-9.IX) [Mufti Jakup Szynkiewicz's report on his journey to Turkey, Syria, Palestine and Egypt in 1932]", *Przegląd Orientalistyczny*, 1 (1977), pp. 41–9.

[38] A. Miśkiewicz, *Tatarzy polscy*, pp. 143–4.

The contacts established by prominent representatives of the Tatar community with the Muslim world led to further cooperation in the academic field. As a result of Szynkiewicz's contacts with high-ranking Egyptian officials, two Tatar graduates from the Oriental Studies Department of Lvov (in Polish Lwów) University were admitted for theological studies in 1933 at Al-Azhar University in Cairo, where they followed a three-year programme designed especially for them. Immediately after their return to Poland one of them, Mustafa Aleksandrowicz, joined the Polish diplomatic service and was sent to Poland's consulate in Jerusalem, while the other, Ali Woronowicz, was appointed Imam in Warsaw in 1937 and became one of the few activists of the Tatar community with a thorough theological training.[39] A second academic link was established with Yugoslavia through personal contacts of the Chairman of the Muslim community of Vilnius, the Volga Tatar Mohammad Waisow.[40] Although a first attempt to send Tatar students to a *madrasa* in Sarajevo in 1927 failed, Waisow established new contacts in 1933. In January 1934 two Tatar students from Warsaw joined the Husrev Beg *Madrasa* in Sarajevo and in December 1935 two further students followed.[41] It might be noted that the expenses of at least the latter two students were met by the Polish state.[42] Apart from Waisow's personal contacts, the fact that Yugoslavia was the closest country to Poland with a complete Muslim infrastructure appears to have played a role in the choice of Sarajevo.

[39] Ibid., pp. 53, 84.

[40] Mohammad Waisow, resident in Poland for more than two decades, had made a fortune as a businessman. It might be noted that he was the son of the founder of the Vaisov sect which in the late nineteenth century had opposed the Tatar clerics and declared the Muslims of the Volga-Ural regions as "Bolghars", not "Tatars". The fate of his father was discussed by him in an article in the yearbook *Rocznik Tatarski*, see Chodżja Muchammed Gajan Wajsow, "Wajsow, Wajsowscy i stosunek do nich Lwa Tolstoja [Vaisov, the Vaisovists and Lev Tolstoi's relationship to them]", *Rocznik Tatarski*, I, 1932, pp. 215–20.

[41] After their return to Poland, these four students did not play any role, neither social or religious, in the life of the community, but we do not know the reason for this.

[42] Ibid., p. 85. Concerning the first two students at the Sarajevo *madrasa* it might be of interest to note that the two brothers came from a family of Volga Tatar origin resident in Warsaw, and the person who established the contact with the *madrasa* was also a Volga Tatar resident in Warsaw.

Publishing activities as identity marker

At the end of the 1920s the Polish Tatars began to engage in publishing activities, with the first publications appearing in 1929. Of special interest both among the Tatar community itself and among Polish scholars was the "Heraldry of Tatar Families in Poland" by Stanisław Dziadulewicz.[43] The book, which was prepared by a special committee with several representatives from the Polish Tatar community, also contained an explanatory list of "Oriental" names by Jakup Szynkiewicz.[44] By reading the list, one comes to the conclusion that the names popular among the Polish Tatar community had almost nothing in common with name giving customs among the Volga Tatars, Turks or Arabs. Names like "Küsmän" (obviously derived from 'Uthman/Osman), "Ibrasz" (as abbreviation from Ibrahim) or "Fen-Dowleć" (from the Arabic *daula)* illustrate that through the centuries the Polish Tatar community had developed independently from other Muslim communities. However, Szynkiewicz's commentaries also revealed his limited competence as several of his remarks were incorrect.[45]

Throughout the 1930s the Tatar community in Poland published a number of journals which provide insights into its structure, main aspirations and ideas. *Życie Tatarskie* (Tatar Life), which appeared from 1934 to 1939 in Vilnius, mainly concentrated on the history of the Tatar community in Poland with a special focus on military history. The Tatars' service in the Polish army as early as the eighteenth century served as a source of pride and a means to foster their own identity.[46] The second Tatar journal, *Rocznik Tatarski* (Tatar

[43] Stanisław Dziadulewicz (ed.), *Herbarz rodzin tatarskich w Polsce*, Vilnius (Wilno), 1929.

[44] Jakup Szynkiewicz, "Tłumaczenia słów i nazw orjentalistycznych [An explanation of Oriental words and proper names]", in S. Dziadulewicz (ed.), *Herbarz rodzin tatarskich*, pp. 457–73.

[45] For a critical review of Szynkiewicz's remarks see Henryk Jankowski, "Nazwy osobowe Tatarów litewsko-polskich [Proper names of the Polish-Lithuanian Tatars]", *Rocznik Tatarów Polskich*, IV (1997), pp. 59–90.

[46] From 1936 until it ceased publication the journal had a permanent column "Military Documents from the history of the Lithuanian Tatars from 1782 to 1792". For an extensive analysis of *Życie Tatarskie* see Bronisław H. Bladocha, "Analiza treści prasy islamskiej w II Rzeczypospolitej [An analysis of the contents of the Islamic press in the Second Republic]", *Rocznik Tatarów Polskich*, VII (2001/2002), pp. 57–66.

Yearbook), appeared three times and had a more scientific character. Again the Polish Tatars' military past was well represented, but the authors of the journal were also interested in subjects such as the loss of their traditional language and the legal situation of Islam in Poland compared to Russia.[47] The third (and last) volume of *Rocznik Tatarski* consisted of a voluminous monograph on the history of the Polish Tatars by Stanisław Kryczyński, one of the editors of the journal.[48] Islamic themes had a defined but very limited place in these journals, and were only covered when they played an important role in the history of the community. Consequently, one can find no more than two articles by Mufti Szynkiewicz on the religious literature of the Polish-Lithuanian Tatar community in *Rocznik Tatarski*.[49] Compared to the numerous articles on the military past of the community, the religious aspect was hardly represented.

However, Islamic subjects were covered by a third journal, *Przegląd Islamski* (Islamic Review), edited by the Caucasian Muslim journalist Wassan-Girej Dżabagi and published from 1930 to 1931 and from 1934 to 1937. Dżabagi had come to Poland in 1922 after marrying a Polish Tatar woman and had immediately begun to engage in journalistic activities. As its goal was defined as bringing Islam closer to a Polish readership, *Przegląd Islamski* covered on the one hand political subjects such as Polish-Arab and Polish-Turkish relations, and on the other it was also interested in cultural issues such as Islamic literature. Although Polish Tatar writers were among those who contributed to the journal, it did not have an ethnic identity. According to Miśkiewicz, the journal was of a poor quality, and many of the texts contained numerous mistakes. Moreover, even that part of the Polish public interested in "Oriental" matters regarded the journal with some suspicion. It is quite revealing that the Orientalist Jan Reychman, who also published extensively in

47 See *Rocznik Tatarski*, I (Vilnius/Wilno, 1932), II (Zamosc, 1935).

48 Stanisław Kryczyński, *Tatarzy litewscy—próba monografii historyczno—etnograficznej* [Lithuanian Tatars—an attempt at an historical-ethnographic monograph], Warsaw: Rada centralna Związku kulturalno-oświatowego Tatarów Rzeczypospolitej Polskiej, 1938.

49 Jakup Szynkiewicz, "O kitabie [On the "kitab"]", *Rocznik Tatarski*, I (1932), pp. 188–93; the same, "Literatura religijna Tatarów litewskich i jej pochodzenie [The religious literature of the Lithuanian Tatars and its origins]", *Rocznik Tatarski*, II (1935), pp. 138–44.

the Polish Tatar press, accused the journal of being simply devoted to missionary propaganda. As the journal was closely linked to its editor, it closed down when Dżabagi went to Turkey in 1937. The journal did not have a wide-ranging influence on the Polish Tatar community.[50]

The Second World War was a turning point for the Polish-Lithuanian community. In 1939 the Germans stopped all its activities, and some of its activists such as Olgierd Kryczyński were murdered. Most members of the community joined the Polish army to fight the German invaders. Others, however, such as Jakup Szynkiewicz and his nephew Edige Szynkiewicz (who later became famous in Crimean Tatar exile circles as Edige Kirimal), engaged in German-sponsored activities. Jakup Szynkiewicz, who stayed in Vilnius during the war, became Mufti of the Ostland, a German territorial creation encompassing Lithuania, Latvia, Estonia, Byelorussia and the Eastern part of Poland.[51] Born in the Crimea, Edige Kirimal was the son of a Polish Tatar. He had spent several years in Turkey and Poland and later emigrated to Turkey. In 1942 he came to Germany where he tried to establish a kind of Crimean Tatar diplomatic mission. From 1944 onwards he led the officially recognised *Krimtatarische Leitstelle* (Crimean Tatar Office) which was supposed to represent the Crimean Tatars in German politics.

The territorial changes which affected Poland at the end of the war, led to a significant reduction in the size of the Tatar community in Poland as the traditional Tatar settlements now belonged to the Soviet Union as Lithuania, now including Vilnius, had been annexed by the Soviets. Consequently, the Second World War led to a break in the process of development which had started in the early 1920s when Poland gained its independence, and it would take the Polish Tatar community some thirty years to reorganise.

COMPARING THE INCOMPARABLE? TATARS IN GERMANY AND POLAND IN THE INTER-WAR PERIOD

At first sight, a comparison between Tatars in Germany and Poland should reveal parallels as both communities professed Islam and

[50] A. Miśkiewicz, *Tatarzy polscy*, pp. 134–5.

[51] J. Tyszkiewicz, *Z historii Tatarów polskich*, pp. 146–7.

constituted a Muslim community in a non-Muslim environment. In addition, both carry the same name. However, both the inner structure and the networking activities of both groups reveal two totally different communities. The community in Germany, which came into existence as a result of exile, became part of a diaspora network in the years following the establishment of the Soviet Union. It continued to be focused on the "homeland" both in a cultural and political sense. "Culture", as perceived by the leading community representatives, consisted mainly of writings expressing determination to defend against "Soviet distortions", and meetings to remember "national" Tatar poets such as Gabdulla Tuqay, intended to strengthen a feeling of belonging to the community. The political part of their activities consisted of following and unmasking Soviet policies both in the Volga-Ural region itself and in the Soviet Union as a whole. Most of the articles in their journal commented on these subjects. Consequently, the Tatar community in Germany was primarily a "national" one, and religion only played a supplementary role in forming community identity. A look at the networking activities of the community can help us to understand this important characteristic. In the first place they strove to hold together the Tatar exile communities dispersed throughout Europe and Asia, and secondly they tried to connect the Tatars with other non-Russian Soviet exile communities.

The Polish Tatar community, in contrast, was at its core a purely religious one. Linguistic assimilation to Polish society had taken place as early as the sixteenth and seventeenth centuries, and integration into Polish social, military and national structures was a source of pride for the whole community. It is not by accident that the participation of Polish Tatars in defending the Polish state militarily was continuously stressed by both the community and the Polish state.[52] As religion was the decisive feature of their ethnicity, the best means to strengthen and reinforce community coherence was to search for Islamic knowledge, a characteristic which is also

[52] In historical context the Tatar community sometimes also called itself "Lithuanian", or "Polish-Lithuanian" with reference to the personal union between the two states from the sixteenth to the eighteenth century. For the period relevant to this article the Lithuanian aspect did not play any role as the cultural integration into Polish society was completed in the early nineteenth century.

confirmed by the networking activities of the community. Thus, students were sent to Egypt and Yugoslavia in order to obtain the Islamic knowledge necessary for the cultural reproduction of the community. It is not by accident that most of the attempts by the Polish Tatars to establish contacts with the Islamic world were sponsored by the Polish state which sought to pursue a double strategy. On the one hand it tried to secure the loyalty of the community, while on the other it wanted to profit directly from the contacts the Tatars were establishing.

There were some contacts between the German and Polish Tatar communities, and the way these contacts did not work out shows the incompatibility of the two communities. First, it should be noted that in the years prior to the First World War Muslims from the Volga region played an important role in the Muslim community on Polish soil, and even in the 1920s and the early 1930s the Warsaw Muslim community recruited imams from the Volga-Ural region. Yet it would be wrong to regard the presence of the Volga Tatars on Polish soil as that of a "national" community. Volga Tatars did not play a role that was in any way different from Caucasian or Crimean Tatar Muslims, and their relative prominence was due not to their national origin, but to their greater knowledge of Islamic matters. Muslims from Russia could only succeed in the Muslim communities in Poland when they agreed to integrate culturally and to communicate in Polish, the language that Polish Muslims had used for centuries.[53]

A second potential contact can be seen from the fact that the Polish state was actively engaged in supporting the political émigré leaders of non-Russian peoples from the Soviet Union. From 1926 onwards it actively promoted the Promethean League which consisted of exiled leaders from Ukraine, Georgia, Turkistan, Azerbaijan, the Crimea and the Volga-Ural region, many of whom settled down in Warsaw, thus building a small-scale political network. The Volga Tatar structures supported by the Polish authorities had their headquarters in Warsaw and also in Berlin. The Tatar journal *Yaña*

[53] For examples of Muslims from the Volga-Ural region who played a prominent role in the Muslim communities in Poland see J. Tyszkiewicz, *Z historii Tatarów polskich*, p. 115.

Milli Yul was one of the Promethean publications, and Ayaz İshaki can be seen as the Volga Tatar representative in the League.[54] İshaki, who lived mostly in Warsaw, published widely in the Promethean journal *Wschód* (Orient), mainly concentrating on the political aspects of Volga Tatar history. It is quite revealing that one can find many articles in this journal by Georgian, Turkistani and other non-Russian exile leaders and by Polish Orientalists, but not one by a Polish Tatar.

İshaki's attempts to establish closer relationships with the Polish Tatar community were however unsuccesful. Although the community was probably grateful for his involvement in the Islamic Sunday school in Warsaw,[55] his other ideas on the development of the Polish Tatar community were rejected by their representatives. At the congress of the Association of Polish Tatars in Vilnius in 1928 he urged Polish Muslims to establish closer contacts with the Muslim world by learning the Tatar language,[56] a call İshaki later repeated in his only article in the Polish Tatar press.[57] His appeal did not go unnoticed, and on the contrary it provoked objections. At the Vilnius congress where İshaki voiced his appeal for the first time, Olgierd Kryczyński, the next speaker, immediately stressed the great cultural influence Western civilisation exerted on the Polish Tatar community—a comment that might be seen as a direct response to İshaki's appeal. Involvement in pan-Turkic activities or in Volga-Ural solidarity movements was the last thing Polish Tatars were thinking about.

However, it cannot be said that the representatives of (Crimean and Volga) Tatar exiles resident in Poland were distrusted by the Polish Tatar community. There was considerable sympathy for the Crimean cause but this was not based on "ethnic" or "national"

[54] The history of the Promethean movement is still to be written. For a good survey see Étienne Copeaux, "Le mouvement 'Prométhéen' [The Promethean movement]", *CEMOTI*, 16 (1993), pp. 9–47; for the Polish involvement see Sergiusz Mikulicz, *Prometeizm w politice II Rzeczypospolitej* [Prometheanism in the politics of the Second Republic], Warsaw: Książka i Wiedza, 1971.

[55] A. Miśkiewicz, *Tatarzy polscy*, p. 87.

[56] Ibid., p. 106.

[57] Ayas Ishaki, "Narodowe zadanie polskich Tatarów [The national task of the Polish Tatars]", *Rocznik Tatarski*, I (1932), pp. 195–9.

feelings, but simply on solidarity for an oppressed Muslim people. Polish Tatars did not see anything wrong in supporting a Muslim people fighting for its national rights, but they did not make it their own cause,[58] and did not feel any need to react to Crimean Tatar demands that they return to their "Turkic past". Pan-Turkic solidarity was not on their agenda.

By comparing the German and Polish Tatar communities, one comes to the conclusion that the first one was an exile community in the true sense of the word, whereas the latter might be seen as the first forerunner of a European Islam. This was certainly the claim of the Tatar community in Poland itself. Its members repeatedly expressed their desire to reconcile their loyalty to the Polish state and their commitment to "Western culture" (which they never tried to define more closely) with their allegiance to Islam. However, Polish Tatars never had an explicit conception of Euro-Islam, and together with their engagement with the Polish state and their interest in "Western culture" they continued to stress the importance of developing contacts with the Muslim world; but in reality the situation looked slightly different. Cultural assimilation continued among the community, and the Muslims of Poland relied heavily on the religious knowledge of Muslim immigrants from Russia. Nevertheless, the emphasis of the Polish Tatar community on Euro-Islam on the one hand, and the fact that the Tatars in Germany had a strong national identity as "exiles" on the other, made mutual networking activities between the two communities impossible. Both communities developed their networks according to their cultural and political needs, and these needs were simply not the same.

[58] See also Katarzyna Warmińska, *Tatarzy polscy. Tożsamość religijna i etniczna* [Polish Tatars. Religious and ethnic identity], Krakow: Universitas, 1999, p. 210.

THE FIRST MUSLIM MISSIONS ON A EUROPEAN SCALE: AHMADI-LAHORI NETWORKS IN THE INTER-WAR PERIOD

Eric Germain

INTRODUCTION: THE ORIGINS OF MUSLIM MISSIONS IN EUROPE

An article first published in Austria and reproduced in 1909 in several Russian Muslim newspapers presented a picture of Islamic propaganda in Western Europe at that time.[1] It shed light on two countries: Germany, where Islam was promoted by a couple of converts, and England with a far more organised propaganda spread by the Liverpool Institute of Abdullah (William Henry) Quilliam (1856–1932). The pioneering work done by this small institute, which paved the way for the various Muslim organisations emerging after Quilliam's departure to Turkey in 1908, must be highlighted. Through weekly and monthly papers, pamphlets, public lectures and letters to the local press, the Liverpool Institute developed a specific communication style in which securing converts became an essential part of its agenda for the defence of Islam.[2] In the last decade of the nineteenth century, the Institute established a correspondence with Muslims from several places across Europe, sending its magazines to Belgium, France, Germany, Switzerland, Hungary, Greece, Bulgaria, and also Crete, Malta and

[1] "Europe", *Revue du Monde Musulman* (*RMM*—Paris), X, 1 (January 1910), p. 103.

[2] John J. Pool, *Studies in Mohammedanism. Historical and Doctrinal. With a chapter on Islam in England*, Westminster: A. Constable, 1892, p. xiv. He mentioned Quilliam's propaganda made in England as threatening the success of Christian missions in India, China, and Africa.

Gibraltar.[3] Shaikh Abdullah Quilliam claimed that "scarcely a week passes without an extract from one of our journals being quoted in some other publication", adding that he regarded this "as one of the most important features of our [missionary] work".[4]

The mission that Khwaja Kamaluddin (1870–1932) founded in Woking (Surrey) reactivated and increased Quilliam's English reading public throughout Europe and within the British Empire. Its propaganda effort was a direct response to the worldwide intensification of Christian proselytism among Muslim populations. This new missionary zeal grew together with an "evangelical Orientalism"[5] exemplified by the periodical *The Moslem World* founded by the Reverend Samuel Zwemer in London in 1911.[6] In the foreword of the first issue of his monthly newspaper, Khwaja Kamaluddin expressed his determination to challenge the "campaign against Islam" orchestrated by this "pseudo-Muslim paper, under the name of the *Moslem World*".[7]

The Indian barrister arrived in London in September 1912 to plead the legal case of a Bombay businessman and started to give public lectures on Islam.[8] A prominent member of the Ahmadiyya movement, Khwaja Kamaluddin quickly gained control of the vacant mosque of Woking—about twenty-five miles to the South-West of London—to base his Muslim Mission and Literary Trust. One may be surprised to see that the launching of this European

[3] "Annual Meeting of the Liverpool Muslim Institute", *The Islamic World* (*IW*—Liverpool), IV, 39 (July 1896), pp. 65–93, see pp. 82, 86. The Institute was on the exchange list of European journals written in English, French, German, Dutch, Russian, Spanish, Bulgarian and Romanian.

[4] W. H. Quilliam, "Our Literature", *IW* (Liverpool), IV, 39 (July 1896), pp. 77–8.

[5] Expression taken from Avril Powell who refers to the way that missionaries like C.G. Pfander studied Arabic and Persian sources in order to demonstrate how Islam "fell short of Christianity"; A. Powell, *Muslims and Missionaries in Pre-Mutiny India*, Richmond: Curzon, 1993, pp. 144–51.

[6] Samuel Marinus Zwemer (1867–1952) founded the Arabian Mission of the Dutch Reformed Church and was for 36 years the editor of the *Moslem World*.

[7] Khwaja Kamal-ud-Din, "Foreword", *Muslim India and the Islamic Review* (*IR*—Woking), I, 1 (February 1913), pp. 1–4, see p. 1.

[8] "To the Memory of Khwaja Kamal-ud-Din", *IR*, 50th anniversary volume (1962). He gave his first lectures at the Hyde Park Speakers' Corner and in meetings of British theological societies.

Muslim mission was initiated from the remote Indian city of Lahore. That was precisely the point questioned by a book entitled *Young Islam on Trek, a Study of the Clash of Civilizations*, stressing in 1926 that "it is Indian Islam that has built the mosques and finances the able propaganda at Woking and at Berlin".[9]

HOW AN INDIAN MOVEMENT BECAME THE VOICE OF ISLAM IN EUROPE

The movement founded by Mirza Ghulam Ahmad (c.1836–1908) was registered by the Government of India in the 1901 Census as a "distinct Mohammedan sect". Soon after the death of its founder, the Ahmadiyya community split in two antagonistic groups. The majority of its members joined the Qadian Party[10] which proclaimed the prophethood of Mirza Ghulam Ahmad, whereas a minority group based in Lahore spoke of the "Promised Mahdi and Messiah" as a *mujaddid* (a renewer of his century, as known in Sunni orthodoxy). In 1914 the latter group founded the *Ahmadiyya Anjuman-i-Isha'at-i-Islam* (Ahmadiyya Society for the Propagation of Islam, Urdu acronym AAII) under the leadership of Maulana Muhammad Ali (1874–1951). When Khwaja Kamaluddin decided to join the Lahore Party, the mission he had just founded in England became the spearhead of an Islamo-Christian dialogue/controversy that soon developed into a distinctive feature of this branch of the Ahmadiyya.

Engaging Christian Churches in an assumed polemical argument

Indian Muslims studying at British universities showed interest in the historical interaction between Europe and Islam. Such curiosity is illustrated by the translation made by the young barrister Haroon Khan Sherwani of the classic French book on the incursions of Saracens into France and Switzerland, a text published as a

[9] Basil Mathews, *Young Islam on Trek. A Study of the Clash of Civilizations*, London: Edinburgh House Press, 1926, p. 120.

[10] The movement was generally called after Mirza Ghulam Ahmad's hometown in Punjab where it had its headquarters.

serial story in the Indian Muslim press.[11] In launching a European Muslim mission, Khwaja Kamaluddin placed his action within a resolute historical perspective, claiming that "the fate of the Moors in Spain awaits us everywhere, and our annihilation is only a question of time".[12] He claimed that it was Christian missionary propaganda that made possible the atrocities currently suffered by Muslims in the Balkan wars. In order to "counteract the poison thus created", Khwaja Kamaluddin called upon his Indian brethren to collect the means to allow the free circulation of his *Islamic Review* among Members of Parliament and within the Church as well as the numerous clubs and libraries of Great Britain. More than simple lobbying work, he expressed the ambition to undertake "the dissemination of Islam in Western lands", saying that "the trend of modern philosophy, ethics and socialism is towards Islam".[13] Such a self-confident attitude was shared by a growing number of intellectuals, including one who lamented in a Lahore paper of 1907 that "in Muslim countries, governments as individuals have abandoned all idea of proselytism".[14]

As a religious minority, Indian Muslims felt particularly threatened by the Christian missionary propaganda conducted since the beginning of the nineteenth century.[15] Mission schools were ironically instrumental in forming the new Western educated elite that engaged itself in "counter-missionary" work. Such was the case of Khwaja Kamaluddin who, during his studies at the Forman Christian College of Lahore, acquired a fairly good knowledge of the Bible.[16] In England, the eloquent barrister was particularly willing

[11] Translation of J. Reinaud's book (1836) by Haroon Khan Sherwani, "Incursions of the Muslims into France, Piemont and Switzerland", *Islamic Culture* (*IC*—Hyderabad), from January to October 1930 (IV/1 to IV/4).

[12] "The Message of the Khwaja", *The Review of Religions* [*RoR*—Qadian] (May 1913), pp. 210–19, on line on www.wokingmuslim.org.

[13] Ibid.

[14] Article from the Lahore-based *The Observer* quoted in "L'Avenir de l'Islam", *RMM*, III, 11–12 (November-December 1907), p. 599.

[15] A. Powell, *Muslims and Missionaries*, p. 229. The Ahmadiyya fought anti-Muslims polemics launched in India by Christian missionaries and Hindu revivalists from the Arya Samaj.

[16] "Can Dogmas Rule The Religious World?", *The Moslem Outlook* (*MO*—Cape Town), II, 58 (13 March 1926), p. 13.

to engage in Islamo-Christian debates. On several occasions he was requested to address Christian audiences about Islam,[17] and in July 1913 he travelled to Paris to speak at an Interfaith Congress convened by liberal Christians.[18] After the war, the founder of the Woking Mission adopted an increasingly polemical discourse targeting evangelists like Samuel Zwemer who was accused of engineering "slanders against Islam".[19] On the one hand, Lahori missionaries questioned the validity of the Christian scriptures by raising contradictions and variations in the accounts of the four Evangelists or mocking some doctrines like the Trinity or the virgin birth of Jesus.[20] The defence of Islam, on the other hand, focused mainly on questions such as the authenticity of the Qur'anic revelation, holy war, slavery, polygamy and the position of women.

On Kamaluddin's rhetorical talents, it is interesting to quote the opinion of William (Muhammad) Marmaduke Pickthall.[21] The famous British convert stated that he "had a gift for summing up a train of arguments in striking form" and "unlike much polemical writing it is not devoid of literary grace".[22] Khwaja Kamaluddin showed a true ability to reach an audience having little or no knowledge of Islam, a quality that, according to Pickthall, was lacking in most "Muslim 'missionary' publications" of the time. Even within the same movement, there was a noticeable difference between publications from Woking and the ones issued in Lahore. Commenting on a book by Maulana Muhammad Ali, the same Pickthall stressed that its argument and style were the ones of *fiqh* (Islamic jurisprudence), which "differ from that of Christian polemics and can only be appreciated in the West by the few who

17 "What Means this Mission", *MO*, II, 62 (10 April 1926), p. 4.

18 *Special Features of Islam, a paper read by Khwaja Kamal-ud-Din at the Sixth Congress of Religions, in Paris, on July 19, 1913*, London: J.S. Phillips, 1913, 16 pp.

19 Khwaja Kamal-ud-Din, *Message of Islam*, London/Woking: Unwin Brothers, 1927, p. 5.

20 Those arguments were often taken from the numerous books written by European rationalist thinkers throughout the nineteenth century.

21 Marmaduke Pickthall (1875–1936) was a novelist and Qur'anic translator known for *The Meaning of the Glorious Koran*, New York: A. Knopf, 1930.

22 Marmaduke Pickthall, "The Claim of Islam", *IC*, VIII, 3 (July 1934), pp. 506–7.

have already made some study of Islâm".[23] Muslim missions in Europe brought a true added value to the worldwide effort of Islamic propaganda by publishing a popular kind of literature rather like those question/answer dialogues and compilations containing favourable references to Islam from famous Western writers.[24]

An apolitical discourse securing official recognition

The little mosque at Woking was built in 1889, as part of the educational complex that Gottlieb Leitner—a former registrar of the University of Punjab, Lahore—dedicated to the study of Oriental languages and civilisations. When the institution closed after the death of Dr Leitner in 1899, the mosque remained open only on rare occasions.[25] One such event was the visit of Abdul Baha to Woking on January 1913.[26] The head of the Baha'i Faith announced, on behalf of the heir of Dr Leitner, that "the mosque would in future be open for Muhammadans to worship at any time they pleased".[27] A Trust for guardianship of the mosque was then created with a membership made up of three public figures having strong connexions with India—the Right Hon. Sayyid Ameer Ali,

[23] M. Pickthall, "The Perfect Polity", *IC*, X, 4 (October 1936), pp. 659–62. In this posthumous article, he reviewed Maulana Muhammad Ali's *The Religion of Islâm*, Lahore: Ahmadiyyah Anjuman Ishâ'at Islâm, 1936.

[24] See Dr. H. Marcus, "The Message of the Holy Prophet Muhammad to Europe", *IR*, XX, 6–7, 8, 9 (June to September 1932), pp. 222–39, 268–78, 281–6. These articles were also edited as a tract distributed by the AAII in thousands of copies; Ezad Bakhsh, *19th Annual Report of the AAII from 1st October 1931 to 30th September 1932*, p. 12.

[25] Such as for the memorial service on the death of the Shah of Persia in 1907 or an '*Id* whose prayers were led by Abdullah Suhrawardy; "First Eid in England (1903)", *Daily Dawn* (Karachi), 10–16 (June 1999), p. 13, quoted in N. Ahmad, "G.W. Leitner", on www.wokingmuslim.org.

[26] The Baha'i Faith was founded by Baha'ullah who was succeeded in 1892 by his eldest son Abdul Baha (1844–1921). Its initial expansion in the West was confined to the USA, despite the founding of branches in Britain and Germany in 1923; Peter Smith, *The Babi and Baha'i Religions*, CUP, 1987, pp. 106, 181.

[27] W.M.C.M., "Abdul Baha's visit to Woking—a memorable gathering", *The Asiatic Quarterly Review* (London), I (New Series), 2 (April 1913), pp. 225–36.

Sir Mirza Abbas Ali Baig and Sir Thomas Arnold[28]—who appointed Khwaja Kamaluddin as imam of the mosque. One could hardly consider that this appointment would have been made without the implicit consent of the India Office.

In his Memoirs, Sayyid Ameer Ali regretted that the inner city of London did not possess a "suitable place of worship for the Moslem subjects of the king and Moslem visitors coming to England".[29] As a matter of fact it was the Woking Mosque that fulfilled the need and, as its first imam, Khwaja Kamaluddin could present himself as the paramount Muslim authority for London and the whole kingdom. In 1924, the mission claimed to assume a spiritual leadership not only over the thirty persons who regularly attended prayers at the mosque, but also over "the thousand British Muslims scattered about the country and the 10,000 Muslims from overseas".[30] The British press acknowledged the pre-eminence of Khwaja Kamaluddin, referring to him as the "Very Reverend", on the analogy of the Chief Rabbi.[31]

The Woking Mission constantly reinforced its status and prestige by visits of diplomats and Muslim dignitaries. The bucolic setting of the Surrey mosque saw princes and begums from India, African chiefs and Arab sovereigns.[32] A trip to Woking became part of the usual agenda of foreign leaders coming to London, such as Emperor Haile Selassie in 1936. In March of the same year, the former Prime Minister Lloyd George chose this mosque to deliver a

[28] Sayyid Ameer Ali was a former member of the Indian Judicial Committee (1849–1928), T.W. Arnold (1864–1930) a renowned Orientalist scholar, and Abbas Ali Baig (d. 1933) acted in the Council of the Secretary of State for India as its Muslim advisory member; Dr. Ashiq Husain Batalvi's account on www.wokingmuslim.org.

[29] "Memoirs of the late Rt. Hon. Syed Ameer Ali", *IC*, VI, 4 (October 1932), pp. 503–25, see pp. 503–4.

[30] Peter Clark, *Marmaduke Pickthall: British Muslim*, London: Quartet Books, 1986, p. 41.

[31] Ibid., p. 40.

[32] Some political activists visited Woking like Muhammad Ali Jinnah and Adil Arslan, brother of Shakib Arslan; Aftab-ud-Din Ahmad, "East meet West in Oriental Road", *IR*, XX, 4 (April 1932), pp. 101–3, see p. 103.

speech on "Islam and the British Empire" in front of an audience made up of "ambassadors and ministers, chargés d'affaires, London mayors, ex-governors of Indian provinces and famous Oriental scholars".[33] Illustrious visitors helped the mission to present itself as the heart of Islam in Great Britain, as is shown by the name chosen for the telegraphic address of the mosque: "Islamabad" (City of Islam).[34]

The Woking Mission gave a positive image of Islam in UK and attested to the benevolent attitude of the Crown towards its Muslim subjects. If Woking publications denounced prejudice against Muslims in the Empire, Khwaja Kamaluddin stated that "sedition and anarchical movements are *haram*, and strictly prohibited in Islam".[35] Wartime censorship influenced the content of *Muslim India and the Islamic Review*, which focused even more on religious and social issues (significantly, the title was shortened to *Islamic Review* in 1921). Such a restrained political stance was common to most Muslim organisations in Britain at that time,[36] but the Ahmadiyya's unequivocal condemnation of *jihad* (in its martial sense) surely made a decisive argument to generate sympathy. With the outbreak of the war, the mission tried to take advantage of its long-claimed loyalty by petitioning the government officially to be in charge of the plot opened for the burial of Muslim soldiers at the Woking Cemetery.[37] The imam supported his demand by pointing to the spiritual task that the mission fulfilled in hosting Indian soldiers coming on leave to Woking.

Khwaja Kamaluddin kept on enlarging contacts with members of influential circles of British society that felt attracted by new

[33] *Morning Post* (9 March 1936), quoted in Simon Naylor and James Ryan, "The Mosque in the Suburbs: Negotiating Religion and Ethnicity in South London", *Social & Cultural Geography*, III, 1 (2002), pp. 39–59, see p. 51.

[34] *The Times*, 12 July 1935, quoted in S. Naylor and J. Ryan, ibid., p. 51.

[35] "Message of the Khwaja" [letter addressed to the meeting of the All-India Muslim League in Lucknow], *RoR* (May 1913), pp. 210–19, on www.wokingmuslim.org.

[36] Commenting on the project of founding Urdu newspapers in Istanbul and in Switzerland, M.H. Kidwai of the London Pan-Islamic Society suggested that those newspapers "shall restrain themselves from discussing Indian politics"; "Journaux ourdous", *RMM*, VI, 11 (November 1908), pp. 571–72.

[37] The Central Islamic Society, *The Central Islamic Society and its Need—An Appeal*, Woking/London: Unwin Brothers, 1916, p. 5.

thought and "exotic" Oriental religions. The Lahori barrister was particularly keen to debate with other faiths and was "often requested to address the Theosophists, Spiritualists, leaders of New Thought".[38] He was one of those Muslim intellectuals who found inspiration in the modern methods deployed by the flourishing alternative spiritualities. This was also the case of the London Central Islamic Society which aimed to "establish branches in England and all over Europe like those of the Theosophical and other world-important societies".[39] This wish was realised by the AAII whose leader announced the launching of a German mission at the Annual Conference of December 1921.[40]

In Germany, a country dispossessed of its colonies, Indians like other Muslims from the British Empire found a space where they could have relative free speech on many political subjects.[41] The presence at the Berlin Mission Mosque of Indian revolutionaries such as Maulvi Barakatullah or the Arab activist Shakib Arslan might have indicated a more political inclination of the German mission. Nevertheless, from reading of their publications, it seems that Berlin missionaries did not use this extraterritoriality to be more critical about British policy towards its Muslim colonial populations.

The first Berlin mosque, to reach to continental Europe

Muslim students in Europe were a key target for Lahori missionaries as those educated young men could bring time and energy to propaganda work. The AAII expressed its willingness to reach this audience by offering special prices to students who subscribed to its publications.[42] Among Indian students, a prominent figure was the great poet and philosopher Muhammad Iqbal who came to

38 "Can Dogmas Rule The Religious World?", p. 13.

39 The Central Islamic Society, *The Central Islamic Society*, p. 6.

40 Nasir Ahmad, *A Brief History of the Berlin Muslim Mission (1922–1988)*, 2004, 52 pp., see p. 3 (on www.aaiil.org).

41 Berlin hosted Egyptian activists fighting British imperialism; Joseph Castagné, "Les Indes et l'Egypte vues de Russie", *RMM*, LIX (1st trimester 1925), pp. 213–71, see p. 264 .

42 For example, students had a 40 per cent discount on the annual subscription to the English weekly *The Light*; Ezad Bakhsh, *9th Annual Report*, adverts appearing on the last page.

Cambridge in 1905 and received his PhD in Munich three years later.[43] Despite the harsh material conditions of the post-war period, Germany remained an attractive place for Indian students. The Muslim press of Lahore encouraged this trend, saying that "if Afghanistan can send twenty-five students in Berlin, India ought to be able to send a thousand".[44] The fact that Germany was the second most popular overseas destination for Indian students surely motivated the opening of a second mission in Berlin.[45]

In the aftermath of the First World War, Khwaja Kamaluddin visited France, Belgium and Germany to study the conditions for extending missionary activities in continental Europe.[46] On his advice, the Lahore headquarters decided to open a mission in Berlin and sent Maulvi Abdul Majid who arrived at the end of 1922, followed a couple of months later by Maulvi Sadr-ud-Din.[47] A missionary from the rival Qadian movement stated that Muslim propaganda expected the greatest achievements "among a people whom defeat and humiliation have sobered a good deal, and whose hearts are now turned from materialism to things spiritual".[48] The success met by the German Mission in the cosmopolitan Berliner Muslim community might be attributed to the "outsider" image of Indian Islam. It allowed the mission to play the benevolent mediator between the numerous Muslim movements organised on national lines.

The building of a superb mosque located in a smart residential area[49] of Berlin was designed to be a landmark asserting the peren-

[43] Muhammad Iqbal (1873–1938) studied at the University of Lahore where he attended Sir Thomas Arnold's lectures; his education illustrates the link between India, England and Germany that we find in the Lahori network.

[44] "Afghan King at Berlin", *The Islamic World* (*IW*—Lahore), VI, 6 (April 1928), p. 226.

[45] This choice was not obvious as one of the capitals of countries with large colonial Muslim populations, such as France or the Netherlands, could also have been a suitable option.

[46] "What Means this Mission", p. 4.

[47] "The Berlin Mosque", *IR*, XIII, 3 (March 1925), pp. 81–2.

[48] "Ahmadia News Abroad", *The Moslem Sunrise* (*MS*—Chicago), II, 2–3 (April-July 1923), p. 196.

[49] This residential area was also chosen, at the same period, for the building of the Berlin Russian Orthodox Church. The minarets of the mosque were completed in 1927; C.H. Seiler-Chan, "Der Islam in Berlin", *MR*, IV (October 1934), pp. 112–19 (cf. p. 116).

nial presence of Islam in the heart of Europe. Drawings and pictures of the Briennerstrasse mosque circulated in the Muslim press all over the world; the architecture of the mosque had to be sumptuous, even if its dimensions made it difficult to heat during the long winter. Despite its lavish Mogul style, the building was in search of symbols of its European character such as those Arabic calligraphies crowning the inside dome of the mosque, reproduced from the Alhambra palace.[50] The reference to the Andalusian "golden age" of European Islam, common in the discourse of Lahori missionaries, was part of the propaganda function assigned to the mosque. The adjacent hostel was built to accommodate the imam and "at least four missionaries", showing that Berlin was expected to become the headquarters for itinerant missionaries to the Balkans, Central and Eastern Europe.[51]

In August 1932, the imam of the Berlin Mosque passed through Austria and Czechoslovakia "with a view to gain insight as to the possibilities of spreading Islam there".[52] He came in contact with several Muslims who were propagating their faith "individually in their circles of influence". At the same time, another missionary from Berlin, S.M. Abdullah, was in Lahore along with Baron Omar (Rolf) Freiherr von Ehrenfels (1901–80).[53] The Austrian convert had first heard about the Berlin Mosque from an imam of Sarajevo, while he was travelling in Yugoslavia.[54] Back from his journey to India, the aristocrat founded the short-lived Vienna Muslim Mission in 1934.[55] The same year, the AAII envisaged launching a new

[50] Those calligraphies may have been drawn from an article by Prof. O. Tallgren on the decorative inscriptions of the Alhambra reviewed by M. Pickthall in *IC*, IV, 2 (April 1930), pp. 329–30.

[51] "The Berlin Mosque", pp. 81–2.

[52] Ezad Bakhsh, *9th Annual Report,* pp. 9–10.

[53] Opposed to Nazis, he left Austria in 1938 for India where he pursued an academic career at the Madras University; S.A. Khulusi, *Islam Our Choice*, Woking: Muslim Mission & Literary Trust, 1963 (2nd ed), pp. 234–5.

[54] Baron Omar Rolf Ehrenfels, "An die Schriftleitung der Moslemischen Revue", *MR*, X, 2–3 (April-July 1934), pp. 43–4. I am grateful to Fikret Karčić for having identified this "imam Knobegović" met by Ehrenfels as Abdullah Effendi Kurbegović (1873–1933) who had been military imam in Vienna from 1904 to 1915.

[55] Syed Muhammad Hussain Shah, *Annual Report for the year 1933–34 of the Ahmadiyya Anjuman-i-Isha'at-i-Islam Lahore* (*A Digest*), 1934, p. 4.

mission in Spain, probably with the idea of securing help from the Arab students in Madrid and Granada who had founded in 1933 a review in Spanish with the evocative title *al-Andalus*.[56] For this purpose a fund was raised and regularly advertised in *The Light* that proposed to name the *'Id al-Adha* of 1934 "Spain Day".[57] At this celebration presided over by Maulana Muhammad Ali, a medical student volunteered to go to Spain. It is interesting to note that articles from the Lahore newspaper dealing with the Spanish Mission were translated into Albanian and published in the Tirana journal *Zani i naltë*.[58]

Albania, the only country in Europe with a Muslim majority, was of great interest to Lahori missionaries.[59] The Muslim press of Punjab expressed concern about the progress made by Christian missions to Muslims in the Balkans, and the AAII was eager to help Muslim communities living in those countries.[60] Among them, Albania was considered as the European outpost of *dar al-Islam* (the land of Islam), a present-day Andalusia, and a gateway to gain access to Muslim populations spread throughout the Balkans.[61] The keen interest in Europe's historic Muslim communities led the Berlin Mission to secure contacts with Tatars from Finland and Poland; a Tatar from Poland had translated several Lahori books and in 1929 contemplated starting a paper in Polish "on the style of *The Light*".[62]

[56] The second volume of *Al-Andalus* was reviewed in *Islamic Culture,* VIII, 3 (July 1934), pp. 508–9, the Hyderabad newspaper being on a list for exchange with the *Moslemische Revue*.

[57] Syed Md. Hussain Shah, *Annual Report*, p. 4.

[58] "The first voluntary for a Mission in Spain" (translated from *The Light* by H. Selami), *Zani i naltë* (Tirana), X, 2 (February 1935), pp. 56–8. Thanks to Nathalie Clayer who brought this article to my attention.

[59] Nathalie Clayer, "La Ahmadiyya Lahori et la réforme de l'islam albanais dans l'entre-deux-guerres", in V. Bouillier and C. Servan-Schreiber (eds), *De l'Arabie à l'Himalaya, chemins croisés*, Paris: Maisonneuve et Larose, 2004, pp. 211–28.

[60] Dr. Freytag, "German Missions to Muslims in the Balkans", *IW* (Lahore), VI, 12 (October 1928), p. 417.

[61] Sheikh Muhammad Din Jan, *Annual Report for the year 1928–29 of the Ahmadiyya Anjuman-i-Isha'at-i-Islam Lahore*, 1929, p. 14.

[62] Ibid.

Opposition to Lahori missions

The desire for control of the financial resources collected among Muslims throughout the British Empire led to increasing competition between the various missionary organisations. In 1936, the ex-Secretary of the London Muslim Society argued that his main objection to Woking's activities was motivated by the fact that the mission was channelling the largest part of funds coming from the Muslim world towards its own trust.[63] Newcomers in the field of Islamic propaganda had to present themselves as more orthodox than their "competitors" and constantly outbid them in a battle of image.

At the time the Woking Mission was launched, the only organisation of some importance in England was the Central Islamic Society. The fact that "the oldest Muslim institution in the British Isles" could not achieve what the Woking Mission did in a short time created a good deal of jealousy among some of its members. This is quite noticeable in the foreword to a leaflet of the Islamic Society. While acknowledging the good work undertaken by the Woking Trust, it recommends "to keep the missionary work separate and limited in its scope".[64] However, such resentment could not have been expressed more openly as the imam of Woking was also a member of the Managing Committee of the Islamic Society. In Berlin, the Lahori mission met with hostility from the *Islamische Gemeinde* founded in 1922 by two Indian brothers,[65] but the most serious competitors were the Qadiani missionaries.

Soon after Khwaja Kamaluddin affiliated the Woking Trust to the newly founded AAII,[66] the Qadian headquarters tried to establish

[63] Ahmed Bennet, "Why I Resigned from the Secretaryship of the Muslim Society in Great Britain", *GI*, I, 1 (January 1936), p. 28, objecting that "the Woking Mission draws its funds from the WHOLE of the Muslim world".

[64] The Central Islamic Society, *The Central Islamic Society*, pp. 5–6.

[65] K. Sheldrake, "The Pioneers of Islam in England, France, Germany and America", *GI*, I, 1 (January 1936), p. 26. The Lahori mission was a direct rival of Abdul Sattar and Abdul Jabbar Khairi's own mosque project.

[66] This affiliation was not clearly stated as the Woking Mission was proud to "count among its zealous supporters Sunnis, Shias, Ahl-i-Hadis, Ahmadis, Bowahirs (Bohras), Khojas, and every other school of thought in Islam"; "Editor's Notes", *IR*, XIII, 3 (March 1925), p. 84.

its own mission in England.[67] Its opening in 1919 may have benefited from the slowing down of Woking's activity after Khwaja Kamaluddin had to depart for India the very same year owing to his deteriorating health.[68] In 1924, the spiritual head of the Qadian movement came to England to lay the first stone of the Mission Mosque in the South-West London suburb of Southfields.[69] The opening two years later of the "first London Mosque" was announced at the same time as the inauguration of the Paris Mosque and the Qadian movement played on this coincidence in its publicity.[70] Qadianis shared with Lahoris a similar approach to the way Muslim propaganda should operate and were struggling to represent the voice of Islam in the interfaith conferences organised in Europe.[71] In 1924, Qadianis were operating in London and Berlin and a third mission was even planned in Greece.[72]

At the grassroots, there was a somewhat blurred frontier between the two branches of the Ahmadiyya. Despite their assumed rivalry, Qadiani newspapers mentioned the work accomplished by Lahori missions, and it was not uncommon to find people who subscribed to both Qadiani and Lahori newspapers.[73] In England, some people attended celebrations in Woking as well as in Southfields.[74] It is difficult to know whether they were fully aware of the conflict

[67] A first missionary from Qadian briefly sojourned in London in 1914; S. Naylor and J. Ryan, "The Mosque in the Suburbs", p. 45.

[68] "Ahmadia Moslem Mission News Abroad", *MS*, I, 1 (July 1921), p. 20.

[69] "The First Mosque in London", *RoR*, XXIII,12 (December 1924), p. 428.

[70] "New London Mosque" and "Islam in Paris", *MO*, II, 82 (28 August 1926), p. 11.

[71] If the Qadiani Abdul Rahim Dard attended the Geneva Universal Congress of Religious Forces for Peace, it was a Lahori who spoke at the Congress of Religious Liberals in St Gallen: Union des Eglises pour la Paix, *Les religions contre la guerre*, Paris, 1929, p. 32. Ezad Bakhsh, *9th Annual Report*, p. 9.

[72] The other foreign missions were in the USA, the Gold Coast, Mauritius and Egypt; *RoR*, XXIII, 12 (December 1924), inside front cover. "Moslem Mission News Abroad", *MS*, I, 1 (July 1921), p. 20.

[73] "One day Christians", in *RoR*, XXIII, 2 (February 1924), p. 75. "Congratulations", *MS*, III, 2 (April 1924), p. 74.

[74] Afghan diplomats as well as Abdullah Quilliam attended '*Id* in Southfields in 1922 and in Woking in 1925; "Ahmadia News Abroad", *MS*, I, 6 (October 1922), pp. 140–2 and "General", p. 3.

between the two groups, but such confusion was somehow more convenient for the Qadianis whose impact on the European scene was less important in the inter-war period. One could not say the same for Lahori missions, which suffered from the "anti-Ahmadi" campaign that grew in India at the beginning of the 1930s.

After Khwaja Kamaluddin's death in December 1932, the Woking Trust came to be attacked more often for its link with the Lahore branch of the Ahmadiyya. Opposition to Ahmadi missions in Europe was supported by the All Malaya Muslim Missionary Society and its newspaper, *Genuine Islam*, published in Singapore.[75] Aiming to carry on work "in Europe, America, Japan, Australia and Africa",[76] this new organisation led by Maulana M.A. Siddiqui became a direct rival to Ahmadi missions. The Society was eager to stress its difference in targeting more specifically "the Lahori sect of the Qadianees".[77] The expression is not innocent because we know that in the 1930s several Egyptian and Indian *fatwa*s had already condemned Qadianis for being "outside the pale of Islam", whereas the Lahore movement was still considered by many as a modernist, atypical, but orthodox Sunni group.

This positive image explains why the Muslim Missionary Society focused on trying to undermine the esteem that Lahori missions had gained all over Europe.[78] The Singapore-based organisation wrote to *Hlas*, the monthly Islamic journal of Prague, to warn Czechoslovak Muslims against translating Muhammad Ali's articles.[79] The first issue of *Genuine Islam* proudly announced the results of a campaign calling on European Muslims to "sever all

[75] The All Malaya Muslim Missionary Society was founded in 1931 by Maulana Muhammad Abdul Aleem Siddiqui Al-Qadri and the first issue of *Genuine Islam* appeared in January 1936.

[76] "Reception to Famous Muslim Missionary", *GI*, III, 9 (September 1938), pp. 304–5.

[77] "Truth about Qadianism", *GI*, III, 1–2 (January-February 1938), pp. 43–5. In the same issue "Islamic pictures from Denmark, Poland and Germany" were published.

[78] The Muslim Missionary Society tried to establish a foothold in Poland and published pictures of the Vilnius Mosque and of the Grand Mufti of Poland, *GI*, III, 1–2 (February 1938), p. 32.

[79] M.A. Brickcius' letter published in *GI*, III, 10 (October 1938), pp. 365–7.

connections with Mirzais".[80] This campaign received support from some leaders of the Muslim Society of Great Britain who were evicted after the Woking Trust took over the association at the end of 1934. Its former secretary argued that "the Woking Mission teaches nothing about Ahmadi doctrines", but denounced an "indirect Ahmadi influence" in the "Salvation Army, milk-and-water, or Christened Islam" presented by the mission.[81]

Attacks were sometimes rather low, such as the publishing of photographs of S.M. Abdullah taken at the stadium during the 1936 Olympic Games; the stolen shots appeared in Indian magazines with the comment: "Mirzai Imam of the Berlin Mosque who has taken the arm of a German unpermitted lady".[82] The level of this campaign of denigration shows the difficulty experienced by its protagonists in tracing any doctrinal influence of Mirza Ghulam Ahmad in the European Lahori propaganda and explains why it is only at the very end of the inter-war period that their anti-Ahmadi arguments gained ground.

ACHIEVING OPTIMAL MOBILISATION OF LIMITED RESOURCES

The success of European Muslim missions owes a great deal to the AAII's organisational skills. The Secretary's Office in Lahore supervised the organisation of *tabligh* (propagation of Islam).[83] This core activity was subdivided under two departments: one dealing with "*tabligh* through literature"—with a Book Depot in charge of correspondence, printing and dissemination of AAII's publications—and the other one managing "*tabligh* through *mubbalighs* (missionaries)" conducted by permanent missions and some itinerant *mubbalighs*. The development of Ahmadiyya activities in Europe and elsewhere increased the need for properly trained missionaries.

[80] "Ahmadi Propaganda", *GI*, I, 1 (January 1936), p. 35. "Mirzai" was the pejorative name given to Ahmadis (Qadianis as well as Lahoris), referring to the founder of the movement Mirza Ghulam Ahmad.

[81] Ahmed Bennet, "Why I Resigned", p. 28.

[82] *Daily Zamindar*, 30 August 1936, quoted in *GI*, III, 1–2 (January-February 1938), p. 56.

[83] Sheikh Md. Din Jan, *Annual Report*, pp. 2, 8, 11.

To respond to it, the AAII created in Lahore in 1914 the Ishat-i-Islam College, which was run in 1927 by Maulvi Sadr-ud-Din who used his experiences gained at the Woking and Berlin missions.[84] Foreign missions benefited from the centralised organisation even if they also demonstrated their ability to channel locally available resources. Indeed they made the best use of the religious zeal manifested in Europe by students and converts and attracted the keen assistance of traders and women.

An attempt to mix converts and foreign Muslim populations

In 1913, Khwaja Kamaluddin made a speech at a meeting arranged by the Islamic Society in front of some two hundred Muslim students resident in London.[85] He called on his young audience "to continue the ceremonial observance of their religion, and to refuse to drink wine" and galvanised their religious pride in announcing the conversion to Islam of Lord Headley (1855–1935). Securing converts was indeed an essential dimension of the European missions' work as they played the role of mediators between the host society and its foreign Muslim population. More than the number, it was the converts' social status[86]—aristocrats, professionals, scientists, etc.—which was of great importance. It helped to deal with racist preconceptions of civil servants and served the religious propaganda in and outside Europe. The most efficient of those "go-betweens" was Lord Headley whose conversion enhanced the leadership position of the Lahori mission in its relations with both the government and other local Muslim organisations. It also had a major impact overseas, giving international fame to the organisation. Following the pilgrimage to Mecca that the aristocrat performed in 1923 in the company of the imam of Woking, the Cairo

84 Sheikh Md. Din Jan, *Annual Report*, pp. 15–16. Some ten students were trained in this institution.

85 "Moslem Missionaries", *Manchester Guardian* (17 November 1913); quoted in *MIIR*, I, 11 (December 1913), p. 412. Most of those who attended were Indians, but there were some Egyptians and Turks.

86 "What Means this Mission", p. 4. When articles referred to Muslim English women, it was mentioned that they were "wearing costly furs"; "East Meets West in London Suburb", *MS*, II, 4 (October 1923), p. 256.

Rabita al-Sharqiyya (Oriental League) announced that it was giving Honorary Membership to "Lord Headley Farooq and his collaborator the Khodja Kamaluddin".[87]

Lahori missions showed concern about preventing the condescending attitude of born-Muslims towards European converts. Therefore, one might notice that the privilege of leading the outdoor '*Id* prayers at Woking was occasionally granted to British Muslims such as Marmaduke Pickthall in 1919 and William Bashyr Pickard in 1932. But those gestures did not prevent some British Muslims from resenting the Indian leadership of Woking and trying to reduce its influence by incorporating the Lahori mission into a broader "United Muslim League". To establish this new body, a conference organised by Omar Wilkins, Reshid Sharp and Khalid Sheldrake was held in London on October 1926.[88] This initiative of "linking together all Islamic Missions and Societies in the West to strengthen and unite Islamic propaganda" was short-lived, but was pursued by Khalid (Bertrand) Sheldrake (1888–1947). First associate with Woking and later with the Qadiani Mission,[89] he finally achieved his ambition in founding and becoming the Life-President of the Western Islamic Association. In 1936, K. Sheldrake blatantly claimed that "the bulk of the 30,000 Muslims of Great Britain, among whom some 5,000 were English by birth, are in the branches of this body", denying any authority to "the little mosque of the distant county of Surrey".[90] In the same way, Khalid Sheldrake minimised the influence of the Berlin Mission and challenged the Lahori Anglo-German connexion by drawing attention to his relations with the French *Fraternité Musulmane*. Nevertheless, Sheldrake could hardly challenge the intellectual stature of

[87] M. 'Ajjan el-Hadîd, "Le Trait d'Union Oriental—Er-Râbitat Ech-Charqîya", *Revue des Etudes Islamiques* (*REI*—Paris), IV (1930), pp. 289–96. Lord Headley was also invested with the Order of the Nahda of Arabia by the King of Hejaz; "The Muslim Mission to South Africa", *MO*, II, 55 (20 February 1926), p. 3.

[88] "London Conference", *MO*, II, 94–95 (27 November 1926), p. 6.

[89] In 1924, Sheldrake helped to organise the visit to the UK of the leader of the Qadian Movement; "His Holiness visits Brighton", *RoR*, XXIII, 12 (December 1924), pp. 446–52.

[90] K. Sheldrake, "The Pioneers of Islam. . ." and "The First Moslem Conference of Europe", *GI*, I, 1 (January 1936), pp. 26, 30–31.

Marmaduke Pickthall or the social prestige of Lord Headley, both of whom were associated with Woking.

If the English mosque was proud of having "Al-Haj El-Farooq" Headley in its congregation, the most famous of the Berlin converts was Baron Omar von Ehrenfels. The aristocrat, who converted in Berlin in 1927, went to Lahore at the end of 1932 and toured India together with the imam of Berlin, Shaikh Muhammad Abdullah. Another famous convert of the Berlin Mission was Dr Hamid (Hugo) Marcus (1880–1966) who played a major role in the running of the mission. He acted as President of the *Deutsch-Moslemische Gesellschaft* (German Muslim Society) which was formed on March 1930 and was open to non-Muslim members.[91] The Society was closely associated to the Briennerstrasse Mission, paying the electric, gas and some other repair bills of the mosque and taking on the expenses of '*Id* functions and other meetings.[92] Having a good command of English, Dr Marcus could also translate Woking's publications into German.[93] With other German Muslims like Dr Khalid Banning and Dr Arif Griffelt, he contributed to the running of the quarterly *Moslemische Revue* launched by Maulvi Sadr-ud-Din in January 1924.[94] Converts with previous experience in journalism (Lord Headley)[95] or as novelists (Marmaduke Pickthall) helped to improve the quality of Muslim publications. In Lahore itself, it was an Englishman, Hamid Snow, who produced a Muslim prayer book and catechism.

The missions' communication policy

Lahori missionaries reached European public opinion by giving lectures, visiting educational institutions,[96] and getting coverage of

[91] Nasir Ahmad, *A Brief History*, pp. 22–3.

[92] Ezad Bakhsh, *9th Annual Report*, p. 9.

[93] Nasir Ahmad, *A Brief History*, p. 8. Hugo Marcus received his PhD in Vienna.

[94] Ibid., p. 11.

[95] He was editor of the *Salisbury Journal* for a couple of years; "Peer of 58 converted to Mohammadism", *The Daily Sketch*, 17 November 1913, quoted in *IR*, I, 11 (December 1913), pp. 405–6.

[96] Missionaries visited the Railway Orphanage of Woking and provided meals to children on the day when the Prophet's birthday was celebrated; *IR*, IX, 10 (October 1921), inside front cover, and *IR*, XIII, 12 (December 1925), p. 428.

their activities in the local press. Between 1931 and 1934, articles about the Briennerstrasse Mosque were published in a dozen German newspapers mostly in Berlin, but also in Hamburg and Essen.[97] Journalists contacted by the mission wrote reports on the *'Id al-Fitr*, *'Id al-Adha* and *Milâd un-Nabi* celebrated at the Berlin Mosque and presented some brief explanations of their religious meaning.[98] Indeed it was an occasion to bring to a large audience some knowledge about Muslim rituals and to create a bond of sympathy and understanding by highlighting affinities with the Christian and Jewish faiths.[99] Visits of Muslim personalities such as the princes of Hyderabad or Shakib Arslan in 1931 were occasions for the mission to attract attention from the German press.[100] Those events, as well as some religious functions, were broadcasted in Pathe film clips and on radio programmes, showing the familiarity of the Lahori missions with the most modern propaganda tools.[101] To serve the mission's communication policy, proficiency in European languages was essential. Young converts were often sensitive to a modern approach to religious propaganda. The style of the *Islamic Review* reveals this curiosity for innovative communication techniques; see for example the statement of faith from a new convert that appeared from 1915 on the first page facing the photograph of a European Muslim.[102]

In the linguistic field, some converts considered the Esperanto language as a practical way to match the medium with the universal character of the message of Islam. Bertrand (latter Khalid) Sheldrake,

97 "Das Echo unserer Arbeit", *MR*, IV (October 1934), pp. 89–98.

98 Such a communication policy was inspired by the one developed by the Woking Mission; see for instance the news reports taken from six British newspapers published *IR*, X, 6–7 (June-July 1922), pp. 250–6.

99 The *Daily Telegraph* of 29 May 1922, reporting the *'Id al-Fitr* celebration at Woking, said: "Fasting, too, was common to the Moslem, Christian, and Jewish faiths. Purification came with fasting"; ibid., p. 252.

100 "Das Echo unserer Arbeit", *MR*, III-IV (October 1935), pp. 89–95.

101 British Pathe Ltd website listed on www.wokingmuslim.org. In 1931, the Berlin Mosque was instrumental in the hour-long programme about *'Id al-Fitr* broadcast on radio nationwide; Nasir Ahmad, *A Brief History*, p. 24.

102 One may also mention the statement entitled "What is Islam?" that appeared on the back-page of the *Review* from the mid-1920s.

who founded a "Crescent Esperanto Group" in 1908,[103] wrote several articles in Esperanto in the Woking review presenting "the common ideal of Islam and Esperanto in breaking down barriers of colour, creed, and caste".[104] Esperanto supporters could also be found among Indian Muslims such as Professor Attaur Rahman and Maulvi Sadr-ud-Din, the future imam of the Berlin Mosque.[105] Nevertheless, the enthusiasm invested in this universal language vanished in the post-war period, even if books in Esperanto on Islam continued to be published.[106] Esperanto was a rather marginal aspect of a strategy—probably modelled on the policy of Protestant missionary organisations such as the Bible Society—to reach local people in their own native tongues. With its limited resources, the AAII had to focus on languages having a status of international *lingua franca* such as English or German.

In 1922, the AAII started a fortnightly four-page journal in English, *The Light*, that soon became a weekly publication. At the end of the decade, the mouthpiece of the Lahore headquarters had a print run a little over 1,500, of which a tenth was supplied free to "some European and American libraries and notable personages".[107] Capitalising on the success of *The Light*, the AAII launched in Lahore two other newspapers in English: the quarterly *Muslim Revival* in 1930 and *Young Islam*, a fortnightly started in June 1934. Those titles were also sent to Europe and added to the publications produced by the Berlin and Woking missions themselves, which were printed on a good quality paper and often illustrated with photographs. Alongside the *Islamic Review*, the free circulation of a

[103] "Muslim and Esperanto", *The Crescent* (Liverpool), XXXI (8 January 1908), p. 28.

[104] K. Sheldrake, "Islam and Esperanto", *MIIR*, II, 6 (July 1914), pp. 298–9.

[105] Professor Attaur Rahman, MA, "Birdperspektivo de la Vivo de la Sankta Profeto", *MIIR*, II, 9 (October 1914), p. 466. Maulvi Sadr-ud-Din, "Mia Studado de la Biblio", *MIIR*, II, 11–12 (December 1914), p. 576.

[106] Isma'il Colin Evans, *Islamo esperantiste rigardata*, London: IKRO, 1946. A Polish convert paid tribute to this book and some Lahore publications; S.A. Khulusi, *Islam, Our Choice*, p. 118.

[107] Sheikh Md. Din Jan, *Annual Report*, p. 19. The *Anjuman* stated that "Each copy of the Light is a Missioner" to justify the money spent on the free distribution of literature.

thousand copies of the quarterly *Moslemische Revue* introduced Islam to a German-speaking audience in Eastern and South-Eastern Europe.[108]

In 1932, the AAII boldly announced that "the work of translating the Holy Qur'an in all languages is under our consideration".[109] The aim was not to publish a translation in languages where none were available—that was not the case for English or German—but rather to present a work made by a Muslim believer and not by a Western scholar. Moreover, the publication of the Qur'an conferred an obvious authority over Muslim communities relying on that edition. As Maulana Muhammad Ali's *English Translation of the Holy Qur'an* published by the Woking Trust in 1917 was too difficult for a non-scholarly audience to handle, the mission started around 1927 to prepare a more accessible edition without the Arabic text. The AAII justified the publication of "a cheap edition by a Muslim author" saying that the several translations already on the market were all by non-Muslims who "failed to present the true Muslim point of view and here and there actually misrepresented it".[110] The same motivation prevailed for the launching of the first German translation of the Qur'an made by Muslims, expecting that it "would reveal the true spirit of the Holy Qur'an to the German-speaking countries of Central Europe".[111] The project launched in 1928 took more than a decade to complete. The German Qur'an was finally printed in 1939, just as the Second World War broke out, when the Indian missionaries had to leave Germany.[112]

108 Ibid., p. 17. During the Second World War, Omar von Ehrenfels translated Maulana Muhammad Ali's works into German.

109 Ezad Bakhsh, *9th Annual Report*, p. 10.

110 Sheikh Md. Din Jan, *Annual Report*, pp. 16–17. *Translation of The Holy Quran (without Arabic text)*, with short notes and introduction by Maulana Muhammad Ali, MA, LLB, President *Ahmadiyya Anjuman-i-Isha'at-i-Islam*, Lahore: Ripon Press, 1929, the book was printed in 3,000 copies.

111 Maulana F.K. Khan Durrani, BA, "A German Translation of the Quran: A Review", *The Truth*, reproduced in *Genuine Islam* (*GI*—Singapore), III, 1–2 (January-February 1938), pp. 46–51.

112 Ezad Bakhsh, *9th Annual Report*, p. 10. *Der Heilige Koran in deutscher Sprache mit gegenüberstehendem arabischem Text. Eingeleitet, übers. u. eingehend erläutert von dem indischen Gelehrten u. bekannten Korankenner Maulana Sadr-ud-Din*, Berlin, 1939.

The publication of newspapers, books and pamphlets was the main activity of the AAII's missions. Besides expenditure on the free distribution of literature, the Lahore headquarters subsidised all its English publications which were constantly in deficit. That was the case of the *Islamic Review*, even if subscriptions represented a substantial income making up about half of the financial resources of the Woking Trust. The deficit was covered by the AAII's central budget which, quite naturally, tried to limit the shortfall by encouraging commercial adverts.

Addressing the trading community

The Woking Mission differed from the previous Muslim organisations in England in not relying primarily on Muslim world leaders and Indian rulers to provide financial assistance for their project.[113] Donations from supporters were centralised in Lahore and members were encouraged to give money on a monthly basis through *sadaqa*. This financial organisation helped to provide the missions with a regular income to maintain their activity throughout the years. By centralising funds, the AAII's headquarters could more easily regulate, organise and rationalise the missions' expenses. Besides regular subscriptions, funds were set up and targeted for a specific foreign mission or translation work.[114]

The Lahori European missions' pragmatic approach to "Muslim Banking"—making a distinction between "interest" and *riba* ("usury", forbidden in Islam)—was appreciated by the Indian Muslim merchant class.[115] The city of Lahore, an important trading centre, was, together with Egypt, at the forefront of the development of

[113] It differed from the Liverpool Institute, supported by the Ottoman Sultan and the Ameer of Afghanistan; Dr Leitner's Oriental Institute of Woking, helped by the Begum of Bhopal and the Nizam of Hyderabad; and Sayyid Ameer Ali's London mosque project, under the patronage of the Ottoman Sultan.

[114] Notwithstanding the publicity given to donors in the AAII's newspapers, generosity was stimulated by the visits of European converts in India or the publication of calendars with photographs of the Woking and Berlin mosques; *IR*, VIII, 12 (December 1920), advert p. 464 and Nasir Ahmad, *A Brief History*, p. 30.

[115] Editor's Notes, "Islam, Usury and Interest", *IR*, XIII, 1 (January 1925), pp. 3–4; and "Letter by Sheikh A. Hafeez of New York", *IR*, XIII, 2 (February 1925), pp. 77–8.

Muslim banking. In 1907, the opening of the Orient Bank of India in the Punjab capital was announced.[116] The next year, a *fatwa* issued by religious scholars from Lahore stated that "a Muslim can rightfully accept to pay a fee to transfer money from one place to another . . . as this fee is a salary and not interest".[117] The Muslim Bank of India, which had its Head Office in Lahore, extended its activities to Europe and, by 1928, opened agencies in London, Berlin and Switzerland.[118] With the advertisements published by this bank in newspapers supporting Lahori activities, one might presume that there was a rather friendly relationship with the Woking and Berlin missions.[119] The AAII was interested in adapting religious principles to the "modern capitalistic and materialistic age", and its leader Maulana Muhammad Ali expressed his liberal theory of banking and private loans for "Muslims living under non-Muslim governments" in a long article on *riba*. The text, originally published in *The New Orient*, was reprinted in *The Light* of Lahore and in various other Muslim newspapers.[120] Not surprisingly, Ahmadi missions gained sympathy among the major Muslim Indian trading communities such as the Memons and Bohras.[121] The spiritual head of the Bohras even financed the stay in England of one missionary, who arrived in Woking in 1925 and remained for five years.[122]

From the beginning, the Woking Trust received support from individual businessmen established in London such as Mirza

[116] *Mulk and Millut*, 18 June 1907; quoted in "Nouvelles diverses", *RMM*, II, 8 (June-July 1907), p. 567.

[117] "La Question des banques", *RMM*, IV, 2 (February 1908), pp. 433–4.

[118] Advert in *IW* (Lahore), VI, 12 (October 1928), inside front cover. The bank incorporated in British India in 1912 offered "special terms for Orphans, Widows, Students and Public Institutions".

[119] One could note that the Qadiani Mission in Berlin was located in the American Express Co. offices; *RoR*, XXIII, 12 (December 1924), inside front cover.

[120] H. Atta Ullah, "The Problem of 'Riba'", *MO*, II, 53 (6 February 1926), pp. 11–12.

[121] Memons and Bohras are trading Hindu castes that converted to Islam around the fifteenth century.

[122] "New Workers in the Mission Field", *IR*, XIII, 3 (March 1925), pp. 82–83. "His Holiness Sayyed Abu Muhammad Tahir Saif-ud-Din", ibid., pp. 83–4.

Hashim Ispahani.[123] He and his wife were active members of the small congregation gathering at the Woking Mosque for *'Id* and had friendly relations with Khwaja Kamaluddin.[124] The businessman was in charge of the foreign activities of his father's firm and was the Managing Director of a firm importing tropical products from East and West Africa, the East Indies, Ceylon and the Straits Settlements.[125] Those international activities are likely to have made him sensitive to the worldwide ambitions of the AAII. He may also have appreciated that advantages were to be gained from an association with the Woking Mission whose activities were very popular among Muslim communities in places where he conducted business. In the same way, the opening of the Berlin Mission was welcomed by Muslim traders who had interests in Germany. For instance, it was the owner of a tannery in Wazirabad in the Punjab who financed repairs to the Berlin Mosque after a stay in Germany where he received advanced training in leather tanning.[126] For its self-financing activities, the Woking Trust was quite innovative in organising its own company named Oriental Products, whose leading sale product was a "Divine Elixir".[127] This general tonic for the brain and body was publicised in newspaper adverts with eulogising testimonials from Sir Mirza Abbas Ali Baig, the Heir-Apparent of Mangrol State and Khwaja Kamaluddin.[128]

To finance its publications, the Woking Mission appealed to the generosity of wealthy Indian traders and their wives throughout

[123] "Biography of Mr. Ispahani, a prominent London merchant", *The African Times and Orient Review* (*ATOR*—London), IV, 2 (February 1917), p. 38. H. Ispahani was Vice-President of the Central Islamic Society in London.

[124] "Eid-ul-Fitr at the Mosque, Woking", *ATOR*, V, 2 (August 1917), p. 45.

[125] Advertisement for Jules Karpelés & Co., *ATOR*, IV, 2 (February 1917), p. ii. Ispahani & Sons was based in Bombay; the family, of Persian origin, had been settled in India for over a century.

[126] Nasir Ahmad, *A Brief History*, p. 29.

[127] The Liverpool Institute initiated this practice in supporting an "Hillal Soap—made especially for the use of Muslims and Brahmins" manufactured by the Ali Othman & Co. of Liverpool; adverts in *The Crescent* in 1908.

[128] "Divine Elixir", *MO*, II, 55 (20 February 1926), p. 3. The elixir could be obtained from: "Oriental Products, Memorial House, Oriental Road, Woking".

British colonies.[129] At the end of his journey in South Africa, Khwaja Kamaluddin wrote a letter to the Moslem Women's Association of S.A. asking "Sisters at the Cape to start a Fund to enable us to publish a book entitled 'The Position of Woman in Islam'".[130] He concluded by giving the assurance "that the book, if spread broadcast, will not only strengthen the position of our Sisters in their own community, but will also do excellent propaganda work". This discourse went beyond securing financial support and expressed the AAII's genuine concern for the improvement of Muslim women's social and educational position.

Gendering the European missions

The Woking Mission was proud to underline that its mosque was named after Begum Shah Jehan, "Queen of Bhopal, the only Indian state where a woman rules".[131] In 1926, when the new Begum came to England, she made promises of help to build the London Mosque and to add an annexe to the Woking Mosque, which her mother had greatly assisted in founding.[132] It was another Indian lady, Mrs Tayyiba Begum, who collected in 1914 a substantial amount of money that was sent to Khwaja Kamaluddin.[133] In the following years, the president of the Islamic Women's Association kept on delivering lectures that urged upper-class women from Hyderabad to give financial support to the "Imam Khwaja". In India, the AAII was well known for encouraging women's education and the Society presented books to female students from all over the country who passed their degree examinations.[134]

[129] Khwaja Kamal-ud-Din, *Islam and Christianity*, 1931, p. vi. Foreword thanking the generosity of Mahomet Allum Khan of Adelaide, Australia, who made possible this publication.

[130] "Khwaja Kamal-ud-Din's Appeal", *MO*, II, 60 (27 March 1926), p. 7. The booklet published in English in Woking was translated into German by the Berlin Mission.

[131] "End of a month's fasting", *Daily News* (29 May 1922), quoted in *IR*, X, 6–7 (June-July 1922), p. 251.

[132] In 1932, these promises had not yet come to fruition; "Memoirs of the late Rt. Hon. Syed Ameer Ali", pp. 503–4.

[133] M.H. Khan Ghori, *Rabitah A'lam-i Islami and Hyderabad Deccan*, Karachi: Darul Adab, 1978; "Liaison with the Muslim World", pp. 181–8, English translation kindly given to us by Mr. Nasir Ahmad.

[134] Sheikh Md. Din Jan, *Annual Report*, p. 6.

Muslim ladies from Indian high society were sensitive to a discourse that opposed the offensive image of Muslim women broadcast in the Western media. In the first issue of his review, Khwaja Kamaluddin blamed the Church's historical prejudice against women. He recalled that "it was the Council of Macon toward the end of the sixth century, and not any Mohammadan assembly, where a bishop raised the question whether a woman really was a human being, and answered the question by the negative".[135] In helping missions in the West, this female elite thought that it would help to strengthen their position at home.[136] Progressive ideas "made in Europe" were in a way more acceptable but, at the same time, they were also suspected of having been "Christianised". This ambiguity was well understood by the mission's people who, speaking to an Indian audience, challenged the equation "modern = Western". For instance, when the Austrian convert Omar von Ehrenfels published in Hyderabad an article entitled "Muslim women in present-day Europe", he stated that it was significant to see "European countries under Islamic rule like Turkey and Albania. . . introducing equal rights for both sexes". He added that "this shows clearly, that the impulse for improvement of the Muslim women's position really was originated by the Muslim centres themselves and not borrowed from the Christian European school of thought".[137]

The relationship of mutual interest was even more obvious in the case of the Indian diaspora which, like its Muslim coreligionists in Europe, had to face a racism which hid behind humanistic considerations. In the colonial discourse, the veil and female segregation replaced slavery to illustrate the backwardness of Islamic societies. This issue was a major argument for Christian propaganda, and several books and articles highlighted the unattractive fate of confined Muslim women.[138] At the time of the foundation

[135] Khwaja Kamal-ud-Din, "Foreword", p. 3.

[136] "Khwaja Kamal-ud-Din's Appeal", p. 7.

[137] Omar Rolf Ehrenfels, "Muslim Women in Present-day Europe", *IC*, X (1936), pp. 471–6.

[138] Ellen Fleischmann, "The Impact of American Protestant Missions in Lebanon on the Construction of Female Identity, c.1860–1950", *Islam and Christian Muslim Relations*, XIII, 4 (2002), pp. 411–26.

of the Woking Trust, a circular was issued by the Australian government warning white women against the "utterly degrading treatment" reserved for those marrying "Muhammadans".[139] Khwaja Kamaluddin took this opportunity to link the type of prejudices found in the Southern Hemisphere with the misconceptions encountered in Europe. He insisted on dissociating polygamy from the tenets of Islam and spoke of the happiness of European wives in Muslim families.[140]

The high proportion of European women in the congregations of the Woking and Berlin mosques helped Lahori missions to challenge the idea that the status of woman in Islam was repulsive to the Western liberal mind.[141] Their publications aimed to dispel the idea "that Islam, as a religion, may appeal to men (because it allows polygamy) but cannot possibly appeal to any civilized, enlightened woman".[142] In 1932, the German Muslim Society sponsored the free distribution of 5,000 copies of S.M. Abdullah's tract on *The Position of Women in Islam*.[143] Muslim missionaries knew how to select arguments that were particularly attractive to women; for example Khwaja Kamaluddin pointed out that when a child "dies at his very birth, he must go to heaven under Islamic teaching, but he is foredoomed to hell according to Christian principles", and concluded that "in other words heaven is our birthright under Islam".[144]

139 "White Wives of Brown Men. Letter by Sir John Rees, M.P.", *MIIR*, I, 8 (September 1913), p. 309.

140 "Polygamy a Ban" and "Interesting Debate at Cambridge on Polygamy", *MIIR*, I, 2 (March 1913), pp. 41, 75. "White Wives of Brown Men. Outcasts in the Harem", *MIIR*, I, 6 (July 1913), pp. 229–32.

141 From a picture taken in the 1930s, women made up half of the Berlin Mosque's congregation; L. Günther and H.-J. Rehmer, *In der Indien und Berlin*, Berlin: Lotos, 1999, p. 125.

142 M. Pickthall, "An English Lady's Pilgrimage", *IC*, VIII, 4 (October 1934), pp. 674–9 (article reviewing Lady Evelyn Cobbold, *A Pilgrimage to Mecca*, London: J. Murray, 1934).

143 Ezad Bakhsh, *9th Annual Report*, p. 9. Aftab-ud-Din Ahmad, "The Status of Woman in Islam", *IR*, XXI, 1–2 (January-February 1933), pp. 49–58.

144 Khwaja Kamal-ud-din, *Islam My Only Choice*, p. 19. The issue of "unbaptised children" had already been addressed by Abdullah Suhrawardy, *The Sayings of Muhammad*, London: A. Constable, 1905, p. 28.

CONCLUSION: IMPROVING THE SELF-ESTEEM OF MUSLIMS IN AND OUTSIDE EUROPE

The activities directed from Woking and Berlin were intended to benefit not only the Muslim population of Europe but all places where Islam felt threatened. This Europe-made discourse found a large audience, and articles from the *Islamic Review* were reprinted in newspapers published in English or in vernacular languages throughout the world. The Woking and Berlin missions played a important role in centralising information from various parts of Europe and gave it an international exposure. One might take the example of the outrageous book by a French activist from the colonial lobby on "Islam and the Psychology of the Muslim", quotations from which, published in *The Islamic Review*, were reprinted in a South African Muslim newspaper.[145] The European missions also had an impact amongst Muslim reformists such as the famous scholar Rashid Rida.[146] In India, the Woking publications reached mainly a Western-educated elite. Khwaja Kamaluddin was, for instance, enthusiastically received at the Muhammadan Anglo-Oriental College of Aligarh when he went to open its Students' Theological Society and delivered a lecture on "Islam in England with Christianity on the Wane".[147]

The extension of Islamic propaganda to Europe and the United States aimed to fight "at home" an evangelical zeal that received most of its political and financial support from the West.[148] On the one hand, Muslim missionaries were borrowing from Christian rhetorical tools and methods while simultaneously denouncing the

[145] André Servier, *L'islam et la Psychologie du Musulman*, Paris: A. Challamel, 1923. The English translation published in London in 1924 was reviewed by Khwaja Nazir Ahmad in *IR*, XII, 4–5 (April-May 1924), p. 170. "Arab Culture—It Is Barbarian?", *MO*, II, 36 (3 October 1925), pp. 10–11.

[146] Rashid Rida was the vice-president of the Rabita al-Sharqiyya that made Lord Headley and Khwaja Kamal-ud-Din honorary members. The famous scholar seems to have borrowed some of his criticisms of Protestant literature from Lahori publications; M. 'Ajjan el-Hadîd, "Le Trait d'Union Oriental", p. 291.

[147] "Al-Haj Khwaja Kamal-ud-Din", *MO*, I, 5 (27 February 1925), p. 2.

[148] Khwaja Kamal-ud-Din accused Churches in Africa of being particularly eager to present Islam as "a barbarian creed and a *menace* to civilisation"; "The Modern Religious World We Live In", *MO*, I, 38 (17 October 1925), pp. 11–12.

Church's insidious propaganda in Muslim lands. On the other hand, their Christian counterparts found in this new Muslim missionary activity arguments to denounce the pan-Islamic menace to Western civilisation, like for example Samuel Zwemer who expressed concern about finding an article on the new mosque in Berlin in a weekly Muslim newspaper from Borneo.[149] The importance given to Ahmadiyya activities in the Christian missionary literature of the time shows how seriously the success gained by the "anti-Christian arguments of this Modernist sect"[150] was taken.

Despite limited resources, the Ahmadi-Lahori movement played a pioneering role in establishing Islam in Western Europe. It helped to bring various foreign Muslim groups—students, traders, workers, sailors, and diplomats—into contact with the local converts, paving the way to an embryonic community feeling. Moreover, Lahori missions set up networks building the very first linkage between the various Muslim communities living in Europe, from Spain to Poland and from England to the Balkans.

[149] Basil Mathews, *Young Islam*, pp. 23–4.

[150] Rev. A.R. Hampson, *The Mission to Moslems in Cape Town*, January 1934, Cape Town, p. 9.

Part II. TOWARDS THE BUILDING OF A 'EUROPEAN ISLAM'

The issue of building a "European Islam" is a highly debated question at the beginning of the twenty-first century, in relation to the question of integration of migrant populations in the countries of Western Europe. This notion is generally related to the process of providing a legal framework for the practice of Islam in some more or less secularised states.[1] It is also bound up with the creation of a common public space in which new interpretations and practices of Islam are emerging, as well as new responses to the minority situation.[2] However, in a more subjective way "European Islam", as a discursive notion, has received support from states and media as they share the general belief that an Islam more deeply rooted in the West would be immune from "fundamentalism", seen as an "imported phenomenon".[3]

THE EARLY EMERGENCE OF THE CONCEPT OF 'EUROPEAN ISLAM' RELATING TO SOUTH-EASTERN EUROPE

In modern history, the concepts of "European Islam" and "European Muslims" first appeared, explicitly or implicitly, in relation to the Balkans, well before the massive immigration of Muslims to Europe after the Second World War. They developed in the nineteenth

[1] Jocelyne Cesari and Sean McLoughlin (eds), *European Muslims and the Secular State*, Aldershot: Ashgate, 2005.

[2] See, for example, Jorgen Nielsen, *Towards a European Islam*, Basingstoke: Macmillan, 1999; Olivier Roy, *Vers un islam européen*, Paris: Editions Esprit, 1999.

[3] See Alain Roussillon, " 'Islam d'Europe' ou 'Musulmans européens': reconduire l'exception musulmane?", *CEMOTI*, 34 (July-December 2002), pp. 331–8.

century, in the context of the decline of the Ottoman Empire in Europe, the creation of Christian nation-states in the Balkans and the penetration of the Great Powers into the region. Some contemporary observers such as Ami Boué (1794–1881) considered the Albanian and Bosnian Muslims as "indigenous Muslims of European Turkey". The geographer even claimed that these Muslims, aware of their Christian origin, could be easily converted back to Christianity, whereas "Asiatic" Ottoman Muslims, being "less subtle" in religious matters, would be more reluctant to convert.[4] In the 1860s Dora d'Istria (1829–88), one of the best examples of a cosmopolitan European intellectual of the time, also presented Albanian Muslims as completely different from their "Asiatic" coreligionists. She explained to a wide European public that the Albanian Muslims, especially those from the Southern Albanian provinces, differed from the "Islam of the Ottomans" in professing Shiism.[5] She considered that they had chosen that form of Islam because it was compatible with their "Aryan race", just as the Persians did for the very same reason.[6] Thus those non-Muslim writers raised the idea of the specificity of "European Muslims" and even spoke of a "European Islam", i.e. an Islam even more compatible with "Europeanness", suggesting that it would ultimately disappear.

This theory evolved at the turn of the nineteenth century, when some Albanian Muslim intellectuals appropriated the task of promoting the genuine European identity of their nation, the only one in the continent to be predominantly Muslim. Indeed, in the framework of Albanian nation building, some intellectuals with a Bektashi background used this mystical, heterodox and syncretistic form of Islam to characterise "Albanian Muslims",[7] who were

[4] Ami Boué, *La Turquie d'Europe*, t. IV, Paris, A. Bertrand, 1840, pp. 181–2.

[5] Here Dora D'Istria referred to the heterodox Islam (which was not Shiism) of some groups of population in Southern Albania, especially to the Islam of some mystical brotherhoods.

[6] Dora d'Istria, "Gli Albanesi Musulmani, Scutari e i Buchatli", *Nuova Antologia* (Florence), VIII (1868), pp. 221–66; "Gli Albanesi Mussulmani. II. Berath e Janina", *Nuova Antologia*, XIV (1870), pp. 27–54; and "Gli Albanesi Mussulmani. II.", *Nuova Antologia*, XV (September 1870), pp. 31–63.

[7] On Bektashism, an Ottoman mystical brotherhood originating from Anatolia, see John Kingsley Birge, *The Bektashi Order of Dervishes*, London: Luzac, 1937;

supposed to be fundamentally different from Turkish Muslims. They presented the Asiatic Turkish Sunni Muslims as fanatical, whereas Albanian Muslims were liberal and even had affinities with Christianity. In their eyes, this characteristic was proof of the Europeanness of the Albanian nation, "the most ancient nation in Europe". Such a discourse was supposed to legitimise the formation of an Albanian nation and an Albanian state after the total collapse of the Ottoman Empire in Europe, despite its Muslim majority.[8]

During the same period, a significant number of Muslims in the Balkans were living under non-Muslim rule. That was the case for the large Muslim population of Bosnia-Herzegovina, under Austro-Hungarian rule since 1878, and for other important Muslim populations living in Romania, Bulgaria, and to a lesser extent Greece and Serbia. These Muslims, who had to adapt to a new predominantly Christian order, did not claim a "European identity" as such, at least not explicitly. Nevertheless, a "European Islam" began to take shape *de facto* with the creation of new institutions recognised by the new non-Muslim governments. In Bosnia-Herzegovina especially, as Fikret Karčić points out in this volume, the incorporation of Shari'a courts into the Austro-Hungarian judicial system led to a substantial transformation of this central Islamic institution, with the introduction of an appellate jurisdiction, a new Code of Civil Procedure and the use of the local language. On the other hand, the adhesion of small groups of Muslim intellectuals to a Croat or a Serbian national identity generated, often implicitly, the introduction of a Western or European dimension into their identity. More generally, the desire for Europe and the desire for progress were implicitly linked, as Europe was considered as a

Alexandre Popovic and Gilles Veinstein (eds), *Bektachiyya. Études sur l'ordre mystique des Bektachis et les groupes relevant de Hadji Bektach*, Istanbul: Isis, 1995.

8 See Nathalie Clayer, "Le bektachisme entre construction nationale albanaise et vision européo-centrée de l'islam", in J. Boulad-Ayoub and G.M. Cazzaniga, *Traces de l'Autre. Mythes de l'antiquité et Peuples du Livre dans la construction des nations méditerranéennes. Bibliotheca Alexandrina, le 19–21 avril 2003*, Pise-Paris: Edizioni ETS-J. Vrin, 2004, pp. 169–88; and N. Clayer, *Aux origines du nationalisme albanais. La formation d'une nation majoritairement musulmane en Europe*, Paris: Karthala, 2007.

model of modernity. However, because most of these intellectuals were secularists, their proposals hardly included considerations about modernising the institutions and practice of Islam.

TOWARDS A 'EUROPEAN ISLAM' IN INTER-WAR EUROPE

During the inter-war period, the institutionalisation of Islam in South Eastern Europe, as well as in Poland, continued, as we can see from various contributions in the present volume (e.g. the chapters by Nathalie Clayer, Yannis Bonos, Xavier Bougarel, Muhammed Aruçi, Fikret Karčić and Sebastian Cwiklinski). Countries such as Yugoslavia, Bulgaria, Greece, Albania, Romania and Poland provided a legal framework for the practice of Islam,[9] and set up "national" Islamic institutions using the vernacular languages. In this context, no explicit reference to a "European Islam" was made. For some Muslim groups, especially in Romania, Bulgaria and Greece, the main reference was not Europe, but rather Turkey. The reform issue was linked to the place of the Muslim minority within the state, as well as to the real or imagined impact of Kemalism among the local Muslim populations.[10] However, the need to adapt to fast-changing societies led some Muslim leaders in other countries such as Džemaludin Čaušević, the head of the Islamic Community of Bosnia-Herzegovina, to claim that Islam should be made compatible with the European type of institutions, and that Islam, in essence, was not opposed to progress, education and modernity.[11] Indeed Bosnian Muslim elites faced the challenge of being Muslim in Europe (see Xavier Bougarel's chapter). Some consciousness of

[9] A statute on "the religious organisation and management of the Muslims in the Kingdom of Bulgaria" was promulgated in 1919. In Romania, the Law on Cults was promulgated in 1928.

[10] On Bulgaria, see the analyses of Mila Mančeva concerning the interplay between perceptions of Bulgarian officials about Kemalism and its real manifestations ('State-minority Relations and the Education of Turks and Pomaks in Inter-war Bulgaria, 1918–1944', unpublished PhD thesis, Central European University, Budapest, 2003).

[11] Sabina Ferhadbegović, "Fes oder Hut? Der Islam in Bosnien zwischen den Weltkriegen", *Wiener Zeitschrift zur Geschichte der Neuzeit*, 5, Heft 2 (Jg. 2005), pp. 69–85 (see p. 84).

belonging to a "European Islam" also emerged through contacts between some Muslims from Europe and Muslims from outside Europe, as Sebastian Cwiklinski points out in the case of Polish Tatars.

However, there were also several examples of an explicit promotion of a "European Islam" in inter-war Europe. Such was the case in Albania, the only predominantly Muslim European state, studied in Nathalie Clayer's chapter. The situation there was characterised by the continuation of the identity building process started in the late Ottoman period and by the beginning of a state building process. In these circumstances, secular and religious reformists agreed on the need to adapt Islam to the European context, but differed about the way to achieve it. Taking into account the fact that the (predominantly Muslim) Albanians were surrounded by Christian neighbours, some secularist intellectuals thought that only radical reforms, such as those introduced by Mustafa Kemal Atatürk in Turkey, would guarantee the independence of the country; otherwise Islam would disappear. In their minds, these reforms mainly concerned the training of new clerics in Western European universities and the greater involvement of laymen in Islamic matters, without any religious authority as intermediary. Banning the veil should symbolically illustrate the modernisation policy of the government and prove Albania's legitimacy to stand side by side with the other European states. Some non-secularist Muslims also wanted to move towards reforms because they considered that improving the educational level of the Albanian Muslim population was the only way to survive among "people of culture". To that end, they accepted the help of the Indian Ahmadi missionary society of Lahore, using its literature disseminated from England and Germany, which promoted the compatibility of Islam with European modernity.

Indeed, the Lahori Ahmadis, as we have seen in the previous part, contributed to the building of a "European Islam" not only by making reference to the Andalusian golden age, but also by their very activities. From their centres in Woking and Berlin, these Indian missionaries considered Muslims living all over Europe as forming a geographical and spiritual entity. This clearly appears both in their publications, in which they presented a picture of the

Muslim presence in Europe,[12] and in their networking activity that helped to create the image of a European Islamic space. European converts were particularly important in their strategy, as Eric Germain points out, not only as go-betweens within European society, but also as agents of the legitimisation of Islam in the European context. The very first aim of the Lahori missionaries was to improve, in Europe as well as in Muslim countries, the image of Islam, and to counter the propaganda of Christian missions, often using the same methods as the latter. But, in doing so, they proposed a rhetorical framework for the assertion of a "European Islam" that answered the basic demands of Muslim living in a minority context. The Woking Mission together with other British Islamic organisations similarly played a decisive role in trying to make Islam indigenous to Europe, asserting its full compatibility with Western modernity (see Humayun Ansari's chapter).

However, the initiative for the most symbolic step towards the affirmation of a "European Muslim" identity during the inter-war period—the 1935 European Muslim Congress of Geneva—did not come from Britain. The mastermind of this meeting, bringing together delegates from all over Europe, was the political activist Shakib Arslan. Raja Adal's contribution in this volume sheds light on the motives of Shakib Arslan who saw this meeting as a way to develop a synthesis of Islam and modernity for teaching in Islamic schools, in order to place Muslims on the same level as non-Muslims. Having been educated in Christian missionary schools, he knew how this issue was crucial for Muslims living as minorities in European countries. Neither Albania nor Turkey participated in the Geneva Congress, because its organisers were not of the opinion that a "European Islam" meant the full acceptance of Western values at the expense of Islamic values, as happened in the modernisation processes carried out in Turkey and Albania. What is interesting in the case of Shakib Arslan is that his efforts to build a "European Islam" did not prevent him from criticising Europe.

Shakib Arslan was a precursory figure, when he critically defined the "Europe" where a "European Islam" was to assert itself. As Raja

[12] Articles about Muslim populations in Europe were also to be found in other journals published in English by the Qadianis or other Muslim missionary societies.

Adal explains, he saw Europe as a coloniser and an inquisitor, and even Andalusia, symbol of the Golden Age of "European Islam", was also regarded as the symbol of the European Inquisition and a policy of conversion which endangered the religious and linguistic identity of Muslims. Nevertheless, Europe was also a land of Islam, not only because of the Andalusian past, but also because of the present Muslim communities living in Europe, especially in Eastern and South-Eastern Europe. Shakib Arslan often helped these communities to assert their presence on European soil.

It is often assumed that the emergence of Islam on public space in Europe is a recent phenomenon. Of course, this was not the case in South-Eastern Europe even if its presence was considerably reduced after the collapse of the Ottoman Empire. But for Western and Central Europe also, one often forgets that pioneering attempts were made by various individuals and groups to mark the presence of Islam in public space in various countries. The mosques built in the centre of Paris and in the suburbs of Berlin and London represented an important symbol of that presence in urban space. With the taste for "Saracenic" and "Mauresque" architectures created by the nineteenth-century Universal Exhibitions,[13] such Oriental buildings generated a rather positive curiosity among the population. Other projects for erecting mosques were made in Prague, Budapest[14] and, as noted by Sebastian Cwiklinski, in Warsaw, but also in Marseilles[15] and in different places in Britain (see Humayun Ansari's and Richard Lawless' chapters).

However, promoting a "European Islam" in the public sphere was not so easily accepted, as is illustrated by the case of the

[13] Lorraine Decléty, 'La représentation de l'architecture islamique à Paris au XIXe siècle: une definition de l'orientalisme architectural', unpublished thesis, Ecole Nationale des Chartes, Paris, 2001.

[14] See Miloš Mendel, "The Islamic Religious Community in Bohemia and Moravia (1934–1945)", *Archív Orientální*, 66 (1998), pp. 127–41; György Lederer, "Sur l'islam à Budapest", *La transmission du savoir dans le monde musulman périphérique*, 6 (November 1986), pp. 23–37 (see pp. 27–32) ; and György Lederer, "Islam in Hungary", *Central Asian Survey*, XI, 1 (1992), pp. 1–23 (pp. 13–15).

[15] Michel Renard, "Aperçu sur l'histoire de l'islam à Marseille, 1813–1962. Pratiques religieuses et encadrement des Nord-Africains", *Outre-Mers*, XC, 340–41 (2003), pp. 269–94 (see pp. 281–6).

neo-Sufi groups, which were, in a way, the very vectors of a new brand of "European Islam". The various "neo-Sufi" and "Sufistical" movements that developed with some success all over Europe also contributed to the "Europeanisation" of Islam. Neo-Sufism differs from Sufism as it is traditionally thought, lived and practised in the Islamic world. It is a new adaptation of Sufism to a European mind and a "Western religious modernity" characterised, according to Mark Sedgwick, by its pluralism, an image-mediated experience, a repeated reference to the final age of mankind, and an emphasis on individual intuition. Furthermore, most of the inter-war neo-Sufis—such as the members of Inayat Khan's Sufi Order or of Frithhof Schuon's Alawiyya—tried publicly, but not necessarily privately, to distance themselves from Islam, because of its predominantly negative image in Europe, even if they themselves did not endorse such a portrayal.

The role of non-Muslims in the shaping of a "European Islam" does not limit itself to the creation of groups whose spirituality resulted from an adaptation of Islam to "European religious modernity". There were also several cases where non-Muslims who did not convert helped to promote Islam in Europe, or even a "European Islam". In England, the renowned scholar T.W. Arnold was among the trustees of the Woking Mosque and, in Germany, the *Deutsch-Moslemische Gesellschaft* was largely opened to non-Muslims. In Hungary, from the beginning of the 1930s, one might mention Andor Medriczky's attempt to organise the Islamic Community in order to gain official recognition. He proposed to build a mosque and a hostel for Muslim students next to the sixteenth century mausoleum of Gül Baba, and tried to find some support from Shakib Arslan, and later on from Ahmadi missionaries.[16] The Gül Baba Society was patronised by some influential Hungarian politicians such as Istvan Barczy, former Mayor of Budapest. The exact motivation of the Society's promoters remains uncertain; only in the case of Medriczky do we know that his interest in Islam developed from the years he spent in Istanbul.

In the case of Germany, the political motivation of the Islamophilia of some German officials is much more obvious and

[16] See the two articles of György Lederer quoted in the footnote 14.

sinister. As Wolfgang Schwanitz will explain in the third part, it was in non-Muslim minds that the idea emerged of using the Islamic concept of *jihad* in a particular sense and for a specific political agenda. The decade of the 1930s ended with the rather extreme case of European professional propagandists acting with '*ulama* and even as '*ulama*, to give a new "Western-made" interpretation of Islam conceived for a wartime discourse.

N.C.—E.G.

BEHIND THE VEIL. THE REFORM OF ISLAM IN INTER-WAR ALBANIA OR THE SEARCH FOR A 'MODERN' AND 'EUROPEAN' ISLAM

Nathalie Clayer

The Albanian case is unique. When the independence of this young European country was again recognised by the international community in 1920,[1] Islam was the religion of the majority of the population (around 70 per cent of an estimated 800,000 inhabitants). Albania was thus the only predominantly Muslim European state. Unlike the majority of Muslims in Western Europe, Albanian Muslims were neither immigrants nor recent converts to Islam. Nor did they form a "surviving minority",[2] as was the case with Muslim groups living in other Balkan countries; rather we could say that they made up a "surviving majority". One of the components of the national identity building process had been to legitimise the existence of a sovereign nation, even if a predominantly Muslim one, in Europe, in case of the collapse of the Ottoman Empire.[3]

Despite this Muslim majority, from 1920 onwards the Albanian state was immediately defined by its political leaders as *afetar* ("without religion"), that is to say "without any official religion". The aim was to strengthen national feeling among a population divided between different denominations, Muslims, Catholic

[1] Albania was first recognised by the European powers as an independent principality in 1913, but it was occupied by different countries during the First World War.

[2] The expression is from Xavier Bougarel.

[3] See my book *Aux origines du nationalisme albanais. La naissance d'une nation majoritairement musulmane en Europe*, Paris: Karthala, 2007.

Christians and Orthodox Christians.[4] In fact, the state was multi-denominational rather than a-denominational. The "a-denominational" character of the state also fitted the wishes of secularist intellectuals and civil servants, who were non-Muslims as well as Muslims—Sunnis or members of the heterodox Islamic brotherhood of the Bektashis. These secularists dominated the intellectual life and the state apparatus, and were working for what they called the "modernisation" and the "Europeanisation" of the country.

The dominant role of secularist elites paved the way for the "reform of Islam". This process was made easier by the nationalisation of the Islamic religious institutions and by the progressive control exerted over them by the state. Indeed, the Albanian state played an important role in the organisation and reform of official religious institutions. For example, it interfered in the organisation of the first national Islamic Congress which took place in 1923, issuing orders concerning the choice of the delegates. It was not essential that they were clerics, but above all they had to be "patriots" and "more or less liberal". The civil authorities themselves even chose some of the delegates, who were supposed to represent one province or another.[5] Government representatives were also present during the meetings. Apart from the congresses, the political view of clerics was closely controlled. Their nomination had to be accepted, and was sometimes even decided, by the civil authorities, who also dismissed some clerics. Finally, with the further reform and centralisation of religious institutions in 1929, the state came to provide a substantial part of the Islamic Community's budget.[6]

The "reform of Islam" was also facilitated by the fact that the authority of the official religious leaders was sometimes even imposed through the intervention of the civil authorities. For instance, in 1926 the head of the Islamic Community informed

[4] Approximately 20 per cent of the population were Orthodox Christians, mainly in the South of the country, and 10 per cent Catholic Christians, mainly in the Northern part.

[5] Arkivi Qendror i Shtetit (AQSh), Tirana, Fondi 152 (Ministri e puneve të Brendshme), Viti 1923, Dosja 31, fl. 1–3.

[6] See for example AQSh F. 152, V. 1925, D. 623 ; F. 882 (Komuniteti Mysliman), V. 1929, D. 3; *Statuti i Komunitetit Mysliman Shqipëtar*, Tiranë, 1929. In this text, "Community" with a capital letter refers to an institution and not to a group of people.

the Ministry of the Interior that propaganda had been launched in Shkodër against the New Madrasa established in that city, as well as against the new organisation of the Jemaat and the collection of money that it implied. The Ministry therefore ordered the head of the Community not to allow sermons to be delivered in mosques without the authorisation of the Community, and promised that the civil authorities would take action against offenders.[7]

The links between the political authorities and the Islamic Community were especially close since Islam and the Islamic religious institutions were also used by the government for social control. As early as 1922, sermons (*vaz*) were used to persuade parents to send their children to school, and to strengthen national fraternity and loyalty to the government. Even in 1936, the official aim of the Islamic Community was to contribute by means of sermons and lectures to the strengthening of national fraternity and national feeling, as well as to advise Muslims to conform to progress and "true civilisation". Islam was also particularly used in the context of the economic crisis. During Ramadan in 1931, for example, preachers had to address this problem, and Islamic charity was encouraged in order to help solve the social crisis. In 1937, the leaders of the Islamic Community called upon wealthy Muslims to give to the poor who were suffering from unemployment in order to show that there was no need for socialism and Bolshevism. Indeed, Islam was certainly considered by the Albanian political authorities as a tool against the diffusion of Communist ideas, which, at that time, were attractive especially for young people.[8] The "harmful nature" of Communism was denounced by Muslim clerics in numerous articles and booklets.[9]

[7] AQSh, F. 882, V. 1926, D. 90, fl. 17–26.

[8] AQSh, F. 882, V. 1922, D. 10, fl. 26 ; V. 1931, D. 106, fl. 3–4 ; V. 1936, D. 53, fl. 1; *Zani i naltë* (Tirana), XII, 2 (February 1937), p. 34. In 1937, measures were taken by the political authorities against Communist groups (cf. Michael Schmidt-Neke, *Entstehung und Ausbau der Königsdiktatur in Albanien (1912–1939)*, Munich: Oldenbourg, 1987, p. 262).

[9] The most significant work in this respect was that of Hafiz Ali Korça (*Bolshevizma. Çkatërimi i njerëzimit* [Bolshevism. The destruction of humanity], Tirana, 1925). From 1933–34 on, atheism was one of the main targets of the Islamic Community in its journal. See also the booklet of Hafiz Ali Kraja (*A duhet feja. A e pengon bashkimin kombëtar* [Is Religion necessary. Does it prevent the national union], Shkodër, 1934).

Among the "reforms of Islam" that were introduced in this context, we should mention firstly the autonomy granted to the Sufi brotherhoods, in particular to the Bektashiyya, which had already been promoted by some Albanian nationalists at the end of the Ottoman period as a liberal form of Islam. These changes, imposed by the political power against the wishes of the leaders of the Islamic Community, were quite different from the developments taking place in Turkey where Sufi orders were banned. Nevertheless, from 1936 onwards, four Sufi networks—the Qadiriyya, the Rifaiyya, the Sadiyya and the Tijaniyya—were grouped within a special organisation, under the umbrella of the Islamic Community.[10]

Another important reform was the suppression of the Shari'a courts, following the adoption of the Civil Code in 1928–29. Their abolition was only reluctantly accepted by the leaders of the Islamic Community, because it erased the religious character of marriages and introduced some provisions concerning inheritance and divorce that were contrary to the Sacred Law. On the other hand, other reforms proposed by the political authorities were well accepted, because they were in accordance with the ideas promoted by reformist '*ulama*s.[11] Thus, in 1929, all the provincial *madrasa*s were closed down and a new General Madrasa was set up in the capital, in order to train a new staff of religious officials, in a "modern" spirit.[12]

However, by using the example of another reform, the ban on the veil, I want to highlight the mechanisms of such reforms and the relations between the various actors involved. More generally, I want to show how these mechanisms reveal the place of Islam within Albanian society during the inter-war period.

[10] Nathalie Clayer, *L'Albanie, pays des derviches*, Berlin: Otto Harrassowitz, 1990. About the reactions of the Muslim religious leaders, see for example AQSh, F. 882, V. 1923, D. 1.

[11] As in Turkey, religious reformists and political reformers had a common goal, to elaborate a "true spiritual Islam", cleansed of its impurities.

[12] See Alexandre Popovic, *L'islam balkanique*, Berlin: Otto Harrassowitz, 1986, pp. 27 ff.

THE PROGRESSIVE LIFTING OF THE VEIL

The ban on the veil only occurred step by step.[13] Between 1920 and 1928, only some actors—intellectuals and politicians—called or asked for such a reform in the press or in parliament, particularly when important political decisions were to be taken. This occurred between 1920 and 1923, a period which represents the beginning of a difficult state building process.[14] It also occurred in 1924, during the short government of Fan Noli, established after the so-called "June Revolution". The question was again debated in 1928, when the Civil Code was introduced and when the political system was transformed from a republic to a monarchy. But during this first phase no action was actually taken, either by the political authorities or by religious leaders.

In 1929, however, at a time of political change and of religious reorganisation under state control, the ban on the veil became part of the radical measures requested by Behxhet Shapati, the new head of the Islamic Community, elected at the close of the national Islamic Congress. Indeed, it has been suggested that Shapati asked the Minister of Justice to ban the *perçe* (veil) and requested that, through the police, he should advise the population to abandon the veil by prohibiting husbands and fathers to go in the company of veiled women.[15] However, it seems doubtful that the new head of the Islamic Community would have taken this initiative which was probably the work of the political authorities. Indeed, the Ministerial Council banned not only the *perçe* (veil), but also the *ferexhe* (*fereje*, a dustcoat worn by women when they went out). The Minister of Justice nevertheless recommended to police stations that they should be very careful not to offend the people, and try to

[13] Here the discussion will be on the veil (*perçe* in Albanian), covering the face, and not on the headscarf. At that time, in Albania, the veil was worn by urban women, whereas in the countryside it was quite rare.

[14] In 1923, following a proposal by Ali Këlcyra, a deputy from Southern Albania, the President of the Albanian Parliament proposed a vote on a recommendation to the government to make propaganda through the Islamic Congress in order to improve the social life of women, taking Turkey as an example. But the proposal was never put to the vote (*Bisedimet e këshillit Kombtar*, III/4, Tirana, 1923, pp. 49–57).

[15] Fatmira Musaj, *Gruaja në Shqipëri* [Woman in Albania] *(1912–1939)*, Tirana: Akademia e Shkencave, 2002, pp. 306–7.

convince them by working together with the district councils responsible for explaining to women why the ban was necessary.[16]

At the same time, during the following years, the political authorities used various means in order to impose this decision: propaganda in newspapers, lectures and, above all, insistence that women working for the state, such as midwives and teachers, must comply. In fact, at least in 1935, punitive measures were taken against those women who did not respect the ban.[17] In addition, initiatives were sometimes taken by local authorities, such as the mayors of Gjirokastër and Tirana.[18]

But the question of the ban on the veil gained new impetus in 1936–37, during a new period of political crisis. At that time, the country's sovereignty was more and more openly challenged by Italy. A liberal government had been set up in October 1935, but lasted only until November 1936. During this "liberal government" led by Mehdi Frashëri, the debate on the veil was relaunched in the press, especially between the Islamic Community's journal and the newspapers of some young intellectuals. Then, in 1937, when an important set of reforms was launched by the Albanian authorities to assert the country's sovereignty, the ban on the veil became the subject of a law.

Here again, the initiative was supposed to have been taken by the official religious authorities. According to this version, the two muftis of the Southern provinces asked the General Council of the Islamic Community to ban the veil. Following this request, the head of the Islamic Community, Shapati, wrote a report containing a *fatwa* by him stating that it was not *haram* (forbidden by religion) for a woman to show her face. On 1 March 1937, the General Council of the Community agreed with this report and the *fatwa*, and decided to make the decision known on one hand to the population by means of sermons, and on the other to the government. The latter immediately presented a draft law to parliament that was approved on 8 March 1937. Under the title "Law on the ban on face covering", it stipulated that it was forbidden for a woman to

[16] Ibid., pp. 309–10.
[17] Ibid., p. 311.
[18] Ibid.

cover her face, totally or partially, with any kind of veil. Offenders, as well as the husbands, fathers or guardians who had not exerted their authority and those who were making a propaganda in favour of the veil, incurred a fine.[19]

In reality, this initiative probably originated in political circles, and it seems that a kind of compromise was achieved between the political and the religious authorities. Indeed, the law concerned only the covering of the face and remained silent about the wearing of the *fereje*, a garment that the police were supposed to have banned since 1929.

What is important to note is that this law had a strong echo abroad, and this had certainly been the true aim of the political authority. In fact, the ban on the veil aimed to symbolise the Westernisation of the country, by making it possible for women to have a place in economic and social life. As a Western country, Albania should be a sovereign country among the other Western countries.[20]

However, in the country itself, the veil did not totally disappear for two reasons. On one hand, there was popular opposition and, on the other, the government remained very cautious. Resistance developed especially in Shkodër, the stronghold of Islam in Northern Albania, and in small cities of Central Albania, such as Tirana, Kavajë, Elbasan and Durrës. Despite the example given by high religious officials and the order given to civil servants concerning their wives, the veil reappeared after a short period. In some places, women began to wear a *xhari*, a piece of material which allowed them to uncover their faces when meeting a policeman and quickly to recover them afterwards. Even in 1940, problems were still noticed in Kavajë by the civil authorities.[21] In fact, these authorities had received instructions that when applying the law they should

[19] *Zani i naltë* [The supreme voice], XII, 3 (March 1937), pp. 65–73. The law was published in the Official Journal (*Fletorja Zyrtare,* Tirana, XVI, 15 (10 March 1937), p. 1).

[20] A special file in the archives of the Albanian Ministry of Foreign Affairs is devoted to the articles collected in the press of various countries on that reform launched in Albania (AQSh, F. 151, V. 1937, D. 75). See F. Musaj, *Gruaja*, pp. 319–21.

[21] F. Musaj, *Gruaja*, pp. 316–19 ; AQSh, F. 882, V. 1937, D. 88, fl.1 ; F. 152, V. 1940, D. 86.

not act brutally. Politically, it was better to convince than to forbid. At the beginning of the campaign, King Zog had sent his three sisters unveiled to Shkodër, along with the Minister of the Interior and other officials, in order to convince the population.[22] Persuasion was also part of the programme of the Albanian Woman Association's local groups, that were in charge of the organisation of conferences.[23]

THE DEBATE AND ITS ACTORS

A multiplicity of actors, with various positions and interests, were involved in this reform, as well as in the debate that surrounded it. There were three categories of actors, all of whom had to take into account the fact that the population was severely affected by the economic and social crisis and that religion was an important reference for the people. These categories, which were not always very clearly separated, were state representatives, secularist intellectuals and Muslim clerics. In fact, these different actors together represented only a tiny proportion of the population. As with the question of the Civil Code, some non-Muslims participated in the debate, while they interfered to a lesser extent in other reforms of Islam. Nevertheless, the main actors remained Muslims. This reveals that the social division implied by the multi-denominational character of the population was still very important, except for a section of the younger generation.[24]

The state representatives

The state representatives did not intervene much in the debate, but they played an important role in the field, because they were responsible for enforcement of the ban at different levels. In general, the policy they had to implement was dictated by a desire for reform. The aim was to "modernise" the country, but above all to

[22] Bernd Fischer, *King Zog and the Struggle for Stability in Albania*, New York: Columbia University Press, 1984, p. 249.

[23] F. Musaj, *Gruaja*, p. 302.

[24] On the political level too, religious diversity was marked. Members of parliament represented proportionally the denominational composition of the population.

built a "faithful nation" and to assert the sovereignty of the country. However, in concrete terms, the implementation of this policy was changing with time and circumstances. Furthermore, the civil servants in charge of its implementation had their own views that could have an impact upon their actions. Mayors, officials, teachers, policemen could act locally according to their own feelings, either enforcing or not enforcing the orders received from above.

Some of the state representatives were Muslim conservatives who were against the ban. In this case they could be still "more cautious" vis-à-vis the population in implementing the ban. But it seems that, as officials, they were often obliged to set an example. It seems also that, in fact, most of the civil servants even anticipated the government initiatives; I have already referred to the local initiatives in favour of the ban taken in 1929 by the mayor of Gjirokastër. He asked the city's population to abandon the veil, because it was the cause of women's isolation.[25] Teachers, especially those belonging to the younger generation, were often more eager for reforms than the government itself. In particular, some of them seem to have called for a clearer and quicker disappearance of religion, and especially of Islam, from the public sphere.[26] This was the case for non-Muslims, but also for young Muslims trained in Western countries or in new schools in Albania. Their attitude reflects both the social competition in which they were involved vis-à-vis the older elites and especially the clerics who had previously exerted a monopoly over education, and the effects of ideas developed by secularist intellectuals.[27]

The secularist intellectuals

The secularist intellectuals, who voiced opposition to the veil in the press (or in parliament) from 1920 onwards, were often guided by a European-centred vision of Islam. They used the question of the veil

[25] F. Musaj, *Gruaja*, pp. 308–9.

[26] In April 1928, the *qadi* of Delvinë (in the South-West of the country) complained that the director of a primary school was opposing the teaching of religion at school (AQSh, F. 882, V. 1928, D. 95).

[27] See, for example the case of Safet Butka (1901–43), trained in Austria (Uran Butka, *Safet Butka*, Tirana, Maluka, 2003, pp. 31–4 and 98).

as a component of the debate on "modernisation", "Westernisation", "secularisation" and strengthening of the state. They generally belonged to the younger generation. Most of them were of Muslim origin, but others were Christians. However, as they were all secularist, their religious origin did not matter so much. Among non-Muslims, there was no specific discourse, even if for them secularisation meant not only the separation of state and religion, but also the end of the hegemony of Islam in society.[28] The young Albanians of Muslim origin who took the floor had a different profile. Some were born to important notable families, such as Ali Këlcyra and Namik Delvina. They had studied in the West or in Istanbul, in modern schools where Positivism was quite widespread. Other secularist intellectuals were of more modest social origin. They had studied in Western Europe or in Albania. Some of them were attracted by Communism, such as Halim Xhelo and Selim Shpuza.[29] However, they all were fighting against the "Eastern mentality and habits", and wanted their country to turn to the West, even though they were debating how to do this and some of them were trying to build a specifically Albanian way to "Westernisation".[30]

For the secularist intellectuals, the veil (as well as the *fereje*) was linked with notions of seclusion, servitude and slavery of women. It was associated, not with the outside Muslim world as in the current

[28] In September 1924, the editors of a Catholic newspaper in Shkodër asked the Democratic government to ban the veil in the name of democracy, politics and morality (*Ora e maleve*, II, 37 (6 September 1924), p. 3).

[29] The set of articles which I took into consideration is that used by F. Musaj for the period 1922–23, with articles from the journal *Drita* (Gjirokastër, edited by a Muslim), *Agimi* (Shkodër, edited by a Catholic), *Mbrojtja kombtare* (Halim Xhelo) and *Kombi në rrezik* (F. Musaj, *Gruaja*, pp. 140–3). Among the most important texts I used are also texts published in the newspaper *Zëri i popullit*, from Korçë in March 1923 (n° 28) and in March-April 1924 (29 March and 6 April), articles published in *Shqipëria e re*, in Romania, in April 1925; various articles from Namik Delvina published in his newspaper *Ora* in 1932 (see n° 541, 544, 561); articles written by Mehdi Frashëri quoted below, as well as some of his texts published in the journals *Illyria* in 1934 and *Minerva* in 1935; two articles published in *Arbënia* (n° 209 et n° 256 of 1936); and the article of Selim Shpuza published in 1936 in the journal *Bota e re*, under the title "*Modernism and çarçaf*" (n° 7).

[30] In 1934 the journal *Illyria* (n° 38, 11 January 1936, p. 1) explained that it was necessary to form a front against Eastern influences, and to assimilate the Western mentality, not by importing it, but by creating an Albanian culture.

debate concerning the veil in Western Europe, but with the Ottoman past, seen as synonymous with "yoke", "barbarism", "backwardness", "fanaticism" and "Asia". It was also closely associated with the socio-political decline of the Islamic community and the backwardness of the nation. Indeed the veil was described by such intellectuals as the cause of the backwardness of the whole nation, because Muslims were the majority of the population, and because girls were not educated and did not participate sufficiently in economic life. But, for them, the question was not only intrinsic. There was also the problem of foreign perceptions, and concern that the first impression gained by "European tourists" (as they wrote) would be to see veiled women in all Albanian cities.

These intellectuals considered that the ban on the veil was necessary in order to make Albania a European country or at least to portray it as such. It could lead Albania towards progress and show that Albanians deserved to live as a free people in the middle of Europe. They considered that the geographical location of Albania in Europe, as well as the fact that the country was living in the twentieth century, were two reasons for the ban on the veil.

Lastly, they used the example given by Kemalist Turkey, or by other Muslim countries (like Iran and Afghanistan), which had made similar reforms. For instance, in 1923, the deputy Ali Këlcyra declared in the middle of the Albanian parliament that Mustafa Kemal went to the Turkish parliament with his unveiled fiancée and that newspaper photographs showed the faces of Mustafa Kemal and "his wife".[31]

The case of Mehdi Frashëri

Among this group of secularist intellectuals, the figure of Mehdi Frashëri occupied a specific place. Deputy, civil servant, minister, president of the Council of State and intellectual, he was one of the main officials responsible for the autonomy of the Bektashi Community, which he represented in 1943–44 on the Regency Council, being himself a Bektashi Muslim. He was also one of the main architects of the Civil Code introduced in 1928–29 in Albania.[32]

[31] *Bisedimet e këshillit Kombtar*, III/3, Tirana, 1923, p. 48.

[32] M. Schmidt-Neke, *Entstehung*, pp. 335–6.

In 1928, the question of the veil enabled him to contrast Bektashism, portrayed as "liberal", with Sunnism, presented as "fanatical" and the enemy of progress. Indeed, in the introduction of his book about the ancient history of Albania, he tackled the question of religion. He depicted Sunnism as a fanatical form of Islam, which considered every type of progress and every change as a threat to religion, while presenting Bektashism as a "protest" against this type of Islam. According to Mehdi Frashëri, Bektashism prohibited polygamy and, whereas Sunni Islam required women to be veiled, Bektashis considered that women had to be veiled only with the "veil of honour", which was not a material veil. Women therefore were only required to be honourable, and were not required to cover their faces.[33]

In a long text published the same year as a serial in a newspaper aimed at "intellectuals and patriots", Mehdi Frashëri explained his ideas about "Muslim reforms".[34] He presented the position of women and the question of the veil, as well as the perception of Christians by Muslims, as the two revealing factors of the evolution of Islam. The veil appeared with the decline of Islam. Therefore, the most radical reform required was the one concerning the position of women.[35] He claimed that such a reform was necessary in order for Albanians to be included among "European people". Since Albanians wanted to live free, independent and advanced lives, Mehdi Frashëri saw only two solutions for Albanian Muslims who represented the part of the Muslim world that was face to face with Christian people: either they would make reforms or Islam would

[33] Mehdi Frashëri, *Historia e lashtë e Shqipërisë dhe e Shqipëtarëve*, Tirana, Phoenix, 2000 (1928[1]), pp. 44–5 and 46–7.

[34] "Reformat Myslimane në Shqipëri", *Gazeta e re*, Tirana, 17 (20 November 1928), p. 1; 26 (1 December 1928), p. 2; 27 (2 December 1928), p. 4; 30 (6 December 1928), p. 2; 31 (7 December 1936), p. 3; 35 (12 December 1928), p. 2; 36 (13 December 1929), p. 2; 37 (14 December 1937), p. 2; 39 (16 December 1928), p. 2.

[35] Mehdi Frashëri also suggested making other reforms concerning the way of performing prayers and the diffusion of knowledge. In a later article, published in 1931, concerning the economic situation of the country and the lack of development of agriculture, he suggested that one of the factors was that the Islamic religion was humiliating women in numerous ways ("Aveniri i Shqipërisë në pikpamje bujqësore", *Bujqsija*, III, 1–2 (January-February 1931), p. 17).

have to disappear from the face of Albania.[36] Only radical reforms like those of Mustafa Kemal in Turkey could bring civilisation and independence, as Christian people had experienced four centuries before, with the Protestant Reformation.

At that time, Mehdi Frashëri was preparing new legislation covering all fields, including family law, previously covered by the Shari'a courts. Thus, his approach to the reform of Islam had another important aspect: that of religious authority. In fact, in the same article,[37] he advocated returning to the sources without the intermediary of an authority, in accordance with Luther's principle. Moreover, he claimed that even some features of the Islamic religion urged him to follow this line. Indeed, in Mehdi Frashëri's view, the Prophet himself did not assume authority, and Islam, as a general principle, opted to have no clergy. Because the educational level of the clerics was too low, and until the arrival of a new educated generation, clerics should confine themselves to the practice of religion, whereas the Muslim councils established all over the country should be made up of educated people, doctors, lawyers, agronomists, professors, etc. Mehdi Frashëri went so far in this direction that he proposed totally new training for muftis. He stated that all the country's *madrasa*s however, should be closed and replaced by the establishment of two colleges (one in the South, the other in the North), with a new educational system where Arabic should be taught according to the American Berlitz method. The best students should be sent to Europe to study philosophy, as well as the Arabic language in the departments of foreign languages. On their return, they should be appointed muftis, since, in Islam, those who are more learned are in a better position to interpret the texts and muftis do not need to wear turbans and *jubes*.

The 'ulama

It is easy to understand that people holding religious authority reacted to a debate in which Islam was often disparaged and their authority challenged. They were also reacting to the measures taken

[36] Mehdi Frashëri considered that the other Balkan Muslims, who were under the domination of the Balkan states, were condemned to emigrate to Anatolia.

[37] See footnote 34.

by the state and its representatives to ban the veil. However, the reactions were expressed in various ways, often depending on the social position of those concerned.

A first group of Muslim clerics was made up of the leaders of the Islamic Community, i.e. of the official religious institutions. These people were themselves reformists. For instance, in 1925, when a national Islamic Congress was convened, they declared that Albania was taking part in the "revival" of Islamic civilisation inaugurated by Muhammad Abduh. They wanted to introduce reforms in order to achieve culture, civilisation and progress. As a result, the political authorities looked favourably on them. Nevertheless they only had a limited room to manœuvre vis-à-vis these political authorities, and when they had differences of opinion with them, especially when reforms implied restrictions to their own authority, they had great difficulty imposing their view.[38] They themselves did not form a totally homogeneous group. For instance, in 1926, when the students of Tirana's *madrasa* asked for authorisation to create a sports association, only one member of the High Council of the Shari'a was in favour of this idea.[39]

The attitude of the leaders of the Islamic Community concerning the veil had fluctuated according to their place in the debate and in the process. Until 1929, they generally defended the veil or at least opposed criticism of it, using two arguments—a woman's honour and religious authority.[40] In 1929 and in 1937, when official measures were taken concerning the ban on the veil, the leaders of the Islamic Community were supposed to have taken the

[38] It was particularly the case when the jurisdiction of Shari'a judges was limited in 1919 and when the Civil Code was introduced in 1928–29.

[39] AQSH, F. 882, V. 1926, D. 71, fl. 1–2. This member was Salih Vuçitërn, a person who belonged both to the religious and to the political field.

[40] In 1924, the Mufti of Shkodër criticised the idea put forward in a Catholic newspaper of banning the veil (see footnote 28), because it undermined Islam, and stated that if the Catholics committed a second offence, there would be a quarrel between the two "elements" (*Zani i naltë*, I, 11 (August 1924), p. 348). Reacting to the same affair, the Muslim editors of the newspaper *Dajti* in Tirana explained that the veil was one of the fundamental means of preserving a woman's honour (*Dajti*, 45 (17 September 1924), p. 3). As we will see below, in 1928, the answer of Hafiz Ismet Dibra to Mehdi Frashëri mainly concerned the question of religious authority.

initiative, but, as I have argued, this does not seem very plausible. In 1929, the argument they used to justify the measures taken by the civil authorities was that the wearing of the veil was not a Qur'anic prescription and that the Islamic religion did not insist on covering the face. Some months later, the Islamic Community published in its journal the translation of a lecture given in the Berlin Mosque on a woman's position in Islam. Here again the interpretation of the Qur'an, inspired by the leader of the Lahori Ahmadiyya, Muhammad Ali, led to the conclusion that uncovering of a woman's face and hands was lawful.[41]

When the veil debate livened up again in the press in 1936, as representatives of the Islamic Community these leaders chose above all to defend the Islamic religion and, for that, to denounce the criticisms made against the veil, since it was associated by their adversaries with Islam. In the Community's journal, they denounced the idea that the veil—and the Islamic religion—was the cause of the lack of progress of the Albanian nation and accused their adversaries of wanting to force Albanian women to live in excessive luxury. In doing so, they inevitably appeared all the more as the champions of the veil. Yet, relying on the Qur'an, the article concluded that a woman could go out with her face unveiled, but without any make-up, and with a cloak (*jilbab*) leaving only the face and the hands uncovered.[42] It shows the ambiguity of their discourse.

With the decision of the political authorities to impose the ban on the veil at the beginning of 1937, the leaders of the Islamic Community were placed in a different position. Again they had to justify such a decision at the religious level, and even to appear to promote it. The arguments presented in these new circumstances were in fact of various types.[43] Some were of course religious. Shapati explained that, according to verses 31–32 of Surat XXIV of the Qur'an, a woman had to be covered in front of strangers. But according to Imam Azam,

[41] "Gjendja e Grues n'Islamizmë", *Zani i naltë*, VI, 4 (March 1930), pp. 966–76.

[42] "Zbulimi i Grues Muslimane", *Zani i naltë*, XI, 5 (May 1936), pp. 142–9. One of the arguments used against their adversaries was also that the latter wanted unveiling only because of shame in the face of foreigners. So they accused the secularist intellectuals of wanting "to destroy the country in order to please the foreigners".

[43] *Zani i naltë*, XII, 3 (March 1937), pp. 65–77.

this prescription excluded the face and hands. All the Hanafi *'ulama* preached this interpretation. Later on, because of the problems that appeared in Muslim societies, Muslim jurists had prohibited women from showing their faces.[44] According to *fiqh* books, a Muslim woman had the right to work outside the home, to trade, to be a witness at the court, etc. Then Shapati wrote:

> Ibn Abidin said that the fact that a free woman shows her face is not *haram* [unlawful], but it is not necessary, it is *meqruh* [not forbidden by God, but looked upon by Muslim teachers with disgust]; According to this prescription, we issue the following *fatwa*: The stranger, Zeyd, when he sees the face of a foreign woman, Hindi, is it *haram*? Answer: it is not *haram*.[45]

Apart from the religious justification, the leaders of the Islamic Community also used the rhetoric of the civil authorities, and eventually that of the secularist intellectuals they had opposed. They presented abandoning the veil as a "social measure". They explained that its main aim was to improve the position of Muslim women within Albanian society, because the country needed such an investment of women in social life in order to achieve, as soon as possible, the level of cultural progress and economic development of a civilised country. Moreover, they did not forget to mention that the measure was taken just at the time when the King promised a set of reforms.

Like the secularist intellectuals, they also structured their arguments around the question of perception. The veil had become a problem because it was misused by some people, and, because it was considered as a prescription of the Islamic religion, the result was a criticism of the Islamic religion itself. Abandoning the veil was therefore necessary to highlight the true nature of Islam in the mind of public opinion. The fact that Albanians, particularly Muslims, wore different clothes made others laugh at them. Every day, "foreign tourists" were taking photographs of Muslim women, showing them to the rest of the world as testimony to the barbarian nature of the Muslim religion. Just like the secularist intellectuals, the leaders of the Islamic Community declared lastly that in the

[44] Shapati argued that some regions, in particular mountainous areas, continued to observe the true prescriptions of the Prophet and did not veil women. Thus, for nationalists, mountainous areas appeared as the bastion of tradition.

[45] Ibid.

twentieth century and in the middle of Europe Albanians had to adapt themselves to all the "good customs" of the civilised nations.

In this way, urged on by the political authorities, the leaders of the Islamic Community henceforth seemed to agree with the young religious Muslims sent to Lahore in India, who had expressed a different position during the debate in 1936. This small group of future '*ulama*, who were not yet involved in the leadership of religious affairs, had published at that time an article about the veil in their small journal—a supplement to the journal of the Lahori Ahmadiyya, *The Light*.[46] Like the leaders of the Islamic Community, the authors criticised those who wanted unlimited freedom for women to mix with any foreigner. They also drew the same conclusions from the analysis of the Qur'an, which they considered as giving the principles of religion and civilisation: there was no prescription concerning the covering of the face and the hands. However, they seemed to hold an opposite position in the debate. Indeed, they were convinced that the progress of Muslims was closely related to "solving the problem of the veil". Like the secularist intellectuals, they even declared that the veil was responsible for the educational backwardness of Muslim women.

But the real difference was between the leaders of the Islamic Community and other '*ulama* who were against lifting the veil. These people did not use the press or any printed matter to express themselves in public space. Nevertheless, we know that the leaders of the Islamic Community had to face opposition from such '*ulama*, which they tried to hide.[47] In fact, a blurred frontier existed between these '*ulama* and those belonging to the official Community who only reluctantly accepted the lifting of the veil. But the

[46] Sherif Putra, "Moda e mbulesës dhe veçimi i grave", *Drita*, Lahore, 6–8 (June-July-August 1936), pp. 6–19. In fact, this text was a translation of an article written by the future head of the Lahori Ahmadiyya, Muhammad Ali, and published in 1905 in *The Review of Religions* (Lahore). This appears in the second part of the text which was published in the journal of the Albanian Islamic Community in 1937, after the ban on the veil (*Zani i naltë*, XII, 5 (May 1937), pp. 202–13).

[47] Whereas a report from Elbasan shows that there were opponents (AQSh, F. 882, V. 1937, D. 88, fl.1), the journal of the Islamic Community published a false report showing that there was no opposition to unveiling (*Zani i naltë*, XII, 3 (March 1937), p. 96).

'*ulama* who opposed the ban on the veil had been against both the other reforms (introduction of the Civil Code and closing down of Shari'a courts and local *madrasas*) and the new religious hierarchy close to the political power. Apart from their real opinion concerning the veil, it provided a good opportunity to oppose the *fatwa* and the law.

It would have been interesting to know how a reformist member of the '*ulama* like Hafiz Abdullah Zëmblaku, who chose to have no relations with the authorities and who remained outside the new religious institutions, reacted in the 1937 debate. A former reader of the Turkish Islamist journals *Beyanülhak* and *Sebilürreşad*, in the 1920s he took as a model the missionaries of the Lahori Ahmadiyya, with whom he was in contact. He claimed to have the same objectives as this network: to make the religious prescriptions and texts accessible to everybody in vernacular languages, to work against the superstitions that entered into religion, to defend the Shari'a and to reinforce the bonds between Muslims, to show that Islam was a modern religion and that the clerics were also acting on the path to civilisation, as well as to oppose the intense activity of Christian missionaries. That is why he worked for the teaching of religion and true beliefs in the Albanian language, through courses, preaching and a set of booklets. He even invented a transcription of the Arabic language into Latin script in order to make it more accessible.[48]

We know that at the beginning of 1938 Hafiz Abdullah Zëmblaku was confined by the political authorities to the city of Vlorë, but we do not know the reason for this.[49] Some years before, however, he seems to have had an intermediary position on the question of the veil, between the young students in Lahore and the leaders of the Islamic Community. He criticised those who were against the veil, as well as those who were in favour of it for the wrong reasons. He considered that religious prescriptions obliged a woman to wear a complete veil, but that the old *fereje* was not

[48] See, for example, H.A. Sëmlaku, *Bilbil i gjashtë. Kanarja*, Korçë, 1930, pp. 41–3, *Bilbil i shtatë*, Korçë, 1931, pp. 15, 24–6; and *Bilbil i tetë*, Korçë, 1931, pp. 15–21.

[49] H.A. Sëmlaku, *Kanar i ri dhe bilbili faqe bardhë*, Korçë, 1938, p. 5.

necessary; a modern thick coat was much better, with a headscarf (*shami*) on the head and a kind of shawl.[50] Three years later, like the leaders of the Islamic Community, he appeared to deny the right of newspapers to address the question of the veil, which he saw as an issue that concerned only the '*ulama*, thus reducing the debate to the question of religious authority.[51]

Therefore, we can see that multiple issues appeared throughout the debate and the way the question was tackled by the different categories of actors.

THE STAKES BEHIND THE VEIL

In the first place, it is clear that the debate and the measures concerning the veil had their climax when political and social events or crisis occurred: at key moments in the state building process, at times when the country's sovereignty was questioned, and during economic and social crises. Whereas Islam was a mean of social control for the political authorities against the spread of Communist ideology in society, notably among young people, the question of the veil had a particular meaning. In 1937 it became a tool of foreign policy deployed to assert Albania's sovereignty. However, because it symbolised the "modernisation" and "Europeanisation" of the country for secularist intellectuals and civil servants, the ban was also a sign given to these groups and to the rest of society that the state building process was progressing. So they had to be faithful to the country and the government. More generally, the problem of the relations between religion and state was crucial.

State and religion

Throughout these debates and measures, the relationship between state and religion was involved repeatedly. In 1923, when the ban on the veil was discussed in parliament along with the prohibition of polygamy, some deputies reacted by saying that such decisions

[50] So it is unclear whether he considered that the face had to be covered or not (H.A. Sëmlaku, *Trëndafil i 1*, Korçë, 1932, pp. 169–70).

[51] See below.

could not be taken by the Assembly and that the government had no right to intervene in religious affairs; time and education would resolve the problem. Others believed in duty of the parliament and the state to take care of the cultural and social development of the nation and thus to solve this kind of question. Using a juridical approach, Mehdi Frashëri sided with the former (claiming that parliament had no authority in religious matters), but explained that other questions, such as the equality between women and men before the courts, and inheritance and divorce, could be debated by the Assembly.[52] In the following years, the Albanian government in fact adopted the second position and often interfered in religious affairs, by directing, controlling or using the religious scene, as illustrated by the question of the veil. That is why we can say that the Albanian state was multi-denominational rather a-denominational. There was no separation of state and church as there was, at least theoretically, in France. But, as in Turkey, only the government could combine religion with politics.[53] The difference with Turkey was that, despite Albania's Muslim majority in demographic terms, the state did not give the nation a Muslim character, which means that the question of the plurality of confessional groups arose.

The problem of building a nation out of several denominational groups appears clearly in the arguments put forward by Mehdi Frashëri in his famous article of 1928 on the reform of Islam. For him, Albania's fate was linked to the progress of the Muslim community, since it formed the majority of the population. In order to achieve a true and non-superficial union of the different parts of the nation, which was a question of survival for a small nation like Albania, the Muslim majority had to be liberal. At the same time Mehdi Frashëri thought that abandoning Shari'a-based jurisprudence was necessary not only because this was "old-fashioned" legislation and because religion concerned the consciousness and legislation of the state, but also because the Albanian people was

[52] *Bisedimet e këshillit Kombtar*, viti III, 4, Tirana, 1923, pp. 49–57.

[53] See Hamit Bozarslan, "Islam, laïcité et la question d'autorité de l'Empire ottoman à la Turquie kémaliste", *Archives de Sciences Sociales des Religions,* Paris, 125 (January-March 2004), pp. 99–112.

made up of non-Muslims as well as Muslims.[54] Like Mehdi Frashëri himself, people who were not Sunni Muslims (e.g. Bektashis or Christians) had of course a specific position towards the former dominant religion. They wanted it to lose its hegemonic status, and demanded more rights for other denominational groups.[55]

In the course of the debate, the question of the secularisation of public space also arose, since the veil was generally considered as a mark of the Islamic religion. Secularist intellectuals, as well as many officials and political leaders, seem to have been extremely sensitive to this, because for them "secularisation" was synonymous with "de-Ottomanisation" and "modernisation". All marks of Ottoman domination, often mistaken for marks of Islam, were to be banned, which led to a certain depreciation of Islam. Public space was partially de-Islamised, especially in schools and in the administration, but also in urban space, even if the state itself contributed to the building of some mosques during the inter-war period. Consequently, the context was not that of re-Islamisation of the public sphere and disillusionment with secularism that characterise Western Europe today.[56]

Another difference from the current situation in some European countries is that education was not the main theatre of the public sphere involved in the debate on the veil. In Albania at that time, the percentage of girls attending school was rather low; veiled girls were simply not sent to school.[57] However, apart from the veil, the separation of religion and education, which was an important facet of state politics, notably where religious teaching was concerned, became a subject of polemics. Hafiz Abdullah Zëmblaku, for instance, saw the state, and particularly the Ministry of Education,

[54] See references in footnote 34. Here the difference between the Albanian and the Turkish case has to be stressed. In Albania, the non-Muslim minorities were larger (approximately 30 per cent of the population), and most of the non-Muslims were also ethnic Albanians.

[55] In 1923, as well as in 1929, the question of relations between the Islamic Community and the Bektashis was at the heart of the question of religion and state.

[56] The expression is from Jocelyne Césari and Jean Baubérot ("Laïcité, communautarisme et foulard: vrais et faux débats", http://lmsi.net).

[57] F. Musaj, *Gruaja*, p. 142.

as enemies of religion and promoters of unbelief. He considered them as "Young Turks" and "Freemasons". He himself had a lot of trouble with the authorities who banned him from teaching the Albanian language, because he taught it together with religion.[58] Here we can perceive of course the problem of the loss of legitimacy for clerics in the educational sphere, mentioned above. As a result, the journal of the Islamic Community strongly denounced the role of teachers in propagating atheism and Bolshevism.[59] But for Hafiz Abdullah Zëmblaku even the head of the Islamic Community, who sided with the political authorities, was an enemy of religion and a promoter of unbelief. Religious authority was thus also questioned in itself.

Religious authority

The question of religious authority came up in the debate on the veil firstly because the ban on the veil was considered as one of the key reforms of Islam to be implemented and because some of the actors raised the following questions: who is able to debate about Islam?, who can decide on reforms?, and who can lead them?

I have already pointed out that the leaders of the Islamic Community very often used the argument of religious authority to answer opponents of the veil. In 1928, when one of the leaders of the Islamic Community, Hafiz Ismet Dibra, had to answer the long article by Mehdi Frashëri, he gave his answer not directly to him, but to "the Muslims who wonder after reading Mehdi's Frashëri on the reforms of Islam". Moreover, instead of criticising the point of view of his adversary, Dibra first denied his authority in the field of religion, pointing out all his "mistakes" as proof of his incompetence. In particular, Mehdi Frashëri's tendency to imagine *ijtihad* (rational interpretation) out of the context of the Shari'a, as well as his failure to show signs of respect towards the Prophet, were

[58] See, for example, H.A. Sëmlaku, *Bibil i Fesë. Sheri-ati Muhamedija*, Korçë, 1930, pp. 77–9 and *Trëndafil i 1*, Korçë, 1932, pp. 83 and 96 ff.

[59] See, for example, "Kundër Ateizmit", *Zani i naltë*, XI, 8–9 (August-September 1936), pp. 287–90.

considered unacceptable.[60] Such an answer, in fact, followed the same lines as that of Mehdi Frashëri, since the latter had advocated returning to the sources without the intermediary of an authority, proposing to establish Islamic councils composed of laymen and to train new muftis using modern educational methods, as we have seen.[61] In the same way, in 1935, Hafiz Abdullah Zëmblaku explained that since the Kingdom had no official religion, religion was free and nobody had the right to meddle with religious matters, except the religious scholars. Thus, he urged the journalists to speak about the economy rather than religion.[62]

The secularist intellectuals were really challenging the religious authority because of their direct access to the Qur'an through translations[63] and their constant attacks on Islam, but also because of widespread ignorance among Muslim clerics. This led some Muslims to react by proposing a plan to train clerics capable of guiding people with an Eastern as well as a Western culture, and more generally to launch reforms based on *ijtihad*.[64]

Furthermore, the question of the veil reveals that the authority of the leaders of the Islamic Community was not only challenged by secularist intellectuals but also by some religious entrepreneurs. The new religious hierarchy had difficulty gaining recognition from all the country's Muslims. Some *'ulama* were unwilling to accept the reforms which the Community had agreed to implement in close collaboration with the civil authorities, or to accept the new hierarchy and the centralisation of the religious authorities. Hafiz Abdullah Zëmblaku, for example, had refused appointment as mufti. Many

60 *Zani i naltë*, V, 10–11 (August-September [November] 1928), pp. 678–90; V, 12 (December 1928), pp. 726–34. H.I. Dibra even pointed out incompetence on the part of his adversary in his own field, diplomacy.

61 Later on, in July 1938, Mehdi Frashëri gathered Muslim intellectuals in the Albanian capital, in order to help the cultural development of the "Muslim element" (*Zani i naltë*, 8 (August 1938), p. 255).

62 *Bilbili besëtar*, Korçë (28 September 1935), pp. 51–2.

63 A first partial translation of the Qur'an had been made by a Christian Albanian (first fascicle, Bucharest, 1921; 2nd fascicle, Korçë, 1928). In addition, an English translation and commentary by Muhammad Ali, from the Ahmadiyya, was circulating in the country.

64 "Persri mbi fonksionarët t'onë fetarë", *Zani i naltë* (August-September 1930), pp. 1121–6.

'*ulama* in Shkodër went on teaching in a traditional way, without any contact with the new Tirana Madrasa. Most of them considered the introduction of the Civil Code and the ban on the veil as being in conflict with the Shari'a.[65]

Europe as reference or towards a 'European Islam'

Despite the opposition, if we analyse the content of the whole debate, it is striking to see "Europe" appearing as a common reference for all the actors, whatever their position concerning the veil.[66] In fact, the relationship between Islam and Europe was at the heart of the debate. The Islam shaped by all the actors was not only an Islam in Europe. At the Paris Mosque, in 1930, Ilyas Vrioni, the Albanian Ambassador, presented his country as "a fortress of the Islamic traditions in Europe".[67] But it was also a "European Islam". For the secularists, as we have seen, the reform of Islam had to be carried out precisely because the country was situated in Europe. On the other side, Hafiz Ismet Dibra, one of the leading '*ulama* of the official Community, agreed with Mehdi Frashëri that Muslims, although a majority in Albania, would not be able to live and to retain their faith without accepting the principles of "modern" and "European" life. In particular, in order to live in the middle of Europe it was necessary for them to make their own all kind of sciences that were the product of progress. Consequently the reform of Islam was essential.[68]

Nevertheless, it seems that the position of the various actors was not exactly the same on the European modernisation reference. For the secularist intellectuals or state representatives, the reference was always positive, whereas for the '*ulama*, it could be positive or

[65] See, for example, the great debate about the required reforms which started in 1927, whose echoes are to be found in the journal of the Islamic Community (*Zani i naltë*). After this period, the only criticism of the leaders of the Islamic Community that appeared in print was that by Hafiz Abdullah Zëmblaku, but it certainly points to a broader opposition.

[66] Here, of course, I cannot take into account the adversaries of the ban on the veil who did not take part in the debate in print.

[67] AQSh, F. 882, V. 1930, D. 114.

[68] See reference in footnote 60. There was never a debate about *dar al-harb* and *dar al-Islam*.

negative. The *'ulama* used it when they wanted something from the government, when they answered the secularists or when they wanted to convince Muslims about the need for reforms. Thus, they often mentioned that European states had realised again the importance of religion, had strengthened the teaching of religion at school or hosted religious congresses. They pointed to the fact that even developed countries did not prevent their people from being "fervent believers". Even Abdullah Zëmblaku, when he was criticised for using too many Arabic words, argued that, in Europe, too, Arabic words had been incorporated into the languages.[69] In this way they were highlighting European realities that the secularists and Westernists did not refer to. However, when the *'ulama* tried to reassert the importance of Islam, they could place "Europe" in opposition to "Islam" in a negative way for the former and a positive way for the latter. In this case, Europe became "materialist", the seat of unbelief, of women's dishonour, of luxury and frivolity.[70] The official Islamic hierarchy, through its journal, denounced the "new trends with a European influence", the "*Oksidentalofilë*" ("those who love the West").[71]

Another important reference in the debate was Turkey, as was the case throughout the Muslim world at that time.[72] The reforms of Mustafa Kemal were quoted as an example by the secularists and the state representatives.[73] On the one hand, the leaders of the Islamic Community, probably with the aim of convincing the

[69] See, for example, "Veprimet e Këshillit të Naltë të Sheriatit dhe nevojat e trupit musliman", *Zani i naltë*, II, 3 (May 1925), pp. 459–64; "Bisedimet e Kongresit Muslyman", *Zani i naltë*, II, 4–5 (June-July 1925), p. 502 ; Hafiz Ali Kraja, *A duhet feja*; H.A. Sëmlaku, *Trëndafil i 1*, Korçë, 1932, p. 154.

[70] See, for example, "Zbulimi i Grues Muslimane", *Zani i naltë*, XI, 5 (May 1936), pp. 142–9.

[71] Ibid.

[72] See Catherine Mayeur-Jaouen and Anne-Laure Dupont (eds), *Débats intellectuels au Moyen-Orient dans l'entre-deux-guerres*, *REMMM*, n° 95–96–97–98, 2002.

[73] In the religious field, the Turkish model could even be followed very concretely. Thus, in 1928, the Albanian Ambassador in Ankara sent a collection of *khutbas* (Friday sermons) for translation into Albanian because "it fitted with the religious principles and to the need of the time". The book was translated as *Këshillet e së premtes* (Shkodër, 1928).

political authorities, explained that Mustafa Kemal was not against Islam.[74] But someone like Hafiz Abdullah Zëmblaku could criticise the "Young Turks" and the "masons" of Turkey as bad examples for the Muslim world, while criticising the state representatives as well as the leaders of the Islamic Community.[75]

On the other hand, references to the Arab world (or to India) posed problems, and arguments based on such references were violently rejected by secularist intellectuals.[76] Even the Arabic script and the Arabic language were stigmatised by the secularists as well as by the state representatives. The political authorities tried to ban prayers (*dua*) in Arabic from the public sphere, arguing that it could make a bad impression on foreigners; that the people had to understand what they were hearing; and finally, that it was contrary to the independence of the Albanian Islamic Community.[77] This last point shows that the authorities, as in France today, were faced with the problem of "domestication in a global religious field".[78]

ALBANIAN ISLAM AND EXTERNAL NETWORKS

During the inter-war period, many Albanian entrepreneurs were in contact with the outside Muslim world: with Turkey, Egypt, India, and with Muslims in the Balkans and in the rest of Europe.[79] These contacts were used in the local field in different ways and for different purposes: to train students, to obtain Islamic literature, to benefit from various debates, etc. Apart from their relations with Egypt,

[74] See, for example, "Vepra e Gazi Qemal Ataturkut", *Zani i naltë*, X, 3 (March 1935), pp. 81–4; "Përsëri Mustafa Kemali flet mbi naltësinë e Islamizmës. . .", *Zani i naltë*, X, 9–10 (September-October 1935), pp. 319–20.

[75] *Trëndafil i 1*, Korçë, 1932, p. 120.

[76] See, for example, the article "Zani i naltë kundra Qytetnimit", published in *Bota e re,* 20 (30 January 1937), where the author, Selim Shpuza, criticised the journal of the Islamic Community for having quoted the discourse of an Arab *shaikh* of Al-Azhar (Selim Shpuza, *Vitet '20-'30,* Tirana, Toena, 1999, pp. 146–51).

[77] AQSh, F. 882, V. 1926, D. 90, fl. 1–2.

[78] John R. Bowen, "Does French Islam Have Borders? Dilemmas of Domestication in a Global Religious Field", *American Anthropologist*, CVI, 1 (2004), pp. 43–55.

[79] A lot of them corresponded with different persons from abroad, the Hajj was performed, and students were sent to Egypt or even to Lahore.

the leaders of the Islamic Community, in particular, made extensive use of their relations with the Lahori-Ahmadi network based in India, as well as in Berlin, Vienna and London. From 1927 onwards, they sent students to Lahore and ordered the translation of many articles and booklets developing the idea of compatibility between Islam and modernity, in order to reply to the arguments of those who downgraded Islam and to stress the compatibility of Islam and Europe embodied by the activities of the Lahori missions in England or Germany.[80] Hafiz Abdullah Zëmblaku, although opposed to the Community, also justified his "missionary action" in highlighting the work of the Lahori-Ahmadi in the Western World and his own contacts with them. He also used their networks to disseminate his method of transcription of Arabic.[81]

However, it seems that official networking was not possible, because of the principle of nationalisation imposed by the state. As early as 1923, the decision to break with the Caliphate had been of specific political importance, with the aim of setting up an independent Islamic Community. Eight years later, when the leaders of the Albanian Islamic Community received an invitation to attend the Jerusalem Congress, they declined it on the pretext that their treasury did not have sufficient funds to send a representative.[82] There was also no delegate from Albania at the Geneva Congress of European Muslims held in 1935.[83] We have to point out that, according to the law, religious communities in Albania could not be financed from abroad and could only have spiritual and cultural relations with foreign individuals or institutions; correspondence with religious centres situated abroad had to be authorised.[84]

[80] Nathalie Clayer, "La Ahmadiyya Lahori et la réforme de l'islam albanais dans l'entre-deux-guerres", in V. Bouillier and C. Servan-Schreiber (eds), *De l'Arabie à l'Himalaya. Chemins croisés en hommage à Marc Gaborieau*, Paris: Maisonneuve et Larose, 2004, pp. 211–28.

[81] See footnote 48.

[82] AQSh, F. 882, V. 1931, D. 116.

[83] The Albanian participants to these congresses came from Macedonia, i.e. from Yugoslavia.

[84] See the text of 1923 on the status of the religious Communities (AQSh, F. 152, V. 1923, D. 855, fl. 15), and Roberto Morozzo della Rocca, *Nazione e religione in Albania (1920–1944)*, Bologna: Il Mulino, 1990, p. 32.

Thus the progressive ban on the veil which occurred in Albania in the inter-war years reveals different phenomena. In order to build and to gain recognition for their state in the "middle of Europe", and despite—or because of—the Muslim majority in the country, Albanian political authorities and secularist intellectuals wanted to built a "modern" and "European" Islam. Their action was also dictated by a wish for secularisation in order to set up a multi-denominational nation, but also by the lower value attached to Islam among the elites. Some leaders of the Islamic Community were also convinced of the need to build a "European Islam", but not exactly in the same way, and not at the expense of a loss of power. The most significant result of their action was the appearance of a new religious elite promoting an Islam of the Qur'an and of progress, such as that presented by the Lahori Ahmadiyya working at that time in the heart of Europe for the promotion of Islam. However, the process of banning the veil shows the complexity of building a European Islam "*à l'albanaise*"—a specific approach to secularisation, submission of the upper levels of the Islamic official hierarchy to the political authorities, the difficulty that this hierarchy had in imposing itself on all Muslims in the country, and the limited impact of the reforms within Albanian society.

SHAKIB ARSLAN'S IMAGINING OF EUROPE: THE COLONISER, THE INQUISITOR, THE ISLAMIC, THE VIRTUOUS, AND THE FRIEND

Raja Adal

INTRODUCTION

For most of those belonging to the Arab and Islamic worlds of the inter-war era, Europe was primarily an image. The word "Europe" signified a broad range of meanings and elicited a range of responses. "Europe" was part of the discourse on modernising of the military and urban planning as much as on household furniture and dress styles. The image of Europe in the colonised world resulted partly from the European colonial apparatus—the sight of the European soldier, priest, or merchant. It also resulted from the writings and commentaries of Arab and Muslim travellers and *émigrés* who could claim to have experienced the "real" Europe.

Shakib Arslan began his exile in Europe in 1917, as an émigré from the ruling class of the defunct Ottoman Empire. He would remain in Europe, moving from Berlin to Lausanne to Geneva, until 1946, the year of his return to Lebanon and of his death. During these twenty-nine years of exile in Europe, Arslan negotiated with European statesmen, attended congresses throughout Europe, and entertained a network of acquaintances and friendships. Arslan's principal mouthpiece in Europe, however, was the journal *La Nation Arabe*. Appearing from 1930 to 1938 in French, the *lingua franca* of the time, *La Nation Arabe* provided Arslan with space to engage with a European audience on Arab and Islamic issues.[1]

At the same time that he participated in Europe's journalistic, political and intellectual life, Arslan was also one of the most prolific writers of the Arab world, publishing about two dozen Arabic language works and thousands of articles. Known throughout the Arab world by his epithet *amīr al-bayān*, "the prince of eloquence", which celebrated his literary talent, Arslan was as much an heir to Ottoman culture as he was a literary and political figure of the Arabic-speaking world. As an admirer of Jamal al-Din al-Afghani, a student of Muhammad Abduh, and a close friend of Rashid Rida he also enjoyed close ties to the Islamic revivalist movement. As a result, Arslan became a fulcrum of both Islamic revivalist and Arab nationalist networks which stretched to every corner of the Arab world and throughout much of the Islamic world.[2] This allowed him to simultaneously claim a central position among the former Ottoman elite, the Arab nationalists of the inter-war period, and the Islamic revivalist thinkers. It also gave him a unique measure of legitimacy that made his representation of Europe all the more authoritative to his Arab, Islamic, and European audiences. For a considerable audience in the Arab and Islamic worlds, Arslan must have stood as the foremost authority on Europe.

Arslan was the representative of the Syrian-Palestinian opposition to colonial rule before the League of Nations. As such, he produced a constant flow of articles, books, and letters assailing colonial Europe. Scholarship on Arslan has all too often been overwhelmed by this anti-colonial literary production, depicting

1 *La Nation Arabe* was co-edited by Arslan and Ihsan al-Jabiri, the two representatives of the Syrian-Palestinian Congress before the League of Nations in Geneva. Arslan was nevertheless the journal's chief contributor and the driving force behind it. All references are to the reprint edition *La Nation Arabe,* England: Archive Editions, 1988.

2 Arslan's transnational network stretched from the former Ottoman possessions of Turkey, greater Syria, Egypt, and Eastern Europe to the Arabian Gulf, the Maghreb, and Western Europe. For more on this network, see Raja Adal, "Constructing Transnational Islam: The East-West Network of Shakib Arslan", in S. Dudoignon, H. Komatsu and Y. Kosugi (eds), *Intellectuals in the Modern Islamic World: Transmission, Transformation, and Communication*, London: Routledge, 2006, pp. 176–210.

Arslan as an inveterate enemy of Europe.[3] In doing so, it has overlooked Arslan's other representations of Europe. This chapter on Arslan's imagining of inter-war Europe is based on an analysis of Arslan's journal *La Nation Arabe,* which contains many of his writings about Europe.[4] It also makes use of Arslan's Arabic language works. Five dominant images of Europe emerged from a reading of these texts.

One important image is certainly that of Europe as the coloniser. Yet Arslan's representation of colonialism was itself not devoid of subtle but essential distinctions. Arslan clearly differentiated between foreign conquest and attempts by the conquerors to transform the linguistic and religious identity of the conquered. His critique of colonialism was grounded in a second image omnipresent in Arslan's works, that of Europe as the Inquisitor. This referred as much to the Inquisition of Ferdinand and Isabella in medieval Andalusia as to contemporary colonial practice, such as the promulgation of the Berber Dahir in Morocco, which Arslan saw as a continuation of the medieval Inquisition.

The third imagining of Europe was as a land of Islam. This is apparent in Arslan's research into Europe's Arab and Islamic past in Andalusia, in his interest in the contemporary Muslim communities

[3] While Arslan appears in a variety of scholarship on Arab and Islamic movements, he is the topic of only one full length monograph, by William L. Cleveland, *Islam Against the West: Shakib Arslan and the Campaign for Islamic Nationalism*, Austin: University of Texas, 1985. Other studies of Arslan in a Western language include Martin Kramer, "The Arab Nation of Shakib Arslan", in M. Kramer, *Arab Awakening and Islamic Revival: The Politics of Ideas in the Middle East*, New Brunswick: Transaction Publishers, 1996, pp. 103–10; and Mahmoud Haddad, "The Ideas of Amir Shakib Arslan Before and After the Collapse of the Ottoman Empire", in N. Yavari, L.G. Potter, and J.-M. Oppenheim (eds), *Views from the Edge: Essays in Honour of Richard W. Bulliet*, New York: Columbia University Press, 2004, pp. 101–15. In Arabic one can find more than a dozen monographs on Arslan. The best known is the biography by Ahmad al-Sharabāsī, *Amīr al-bayān shakīb arslān,* 2 vols., Cairo: Dār al-kitāb al-'arabī, 1963.

[4] A systematic analysis was made possible by indexing all proper names and journal titles appearing in the 38 volumes of *La Nation Arabe* reprinted by Archive Editions. This index was published as Raja Adal, *Index of* La Nation Arabe, Tokyo: Islamic Area Studies Project, 2002.

of Eastern Europe, and in his presiding over the European Muslim Congress of 1935. For Arslan, Europe was exceptional because it was the cradle of modernity, and at the root of European modernity Arslan saw the lost virtues of early Islamic societies. Arslan's fourth image was therefore that of Europe as the virtuous.

Arslan also portrayed Europe as a place pregnant with cultural affinities and friendships. His fifth image is of Europe as a friend, although political circumstances often limited these friendships to anticolonial activists in colonial states and political figures in non-colonial states. These multiple representations of Europe can be seen ebbing and flowing in Arslan's works, according to his audience, to political circumstances, and to the message which he sought to convey at any given time. It is hardly surprising, however, that this layered rendering of Europe was the product of an exiled Ottoman emir from the Lebanese mountain, born a Druze, educated in American Protestant and Maronite Christian schools, married to a non-Arab, and inspired by the transnational Islamic revivalist thought of al-Afghani and Abduh.

EUROPE AS THE COLONISER

As the representative of the Syrian-Palestinian Congress to the League of Nations, Shakib Arslan's official function in Geneva was to present the case of those opposed to the French and British mandates over Syria, Lebanon, and Palestine.[5] Yet his travels, writings, and correspondence went far beyond the task of a representative. In a typical attack against the philosophy underpinning the colonial system, Arslan wrote:

[5] The Syrian Congress, later renamed the Syrian-Palestinian Congress, met in 1921 in Geneva to petition the League of Nations Permanent Mandates Commission for an end to the French and British mandates over Syria and Palestine. The delegates to the Congress elected a permanent executive committee with Michel Lutfallah as president, Rashid Rida as vice president, and Shakib Arslan as secretary. They also established a permanent delegation to the League of Nations in Geneva headed by Shakib Arslan and Ihsan al-Jabiri. For more information on the Congress, see Marie-Renée Mouton, "Le congrès syrio-palestinien de Genève (1921)", *Relations Internationales*, 19 (autumn 1979), pp. 313–28.

It is thus that all of that which an authentic history of colonisation by the French, British, Dutch, Italians, and others . . . would call injustices, cruelties, spoliations, thievery, massacres, and absurdities of all kinds is called 'a will to civilize and co-opt in view of a better future!'[6]

Every issue of Arslan's journal sought to take apart the colonial discourse of civilisation and benevolence. More often than not, wrote Arslan, colonial policies could be traced to a power struggle among European states carried out through the plunder of Asian and African nations.[7]

The content of Shakib Arslan's anti-colonialism is perhaps best understood by looking at the more problematic margins of Arslan's anti-colonial discourse, where the colonial ceases to appear as exclusively evil. One such case is Arslan's own confession of his "enormous respect which borders on a cult" for Marshal Lyautey, France's Resident General in Morocco. In Arslan's eyes, Lyautey was the quintessentially good colonial ruler, whose intelligence and tact contributed as much to the success of French policy as they impaired nationalist efforts at ending French rule over Morocco:

One cannot explain [. . .] my esteem, along with sympathy, for a man who subjected Morocco to France, reducing this great Islamic heritage to a simple French colony [. . .] Lyautey is, from an indigenous point of view, the most dangerous Frenchman which Northern Africa has ever known, because he is the wisest. By his wisdom he knew how to calm the Arabs; he attracted them by every means towards France; he upheld their self-esteem and avoided as much as possible wounding them so as better to harness them.[8]

Thankfully, added Arslan, Lyautey was not in charge of Syria, for his know-how and wisdom would have prevented Syrian nationalism from emerging.[9]

While Lyautey never represented France in Syria, Arslan did encounter a relatively conciliatory French High Commissioner of Syria, Henry de Jouvenel. At the start of the Syrian revolt of

[6] Chekib Arslan, "Une nouvelle philosophie coloniale", *La Nation Arabe*, February 1931, p. 1. Unless otherwise noted, all translations are my own.

[7] Ibid., p. 5.

[8] Chekib Arslan, "Le plus grand et le plus fin colonial de France", *La Nation Arabe* (May-June 1931), p. 30.

[9] Ibid., p. 31.

1925–26, which shook French rule in Syria, the unpopular French High Commissioner, Maurice Sarrail, was replaced with the more liberal Jouvenel. In November 1925, Jouvenel invited Arslan to travel from Geneva to Paris for negotiations on Syrian independence. Arslan's moderation apparently impressed Jouvenel, who invited him the following year for further talks with two other members of the Syrian-Palestinian Congress executive committee, Ihsan al-Jabiri and Michel Lutfallah.[10] Arslan's writings reveal his esteem for Jouvenel, whom he describes as "intelligent" and "realistic", blaming the failure of the talks on the French Prime Minister Poincaré.[11] Upon hearing of the discussions with the Syrian nationalists, Poincaré is said to have exclaimed against "[discussions with] the enemies of France", whereupon the talks were cancelled and Jouvenel was replaced as High Commissioner of Syria by Henri Ponsot.[12] Ten years later, when France agreed to sign a treaty with the Syrian nationalist leaders, Arslan was no longer considered the enemy of France but its strategic ally. The French Vice-Minister of Foreign Affairs Viénot, who met Arslan in Geneva, considered his support for the treaty crucial to obtaining its ratification by the Syrian Chamber of Deputies.[13]

[10] For the first meeting between Arslan and Jouvenel, see Philip S. Khoury, "Factionalism Among Syrian Nationalists During the French Mandate", *International Journal of Middle East Studies*, XIII, 4 (1981), pp. 441–69. For a description of the sessions of the subsequent meetings, see Chekib Arslan, "Le traité franco-syrien", *La Nation Arabe* (September-November 1936), pp. 641–8; and by the same author, "Le départ de M. Ponsot", *La Nation Arabe* (July-September 1933), pp. 37–8. Arslan's version of events is partly confirmed by the French Socialist Robert-Jean Longuet's article in the journal *Clarté* of March 1938, reprinted as Robert-Jean Longuet, "A propos de la Syrie", *La Nation Arabe* (January-April 1938), pp. 891–7; by E. Lévi-Provençal, "L'Émir Shakib Arslan", *Cahiers de l'Orient contemporain* IX-X (1st and 2nd trimester 1947), pp. 5–19; and by Meir Zamir, *The Formation of Modern Lebanon*, Ithaca: Cornell University Press, 1985, p. 198.

[11] C. Arslan, "Le traité franco-syrien", p. 642.

[12] Chekib Arslan, "Il y a, paraît-il, un comité franco-musulman: Toujours l'Afrique du Nord", *La Nation Arabe* (November-December 1934), pp. 133–4.

[13] Bureau Politique, état-major, théâtre d'opérations de l'Afrique du Nord, *Contribution à l'étude de l'activité politique de l'émir Chekib Arslan*, Aix-en-Provence, 29H35, 1940, pp. 28–9; also see Arslan, "Le traité franco-syrien", p. 645; and Arslan, "L'ennemi de la France que je suis?", *La Nation Arabe* (January-April 1938), pp. 801–2.

An inveterate politician, Arslan's attitude towards a colonial power could also change. Arslan's critique of Italy's treatment of Arabs in its Libyan colony led Mussolini, who was concerned about Italy's image in the Arab world, to seek a dialogue. Arslan responded to Italy's overtures, moving from a highly critical to a more conciliatory attitude. From 1930 to 1933 at least twelve articles in *La Nation Arabe* contained scathing critiques of Italy's policies in Libya. While retaining its critical tone, 1933 saw the journal begin to point toward specific ways in which Italy could improve the conditions of Arabs in its colonies. In mid-1933, *La Nation Arabe* printed several Italian documents announcing an Italian policy of non-interference in local and religious affairs, the abolition of prison camps, and amnesties. Arslan touted this as a "radical change in Italian policy" that could usher an era of collaboration between Libyans and Italians "for the prosperity of Libya".[14] On a trip to Rome in 1934 Arslan met Mussolini twice, as well as Marquis Theodoli, President of the Permanent Mandates Commission of the League of Nations. Arslan described his change of attitude in the following terms:

> When we cried out in condemnation against the unbelievable acts which General Graziani had committed, Mussolini sought to have a conversation with us and sent us an envoy to find out what should be done to repair these wrongs. We answered that before anything else, the Arabs should be reintegrated into their homes. He did it and saved them from a certain death [. . .] also upon our request, three to four hundred Arabs condemned to twenty to thirty years of prison term were amnestied. On our request also, the properties which are called 'waqf' [. . .] were restored to the Muslims [. . .] Muslim education. . .was restored in all state schools [. . .] We asked for the prohibition of all Christian religious propaganda among Muslims [. . .] Mussolini himself told us that it was absolutely forbidden and that he would never tolerate such propaganda.[15]

Thereafter, Arslan's stance towards Italy warmed considerably. At the European Muslim Congress of 1935 presided by Arslan, the Italian scholar Laura Vaglieri was the only non-Muslim allowed to

[14] Chekib Arslan, "L'Italie et le Monde Arabe", *La Nation Arabe* (April-June 1933), pp. 23–31.

[15] Chekib Arslan, "Le problème éthiopien", *La Nation Arabe* (January-April 1936), pp. 514–15.

speak. On the same occasion, Arslan himself read a letter from a Libyan Arab praising the great improvements in Italian policies towards the local population, while concluding that much remained to be done.[16]

Arslan's praise of Italy in *La Nation Arabe* and in the Arab press gave his opponents a unique opportunity to discredit him. In 1935, a journal opposed to Arslan published what it claimed was a letter from Arslan to Hajj Amin al-Husaini, Mufti of Jerusalem and President of the Supreme Muslim Council of Palestine, outlining a plan for making Italian propaganda in the Arab world. Arslan's efforts to demonstrate that the letter was a forgery provide us with a rare insight into the pan-Arab concerns that guided his policies.[17] Arslan certainly credited Mussolini for improving the actual conditions of Arabs in Libya. Beyond Libya, however, Arslan saw in a European Great Power such as Italy a useful ally in promoting Syrian independence, in opposing Jewish immigration into Palestine, and in securing Iraqi independence:

> Having played a very obliging role on the issue of Iraqi independence, Italy could also help us in Syria and in Palestine with a pro-Arab policy. Our [Arslan and Jabiri's] mission as representatives of the Arabs in Europe, gives us the duty to look out for Arab interests everywhere. We have been several times to Paris. We have been several times to London. We can therefore, for the same cause, go to Rome.[18]

Arslan's ultimate concern, however, was not limited to the liberation of Syria from colonial rule. Nor was it limited to the abolition of colonialism for its own sake. Its ultimate objective was the preservation of the cultural and religious values of Arabism and Islam. More often than not, European colonialism endangered these values. This explains both Arslan's adamant resistance to colonialism and his willingness to negotiate with colonial powers for the protection of these core values.

[16] "Urkunden: Der Muslimische Kongreß von Europa", *Die Welt des Islams*, XVII, 3–4 (1935), p. 101; "Le Congrès Musulman d'Europe", *La Nation Arabe* (October-November 1935), pp. 417–24.

[17] Chekib Arslan, "Une perfidie inouïe : On nous fait la guerre avec des faux", *La Nation Arabe* (March-April 1935), pp. 277–81.

[18] Ibid., pp. 278–9.

EUROPE AS THE INQUISITOR

Colonialism could cause Arab and Islamic identity to disappear into thin air. Muslim Spain represented the quintessential example of both the construction of an Arab Islamic civilisation and its disappearance. It was a subject which Arslan revisited in no less than three works.[19] He also wrote on the history of Andalusia in the Arab press and in a series of articles that appeared in *La Nation Arabe* in 1930–31.[20] In Arslan's writings on Islamic Spain, the Inquisition is seen imposing a religious and linguistic conversion upon the conquered Muslim populations. Contemporary European colonial practices, Arslan argued, engaged in a similar project:

> Some of them [Europeans] say that such things [as the Inquisition] happened in the Middle Ages. If we concede that these incidents happened during the Middle Age, what would they say then of the crimes and atrocities that were committed by the white European race in the course of this very century, whether in the nineteenth century or the twentieth century, of what they did in their colonisation of Central Africa, Northern Africa, the Congo, the Egyptian Sudan, and of what they have done in India and elsewhere in Asia, and of what happened with their knowledge in Rumelia during the Balkan War, even what they did to each other during the World War . . . all of this did not occur in the Middle Ages, nor in the European Dark Ages, but occurred in the Age of Enlightenment and at the pinnacle of European civilisation and of pride in its refinement.[21]

Although the values of the Enlightenment touted by the French left regularly found their way into Arslan's writings in *La Nation Arabe,* they were mixed with cynicism and a pervading sense of

[19] Shakīb Arslān, *Al-hulal al-sundusiyya fī al-akhbār wa al-athār al-andalusiyya,* 1936–1939; repr., Beirut: Dār maktabat al-hayāh, 1966; Shakīb Arslān, *Khulāsat tārīkh al-andalus,* 1925, repr. Beirut: Dār maktabat al-hayāh, 1983; Al-Fīkūnt dū Shātūbriyyān, *Al-islām fī al-andalus: ākhir banī sirāj,* trans. Shakīb Arslān, 1925, repr. Beirut: Dār maktabat al-hayāh, 1985.

[20] Chekib Arslan, "Une page sur l'effort constructif des Arabes en Espagne", *La Nation Arabe* (June 1930), pp. 186–91; Chekib Arslan, "A la recherche des vestiges de la civilisation arabe en Espagne", *La Nation Arabe* (July 1930), pp. 193–200; and Chekib Arslan, "A la recherche des vestiges arabes en Espagne et dans le Midi de la France", *La Nation Arabe* (March 1931), pp. 19–31.

[21] Lūthrub Stūdārd, *Hādir al-'ālam al-islāmī,* trans. 'Ajjāj Nuwayhid, comp. Shakīb Arslān, 1924, repr. Beirut: Dār al-fikr, 1971, p. 209.

hypocrisy. "We have suspicions, even about you, statesmen of the left", wrote Arslan, that "once in power, you become dreadfully imperialist".[22] Arslan had little faith in the ethical values of European modernity once they were projected into Europe's colonial possessions.

Some of Arslan's greatest conflicts with the colonial powers were about what he saw as attempts to convert Muslims to Christianity and to prevent Arabs from learning Arabic. In May 1930, the French Protectorate authorities in Morocco promulgated the Berber Dahir. The Dahir placed Moroccan Berber populations, which had been Islamised in the early days of Islam, under the jurisdiction of French courts and Berber tribunals, which applied a revived Berber customary law antecedent to Islam. This, in effect, withdrew Berbers from the jurisdiction of Islamic courts. The impression of many Muslims was that this was the French colonial authority's attempt to de-Islamise the Berber communities. This impression was reinforced when a special permit was required for Moroccans to travel between the "Arab regions" and "Berber regions" of Morocco, Muslim religious education was banned in the Berber regions, and French missionary activity in the Berber regions increased.[23] For his part, Arslan lamented how "the [French] civilian, democratic, and secular Republic *par excellence* could lend itself to such an unfortunate game".[24]

For Arslan, contemporary French authorities in Morocco were pursuing the work of the Spanish Inquisition:

[The French Resident General of Morocco] Mr Saint needs to justify himself and appear as completing the work of Ferdinand and Isabella in this century. They converted the Moors of Spain, and he will convert the Moors of Africa. . . . Why not? Was the conversion of the Moors of Spain not the consequence of the fall of Muslim political power in Spain? Well, now it is Muslim political power in Africa which is in decline [. . .] This is the reasoning of Mr Saint and Co.: to exploit French political power with

22 C. Arslan, "L'ennemi de la France que je suis?", p. 809.

23 John P. Halstead, *Rebirth of a Nation: The Origins and Rise of Moroccan Nationalism, 1912–1944*, Cambridge, MA: Harvard University Press, 1967.

24 Chekib Arslan, "Tribunaux Berbères", *La Nation Arabe* (August-September 1930), pp. 27–8.

the aim of detaching the Berbers, who consist of approximately eight million souls, from the Islamic religion.[25]

In response, Arslan launched an international campaign against the Berber Dahir. It consisted of approximately a dozen articles in *La Nation Arabe,* numerous others in the Arabic press, and the co-authoring of a resolution that was sent to the League of Nations by the Universal Muslim Congress in Jerusalem. According to Le Tourneau, it was because of Shakib Arslan that what had been an exclusively Moroccan issue was catapulted into the headlines of the Islamic press.[26] The fight over the Berber Dahir also contributed to establishing a boundary for religious policy beyond which a colonial power could not proceed without instigating a storm of protests.

Among the range of conceivable colonial practices, Arslan made a careful distinction between what he considered egalitarian and benevolent colonial policies and the policies of the Inquisition. When the Berber Dahir was repealed in 1934, partly as a result of his efforts, Arslan praised the wisdom and enlightened attitude of Ponsot, the new French Resident General in Morocco, who "would be capable of causing much appeasement in Morocco if there were not beside him soldiers, priests, and colonists".[27] For Arslan, these "new Inquisitors" represented the vilest face of colonialism.

Some of Arslan's writings go as far as to suggest that he was fundamentally opposed to colonialism only to the extent that it implied a contemporary "Inquisition" which endangered the religious and linguistic identity of Muslims and Arabs. Arslan's reaction to the Blum-Viollette plan established under the Popular Front government of Léon Blum in 1936 is revealing of his intricate stance regarding French Algeria. The Blum-Viollette plan sought to allow a limited number of Muslim Algerians to acquire French citizenship without having to give up the Islamic personal legal status

25 Ibid.

26 Roger le Tourneau, *Evolution politique de l'Afrique du nord musulmane, 1920–1961*, Paris: Armand Colin, 1962, p. 185.

27 Chekib Arslan, "Et le fameux Dahir berbère?", *La Nation Arabe* (September-October 1934), p. 66.

which governed their personal and family matters. To some, it was a first step to granting all Algerians French citizenship. In a short but approving article, Arslan endorsed Maurice Viollette, the co-author of the plan, as "a man who is sincere and a realist", and sharply criticised the opposition of the French colonists in Algeria and the French press.[28] This article leaves open the very interesting question: how accommodating would Arslan have been to the creation of a French Algeria where all Muslims could become Frenchmen without losing their Islamic personal legal status?

Considering that the Blum-Viollette plan sought to make Algeria a permanent part of France, Arslan's approving tone seems to indicate that he preferred supporting a French and Muslim Algeria to sabotaging any rapprochement with France in the name of future Algerian independence. This stance contradicts Arslan's previously mentioned position vis-à-vis Lyautey, the "most dangerous Frenchman [. . .] because the wisest".[29] Yet it matches another position taken by Arslan in 1935, when he writes that for the feelings of indigenous politicians vis-à-vis France to change, it was necessary for "the Muslim [to] be conscious, while remaining Muslim, of his dignity, of his rights, and of his equality with the Frenchman".[30] This discrepancy may be due to the difference between Morocco and Algeria, the latter being an integral part of France, where Arslan only hoped to salvage its religious and cultural identity by opposing its subjugation in a contemporary Inquisition. Or it may be that between 1931 and 1938 Arslan came to terms with the possibility of being fully Arab, Muslim and French, not only on the European continent but also in such a thoroughly Gallicised region as colonial Algeria.

EUROPE AS A LAND OF ISLAM

If Arslan represented Europe as Coloniser and Inquisitor, he also portrayed it as a land of Islam. His last two historical works on

[28] Chekib Arslan, "Le Projet Viollette pour l'Algérie", *La Nation Arabe* (January-April 1938), p. 882.

[29] C. Arslan, "Le plus grand et le plus fin colonial de France", p. 30.

[30] Chekib Arslan, "Ce n'est pas par l'assimilation mais par la justice et l'égalité que la France peut réussir dans le nord de l'Afrique", *La Nation Arabe* (March-April 1935), p. 263.

Islamic Europe were written after a trip to Southern France, Spain, and Morocco in 1930. On his way to Tangier in Morocco, he stopped in Toulouse, Carcassonne, Narbonne, Montpellier, Nîmes, Avignon, Marseilles, Antibes, Cannes, Nice, Madrid, and Cordoba to collect documents for his historical projects. He was joined in Cordoba by two young Moroccan nationalist leaders studying in Paris, 'Allal al-Fassi and Ahmad Balafrej.[31] Arslan then continued to Morocco, where his passage would be short but politically consequential, making him one of the principal international advisers and promoters of the Moroccan anticolonial campaign.[32] His two young companions in Cordoba would later become the two most prominent figures of the Moroccan nationalist movement.[33] It must have been largely for such nationalist leaders studying in Europe that, in the early 1930s, Arslan wrote his two works on the history of Moorish Spain. For Arslan, the history of Islamic Europe as written by Christian authors told of the triumph of Western Christian civilisation in repelling the Arab and Muslim Other. Arslan mentions that his several volumes on the history of Muslim Arabs in Europe would allow "that [history] which is ours to be returned unto us".[34] A transformation of the relationship between the Arab-Islamic world and modern Europe entailed a reclamation of the Medieval Arab and Islamic past in Europe.

For Arslan, Islamic Spain was a splendid civilisation. Cordoba was a jewel of Europe, a city with which no other European city of its time could compare in size and grandeur.[35] The Muslim Arab conquerors of yore were few but brave. Although there were relatively

[31] C. Arslan, "A la recherche des vestiges de la civilisation arabe en Espagne", p. 193.

[32] W. Cleveland, *Islam Against the West,* chap. 5 and R. Adal, "Constructing Transnational Islam".

[33] John P. Halstead, *Rebirth of a Nation*, p. 165.

[34] C. Arslān, *Khulāsat tārīkh al-andalus*, p. 9. In addition to his three works on Islamic Andalusia (see note 19), Arslan wrote *A History of the Arab Conquests in France, Switzerland, Italy, and the Mediterranean Islands*: Shakīb Arslān, *Tārīkh ghazawāt al-'arab fī faransā wa suwīsrā wa ītāliyā wa jazā'ir al-bahr al-mutawassit,* Cairo: Matba'at 'Īsa al-bābī al-halabī, 1933.

[35] Shakīb Arslān, *Limādhā ta'akhkhara al-muslimūn wa limādhā taqaddama ghayruhum,* 1930; repr. Cairo: Matba'at 'Īsa al-bābī al-halabī, 1358 [1939–40], p. 111.

small numbers of them in Spain or even the Alps, their ventures were crowned with success, for they possessed virtues which contemporary Muslim Arabs had lost.[36] To an Arab and Islamic world where it was becoming commonplace to see Europeans as the conquerors, the rulers, and the source of enlightened civilisation, there was something profoundly tantalising about a past in which the exact opposite had been true and Muslim Arabs had held political power on the European continent. Arslan's several volumes on medieval Islamic Europe sought to use this historical capital to urge his contemporaries towards a political and economic revival.

While Arslan shared a historical interest in medieval Islamic Europe, and a close relationship with several leaders of the immigrant Arab communities,[37] he also enjoyed exceptionally close personal ties to the contemporary Islamic communities of Eastern Europe. Arslan was himself of Circassian origin on his mother's side, and his wife Salima, whose parents had emigrated from the Caucasus, was also Circassian. As a former Ottoman parliamentarian, soldier, and diplomat who had coordinated the activities of the Red Crescent benevolent society in the Balkans at the time of the Balkan war, Arslan also had longstanding acquaintances and friendships in these former Ottoman possessions.[38] In the early 1930s,

[36] Ibid., pp. 61–2. For Arslan's comments on an article about the Arabs in the Alps, see Chekib Arslan, "Les Arabes dans les Alpes : Étude historique", *La Nation Arabe* (November-December 1931), pp. 63–4.

[37] They included several leaders from the Maghreb, such as 'Allal al-Fassi and Ahmad Balafrej, mentioned above, as well as Messali Hadj, whose break with the French Communist Party and "conversion" to an Islamic ideology of resistance followed six months spent with Arslan in Geneva (see R. Adal, "Constructing Transnational Islam"). Although *La Nation Arabe* often mentioned immigrant Arab leaders in Europe and gave them a forum to publish their manifestos and positions, it eschewed references to class divisions within the immigrant population in favour of an image of Arab and Muslim unity.

[38] Arslan's extensive focus on the Muslim populations of Eastern Europe can be explained by his extensive network in these former Ottoman possessions and by his having maintained an Ottoman ideal of ethnic pluralism long after the fall of the Empire. In the last years of the Empire, Arslan parted ways with many other Ottoman Arabs, such as his longtime friend Rashid Rida, and did not join the Arab revolt. His strategic shift to Arabism from 1921 onwards was grounded in the Arab literary past and the Islamic religion rather than in any idea of racial unity or even of political unity between the Eastern and Western Arab worlds.

Arslan once again undertook a series of trips to the region. He worked tirelessly at bringing what were, with the exception of Yugoslavia and Albania, relatively small Muslim communities into the limelight of the Arab and Islamic press.[39]

Despite its name, between 1932 and 1936 *La Nation Arabe* devoted at least twelve articles to the Muslim communities of Bulgaria, Romania, Poland, Yugoslavia, and Hungary. These articles were both descriptive and ascriptive. They often began by giving the history and statistics of a Muslim community in each Eastern European state, and ended by evoking the community's attachment and fidelity to the state. Yet the way in which relations between each Eastern European state and its Muslim minority were represented in *La Nation Arabe* was itself a politically contentious issue. This can be seen in the polemic between Smail Dchemalovitch and André Girard, law professor at the University of Paris, on the conditions of Muslims in Bulgaria. While Dchemalovitch offered a rather bleak image of the treatment of Bulgarian Muslims by the state, Girard questioned Dchemalovitch's motives and offered a much more positive assessment of Bulgarian state policies.[40]

Arslan's focus on Eastern Europe may also have reflected a certain natural process of specialisation among Arab nationalist and Muslim revivalist writers. His exile in Switzerland, where his visa prohibited him from expressly engaging in political activities, only allowed him to reach the immigrant Arab and Muslim communities in Europe through his journal and through his personal influence upon the political leaders of these communities. On the other hand, very few in the Arab and Islamic worlds were better equipped to engage with Eastern Europe's Muslim communities.

[39] Alexandre Popovic, *L'Islam balkanique: Les musulmans du sud-est européen dans la période post-ottomane*, Wiesbaden: Harrassowitz, 1986, p. 191.

[40] The polemic begins with a short introduction by Arslan in Chekib Arslan, "La vérité sur la situation des Musulmans en Bulgarie", *La Nation Arabe* (October-December 1932), pp. 10–12; this is followed by the argument of Dchemalovitch in Smail Aga Djemalovitch, "Les Musulmans en Bulgarie", *La Nation Arabe* (October-December 1932), pp. 12–20; the answer by Girard can be found in André Girard, "La situation des Musulmans en Bulgarie", *La Nation Arabe* (January-March 1933), pp. 37–46 (including a preface by Arslan); finally, there was a counter-reply by Dchemalovitch in Smail Aga Dchemalovitch, "Les Musulmans en Bulgarie", *La Nation Arabe* (April-June 1933), pp. 36–44 (including a preface by Arslan).

The European Muslim Congress of 1935, in which Arslan played a key role, also sought to represent the totality of European Islam. This included giving equal attention to the Eastern and Western European Muslim communities. The approximately seventy representatives to the Congress, as well as the list of speakers at the Congress, reveal an almost equal distribution between Eastern and Western Europe. The Council of Delegates, which consisted of one representative for each state, was also largely balanced. It included delegates from five states in Eastern Europe (Bulgaria, Romania, Poland, Yugoslavia, and Hungary) and seven states in Western Europe (England, Scotland, Holland, France, Switzerland, Austria, and Italy). Thus did the organisers of the European Muslim Congress attempt, at least symbolically, to bring together members from across Europe, giving voice to an ostensibly common Islamic European identity. The congress sought to represent Europe in all its geographic breadth, not as a foreign or hostile territory but as a land of Islam. Opening with a prayer by the imam of the Paris Mosque, it closed with a prayer by the president of the Council of 'Ulama in Sarajevo.[41]

Although the European Muslim Congress was not Arslan's idea, it largely became his project once he was asked to preside over it. With a few exceptions, the Permanent Committee of the Congress consisted of Arslan's friends and associates. While Arslan himself was president, Ihsan al-Jabiri, his colleague on the permanent delegation of the Syrian-Palestinian Congress and the co-editor of *La Nation Arabe,* was vice president. The secretary was Ali al-Ghayati, the editor of the Geneva journal *La Tribune d'Orient* and a friend of Arslan. Finally, the adjunct secretary was Dr Zaki Aly, a physician, who for a time was Arslan's private secretary. The other members of the Permanent Committee were the treasurer Abd al-Baki al-Omari, a lawyer from Egypt; Ziya' al-Din Tabataba'i, the secretary general of the Universal Muslim Congress in Jerusalem and a former prime minister of Iran; and Mahmud Salim, an Egyptian journalist residing in Paris, who had originally promoted the

[41] For more details on the European Muslim Congress, see Martin Kramer, *Islam Assembled: The Advent of Muslim Congresses*, New York: Columbia University Press, 1986, pp. 129–31.

Congress and offered Arslan the presidency. Thus, Arslan was largely uncontested in his leadership of the European Muslim Congress, which in many ways came to reflect his vision of a European Islam.

The declared purpose of the Congress was to develop a synthesis of Islam and modernity for teaching in Islamic schools, with the goal of placing "Europe's Muslim populations at the same level of instruction and education as that of other confessions".[42] Yet in bringing Muslims living on European soil together for the first time, the Congress symbolically established Islam as a European religion while simultaneously defining the contents of a European Islam. While the above paragraphs described the participants in the Congress, those excluded from it may reveal even more about the ways in which the Congress and its president, Shakib Arslan, simultaneously formulated and represented a European Islam.

The most conspicuous exclusion from the European Muslim Congress was the Turkish Republic.[43] This was not for lack of official Turkish interest in attending the congress. On the contrary, Republican Turkey was the only state to express strong interest in participating. In the early stages of preparation for the congress, the Turkish Ambassador to Switzerland, Cemal Husni, requested an official invitation for Turkey. In exchange, he promised to allow Muslim representatives from the province of Edirne, which lay on the European side of the Bosporus, to attend. Arslan was persistent in his opposition to Turkey's attendance. He unceremoniously sought to put an end to the ambassador's overtures by telling him:

[42] Declaration by I.S. Hakky at the Commissariat de Police, Geneva, Swiss Federal Archives, Doc. C10.3 E 4320 (B) 1984/29, vol. XIII, 19 March 1935.

[43] Albania, the only other European country with a Muslim majority, also did not participate in the Congress, although the reasons for its absence are unknown. In the pages of *La Nation Arabe* the most conspicuous element about Albania is its almost complete absence. In the journal's eight years of publication, not a single article was written about Albania, despite the fact that other Central and Eastern European states with the smallest of Muslim minorities were thoroughly discussed. For some possible reasons regarding Albania's absence from the Congress, see in this volume Nathalie Clayer, "Behind the Veil: The Reform of Islam in Inter-war Albania or the Search for a 'Modern' and 'European' Islam". It can be surmised that the reasons for Albania's non-participation in the Congress were fairly similar to those that led to Turkey's exclusion.

"In short, we have excluded you from our activities".[44] The Turkish Ambassador made further requests to Arslan's colleague Ihsan al-Jabiri, and a majority of the preparatory committee of the congress seems to have favoured sending Turkey an official invitation. Yet Arslan remained intractable, and the committee sent a letter of invitation to the Mufti of Edirne instead.[45]

The reasons for Arslan's exclusion of the Turkish Republic can be most directly traced to its opposition to the 1931 Universal Muslim Congress in Jerusalem. The Turkish government in Ankara had done everything to foil the activities of that congress. It had exhorted the British authorities to outlaw it, prevented Iran and Afghanistan from participating, and removed the Turkish flag from among the flags of Muslim countries hanging at the congress. Arslan was deeply resentful of these obstructions. The only reason that the Turkish government now coveted a place at the European Muslim Congress, he wrote, was so that it would not be said among Balkan Muslims that Turkey was denied an invitation.[46]

Yet upon closer examination, Arslan's refusal to allow Republican Turkish representatives to participate in the European Muslim Congress may have been caused by more than the memory of Turkey's opposition to the Universal Muslim Congress in Jerusalem. It revealed a fundamental difference in visions of European Islam. The European Muslim Congress presided by Arslan called for assistance in building mosques and Islamic schools in Warsaw, Budapest, Amsterdam, and Geneva; discussed the rights of Muslims in various European

[44] Arslān to Rashīd Riḍā, Geneva, 8 Rabiʿ al-thānī 1352 [1 August 1933], quoted in al-Sharabāsī, *Amīr al-bayān shakīb arslān*, II, p. 816.

[45] Ibid., pp. 817–18. Arslan was personally acquainted with many Turkish representatives from his days as an Ottoman parliamentarian and close associate of the Ottoman leadership. At that time, Arslan was perhaps the most eloquent Arab advocate of associating the political destinies of Arabs and Turks within the framework of the Ottoman Empire. He participated in campaigns with Ottoman generals to defend the empire, and developed friendships with Talat Pasha, Enver Pasha, and Mustafa Kemal (the future Atatürk). For the story of his encounter with Mustafa Kemal at the Green Mountain in Libya and again in Paris, see Chekib Arslan, "Congrès Pan-Islamique", *La Nation Arabe* (November-December 1931), pp. 9–13; and R. Adal, "Constructing Transnational Islam".

[46] Arslān to Riḍā in al-Sharabāsī, *Amīr al-bayān shakīb arslān*, II, p. 817.

countries; and read a message by the Austrian scholar Herbert Jansky encouraging Islamic countries to follow Europe in science and technology but not in social and cultural matters.[47] The congress' promotion of Islamic educational, religious, and social institutions contrasted with the social policies of Republican Turkey as depicted by *La Nation Arabe*. These included the abolition of the Caliphate; the suppression of religious education; the closing of mosques; the banning of religiously inspired clothing outside mosques; the adoption of European names; and the obligation to wear a European hat.[48]

Arslan's conversation with the Turkish Ambassador Cemal Husni and the writer Necmeddin Sadak in Geneva in 1933 also illustrated these differences regarding European Islam. When the ambassador asked Arslan why Turkey was not being invited to the congress despite the fact that the province of Edirne was in Europe, Arslan replied: "Because we have seen Turkey eschew involvement in Islamic issues". The response came from the ambassador's companion, Necmeddin Sadak: "But we have interest in this congress from a social perspective".[49] For Arslan, Islam was more than a social policy.

Arslan's critique of inter-war Turkey centred on its active removal of Islam from public life and on its suppression of Islamic symbols in favour of "European" ones. For Arslan, an authentic European Islam could not compromise Islamic traditions in order to become more European. Instead, he sought a syncretism of the "Islamic" and the "European" that would eliminate incongruities between the two terms. In his eyes, Republican Turkey was creating a dichotomy between the European and the Islamic by creating opposition between Islamic and European clothes, Islamic Arab names and European names, and European hats and late Ottoman headwear. With such conflicting visions of a European Islam, it was only consistent for the European Muslim Congress presided over by Arslan to exclude Republican Turkey from its proceedings.

47 "Le Congrès Musulman d'Europe", pp. 417–24.

48 Chekib Arslan, "La piété en Turquie", *La Nation Arabe* (February 1931), p. 16; Chekib Arslan, "Les innovations continuent dans la Turquie kemaliste", *La Nation Arabe* (January-February 1935), p. 181.

49 Arslān to Riḍā in al-Sharabāsī, *Amīr al-bayān shakīb arslān*, II, p. 816.

EUROPE AS THE VIRTUOUS

Arslan's writing did not give Muslims a monopoly on virtue. In a series of articles in Rashid Rida's journal *al-Manār* in 1929, Arslan responded to a question asked of him by an imam from the island of Borneo in Indonesia. The gist of that question became the title of Arslan's best known work, *Why Have Muslims Fallen Behind While Others Progressed*.[50] In a tightly argued response, Arslan compared the contemporary condition of Muslims to three models: the Islamic past, Europe, and Japan. All three represent the virtues of sacrifice and effort. The virtues of the early Muslim conquerors are the same as those of the Europeans (*ifranj*) and the Japanese, who are always ready to sacrifice lives and money for their nation (*watan*). Arslan makes careful comparisons of the per capita sacrifice in lives and wealth incurred by various European nations during the First World War, concluding that contemporary Muslims have comparatively little solidarity with their coreligionists or desire to help any cause greater than their petty personal interests. It would be abnormal, he concludes, for contemporary Muslims, who share little of the virtues of their forefathers, to benefit as much from the bounty of God. On the contrary, "if Muslims revive their determination, they can achieve what their Book urges them to do, namely to reach the level of Europeans, Americans, and Japanese in knowledge and progress".[51]

Arslan's work made abundant use of European and Japanese history, mixing it with Islamic historical and textual sources, to construct a logic which explained the power and wealth of the colonisers and the helplessness and destitution of much of the contemporary Islamic world. By making constant references to well-known Islamic scriptures and historical events, Arslan made his work easily intelligible to Muslim audiences. At the same time, his use of the scriptural tenets contained in the Qur'an and *hadith*s gave these texts new explanatory power in elucidating what Arslan

[50] Arslān, *Limādhā ta'akhkharā al-muslimūn wa limādhā taqaddama ghayruhum*. This work has been translated into several languages including English, Malay-Indonesian, Serbo-Croat, and Turkish.

[51] Ibid., p. 166.

saw as the decline of Muslim civilisation in all of its aspects, spiritual as much as intellectual and material.

Although Arslan does not elaborate a concept of modernity, he establishes a clear commensurability between what is considered novel today and what was considered novel in previous times. The contemporary age does not have any particular quality that differentiates it from previous ages. Nor is it necessary for modernity to instigate a Hegelian break with the past, to stop referring to models of another age and to create its own norms. The values of the European Enlightenment may have held some appeal for Arslan, but the Enlightenment was not a universally relevant seminal moment when humanity achieved maturity. In Arslan's *Why Have Muslims Fallen Behind While Others Progressed*, history functions neither according to a teleology of decline nor according to one of progress. This leads Arslan to criticise those Muslims who, stuck in the past, do not engage with the new. It also leads to a critique of Muslims who believe in the necessity of abandoning their linguistic or religious heritage in order to be modern. In the end, for Arslan religion is neither a cause of decline nor a cause of progress. Just as Christianity was not the cause of the decline of Greek culture in the Middle Ages, Islam is not the cause of the decline of Arabs in contemporary times. On the contrary, he argues, Islam enjoins Muslims toward rejuvenation and solidarity, both of which are universal virtues which can be seen in contemporary Japanese and European civilisations.[52]

The conclusion to *Why Have Muslims Fallen Behind While Others Progressed* was penned in Lausanne, in Switzerland, in 1930. It is likely that the body of that work was written there. It took someone like Arslan, who resided in Europe and had in many ways already internalised the value system of the modern developed world and its hierarchy of civilisations based on material prosperity and military power, to see in the economic and military subjugation of the Islamic world a sign of its spiritual decadence. Europe and Japan became the backdrop, the virtuous societies comparable to early Islamic society, against which the contemporary Islamic world was critiqued. Yet their success was not only congruent with

[52] Ibid., pp. 113–17.

the teachings of Islamic scriptures: the keys to that success would have been found by Muslims on their own had they remained true to the teachings of their scriptures. While throughout his writings Arslan sympathetically refers to the values of the Renaissance and Enlightenment, he would probably have argued that their equivalent in the Muslim world was the Islamic revelation itself, in both its scriptural and historical traditions. For Arslan, what was needed in order to escape colonial subjugation and social lethargy was a revival of that tradition.

EUROPE AS THE FRIEND

Europe was also a deeply familiar place, in terms of both culture and personal friendships. In 1917, when Arslan was sent by the Ottoman government to investigate the condition of its ally Germany, he visited the Goethe House in Frankfurt. In Goethe's memory he penned a poem in Arabic:

> I bowed the head of my muse before his gate
> Before his doorstep how many have lain prostrate
> Although he is not of my community nor my kin
> The community of man in literature is one
> (For if a common genealogy we do not share
> Between us literature holds the place of the father).[53]

During the centennial commemoration of Goethe's death in 1932, Arslan wrote of his "infinite regret" that, while many countries were represented, "governments from the Orient" did not take part in the remembrance of "the greatest German poet and perhaps the greatest European poet".[54]

As one of the few European Great Powers with almost no colonial possessions, Germany offered Arslan a rare chance for fraternal

[53] Guest book, Das Goethe Haus, 10 October 1917. For the full Arabic text, see Shakīb Arslān, *Sīra dhātīya*, Beirut: Dār al-talīʿa, 1969. For a French translation, see Chekib Arslan, "Le Centenaire de Gœthe", *La Nation Arabe* (March–April 1932), p. 55.

[54] Arslan, "Le Centenaire de Gœthe", p. 55.

relations. When Kaiser Wilhelm II visited Damascus in 1898, Arslan was appointed by Sultan Abdulhamid II as his escort in the city.[55] More than thirty years later, Arslan met the now deposed Kaiser again, visiting him at his residence in Doorn in the Netherlands.[56] Soon thereafter, Arslan used the pages of *La Nation Arabe* to engage in a lengthy defence of the Kaiser against charges of having initiated the First World War.[57] For a journal dedicated to the Arab nationalist cause, this was, to say the least, an unlikely foray into a European polemic. Arslan justified his sympathy for the Kaiser in two ways. First, it was in the name of justice and truth, for he found it devious for the Allies to conveniently throw responsibility for the war on the shoulders of a defeated Germany and its emperor. Second, it was in appreciation of the Kaiser's stance vis-à-vis Islam:

> This man has, for his entire career, shown an unshakable impartiality with regard to Muslims. He was the only sovereign of Christian Europe—despite his attachment to his religion and despite being himself head of the Lutheran Church—who could see Islam as a good religion that could inspire consideration and respect.[58]

The alliance between Wilhelmian Germany and the Ottoman Empire had, for Arslan, been rooted in more than political expediency. Arslan must have deeply appreciated the respect and consideration which Kaiser Wilhelm II had for Arab and Islamic civilisation. This might explain why in 1934, at a time when both the Ottoman Empire and Wilhelmian Germany belonged to the annals of history, Arslan travelled to Holland to pay a visit to the deposed Kaiser and engaged his journal in his defence.

Arslan's greatest friend and ally in inter-war Germany was probably Baron Max Freiherr von Oppenheim. The two met in the closing years of the nineteenth century, when Oppenheim was a young foreign service officer under Kaiser Wilhelm II and Arslan

[55] R.L Melka, "Max Freiherr von Oppenheim: Sixty Years of Scholarsip and Political Intrigue in the Middle East", *Middle Eastern Studies*, 1 (1973), p. 81.

[56] *Procès-verbal d'audition*, Geneva, Swiss Federal Archives, Doc. C10.7 E 4320 (B) 1984/29, vol. XIII, 6 October 1938, p. 3.

[57] Chekib Arslan, "Qu'est-ce que vous voulez qu'un homme d'Etat français dise de Guillaume II", *La Nation Arabe* (March-April 1935), pp. 236–55.

[58] Ibid., p. 249.

was a leading figure in Lebanese mountain politics with close ties to the Ottoman government. Each of these two young civil servants, enrolled in the service of their respective governments, became committed to the Ottoman-Wilhelmian alliance. Each of them also had their private interests. Oppenheim had a passion for Hittite archeology, which led him to resign from the German Foreign Office in 1910 to excavate the Hittite city of Tell Hallal that he had discovered. Arslan was known for his works on history and for his poetry, which played a far from negligible role in gaining him the admiration and allegiance of Arab audiences.[59] In 1917, during Arslan's tour of Germany on behalf of the Ottoman state, Arslan was feted by Oppenheim in Berlin, and then received at the latter's family residence in Cologne.[60] While Arslan was probably Oppenheim's primary Arab adviser on Middle Eastern affairs, Oppenheim appears to have been Arslan's primary link to the German Foreign Office. Arslan declared Oppenheim to be a "famed Orientalist and friend of the Orient", and, in a more personal tone, referred to him as "our friend for forty years".[61] Arslan only used the figure of forty, with its symbolic value in the Islamic tradition, to refer to his closest, and certainly oldest, friends. It was included in the titles of his commemorative biographies of Ahmad Shawqi and Rashid Rida.[62]

In addition to political and diplomatic figures in non-colonial states, Arslan also fraternised with anti-colonialists in colonial states. He shared longstanding ties with some French Socialists, and among these, the figure of Jean Longuet stands out. The grandson

[59] R.L. Melka, "Max Freiherr von Oppenheim", pp. 81–93.

[60] C. Arslān, *Sīra dhātīya*, pp. 221–2. After the fall of the Empire, Arslan was unable to return to the former Ottoman Empire and remained in Europe. He resided in Berlin between 1921 and 1923, associating with the other members of the exiled Ottoman leadership, who elected him president of the Berlin Oriental Club. The club was a meeting point for Muslims and Ottoman exiles who dreamed of a restoration of the Empire.

[61] Chekib Arslan, "Les Hittites ne sont pas Turcs et les Turcs ne sont pas Hittites", *La Nation Arabe* (January-April 1937), p. 780.

[62] Shakīb Arslān, *Shawqī aw sadāqat arba'īn sana*, Cairo: Matba'at 'īsa al-bābī al-halabī, 1355 [1936]; Shakīb Arslān, *Al-sayyid rashīd ridā aw ikhā' arba'īn sana*, Damascus: Matba'at ibn zaydūn, 1356 [1937].

of Karl Marx and vice-president of the Foreign Affairs Commission in the French Chamber of Deputies, Longuet had known Arslan for some twenty years when he died in 1938. At the news of his death, Arslan wrote of a "real sense of emptiness, like at the death of our other still regretted friend Pierre Renaudel". For Arslan, Longuet was memorable for his "sincerity, frankness, elevated mind, loyal character, guiltless conscience, complete disinterest [in personal gain], and friendship for us, Arabs, and for us, Muslims". Both Longuet and Renaudel, lifelong leaders of the French Socialist movement, are said to have hoped that France would one day "win the hearts of Muslims".[63]

No mention was found, however, of Shakib Arslan's European teachers. While Arslan surely could not have acquired his mastery of the French language, literature, and general culture on his own, colonialism may have prevented his French teachers from eliciting a more public display of gratitude. Although Arslan doubtlessly learned much from Europe, and advocated its virtues, he may have been loath to admit to a teacher-student relationship, an analogy undoubtedly reminiscent of arguments used to justify the mandate system.

CONCLUSION

In the first and only monograph on Shakib Arslan in a Western language, *Islam Against the West: Shakib Arslan and the Campaign for Islamic Nationalism*, William Cleveland characterised Arslan as distrustful of Europe and as opposed to the West in general:

> In 1892, Arslan left the Ottoman capital for Europe on the trip which had become nearly obligatory for the educated young men who aspired to lead Ottoman-Arab society. He was neither intrigued nor awed. He had been raised to distrust the West, and his exposure to the centers of Western culture [. . .] evoked no commentaries on European political systems, no descriptions of cities or their architecture, no comparative discussions of morals, manners, or behaviour. To Arslan, Europe represented an imperial threat, not an admirable culture. He held to this view for the next fifty years.[64]

[63] Chekib Arslan, "La perte douloureuse de M. Jean Longuet", *La Nation Arabe* (September-December 1938), pp. 1192–3.

[64] W. Cleveland, *Islam Against the West*, p. 11.

While Europe certainly represented an imperial threat for Arslan, it also represented much more than that. Extolling the virtues of European civilization was considerably more difficult in the inter-war era than for writers such as Rifa'a al-Tahtawi, who a century earlier was enthusiastic for what could still be seen as a benevolent Europe. In the inter-war years, "Europe" was a particularly contentious image in the Arab and Islamic worlds, for alongside the prospect of European modernity there stood the fear of European colonialism.

A writer such as Arslan was most secure among his nationalist readership when critiquing colonial Europe. Anything beyond a critique of Europe required expending political capital. Such an author risked being accused of forsaking what his readership considered the core values of Arabism and Islam. This was a charge sometimes brought against Arslan, most notably when a letter outlining a plan for making Italian propaganda in the Arab world was attributed to him. Yet Arslan seems to have withstood these charges, and his political capital developed throughout the inter-war era. This was visible in his continued patronage of nationalist leaders from the Maghreb to Syria and the Arabian Gulf. It was also evidenced in the jubilant homecoming he received on his temporary return to Syria in 1937.

Arslan's anticolonial struggle, and his single-mindedness in defending what he saw as the core values of Arabism and Islam, won him a reputation of integrity before his Arab and Muslim audiences. He was asked to preside over the European Muslim Congress of 1935 precisely because his network and years of activism on behalf of Islamic causes had made him an emblematic figure of the Islamic revivalist movement of Muhammad Abduh and Rashid Rida. In turn, his appointment to the presidency of the Arab Academy of Damascus in 1938 testified to his reputation as a symbol of Arabism. It was as an established member of the Arab nationalist and Islamic revivalist political communities that Arslan engaged with Europe.

Arslan represented Europe in a constellation of five images. Europe as the Coloniser was the most widely accepted image among Arslan's readership. It also corresponded to Arslan's official function in Geneva, as the League of Nations representative of the

Syrian-Palestinian nationalist opposition to colonial rule. As such, it permeated most of Arslan's works. The justification for Arslan's anticolonialism, however, lay in his attachment to what he considered the core values of Arabism and Islam, the loss of which could come through the nightmare of the Inquisition. For Arslan, Europe as the Inquisitor was an unmitigated enemy. Yet to the extent that it harboured Islamic communities, Europe also belonged to the Islamic world. The European Muslim Congress represented Europe's Islamic communities as encompassing the European continent, in Eastern Europe but also within the borders of the colonial states. The image of Europe as the colonial Other was thus complemented by the image of Europe as the Islamic self.

For Arslan, Europe was also a site of exemplary virtue and real friendship. Arslan could introduce these alternative representations of Europe because he possessed a political capital accumulated during a lifetime defending the core values of Arabism and Islam. It was this political capital of Arab and Islamic authenticity that enabled him to move beyond the anticolonial and anti-European discourses of most other advocates of Arabism and the Islamic revival. In transgressing these discursive boundaries without losing his capital of authenticity, Arslan contributed to inaugurating the postcolonial era. He helped usher in the new era not only by opposing the colonial mandates, but also by expanding the range of legitimate representations of Europe authorised by Arab nationalist and Islamic revivalist orthodoxy. His writings foreshadowed postcolonial reformulations of Europe as a home of Muslims, a model for achieving modernity through virtue, and a site of potential associations and fraternity.

EUROPEAN NEO-SUFI MOVEMENTS IN THE INTER-WAR PERIOD

Mark Sedgwick

Sections of the Western European public first discovered Sufism long before the First World War. A Sufi first appeared on a European stage in 1779, as a character in Gotthold Ephraim Lessing's play *Nathan the Wise*. In 1812, Goethe was reading Hafiz in German. Neo-Sufism, however, did not really emerge in Europe until after the First World War.

"Neo-Sufism" may be defined as any form of Sufism that differs significantly from "regular Sufism", the standard models found in the Islamic world, especially when the differences result from factors extraneous to the Islamic world. Neo-Sufis are generally born into religions other than Islam, but this need not be the case. Neo-Sufism is, in fact, found in the Islamic world as well as in the West, as a result of the impact in the Islamic world of aspects of modernity of Western origin.[1] This chapter, however, deals only with neo-Sufism in Europe.

The growth of neo-Sufism during the inter-war period was a very "modern" development. There had been Sufis of European

[1] For one example, see Mark Sedgwick, "In Search of the Counter-Reformation: Anti-Sufi Stereotypes and the Budshishiyya's response", in C. Kurzman and M. Browers (eds), *An Islamic Reformation?*, Lanham: Lexington Books, 2004, pp. 125–46. Neo-Sufism in this sense must be distinguished from what is generally meant by "neo-Sufism" in the context of the Arab world in the eighteenth and nineteenth centuries—*turuq* such as the Tijaniyya and Sanusiyya. Those *turuq* do indeed exhibit novel features, but these result from factors which are not extraneous to the Islamic world. See discussion in Mark Sedgwick, *Saints and Sons: The Making and Remaking of the Rashidi Ahmadi Sufi Order, 1799–2000*, Leiden: Brill, 2005, pp. 27–49.

origin for many centuries, "renegades" who for one reason or another defected to the Ottoman, Mamluke or Moroccan sultanates (sometimes, freed slaves). These Europeans integrated into their new societies, becoming Muslim and often joining Sufi *turuq*. They were thus regular Sufis, not neo-Sufis. Similarly, Sufi *turuq* were also established in geographical Europe—in the Balkans, in Spain before that area's loss to the Christians, and then during the early twentieth century among Arab communities in various European countries. Again, there was nothing "neo" about these *turuq*. They were simply extension into Europe of standard models of Sufism, as found for centuries in the Islamic world and in areas such as Central Thailand, where there are significant Muslim minorities.

Towards the end of the nineteenth century, however, a small number of Europeans became Sufis and yet kept their former, European identities, social ties, and intellectual worlds. Unlike previous European Sufis, they did not vanish into the Islamic world, but remained firmly European. The earliest of these who has come to my attention was Isabelle Eberhardt, a journalist and writer who joined the Qadiriyya *tariqa* in Algeria in 1899 or 1900. Eberhardt not only retained her cultural connections with Europe, but also continued her distinctly un-Islamic lifestyle—dressing in male clothes, consuming hashish and alcohol, and practicing "free love".[2] Islam was clearly not her only path, which distinguishes her from earlier European Sufis.

The difference between regular Sufism and neo-Sufism is even more clearly visible in another early neo-Sufi, now famous today only in his native Sweden, Ivan Aguéli. Aguéli was a painter who joined the Shadhiliyya *tariqa* in Cairo in 1907, and then established the first ever neo-Sufi group in Europe, in 1911, when he transmitted his Shadhili "initiation" to a few of his Parisian associates. These associates were all members of the so-called Universal Gnostic Church, and also shared Masonic and Taoist initiations.[3] For Aguéli and his associates, Islam was explicitly only one of a number of

[2] Eberhardt is relatively well known. See Mark Sedgwick, *Against the Modern World: Traditionalism and the Secret Intellectual History of the Twentieth Century*, New York: Oxford University Press, 2004, pp. 63–5.

[3] Ibid., p. 60.

paths to be investigated simultaneously. Aguéli's neo-Sufi group was short-lived. It had vanished by 1912, and so falls beyond the scope of this chapter. Aguéli himself was killed in a railway accident in 1917.

A third early neo-Sufi was Etienne Dinet, the celebrated Orientalist painter, who visited the Rahmaniyya *tariqa* at Bu Sada in Algeria in 1884, subsequently settling there and becoming Muslim in 1913. Unlike Eberhardt and Aguéli, Dinet seems to have been a reasonably orthodox Muslim, praying and making the Hajj pilgrimage,[4] but he remained a European despite his Islam, continuing to return to France and exhibit in Paris much as before.

Eberhardt, Aguéli and Dinet made no secret of their Islam. In all three cases, it became part of their public personas as creative artists. This, however, would not be the case for later, inter-war neo-Sufis, who took pains to distance themselves from regular Islam, as a result of what one of them called European "prejudice" against Islam.

EUROPEAN RELIGIOUS MODERNITY

Religious pluralism

Sufis, Masons and Taoists simultaneously, Aguéli and his colleagues exemplify religious pluralism, which is generally recognised as an important aspect of postmodern religiosity.[5] In Aguéli's case, one immediate source of this pluralism was Helena Blavatsky's Theosophical Society,[6] but similar views can be found in the eighteenth century, for example in Lessing's *Nathan the Wise*, first produced in 1779. "Modern", then, should perhaps replace "postmodern" in describing religious pluralism.

[4] Denise Brahimi, *Les terrasses de Bou-Saada*, Algiers: Entreprise Nationale du Livre, 1986, pp. 11–12, 18, 54–5.

[5] See, for example, Phillip C. Lucas, "New Religious Movements and the 'Acids' of Postmodernity", *Nova Religio*, VIII, 2 (November 2004), p. 29.

[6] The Theosophical Society was the single most important body in the history of alternative religion in the nineteenth-century West. Established in New York but then run from India, it flourished throughout the West during the 1870s and 1880s. Its success derived partly from Blavatsky's teachings, and partly from the way in which it provided a forum for all varieties of spiritual explorer.

The central message of *Nathan* (the play in which a Sufi first appeared on the European stage) is that moral and ethical worth are independent of creed, that reason matters at least as much as revelation, and that one of the greatest of all evils is "the pious rage/To own the better god".[7] The question of which god is better—the Jewish, Christian, or the Muslim one—is answered by a re-telling of Boccaccio's parable of the three rings.[8] At the end of Lessing's version, a judge tells the three claimants to possession of the "real" ring that

Ye're all deceived deceivers,
None of your rings is true. The real ring
Perhaps is gone. To hide or to supply
Its loss, your father ordered three for one.[9]

The spokesmen for this somewhat Deistic view of religious pluralism are a Jew, a Templar, and a Muslim.[10]

Over the next forty years, Deistic readings of Sufism (and Hinduism) became increasingly popular among European intellectuals.[11] Partly as a result of an oversight during fieldwork in about 1800, Captain Sir John Malcolm's monumental *History of Persia* was responsible for spreading a view of "the Sooffee doctrine" as unconnected with Islam and as something "to be found in the most splendid theories of the ancient schools of Greece, and in those of the modern philosophers of Europe".[12] Later and more rigorous

[7] Gotthold Ephraim Lessing, *Nathan the Wise: A Dramatic Poem in Five Acts*, trans. William Taylor of Norwich, Guttenberg ebook, act 2, scene 2

[8] The parable is actually found before Boccaccio, but it was Boccaccio who made it famous. W.H. Carruth, "Lessing's Treatment of the Story of the Ring, and its Teaching", *Transactions and Proceedings of the Modern Language Association of America*, XVI, 1 (1901), pp. 107–13.

[9] G.E. Lessing, *Nathan*, act 3, scene 2.

[10] The Muslim is Saladin, not the Sufi. The Sufi addresses not the problem of religious diversity but the tension between power and spirituality.

[11] Mark Sedgwick, "Quelques sources du dix-huitième siècle du pluralisme religieux inclusif", in J.-P. Brach and J. Rousse-Lacordaire (eds), *Etudes d'histoire de l'ésotérisme: mélanges offerts à Jean-Pierre Laurent*, Paris: Editions du Cerf, 2007, pp. 49–65.

[12] John Malcolm, *The History of Persia, From the Most Early Period to the Present Time, Containing an Account of the Religion, Government, Usages and Character of the Inhabitants of that Kingdom*, 1815; new edition, London: John Murray, 1825, p. 383.

research by Western scholars corrected this view, but the earlier misunderstanding was preferred to the later correction by much of the Western public. It is found, in one form or another, in all the groups considered in this chapter.

Image-mediated experience

Returning to the first prewar neo-Sufis, it is striking that all were creative artists—Aguéli and Dinet were painters, and Eberhardt was a writer. This points to a second important aspect of postmodernity, what Baudrillard called "the domination of simulation", glossed by Philip Lucas as "the increasing mediation of experience through synthetic images".[13] One of the most important of these synthetic images during the nineteenth century was that of the Orient. As was demonstrated by Edward Said, Europe's image of the Orient derived in part from Europe's own self-imagining. Said's and Baudrillard's perspectives were combined by Timothy Mitchell in *Colonising Egypt*, a book which examines the role of universal exhibitions such as the 1889 Paris exhibition in creating a synthetic image of Egypt as chaotic, to which Westernised Egyptian elites responded by trying to introduce discipline and order into Egypt.[14]

An equally important pair of images is that of the West as materialistic and of the Orient as spiritual. This pair of images is the reverse of that discussed by Said and Mitchell, and has had much less attention paid to it. In different ways, it is equally important—and has lasted rather longer. Aguéli's and Dinet's Orientalist painting and Eberhardt's writing, then, both drew on and reinforced the image of the spiritual Orient. All the groups considered in this chapter derive their legitimacy, at least in part, from the image of the spiritual Orient.

Angst

A third aspect of modernity, equally important though not as widely recognised as the pluralism we see emerging with Lessing and the mediation of synthetic images identified by Baudrillard, is existential angst. Angst is itself one of the bases of the image of the

[13] P.C. Lucas, "New Religious Movements", p. 29.
[14] Timothy Mitchell, *Colonising Egypt*, Cairo: AUC Press, 1989.

West as excessively materialistic, and so of the Orient as spiritual. It is associated with individual anomie and alienation, seen by some as characteristic of modernity. It may find expression in millenarianism, and in inter-war Europe there were widespread feelings of approaching salvation (chiefly among Marxists) and of approaching doom. Inter-war millenarianism is evidenced both by books such as Spengler's *Decline of the West* and by the repeated reference to the final age of mankind by almost all the inter-war groups considered in this chapter. The inter-war period was frequently identified by them as the *kali yuga*, the fourth and final age of Hindu cosmology.

Originality

A fourth important aspect of modernity is preference for originality over received wisdom, whether "original" is taken in its primary sense of "first" ("this is the original view") or in its superficially contradictory sense of "novel" ("I've just had an original idea").[15] This respect for originality is linked to the Romantic movement's emphasis on individual intuition. In religious terms, it expresses itself as a preference for direct religious experience over unoriginal organised religion, visible both in Emerson and in William James' *Varieties of Religious Experience.*[16] This results in the conviction that each individual must search for an individual answer to the great spiritual questions, rather than "merely" accepting established orthodoxy as a member of a larger group. The preference for originality is one aspect of modern individualism, and is reflected in all the inter-war groups this chapter considers.

The displacement of God

Another aspect of individualism, and so of modernity, is the displacement of God, an emphasis on the development of the individual rather than on God. L. P. Elwell-Sutton saw this as one of the main ways in which the neo-Sufism of Idries Shah (a leading neo-

[15] Reinhard Schulze, "The Birth of Tradition and Modernity in 18th and 19th Century Islamic Culture", *Culture & History*, XVI (1997), pp. 29–72.

[16] William James, *The Varieties of Religious Experience: A Study in Human Nature (being the Gifford Lectures on Natural Religion delivered at Edinburgh in 1901–1902)*, New York: Random House, 1936.

Sufi of the postwar period) differed from Sufism in the Islamic world. The works of Idries Shah, wrote Elwell-Sutton with feeling in 1975, were primarily "prescriptions for self-improvement, directions for the achievement of personal happiness, guide-lines for a worldly elite", since "the Western intellectual of today is above all else a humanist, and is usually incapable of swallowing the idea of a transcendent God more omnipotent than himself".[17] Something similar is visible in the inter-war period as well.

Some echoes of these aspects of modernity may be found in regular Sufism in the Islamic world, though not in mainstream Islam, which may be why it is neo-Sufism that developed in inter-war Europe, and why neo-Islam is unknown. Classical Sufism is Islamic rather than pluralist, but at times may show somewhat more respect for other religions than is found in mainstream Islam. Synthetic images are of great importance for classical Sufism, notably the image of the *wali* (saint). Angst, in the sense of an awareness of the nearness of the final days, is also often found among Sufis. Finally, even though God is never displaced, classic Sufism both concentrates on individual spiritual development and explains the Shari'a in terms of individual spiritual self-improvement.

Aspects of modernity are echoed in regular Sufism, then, but are present in full rather than merely echoed in inter-war European neo-Sufism. European modernity is both the context in which neo-Sufism developed and the principal extraneous factor that led to significant differences between European neo-Sufism and the standard models of Sufism found in the Islamic world.

This chapter will now examine the five major instances of inter-war European neo-Sufism. Two of these groups are clearly neo-Sufi, and three are perhaps best described as "Sufistical". The first inter-war European neo-Sufi group was the pan-European Sufi Order of Inayat Khan, some contemporary branches of which accept the label "neo", though some reject it.[18] The second neo-Sufi group was the Swiss and French Alawiyya of Frithjof Schuon,

[17] Laurence Paul Elwell-Sutton, "Sufism & Pseudo-Sufism", *Encounter*, XLIV, 5 (May 1975), p. 16.

[18] In 2000 in email correspondence with the author, who was then preparing an article on "Neo-Sufism" for the Brill *Dictionary of Gnosis and Western Esotericism*.

a *tariqa* that claimed (and claims) to abhor anything at all "neo", but which this chapter will nevertheless classify as neo-Sufi.

The classification of the three groups that I label as "Sufistical" is more difficult. None described itself as "Sufi" during the inter-war period, but two accepted the "Sufi" label after the Second World War. The groups in question were those led by Rudolf von Sebottendorff in Germany, by Georges Gurdjieff in France, and by Meher Baba from India. It might be argued that none of these groups is or was Sufi at all, but I include them in this chapter partly because Sufism played a part in their origins and perhaps also in their teachings, and partly because their inclusion enables a wider view of inter-war alternative spirituality, the context in which the two clearly neo-Sufi groups emerged.

NEO-SUFI GROUPS

Inayat Khan's Sufi Order

The earliest neo-Sufi group in Europe was Inayat Khan's Sufi Order. Khan was an Indian Muslim who for short time followed a *shaikh* of the Madaniyya, a major *tariqa* of the time.[19] Khan was never a standard Sufi, however, as some of his *shaikh*'s other followers complained. Not only was he a musician and strangely dressed, but he prayed in the mosque only rarely, and was friends with all sorts of strange people—Hindus and Parsis and Christians and Jews.[20] On top of this, by his own account, Khan approved not only of the ultra-modernist reforms of Sir Sayyid Ahmad Khan (no relation) but also of the Qadiani Ahmadiyya, another ultra-modernist group later widely regarded by most Muslims as having left Islam. He even approved of the Brahmo Samaj, a modernist Hindu group influenced by European Deism.[21] These are hardly the positions of a standard Sufi.

[19] The *shaikh* was Muhammad Abu Hashim Madani, in Hyderabad. Inayat Khan, *Biography of Pir-o-Murshid Inayat Khan* (1923), [Germany]: Centrum Universel, 2005; ebook, pp. 53–60. Pirzade Zia Inayat Khan identifies him as a Chishti (email to the author, 28 July 2000), but this seems unlikely, given his *shaikh*'s name. Khan's grandfather, however, was connected with the Chishtiyya.

[20] I. Khan, *Biography*, pp. 55–6.

[21] Ibid., p. 2.

After the death of his *shaikh*, Khan traveled to visit a Hindu *guru* with whom he discussed religious pluralism. "Moslim or Hindu are only outward distinctions", he later remembered telling this *guru*, "the Truth is one, God is one, life is one". "Call it Sufism or Vedantism", he went on, "it is the one and only Truth, perhaps given in different forms, but as it all comes from one source, it cannot be different, it is all the same".[22]

These are unlikely to have been Khan's exact words at the time, and it is impossible to say to what extent Khan's later views influenced his recollection of this conversation. It is also hard to be certain of the source of these views. They might derive from Deism through the Brahmo Samaj, or they might derive from Khan's contacts with the Theosophical Society. These contacts were important once Khan arrived in Europe, and had already been made in India; Khan lectured to the Theosophical Society in Madura, and in Calcutta was friendly with Ektadarul Huq, an unidentified Indian described by Khan as "a Sufi who was addressing large gatherings on theosophical subjects".[23]

Khan travelled from India to America in 1910, and after a musical lecture tour of America went on to Europe, where he spent the rest of his life. His autobiography gives no indication of what prompted this move. It refers to an "injunction" from his Madani *shaikh* to "harmonize the East and West . . . [and] spread the wisdom of Sufism abroad",[24] but this seems to have been inserted into the text in the light of his subsequent attempt to do precisely that.[25] In fact, it may well have been the spiritual interests of one member of an audience he addressed on Indian music in San Francisco, Rabia (Ada) Martin, that drew him to spiritual teaching.[26]

[22] Ibid., pp. 60–1.

[23] Ibid., pp. 71 and 77.

[24] Ibid., pp. 79–80.

[25] The "injunction" is not mentioned at all in the earlier discussion of his shaikh, and would fit oddly with the relationship that between Khan and the *shaikh* that is suggested by that discussion. The "injunction" is first referred to in Khan's comment on a "Brahmin Seer" who told him that he was to "do a great work" in the West. I. Khan, *Biography*, pp. 78–80. The *Biography* seems never to have been properly revised or edited, and there are a few other such internal contradictions in it.

[26] I. Khan, *Biography*, p. 86. This is also the view of Andrew Rawlinson, "A History of Western Sufism", *Diskus*, I, 1 (1993).

Between 1912 and 1914, Khan travelled in England, France and Russia, performing Indian music and lecturing on both music and spirituality. Many of his lectures were given under the auspices of the Theosophical Society, and it was the Theosophical Publishing Society that published the English edition of his *Sufi Message of Spiritual Liberty*, which was also translated into French and Russian. A Sufi Publishing Society was established in Southampton during the war, but it was not until after the war that a formal "Sufi Order" was founded, in about 1920.[27] This may well have been the initiative of Khan's leading English follower, Sophia Saintsbury-Green, a former Theosophist. Saintsbury-Green was responsible in 1921 for establishing the Church of All, an organisation which practiced "Universal Worship" as an exoteric complement to esoteric Sufism.[28] This dual exoteric/esoteric structure presumably followed the example of the Theosophists, for some of whom an esoteric Order of the Star in the East complemented the exoteric Theosophical Society. Most practitioners of Universal Worship were members of the Sufi Order, and most members of the Sufi Order practiced Universal Worship, but the two bodies remained formally separate.

A system of ranks was also introduced: *cherags* (from *charagh*, the Urdu for lamp) were "ordained" as priests for the Church of All, and *murshids* and *khalifas* (standard Sufi terms) were appointed for the Sufi Order. By the time of Khan's death in 1926, he had appointed "national representatives" for the Sufi Order (from 1923 also called the Sufi Movement)[29] in England, Switzerland, France, the Netherlands and Belgium, Germany, and Norway, as well as in the United States and Brazil.[30] His following was probably in the hundreds, and may even have been in the thousands. In 1939 regular Universal Worship in Europe was being held in England and the Netherlands,

[27] I. Khan, *Biography*, pp. 88–96.

[28] Ibid., p. 100.

[29] The Sufi Order and Sufi Movement were in fact separate entities, but the relationship between them is complex and not relevant to the concerns of this chapter.

[30] This list is compiled from the "Biographical Sketches" in I. Khan, *Biography*, pp. 180–214. For Brazil, p. 96.

and probably elsewhere in Europe as well.[31] To judge from Khan's autobiography and from incidental references in the Order's publications, nearly all Khan's followers were from the upper or upper-middle classes, and perhaps two thirds were female. This social profile is strongly reminiscent of what are today sometimes light-heatedly called "the yoga classes". Universal Worship has little if anything to do with Sufism. It uses texts from all the world's religions, and is dedicated to universal brotherhood, Khan's principal social objective.

Khan's neo-Sufism, however, has much to do with regular Sufism, despite being superficially very distinct from it. Khan presented Sufism rather as he claimed to have presented it to the Hindu *guru* in India, as "the essence of all religions and philosophies",[32] a phrase much used by his followers that echoes Captain Sir John Malcolm and which Lessing might have found appealing. Regular Sufis in the Islamic world would subscribe to this statement to a certain extent: Sufism is for them the quintessence of Islam, and Islam is the quintessence of religion—a view that Malcolm rejected and Lessing would have found repugnant. As we will see, Khan probably believed something of this kind privately, but publicly proclaimed something rather different. As a result, for most of Khan's followers, Sufism was not part of Islam, but something above and beyond Islam.

Despite this, Khan's teaching is recognisably Sufi in the classic Islamic fashion. He writes, for example, of the need to subdue the *nafs* (ego) in order to achieve *fana* (spiritual union) in God. He does not use these terms, however, but speaks rather of the development of "personality".[33] *Fana* is described as follows: "In that moment of supreme exaltation one is not only united with the source of all beings, but dissolved in it".[34] The path to this is the attainment of

[31] The list of locations for regular Universal Worship given in *The Sufi*, V, 1, (January 1939) included ten cities in the Netherlands and five in England. There may have been other European locations, of course, not listed in an English-language publication.

[32] This succinct formulation is found, for example, in Angela Alt, "An Open Letter on Sufism", in *The Sufi*, I (September 1934), p. 223.

[33] The original title of Khan's important *The Art of Being and Becoming* was *Personality: The Art of Being and Becoming*.

[34] Inayat Khan, *The Art of Being and Becoming*, New Lebanon, NY: Omega, 1982, p. 41.

purity, a concept from which Khan (with little justification) derives the word "Sufi".[35] One variety of purity is to "mak[e] the heart free from all impressions that . . . are foreign to one's nature", an idea which at first looks rather like Elwell-Sutton's "prescriptions for self-improvement". However, what is "against one's nature" has previously been defined by Khan as "a fault", and one example of such a fault is "every rising wave of passion [which inevitably] carries away one's reason".[36] The need to control the passions to cleanse the heart is a central message of regular Sufism, and is not characteristic of modernist self-improvement. Similarly, Khan writes that a greater variety of purity is "to keep one's mind away from all but God. Then all one thinks about, all that one sees and admires, all that one touches and perceives, is God". This leads to "freedom from the thought of oneself, . . . of one's limited self".[37]

This is classical Sufism. It is presented, however, in terms that can appeal not only to the non-Muslim (references to the Bible outnumber references to the Qur'an) but to inter-war religious individualists. Khan contrasts his understanding of purity, "the exaltation of the spirit", with the "manmade purity" that may come from the "rigid principles" of "the churches, the religions, national and social laws".[38] Khan is providing materials for constructing individual solutions through individual searches, and also has in a sense displaced God, at least publicly. He also speaks to inter-war angst: although Khan did not use the phrase *kali yuga*, he described modernity as an "iron age", referring explicitly to Hindu conceptions: "Never before in any period of human history has there been such grossness and denseness as mankind shows today. And this has come about by the law of gravitation".[39]

In his autobiography, Khan by implication admits that he has adjusted Sufism for contemporary Western consumption:

> Western nature is self-assertive and demanding. That is why spiritual attainment becomes difficult for the people in the West, as it is only

[35] Ibid., p. 4.
[36] Ibid., pp. 8–9.
[37] Ibid., pp. 10–11.
[38] Ibid., pp. 5–6.
[39] Ibid., p. 39.

attained by self-effacement and self-denial. The idea of crushing the I, to become selfless, to become indifferent to the life around one, . . . to feel that one must lose oneself in God and to think that this individuality is an illusion and to imagine it to be four days, these things frighten many from a deeper understanding of the philosophical thought of the East. Therefore those who have worked in the West in spreading the spiritual thought have to keep back many deep ideas of philosophy in order to cope with the people.[40]

He also acknowledges the problems raised by the Western "prejudice against Islam", which he ascribes (in very Muslim fashion) to "the Christian missionaries, [who] knowing that Islam is the only religion which can succeed their faith, have done everything in their power to prejudice minds of the Western people against it".[41] As a result, even "a Western person of good intention who has given up all prejudices against other religions and is trying to overlook all he has heard against Islam, cannot very well comprehend the ideas of the Qur'an as they are put. For he wants the ideas to fit in with the standard of the day and to be expressed in the language of the present time".[42] This, then, may be exactly what Khan was trying to do: to express Sufism, or at least his understanding of Sufism, in the language of his time, avoiding prejudice against Islam by dissociating himself from Islam. He was aware of other approaches, notably those of the Woking Mosque and the Ahmadiyya, but knew little of them.[43] His conclusion on them was that "these Missions could not exist in the West were they not provided for by the hopeful Moslims [*sic*] of Islam, who out of their good faith in the furtherance of Islam try to give a part of the only loaf of bread they have".[44] The implication is that such Muslims would be better advised to keep their loaves to themselves, not to waste them on hopeless causes.

[40] I. Khan, *Biography*, p. 164.
[41] Ibid., p. 138.
[42] Ibid., p. 136.
[43] Of Woking, for example, he wrote that it "is *supposed* to have made a great many converts to Islam" (my emphasis). The Ahmadiyya was "*seeming* to stand apart from" Woking (again, my emphasis). Ibid., p. 149.
[44] Ibid., p. 150.

I have no idea whether or nor Khan prayed and fasted as a Muslim should, but he seems to have remained essentially Muslim despite his public separation of Sufism from Islam. Not only does he ascribe Western incomprehension of Islam to the efforts of Christian missionaries, but he also suggests that Islam inspired Protestantism and Sufism inspired Freemasonry, though all that Protestantism took from this was "the shadow of the outer form of Islam".[45] This is almost the reverse of the position taken by his followers, making not Sufism but Islam the quintessence of religion. Khan occasionally criticises individual Muslims or groups of Muslims (he compares the Ahl al-Hadith to Protestants, for example),[46] but never criticises Islam. One of the few criticisms he makes of Muslims as a whole is that they do not understand rightly the concept of the Seal of Prophecy. "They do not seem to realize that it does not mean at all that he [Muhammad] was the last prophet to come, it only means that he was the last of claimants of prophecy; and that according to the nature and character of humanity after his time it would not be advisable for his successor to make an open claim".[47] This might be interpreted as a reformulation of one version of the classic Sufi doctrine of *walaya* (sainthood), or might alternatively be interpreted as Khan supposing that he himself is in some sense a lesser, latter-day prophet.

The practice of Khan's followers was less Sufi than Khan's teachings, however, presumably because standard Sufi practice involves too much Islam. It consisted in part of Universal Worship, and in part of their original religious practice—since Sufism was above and beyond all other religions, there was no need to abandon one's previous religion. In addition, however, there is also said to have been an important Sufi element, consisting of standard Chishti practice.[48] Some sources also speak of exercises of Hindu origin. Further research is needed to establish to what extent the practice

[45] Ibid., p. 134. Khan has a low opinion of Protestantism, "a religion which is void both of spirit and form, a flower without colour or fragrance. It is a rattle given into the hand of a child to keep him quiet, when he was crying for candy". Ibid.
[46] Ibid.
[47] Ibid., p. 143.
[48] Notably "*namaz*, *muraqaba*, *tawajjuh*, *wazifa*, *fikr*, *dhikr*, *kasab*, *shaghal*, and *'amal*". Pirzade Zia Inayat Khan, email to the author.

of Khan's followers was, like Khan's teaching, Sufism dressed up in non-Islamic garb.

The greatest long-term importance of Khan's neo-Sufism is that his books achieved a far wider European readership than those of any other writer on Sufism until the 1960s, and firmly established the view of Sufism as above and beyond Islam. This view was then further promoted after the Second World War by an Englishman of Indian extraction, Idries Shah, whose books on Sufism sold even better than Khan's—they have by now sold some 15 million copies in twelve languages.[49] If an average European today has any acquaintance at all with Sufism, it is most likely to be with the work of Khan or Shah, and perhaps with the poetry of Rumi, interpreted in the light of the Khan-Shah understanding of Sufism. More serious spiritual seekers, however, will probably also have encountered the books and articles of the followers of Frithjof Schuon, our second major neo-Sufi.

Frithjof Schuon's Alawiyya

The Alawiyya was one of the two most widespread and important regular Sufi *turuq* in inter-war Europe.[50] It was founded in about 1909 in Mostaganem in Algeria by Ahmad al-Alawi, an Algerian who had previously spent fifteen years following Shaikh Muhammad Bu Zidi of the Darqawiyya.[51] The practice of this *tariqa* did not differ from established Sufi norms in any significant way, and al-Alawi's teachings differed from the norm only in that they favoured cooperation with the French authorities. Many Algerian Sufis had previously been involved in armed resistance to the French, but had invariably been defeated. Al-Alawi recognised that continued resistance was fruitless. He instead called for acceptance of the fact of French rule, and even for respect for Christianity. This was not pluralism of the sort found in modern Europe, however, since the basis

[49] This is the estimate of Shah's contemporary followers.

[50] The other was the Mourides (Muridiyya), said to have been present in Britain and France in the 1930s. I have no further information about the Mourides in Europe at present.

[51] Date from Karima K. Stauch, 'Ein maghrebinischer Sufi-Shaykh des 20. Jahrhunderts: Shaykh Ahmad al-'Alawi', unpublished thesis, Rheinische Friedrich-Wilhelms-Universität Bonn, available http://www.abc.se/~m9783/alawi.html.

al-Alawi envisaged for a rapprochement between Christianity and Islam was Christian abandonment of the doctrine of the Trinity.[52] This was well within the classic interpretations of Islam.

Mostaganem being a port, al-Alawi's followers included sailors, and this led to the spread of his *tariqa* from Algeria and Morocco to Aden. It also led to Alawi *zawiya*s being established in Europe, notably in France (among Algerian immigrants), Belgium and the Netherlands (among Moroccan immigrants), and Britain (among Yemeni immigrants).[53] Like the Algerian Alawiyya, the British and French Alawiyyas of the inter-war period were Sufi rather than neo-Sufi. There is no record of any participation in these *zawiya*s from outside the Arab community.[54] Indeed, the leaders of the Yemeni Alawiyya in Britain thought that one important function of their *tariqa* was to prevent Yemeni integration into the surrounding community.[55] Although some individual Europeans such as Jean-Henri Probst-Biraben[56] and Frithjof Schuon found their way to the Alawiyya in Mostaganem, they were exceptions, and had no impact on the character of the *tariqa*.

Frithjof Schuon's Alawiyya differed significantly from other *zawiya*s of the Alawiyya in Europe. Although its immediate origin was an unusual *ijaza* (certificate of appointment) that al-Alawi's senior *muqaddam* (lieutenant) and successor, Adda Bentounès, gave

[52] Eric Geoffroy, "Le rayonnement spirituel du cheikh Al Alaoui en Occident", in *Al-tarbiya wa al-ma'rifa fi maathir al-shaykh Ahmad bin Mustafa al-'Alawi*, Mostaganem: n. p., 2002, pp. 359–60.

[53] K.K. Stauch, *Ein maghrebinischer Sufi-Shaykh*.

[54] "Arab community" here includes working-class European wives who had converted to their husbands' religion. The French *zawiya*s were said to be "*réservées aux Arabes et aux Kabyles*" (Massignon, quoted in E. Geoffroy, "Rayonnement spirituel").

[55] Obituary of Shaikh Muhammad Qasim al-Alawi, British Yemeni Society website, www.al-bab.com/bys/obits/alawi.htm.

[56] Little is known about Probst-Biraben. He frequented Guénon's circle in Paris (*Against the Modern World*, p. 86), and wrote both scholarly articles such as "Les rites d'obtention de la pluie dans la province de Constantine", in *Journal de la Société des Africanistes*, II, 1, 1932, pp. 95–102, and popular works such as *Rabelais et les secrets du Pantagruel*, Nice: Editions des Cahiers Astrologiques, 1949. He was probably a freemason. Serge Caillet, *La Franc-Maçonnerie égyptienne de Memphis-Misraïm*, Paris: Cariscript, 1988, Avant-propos. www.france-spiritualites.com.

Schuon in about 1933,[57] Schuon never acted as a junior associate of Bentounès, which would have been the normal relationship between *shaikh* and *muqaddam*. Four years after establishing an Alawi *zawiya* in Basel on the authority of his Alawi *ijaza*, Schuon received a second appointment as "shaikh"—i.e. as an independent leader—directly from heaven.[58] In Sufi terms, such an appointment is not necessarily problematic. Al-Alawi himself had received a direct appointment in a similar way, though after rather more years on the Sufi path than Schuon. After Schuon's appointment from heaven, the Schuonian Alawiyya was both in theory and practice a distinct entity. Schuon's relations with Mostaganem were thereafter distant, and after the Second World War they ceased altogether.[59]

The Schuonian Alawiyya was also different from the Alawi norm because its members were without exception Europeans, mostly Swiss and French (though a few non-Europeans were to follow Schuon after the Second World War). As has been said, this alone need not make a *tariqa* neo-Sufi rather than Sufi, but in this case the prior convictions of the Europeans in question did lead to significant differences between the Schuonian Alawiyya and the standard models of Sufism found in the Islamic world.[60] Schuon's followers were all devoted readers of the works of René Guénon, the French philosopher who is central to the movement known either as Guénonianism or Traditionalism.

Traditionalism sees itself as anything but modern, but despite this is really a quintessentially modern philosophy. Its immediate origins have much in common with those of Aguéli's neo-Sufi group of 1911–12, mentioned above, to which Guénon had belonged. Guénon had formerly been a member of Encausse's Martinist Order,[61] one source for his views on religious pluralism, which were in some ways similar to those of the Theosophists. Traditionalism sees individual religions as expressions of the same central

[57] M. Sedgwick, *Against the Modern World*, p. 88.

[58] Ibid., p. 92.

[59] Khaled Bentounès, interview, Alexandria, April 2003.

[60] For this and other discussion of Schuon's Alawiyya, see M. Sedgwick, *Against the Modern World*.

[61] For Encausse, see M. Sedgwick, *Against the Modern World*, esp. pp. 43–6.

perennial religious truth, the esoteric form of which is the important one. After moving from Paris to Cairo in 1930, Guénon advised the more serious followers of his philosophy to seek Sufi initiation, since Sufism was more accessible to a European born outside the Hindu caste system than was Hinduism. It was Guénon's advice that had sent Schuon to a Sufi *shaikh*, and Guénon's advice that sent many others to Schuon.[62] Modern religious pluralism, then, was central to Schuon's Alawiyya.

Other modern characteristics of Traditionalism, and so of Schuon's Alawiyya, include a strong emphasis on the materialism of the West and the spirituality of the Orient, the reverse Orientalism discussed above.[63] Inter-war angst was reflected in the Traditionalist conviction that the West was in a state of terminal decline, in the *kali yuga*, and that religions such as Catholicism had lost all their original esoteric content. The Traditionalists' stance on individualism is more complex, however. Both Guénon and Schuon saw individualism as one of the prime characteristics of the *kali yuga*, as a form of fragmentation where mere quantity comes, through a process of inversion, to be valued more than quality. Truth was not available as the solution to an individual search, but rather was contained in immemorial tradition. Even so, there was an unrecognized element of continuing individual search in Traditionalist neo-Sufism. The Traditionalists were in a sense all engaged in a gigantic research project to excavate truth from tradition, as is suggested by the important role played in Traditionalism by quasi-scholarly journals such as *Études Traditionnelles*. Although theoretically static, Traditionalist truth was thus in practice dynamic, to be uncovered by a continuing process of spiritual research, if not of spiritual search. It might also be argued that a further variety of individualism was present: the displacement of God. Traditionalists speak not so much of God as of tradition.

[62] These matters are discussed in detail in M. Sedgwick, *Against the Modern World*.

[63] This was Guénon's original position, though he modified it somewhat after moving to Egypt in 1930, distinguishing between the metaphysical Orient and the physical Orient. In later Traditionalism, "tradition" replaces the Orient as the source of truth.

At the doctrinal level, Traditionalism and Guénon mattered far more to the Schuonian Alawiyya than Mostaganem or Sufism. A small number of Schuon's followers learned Arabic and travelled to experience Sufism at its source, among whom the most important were Titus Burckhardt and Martin Lings. Most, however, remained in Europe, and read Schuon and Guénon in the pages of *Études Traditionnelles*, the Traditionalist journal for which Schuon had even composed an article on the "trinitary aspect" of the three monotheistic religions during his first visit to the Alawiyya in Mostaganem. This suggests to what extent his experience of regular Sufism left his earlier views untouched.

The Sufi practice of the Schuonian Alawiyya, however, did not differ in any important way from the practice of regular Sufism, although some minor differences between the Schuonian Alawiyya and regular Sufism resulted from a striving after authenticity, after the synthetic image of the spiritual Orient. Schuon, for example, insisted that his followers wear "traditional" Arab clothing for the *dhikr* ceremony, and enhanced these ceremonies with devices such as incense that led some critics to complain of excessive theatricality.[64] While it is impossible to say whether or not this was the case with the inter-war Schuonian Alawiyya, the *dhikr* ceremony of one contemporary European neo-Sufi *tariqa* of Schuonian origin has a sober formality about it that is more reminiscent of a Catholic mass than of Sufi practice in the Islamic world.[65]

There were, however, certain unusual characteristics in the Islamic (as opposed to purely Sufi) practice of the Schuonian Alawiyya. One was the relaxation of the Shari'a in ways that Schuon felt appropriate for Europe in the *kali yuga*, but that had never been permitted by any Sufi *shaikh* in the Islamic world. There was a general discouragement of praying *sunna* prayers, on the basis that *dhikr* was more important than prayer, a stance justified by an interpretation of Qur'an 29:45 unknown in regular Sufism. More interestingly, Schuon also gave dispensations from fasting during Ramadan, and general permission to drink beer in public in order

[64] Such a complaint was made by Michel Vâlsan in 1950. M. Sedgwick, *Against the Modern World*, p. 122.

[65] The Milan Ahmadiyya of Abd al-Wahid Pallavicini, observed in 1996.

to disguise the fact that one was Muslim. Like Khan, and presumably for the same reasons, Schuon was actively seeking to distance his group from regular Islam.[66]

Schuon's Alawiyya, then, was neo-Sufi rather than Sufi, and modern despite its abhorrence of modernity. During the inter-war period, it was not of great importance in Europe. It had *zawiya*s in Basel, Amiens, and Paris, and a few hundred members. Its wider influence was limited to the narrow circle of subscribers to *Études Traditionnelles*, which extended beyond France to small groups in Italy and Romania. Like Khan's followers, these subscribers were almost exclusively from the upper or upper-middle classes; unlike Khan's, they were generally male.

After the Second World War, however, the Alawiyya's importance grew considerably. It gave rise to numerous other Traditionalist *turuq*, of which the most important in Europe was that in Paris directed by the Romanian Michel Vâlsan, a *tariqa* which has influenced the direction of French Islamology. As a result of a series of visions starting in 1965, the Schuonian Alawiyya itself became the Maryamiyya, a much less Islamic group. By Schuon's death in 1998, the Maryamiyya had thousands of members worldwide, many of whom were themselves influential as writers or academics. Some Maryami *zawiya*s remained relatively close to the inter-war model of the Alawiyya, but some others came to see Schuon as an *avatar*, a Hindu concept which approximates that of a divine incarnation. For these Maryamis, both teaching and practice moved so far from regular Sufism that the label "neo-Sufi" may no longer be appropriate.

SUFISTICAL GROUPS

Khan's and Schuon's groups were neo-Sufi, describing themselves as Sufi but differing significantly from the standard models found in

[66] When asked about this during an interview, one of Schuon's earliest followers responded that in those days there was no regular Muslim community in Europe, and that admitting one's conversion to Islam would have been inconceivable. Harald de Meyenburg, interviewed in Lausanne, September 1998. Regular Muslims might have been found, though, had an effort been made. The "inconceivable", however, was probably an oblique reference to anti-Islamic prejudice.

the Islamic world. These differences followed from the characteristics of modernity that were identified at the start of this chapter. We will now consider the more difficult cases of three "Sufistical" groups that did not describe themselves as Sufi during the interwar period, but had Sufi origins, and in two cases did claim a Sufi identity after the Second World War.

Sebottendorff's group

The first Sufistical group to emerge after the First World War was in most respects atypical, but is notable for the accidental role it played in world history. It was established in Munich by Rudolf Freiherr von Sebottendorff, a German somewhat after the model of Aguéli.

Sebottendorff was born Adam Glauer, the son of a train driver, and acquired his alias and title of nobility (Freiherr) under controversial circumstances. His spiritual interests were mainly in Freemasonry (which also interested Guénon and Aguéli, though not Schuon), but during several decades in Turkey (during which he acquired Ottoman citizenship) he encountered regular Sufi *turuq*, and possibly also the unusual Bektashiyya, which was itself linked to late Ottoman Freemasonry. Sebottendorff became convinced that Sufism was an ancient form of Freemasonry, the reverse of Khan's suggestion that Freemasonry was inspired by Sufism, and returned to Germany shortly before the First World War to spread a form of neo-Sufism that concentrated more than anything else on numerology. He was initially unsuccessful, but after the end of the war he joined forces with a pre-existing group with esoteric and racialist interests, the *Germanen-Orden*. Under these auspices, Sebottendorff established in Munich the *Thulegesellschaft*, which he intended this to be a vehicle for spreading his quasi-Masonic, quasi-Sufi numerological doctrine.[67]

The vision of Sebottendorff's sponsors in the Germanen-Orden proved more influential than Sebottendorff's intentions, however, and the *Thulegesellschaft* became instead a primarily racialist and political body. As such, it published a newspaper—the *Münchner Beobachter und Sportblatt*—and sponsored a political party, the *Deutsche Arbeiterpartei*. Sebottendorff finally resigned from the

[67] M. Sedgwick, *Against the Modern World*, pp. 65–7, 95–8.

Thulegesellschaft as the result of a scandal relating to the loss of the group's membership lists to the authorities of the short-lived Bavarian Soviet Republic, and returned to Turkey. Shortly after this, the Deutsche Arbeiterpartei was joined by Adolf Hitler. Hitler transformed that party into the Nazi party, the *Münchner Beobachter und Sportblatt* into the *Völkische Beobachter*, and the logo of the *Thulegesellschaft* into the swastika.[68]

It would be ridiculous to argue that the Nazi Party was originally a neo-Sufi group in anything more than accidental form. Sebottendorff's Sufism played little role in the *Thulegesellschaft*, and none in the *Deutsche Arbeiterpartei*. Had the *Deutsche Arbeiterpartei* not existed, Hitler would doubtless have used any one of dozens of other such groups as his vehicle. The *Thulegesellschaft*, then, tells us less about neo-Sufism than it does about some of the possibilities inherent in the general milieu in which neo-Sufism emerged. It will not be referred to again.

Meher Baba's group

More typical is the Sufistical group established by Meher Baba, which began to define itself as partly Sufi in the 1940s, when it subsumed the Sufi Order in California. This section of Khan's Sufi Order had been established during the early inter-war period by Rabia Martin, Khan's first American follower. After meeting Meher Baba in 1942 and reading his works, Martin became convinced that Meher Baba was "the living embodiment of Sufism"[69] and consigned herself and her followers to his care in 1945.[70]

Meher Baba was born in 1894, the son of Persian Zoroastrian parents residing in India.[71] His spiritual awakening was at the hands of a female Indian Sufi saint, Babajan, in 1913.[72] He subsequently followed another great Sufi, Taj al-Din, described as the *qutb* (pole)

[68] Ibid., pp. 96–7.

[69] Quoted in Bhau Kalchuri, *Lord Meher*, Avatar Meher Baba Perpetual Public Trust, p. 3067. www.lordmeher.org.

[70] B. Kalchuri, *Lord Meher*, p. 3068. The *Religious Movements Homepage*, religious-movements.lib.virginia.edu, gives 1952.

[71] He was originally named Merwan Sheheriarji.

[72] B. Kalchuri, *Lord Meher*, p. 195.

of his age,[73] as well as several Hindu gurus. Despite these Sufi origins, however, Meher Baba did not present himself as a Sufi during the inter-war period, but rather as an *avatar*, a divine incarnation, and also as the reincarnation of Zoroaster, Moses, Jesus, and Muhammad. It was as an *avatar* that he was followed by thousands in India, and by some dozens in Britain and America. His Western following grew dramatically after the Second World War, when it included such counter-cultural icons as Pete Townsend of *The Who*.[74]

Meher Baba's teaching concentrated on love—love of Meher Baba that would spill out to become love among all his/His creation, and would result in "union with God".[75] Many Sufis, of course, teach love of the *shaikh* as a means to love of God and thence to union with Him, but love of the leader of a religious group is not in any sense exclusive to Sufism. Sufism seems to have played little part in Meher Baba's inter-war identity or that of his followers. For European followers, his identity as the reincarnation of Jesus was perhaps more important, to judge from the attention they paid to the reminiscences of his time on the cross that he delivered during a visit to a church in Switzerland in the 1930s.[76]

Sufism, then, played some part in Meher Baba's initial legitimisation, but no real part in his teachings, though an article of his on the regular Sufi understanding of "certainty" was published in 1935 in *The Sufi*,[77] the journal of Khan's Sufi Order (by then led by his sons). Meher Baba's later identity as "the living embodiment of Sufism" resulted, in the words of Abdul Ghani Munsiff (a senior

[73] Ibid., p. 213.

[74] *Religious Movements Homepage*. For a description of the Meher Baba centre in South Carolina in this period, see Thomas Robbins and Dick Anthony, "Getting Straight with Meher Baba: A Study of Mysticism, Drug Rehabilitation and Postadolescent Role Conflict", *Journal for the Scientific Study of Religion*, XI (1972), pp. 122–40.

[75] This is the summary of J. Gordon Melton, *Biographical Dictionary of American Cult and Sect Leaders*, New York, Garland, 1985, quoted on the *Religious Movements Homepage*.

[76] B. Kalchuri, *Lord Meher*, p. 599.

[77] Shri Meher Baba, "What is Love?", *The Sufi*, I, 5 (March 1935), pp. 260–5. The article is almost entirely in line with regular Sufi doctrine, though towards the end it states that "divine love knows no law. It is above all rules and regulations, above dogmas and rituals" (p. 264).

Indian follower and a former "fanatic Muslim"),[78] from the fact that "Sufism, Vedanta and Christian mysticism are one and the same in the matter of dealing with the esoteric life",[79] a form of religious pluralism. It also results from Rabia Martin's equating the *avatar* with the *rasul*, with *rasul* most unusually defined as "the divine incarnation of God",[80] and from Meher Baba's contention that "Sufism, as understood by ninety-nine percent of the people, is not real Sufism".[81]

The aspects of modernity that were noted in the cases of Inayat Khan and the Schuonian Alawiyya are also visible in Meher Baba's teaching. Like them, he addressed the problem of religious plurality—all religions were indeed one, incarnated in himself.[82] He subscribed to the view of the West as "more inclined toward the material side of things", and although he did not refer to the *kali yuga*, he linked this image of the West to the angst of the age, adding that materialism "has from untold ages brought in its wake wars, pestilence and financial crises".[83] Financial crises were of course much on people's minds in the wake of the Wall Street crash. Concessions to individualism of the sort condemned by Elwell-Sutton may also be discerned in the way in which Meher Baba's leading disciple in inter-war Europe, Meredith Starr, told the *Empire News* that his centre at East Challacombe in England provided "individual help and instruction in meditation and practical psychology".[84]

As well as being characteristically modern, however, Meher Baba was also characteristically subcontinental. Indian popular religion makes little distinction between *sadhus* by denomination, and a fusion of Hinduism and Islam had even been attempted in the

[78] B. Kalchuri, *Lord Meher*, p. 3219.

[79] Abdul Ghani Munsiff, undated letter [to Rabia Martin], quoted in B. Kalchuri, *Lord Meher*, p. 3233.

[80] Ibid., p. 3067.

[81] Ibid., p. 3792.

[82] This may derive from Sai Baba, who first presented Zoroaster to Meher Baba as an *avatar*. B. Kalchuri, *Lord Meher*, p. 223. Acceptance of this idea in one sense constituted Meher Baba's conversion from Zoroastrianism to a Hindu universalism.

[83] B. Kalchuri, *Lord Meher*, p. 554.

[84] Starr, *Empire News* (10 April 1932), quoted in B. Kalchuri, *Lord Meher*, p. 1575.

sixteenth century by the Emperor Akbar. This lack of distinction played a part in Khan's early understanding of religious plurality. Both of Meher Baba's Sufis—Babajan and Taj al-Din—belong more to Indian popular religion rather than to the literate "high tradition" of Sufism, where a distinction between religions is commonly made even more rigorously in India than elsewhere. We know of Babajan, Meher Baba's spiritual awakener, only from the accounts of Meher Baba's followers, but she appears as the type of saint that a regular Sufi would class as *majdhub* ("attracted" and thus spiritually intoxicated); she was certainly not the *shaikh* of any *tariqa*. Similarly, Taj al-Din is otherwise unknown, but does not sound at all like a regular *qutb*. Meher Baba, in the end, is more neo-Hindu than neo-Sufi, connected to neo-Sufism most importantly through the aspects of modernity that he addressed.

Gurdjieff's group

A third and more complicated Sufistical figure is George Gurdjieff, a Greek Armenian (Gurdzhaev is the Russianisation of Gurdjian).[85] Gurdjieff is today one of the major figures in alternative spirituality.[86] As with Meher Baba, his Sufi identity was stressed after the Second World War as a result of a takeover. The group taken over was that at Coombe Springs, Britain, in 1962, directed by John Bennett, a former disciple of Gurdjieff (who had died in 1949). Bennett passed his Gurdjieff group to Idries Shah, a British postwar neo-Sufi somewhat on Inayat Khan's model.[87] Justifying this, Bennett (perhaps encouraged by Shah) maintained that "Gurdjieff was, more than anything else, a Sufi".[88] According to Shah, Gurdjieff's

[85] James Moore, *Gurdjieff: The Anatomy of a Myth*, Shaftesbury: Element, 1991, p. 340, n. 2.

[86] Google hits for "Gurdjieff" on 6 December 2004: 250,000 (one benchmark is 600,000 hits for Trotsky).

[87] This transaction did not have a happy ending. Shah sold Coombe Springs for £100,000, perhaps $2,000,000 in today's terms, shortly after acquiring it. Anna T. Challenger, *Philosophy and Art in Gurdjieff's Beelzebub: A Modern Sufi Odyssey*, Amsterdam: Rodopi, 2002, p. 21. Many felt that Shah had deliberately deceived Bennett, which does not seem to be impossible.

[88] John G. Bennett, *Gurdjieff: Making a New World*, New York: Harper & Row, 1973, quoted in Challenger, *Philosophy and Art*, p. 12.

work "abound[s] with references, often semi-covert, to the Sufi system".[89] Since Shah is indisputably a neo-Sufi, and since Bennett had some prior experience of Sufism (he had spent some time with regular Naqshbandi *shaikhs* in Damascus and Beirut in 1953–55),[90] these views might carry some weight.

One immediate difficulty is that it is hard to establish anything about Gurdjieff with much certainty, since obfuscation was an important element of his method, found not only in his teachings but even in his group's practice. His writings were often autobiographical in form, but much of this autobiography was overtly fictional, as is indicated by the prevalence of fantastical names such as "Hadji-Zephir-Bogga-Eddin".[91] Many of Gurdjieff's followers, however, seem to have failed to get this point, and have taken at face value stories that were surely fictional.[92] Most important among these is Gurdjieff's account of an encounter with a Sufi *tariqa* in Central Asia, the Sarmoung Order, from whom Gurdjieff said he had learned many of his teachings and spiritual exercises.

Although few commentators on Gurdjieff would put it so bluntly, it seems clear to me that the Sarmoung are entirely imaginary. No Sufi *tariqa* of such a name is known, and in fact "Sarmoung" is a typically Gurdjieffian fantastical name. It is immediately obvious to anyone who knows anything about regular Sufism that there is nothing remotely Sufi about the Sarmoung Order as described by Gurdjieff. Its supposed foundation in Babylon in 2120 BC would predate the emergence of anything generally

[89] Idries Shah, *Way of the Sufi*, London: Cape 1968, quoted in A.T. Challenger, *Philosophy and Art*, p. 20.

[90] In 1952–53 with Emin Chikhou in Damascus. See J.G. Bennett, *Journeys in Islamic Countries*, Sherborne: Coombe Springs Press 1976. In 1955 he visited Abdallah Daghestani in Beirut. A. Rawlinson, "History". Daghestani was the *shaikh* of Muhammad Nazim al-Qubrusi, probably the *shaikh* with the largest following in the West at the start of the twenty-first century.

[91] This character, who is one of those with "a tendency to enthuse over . . . 'higher matters' . . . with anyone they meet, on opportune and inopportune occasions", appears in G.I. Gurdjieff, *Beelzebub's Tales to his Grandson: An Objectively Impartial Criticism of the Life of Man*, 1950; reprinted New York: Penguin Compass, 1999, p. 871.

[92] One exception was Piotr Ouspensky: "What was true in these stories I could never decide exactly". Piotr D. Ouspensky, *In Search of the Miraculous: Fragments of an Unknown Teaching*, New York: Harcourt/Brace, 1949, p. 36.

recognised as Sufism, and no known regular Sufi *tariqa* has a pre-Islamic foundation myth. More importantly, the central feature of the community Gurdjieff claimed to have visited was a temple where priestesses performed sacred dances.[93] Temple dancing was important to Gurdjieff, who famously described himself as "a rather good teacher of temple dances",[94] but no sort of dancing by females has anything to do with any variety of regular Sufism ever recorded. Similarly, the Enneagram (the other famous innovation of Gurdjieff's which was given a Sarmoung provenance) has no echo anywhere in regular Sufism. Gurdjieff's works do frequently refer to Sufism, as Shah suggested, but usually in ways designed to add an air of mystery and playful authority to his stories (as with the Sarmoung).

Sufis, Gurdjieff explained in 1923, are

> wise men who tried to realise for themselves every religion, and all legends and doctrines dispassionately. They did not blindly submit. Before accepting anything, they before had realised it for themselves. Whatever they could realise for themselves, they accepted. What they could not, they rejected. In this way a new religion was formed, although the material of which it was formed was adopted from other religions.[95]

This is not a description of Sufism as found in the Islamic world, but may be a description of Gurdjieff's own ideal.

Taken together, Gurdjieff's teachings are hard to encapsulate[96]—one consequence of the element of obfuscation in them. If any principle predominates, it may be the idea of learning through experience, of the "examined life",[97] of "mobilised attention equipoised among intellect, feeling and body".[98] Static "self awareness" must be

[93] G. I. Gurdjieff, *Meetings with Remarkable Men*, 1963; reprinted New York: Penguin Compass, 2002, pp. 154–62.

[94] Often quoted; see J. Moore, *Gurdjieff*, p. 351.

[95] J. Gurdjieff, 1923 lecture, quoted in A.T. Challenger, *Philosophy and Art*, p. 16.

[96] As Moore put it, they have "proved 'in the depths too deep and in the shallows too swift' to be netted and anatomized by historians of religion". J. Moore, *Gurdjieff*, p. 57.

[97] A.T. Challenger, *Philosophy and Art*, p. 117.

[98] J. Moore, *Gurdjieff*, p. 352. Moore uses the phrase in explaining the impact of Gurdjieff's dances, which are "interior exercises in sensation". "Counting in common may be added, and silent or spoken prayer. These diverse demands are reconcilable only by the dancer's mobilised attention equiposed among intellect, feeling and body".

combined with "self remembering" in action.[99] At one level, this might derive from Sufism: it is certainly not incompatible with the classical Sufi approach, and some individuals do manage to combine Gurdjieff's approach with regular Sufism.[100] At another level, the resemblance between these principles and Sufism is so general that parallels might with equal justice be drawn with several other spiritual traditions. More precise echoes of the teachings of regular Sufism can sometimes be found,[101] but do not in any way predominate. Gurdjieff named the grandson of his important semi-prophetic figure Beelzebub "Hassein", a name that combines Hasan and Hussein, the grandsons of the Prophet Muhammad.[102] This might, however, be read either as homage to the Prophet Muhammad or as disrespect for him. As a Transcaucasian Christian whose father had been killed by Turkish troops,[103] Gurdjieff might not be expected to be an enthusiast of regular Islam.[104]

The practice of Gurdjieff's followers clearly owes something concrete to regular Sufism, however. Although the Sarmoung is obviously fictional, Gurdjieff did know something about Sufism. There are other stories of Sufis in his writings which sound much more like the real thing, notably stories of a Persian Sufi met in Central Asia.[105] Gurdjieff had probably spent some time in Turkey as a child, and spoke Turkish.[106] One practice used by his followers

[99] This was the summary of Shems Friedlander, a former Gurdjieffian Mevlevi, interview, Cairo, 6 December 2004.

[100] Friedlander, for example, is a long-term Mevlevi (of a Turkish *tariqa*) and devout Muslim who continues to read Gurdjieff for spiritual illumination. Interview, Cairo, 6 December 2004.

[101] For example, the idea of the *shaikh* as a route to God. See Gurdieff's answer to the third question put to him on "Contact with God". www.gurdjieff-internet.com/article_print.php?ID=129&=19.

[102] A.T. Challenger, *Philosophy and Art*, p. 69.

[103] J. Moore, *Gurdjieff*, p. 109.

[104] He does recommend Muslim bathroom hygiene as superior to Western slovenliness in *Beelzebub's Tales* (p. 977), but this recommendation may have been somewhat playful. "Gurdjieff, Sufism and Mohammed" (*Gurdjieff Journal*, XXXI (n. d.), pp. 9–10) argues for Gurdjieff's essentially Christian identity.

[105] G.I. Gurdjieff, *Meetings with Remarkable Men*, pp. 183–91.

[106] A.T. Challenger, *Philosophy and Art*, p. 1. Gurdjieff is also reported by Ouspensky to have done extempore translations of Persian verses he knew by heart

is almost identical to Sufi *dhikr*, except that the phrase used ("Lord have mercy") is Christian.[107] His dances, which were first practiced as "sacred gymnastics" in 1918,[108] owe much to the Mevleviyya. An analysis of this debt is now being prepared by Pierre Lory.

Gurdjieff had probably encountered the Mevleviyya by 1912; he was in Istanbul between 1908 and 1912, in contact with a Young Turk Theosophist, Prince Mehmed Sabaheddin, founder of the Society for Personal Initiative and Administrative Decentralisation.[109] During the early 1920s, when Gurdjieff and a number of his followers were living in Istanbul (where they had arrived as refugees from the Red Army, then advancing into Georgia),[110] Gurdjieff was a regular visitor to a Mevlevi *sama* at the Kapoussou *tekke*. He often took with him two close Russian followers, a former Theosophist (Piotr Demianovich Ouspensky) and a musician (Thomas Alexandrovich de Hartmann).[111]

The visits to the Mevleviyya of Gurdjieff, Ouspensky and de Hartmann in the 1920s are not those of Sufi *murids*, but of interested observers. Given that de Hartmann was a musician, the visitors might even have been artistic observers. In fact, the Gurdjieff circle in Georgia in 1919 often looks more like a group of performance artists than of spiritual seekers.[112] Gurdjieff's dances were being developed in conjunction with Jeanne de Salzmann, formerly a successful teacher of experimental dance in Russia. They were actually

(Challenger, p. 16), but Bennett is clear that Gurdjieff did not know Persian. J.G. Bennett, *Journeys in Islamic Countries*, I, p. 7.

107 For this exercise, Friedlander, interview, Cairo, 6 December 2004.

108 J. Moore, *Gurdjieff*, p. 107. The "stop exercise", first recorded in 1917 (p. 101), is also ascribed to the Mevlevis, but Friedlander knows of no Mevlevi practice that resembles the "stop exercise"; interview, Cairo, 6 December 2004. Bennett observed what he thought was a "stop" during a Mevlevi *sama* in the 1950s. J.G. Bennett, *Journeys in Islamic Countries*, II, p. 95. During any *hadra*, whoever is directing the *dhikr* sometimes issues signals to stop a part of the liturgy and pass on to the next.

109 J. Moore, *Gurdjieff*, pp. 149, 362.

110 This period of Gurdjieff's life is documented, and outside the realms of fictional autobiography. See J. Moore, *Gurdjieff*, pp. 139–53.

111 Ibid., pp. 144–5. J.G. Bennett, *Journeys in Islamic Countries*, p. 5.

112 Of course, the two are to some extent combined in surrealism.

"performed" in the Tbilisi Theater, while the group worked on a ballet provisionally entitled *The Struggle of the Magicians*.[113]

Mevlevi influence on the dances is well established, then, and regular Sufism was evidently an element in Gurdjieff's general inspiration, as well as in his construction of legitimacy. In the end, though, like Meher Baba, he appears more Sufistical than neo-Sufi. There were sufficient elements of Sufism in the teachings and practice of both men to make later claims of Sufism somewhat plausible, but the real link between them and the neo-Sufi groups considered earlier is not so much Sufism as the inter-war European environment in which they operated. Like the others we have looked at, Gurdjieff addressed religious plurality through a pluralism that has something of the Theosophical Society about it. He wrote that "fragments of [ancient] knowledge remained intact and passed from generation to generation through a very limited number of initiated beings",[114] the implication being that he himself was such an initiated being, perhaps through the Sarmoung. The Traditionalists' understanding of the transmission of ancient knowledge, of course, was deadly serious, while Gurdjieff's was as ever somewhat playful. As one might expect, Gurdjieff's and Guénon's followers were not on good terms.[115]

As well as addressing religious plurality, Gurdjieff also addressed individualism, perhaps more effectively than any other inter-war group. His method institutionalised not only the continuing individual search but also the individual discovery of personal truth (an approach, as have seen, that Gurdjieff ascribed with little justification to Sufis). One of Gurdjieff's trademarks was his emphasis on "the simultaneous and harmonious development of body, emotions and intellect".[116] This was well suited to the times, and was echoed by Meher Baba, who told his followers that "you will find in my

[113] J. Moore, *Gurdjieff*, pp. 128–9, 134.

[114] G.I. Gurdjieff, *Beelzebub's Tales*, p. 872.

[115] Moore gives an account, probably somewhat imaginary, of a hostile encounter between Alexandren de Salzmann and René Guénon in Paris (*Gurdjieff*, p. 229). The point of the account is the humour of Salzmann and the humourless pomposity of Guénon.

[116] J. Moore, *Gurdjieff*, p. 57.

teachings and activities both renunciation and involvement in the world and its affairs . . . Materialism and spirituality are both combined".[117] The one aspect of modernity we have come to expect that is not apparent in Gurdjieff is angst. Perhaps angst is incompatible with playful humour and lightness. Even Gurdjieff at times criticised modernity, however, telling Ouspensky in 1916 that "there is no progress whatever. . . Modern civilisation is based on violence and slavery and fine words".[118] This, as Ouspensky remarked, was a view that easily seemed persuasive as the First World War entered its second year. Gurdjieff also later criticised the American incarnation of modernity at some length, seeing it as characterised by the blind pursuit of profit, advertising, the consumption of canned food, and the prevalence of venereal disease and talk of "equal rights" for women.[119]

CONCLUSION

Inter-war neo-Sufism addressed circumstances and concerns that were characteristic of European modernity. An angst-ridden awareness of the *kali yuga* is found in each group, though it is less pronounced in Gurdjieff. Khan and Schuon both embraced religious pluralism, as (in different ways) did Meher Baba and Gurdjieff. Gurdjieff celebrated individualism and originality, and presents a clear example of Elwell-Sutton's displacement of God in favour of an emphasis on the development of the individual.[120] Khan publicly accepted individualism and originality, though his emphasis on the development of the individual rather than on God seems to have been more presentation than substance. Schuon invoked tradition rather than God, and it might be argued that Traditionalist truth was dynamic, introducing an element of originality. No-one save Meher Baba (a special case, as an *avatar*) makes much explicit reference to God.

[117] B. Kalchuri, *Lord Meher*, p. 1547.
[118] P. Ouspensky, *In Search of the Miraculous*, p. 51.
[119] G.I. Gurdjieff, *Beelzebub's Tales*, pp. 918–89.
[120] It might be argued that this was only superficial, and that Gurdjieff retained an awareness of transcendent reality.

As well as reflecting a modernity that was not so different from our own modernity, inter-war neo-Sufism was also a product of its period. Khan, Gurdjieff and Schuon were all indebted to the Theosophical Society—Khan directly, Gurdjieff through Ouspensky,[121] and Schuon through Guénon and Encausse. Guénon and Khan later condemned Theosophy— Guénon in an early book[122] and Khan in at least one quip—,[123] and all went far beyond Theosophy in their teachings and practice, but the common factor is there.[124]

Neo-Sufism was also a product of the inter-war period because regular Sufism and regular Islam were then almost entirely absent from the European public sphere (outside the Balkans). As a result, neo-Sufis such as Khan or Schuon could make almost any assertion they felt like about Sufism or Islam, and get away with it. Once Islam became more present in the European public sphere after the Second World War, this approach ceased to be possible. Italy was one of the last Western European countries in which this happened. Even in the early 1990s, Shaikh Abd al-Wahid Pallavicini, a former Schuonian Alawi, enjoyed unchallenged authority there as a public interpreter of Sufism. Once immigrant Islamic associations were established in Italy, however, a growing chorus of objections began to drown out his Traditionalist neo-Sufi explanations of Sufism and Islam.[125]

The inter-war neo-Sufis had no wish to bring regular Islam into the public sphere. Khan regretted the obstacles to his teaching presented by what he saw as European "prejudice" against Islam. His solution was to avoid this prejudice by separating his teaching from

[121] It was under Ouspensky's patronage that Gurdjieff first emerged as a spiritual teacher.

[122] *Le Théosophisme, histoire d'une pseudo-religion*, Paris, 1921.

[123] When asked how Sufism "works upon him once a person has studied Theosophy", Khan replied: "As a disinfectant", I. Khan, *Biography*, p. 178. In writing, Khan was generally more polite.

[124] Another link is Khan's meeting in Boston in 1923 with Ananda Commaraswamy. I. Khan, *Biography*, p. 107. Coomaraswamy was second only to Guénon himself in the early development of Traditionalism. Nothing, however, is known of what transpired at this meeting, and there seem to be no other significant links between Traditionalism and Khan's neo-Sufism.

[125] M. Sedgwick, *Against the Modern World*, pp. 140–1.

Islam. Schuon, likewise, separated his Alawiyya from other European branches of that *tariqa*, and he and his followers concealed the fact that they were Muslim, feeling justified in breaking the Shari'a to do this (by drinking beer). Schuon does not refer specifically to European "prejudice" against Islam as his reason for this, but rather to the circumstances of the *kali yuga*. The most relevant circumstances, however, must have been those that Khan identified.

As an aspect of today's globalised Islam, neo-Sufism is not statistically significant. Its roots in European modernity, however, make it more important than numbers alone would. As more and more European Muslims, of whatever origin, enter the social classes to which inter-war neo-Sufism appealed, neo-Sufism may prove to be one possible future direction for the development of European Islam.

Part III. FROM STATE CONTROL TO FOREIGN POLICY

During the inter-war period, Muslim populations in Europe lived in different political contexts and experienced various kinds of relations with state authorities. Each situation depended on the socio-economic profile of Muslims themselves (migrant workers, soldiers, political refugees, students, merchants, converts and "surviving minorities" from the Ottoman Empire), but was also related to the very nature of the state (colonial or not) in which they were living and the local tradition of relations between state and religion.

BETWEEN AUTONOMY AND STATE CONTROL

In South-Eastern Europe, Muslim minorities generally enjoyed a religious autonomy or some religious rights granted by international treaties and, in certain cases, by the state Constitution and laws. In Yugoslavia, as recalled by Fikret Karčić, the St. Germain Agreement of 1919 and the Yugoslav constitutions of 1921 and 1931 provided such rights. Similar rights were guaranteed for the Muslims in Greece by the Lausanne Treaty of 1923 and some earlier laws (mentioned in Yannis Bonos' chapter), and in Bulgaria by the Neuilly Treaty, the "Statute on the Spiritual Arrangement and Government of Muslims" of 1919 and various laws on education.[1]

[1] Maria Koinova, *Muslims of Bulgaria*, Centre for Documentation and Information on Minorities in Europe—Southeast Europe, www.greekhelsinki.gr/pdf/cedime-se-bulgaria-muslims.pdf, who relies on Krassimir Kănev, "Zakonodatelstvo i politika kăm etničeskite i religioznite malcinstva v Bălgarija [Legislation and Politics towards the Ethnic and Religious Minorities in Bulgaria]", in A. Krăšteva (ed.), *Obštnosti i identičnosti v Bălgarija*, Sofia: Petekston, 1998.

As for Romania, Muslims' rights were specifically set out in the Paris Treaty and reiterated in the Law of 26 December 1920, the Constitution of March 1923 and the Law on Cults of April 1924.[2] This legal corpus not only recognised freedom of religious beliefs and practices, but also ensured that Shari'a courts were given jurisdiction in matters of Muslim personal status, family and inheritance. In addition, they guaranteed the existence and functioning of private schools and pious foundations (*waqf*).

In fact, throughout the period under consideration, the existence of Muslim communities in the Balkans continued to be called into question regularly by some officials and politicians. Their degree of autonomy varied considerably from one country to another and even from one period to another. It ranged from a rather large autonomy guaranteed by international treaties and national laws—which also resulted from some indifference by the state authorities—to determined interference in minority affairs and close governmental control of the various Muslim institutions. In Yugoslavia, the *Reis ul-Ulema* (head of the '*ulama*) Džemaludin Čaušević regularly fought against the political authorities to safeguard the autonomy of Islamic religious institutions (see Xavier Bougarel's chapter). Following the establishment of King Alexander's authoritarian regime, the status of the Islamic community was altered in 1929–30, the outcome being a stronger hierarchical organisation of religious institutions throughout the country and limitations on their autonomy. But in the new Yugoslav political context following the assassination of the King in 1934, Muslim leaders found a more favourable ground when dealing with the Serbian parties in power. A new law passed in 1936 re-established the autonomy of their religious institutions (i.e. the right of electing members of all the Muslim institutions and managing the pious foundations themselves). The King only retained the prerogative of appointing persons to the most important posts.[3] With such changing policies,

[2] Giuseppe Cossuto, *Storia dei Turchi di Dobrugia*, Istanbul: Isis, 2001, pp. 96–7.

[3] Alexandre Popovic, *L'islam balkanique*, Berlin-Wiesbaden: Otto Harrassowitz, 1986, pp. 318–19; Xavier Bougarel, "Un courant pan-islamiste en Bosnie-Herzégovine", in G. Kepel (ed.), *Exil et Royaume. Les appartenances au monde arabo-musulman aujourd'hui*, Paris: Presses de la FNSP, 1994, pp. 278–9; Dragan Novaković, *Školstvo*

the reform of Shari'a Courts and Islamic Law went on during the inter-war period, but could not be completed entirely (see Fikret Karčić's chapter). In the same way these unstable circumstances explain how in Southern Yugoslavia, the political authorities and later on the religious authorities opened modernist and reformist *madrasa*s, while local '*ulama* were allowed to manage their own "old ottoman-style" *madrasa* (see Muhamed Aruçi's chapter).

In Bulgaria, the new Statute of 1919 allowed the state to intervene in the election of local and national representatives of the Muslim Community. Moreover, the government had the power to dismiss them and to monitor closely the management of the *waqf*s and the relations of the Community with foreign organisations.[4] However, state-minority relations continued to be based on a compromise between the religious elite and the government. The spiritual leaders tried to retain religious unity among Muslims and to prevent them from succumbing to secular mobilisation. In return, the Bulgarian state rewarded them by not interfering in religious affairs.[5] But, at least from 1933 onwards, the government suspended elections of local Muslim representatives in order to eliminate Kemalists. After 1938, however, as a result of the relaxation of King Boris' authoritarian rule instituted in May 1934 and a rapprochement with the Balkan Entente, which included Turkey, some measures were officially taken, this time in favour of the Kemalist trend; these included the nomination of pro-Kemalist or rather "non-anti-Kemalist" representatives, the official introduction of the Latin script, and restrictions on the jurisdiction of Shari'a courts.[6]

Islamske zajednice: školski sistem Islamske zajednice na jugoslovenskim prostorima od 1879–1991 godine, Niš: JUNIR, 2004.

[4] M. Koinova, *Muslims of Bulgaria*.

[5] Wolfgang Höpken, "From Religious Identity to Ethnic Mobilisation: the Turks of Bulgaria before, under and since Communism", in H. Poulton and S. Taji-Farouki (eds), *Muslim identity and the Balkan State*, London: Hurst, 1997, pp. 60–61.

[6] See Mila Mancheva, "State-minority Relations and the Education of Turks and Pomaks in Inter-war Bulgaria, 1918–1944", unpublished PhD thesis, Central European University (Budapest), 2003.

In Greece, there was the same discrepancy between the autonomy provided by treaties and law and the situation at grassroots level, characterised by the nomination by the Greek authorities of muftis (who acquired the functions of the *qadi*s) and other local representatives in charge of the management of mosques, *waqf*s and schools (see Yannis Bonos' chapter).[7] As for Romania, the Muslim community was supposed to be self-governing, although *qadi*s and muftis were appointed by the government which also paid the salaries of the religious staff after the *waqf*s' properties had been nationalised. The office of Grand Mufti (*baş müfti*) was created in 1928, but the position was not filled until 1937. The minority benefited from private elementary schools where Turkish was the language of instruction, and from the *madrasa* of Medgidia dedicated to the training of religious staff, which functioned thanks to a state grant. It is not clear whether the political authorities were responsible for the introduction of the Latin alphabet in these schools, but one should note that the reform was introduced in 1935, the year when the government abolished Shari'a courts (despite their previous reorganisation).[8]

Even in the case of Albania, which was an exception because of its Muslim majority, one can observe the same phenomenon ranging between autonomy and interference, if not control, by the political authorities in Islamic religious affairs. Despite the secular nature of the state, the Albanian government was the main actor in the transformation of Islamic institutions and initiated the establishment of a centralised religious organisation that was easier to control (see Nathalie Clayer's chapter).

Outside the Balkans, in Hungary and Czechoslovakia, Islam was an officially recognized religion, but the authorities were extremely reluctant to give formal approval to associations claiming to represent the Muslim community. The reason might have been that such official endorsement would have bestowed an unjustified status on the Muslim leaders of those associations. The "Muslim Religious Community for Czechoslovakia" (*al-Ittihad al-Islami*) formed by a

[7] See also A. Popovic, *L'Islam balkanique*, pp. 155–64.

[8] A. Popovic, *L'Islam balkanique*, pp. 222–48; Frederick de Jong, "Turks and Tatars in Romania", *Turcica*, XVIII (1986), pp. 165–89 (see pp. 176–8); Gyorgy Lederer, "Islam in Romania", *Central Asian Survey*, XV, 3–4 (1996), pp. 349–68.

group of Muslims of Prague in November 1934 was not recognised by the inter-war state authorities.[9] The Czechoslovakian Ministry of Interior and Ministry of Education and National Culture, together with the Land Council of Prague, opposed the claims of this association to conduct marriages and burials. They also contested the territorial extent of the Community's activity, argued about the language that should be used for the keeping of records and which legal rite (Hanafi, Hanbali, Maliki or Shafi'i) should be allowed. In Hungary, the two communities made up of Bosnians on the one hand and Turks on the other were also merely tolerated, even if their leaders, Huszein Hilmi Durics and Abdul Latif, had been very officially appointed as "Guardian of the Muslim tombs" and "Inspector of the Muslim cemetery" respectively.[10]

In Western Europe, the states often considered their Muslim populations as temporary sojourners and were less concerned with educational or legal issues. Their main focus was on politics as Muslim workers and students were considered to be a highly sensitive population. The migration process and growth of Muslim diasporic communities throughout the European colonial empires facilitated the circulation of information. In this context, the official policies towards Muslims residing in Europe as well as their activities in the metropolis acquired an increasing symbolic value in the eyes of colonial populations. Islam was always controlled in some degree by the political authorities. In places where Muslim migrants made up significant groups within certain sectors of the industrial labour force, as in France and the UK, some religious organisations were suspected of offering support to social and political unrest while others were considered as a useful means to counter communist and trade union influence.

Such control was often enforced through the housing system favoured by the local state authorities, such as the boarding houses where Arab and Somali seamen in British ports lived, and which

[9] Miloš Mendel, "The Islamic Religious Community in Bohemia and Moravia (1934–1945)", *Archív Orientální*, 66 (1998), pp. 127–41. The Community was officially recognised in 1941 in the context of Nazi occupation.

[10] György Lederer, "Sur l'islam à Budapest", *La transmission du savoir dans le monde musulman périphérique*, 6 (November 1986), pp. 23–37.

were often run by men from their own tribes. In France, where a special government agency (the *Commission Interministérielle des Affaires Musulmanes* or CIAM)[11] was in charge of the supervision of Muslim Affairs from 1911, a Department of North-African Native Affairs (*Service des Affaires Indigènes Nord-Africaines* or SAINA) was created in 1924 in Paris, with branches in the provinces established later on. The department provided assistance to North African immigrant workers (accommodation, medical facilities and employment bureaus) but was primarily concerned with surveillance and control.[12] North African immigrants were under surveillance by special police units, and also through the health care system and the boarding houses that were specifically assigned to them. In the Parisian region, seven boarding houses specifically for North-African workers were created during the 1930s.[13] In Marseilles, a Special Department (*Service Spécial*) was in charge of the collective housing of the foreign work force. One should also mention the Bobigny Franco-Muslim hospital, which was strictly for use by North Africans. It was conceived to serve France's "civilising mission" aimed at wining over colonial populations and persuading them of the superiority of Western civilisation, as well as to address social problems among the poor immigrant population. Such "positive segregation" which this establishment represented was also meant to serve as a tool to protect the French population from North African immigrants who were generally seen as a potential threat to public health. For practical purposes, the hospital was partly administered by the police and played a part in the surveillance of a Muslim immigrant population mainly composed of young single men.[14]

[11] The Commission gave advice to the four ministries interested in such matters: Foreign Affairs, Interior, War and Colonies.

[12] Pascal Le Pautremat, *La politique musulmane de la France au XXe siècle*, Paris: Maisonneuve and Larose, 2003, pp. 33 ff. and pp. 294–7.

[13] Jalila Sbaï, "La République et la Mosquée: genèse et institution(s) de l'islam en France", in P.-J. Luizard (ed.), *Le choc colonial et l'islam. Les politiques religieuses des puissances coloniales en terres d'islam*, Paris: La Découverte, 2006, pp. 223–36; Louis Milliot, "Les Kabyles à Paris", *Revue des Études Islamiques*, VI (1932), pp. 162–74.

[14] Clifford Rosenberg, "The Colonial Politics of Health Care Provision in Interwar Paris", *French Historical Studies*, 27, 3 (Summer 2004), pp. 637–68.

ISLAM AS A TOOL FOR STATE AUTHORITIES

Whether it was officially recognised or only tolerated and more or less controlled, Islam was occasionally used as a tool by the European political authorities for different purposes, in particular in the context of the economic crisis following the Great War or during the depression of the 1930s. In the present book, Nathalie Clayer's chapter on Albania shows how the political authorities used Islam to strengthen social solidarity in the face of economic hardship, but also as a weapon against the spread of Communism. In Britain Richard Lawless observes a similar strategy and highlights some attempts by the British authorities to use Islam for the social control of the Muslim population. In the context of the economic depression, state authorities were first seeking to safeguard social order, and wanted to eliminate the influence of the Communist-led Seamen's Minority Movement active among Arab workers.[15] For that purpose, they relied on the London-based Western Islamic Association to campaign among Yemeni seamen in order to persuade them to accept the government's policy. In France, state authorities adopted another strategy, preferring to use a combination of social assistance and police surveillance to "protect" Muslims from Communist influence.[16] Actually SAINA's role was to gather intelligence on, and to disrupt the activities of, both the French Communist Party and Algerian nationalist movements such as the *Étoile Nord-Africaine* among immigrant workers. It was also not averse to using representatives of Sufi brotherhoods living in France in the surveillance work.[17]

European Islam was also used in the larger framework of colonial politics. In several countries, the visible presence of Islam in the metropolis was recognised as a way of expressing gratitude to the

[15] We do not possess similar studies in the case of France and, for instance, we do not know whether the not insignificant number of Muslims among the dockers at French ports had an impact on the mobilisation for the dockers' strikes organised in 1925 by the French Communist Party against the War in Morocco.

[16] P. Le Pautremat, *La politique musulmane*, p. 294.

[17] Neil MacMaster, *Colonial Migrants and Racism: Algerians in France 1900–62*, London–New York: Macmillan, 1997. We are grateful to Richard Lawless for this reference.

large number of Muslim soldiers from the colonies who died or were wounded during the Great War.[18] During and after the war, Muslims themselves made vocal reference to their loyalty when demanding official recognition and permission to build mosques (see Eric Germain's chapter for Britain). This was presented as of some mutual benefit, and it was, as the French and the British Foreign Offices took advantage of the mosques built in Paris and around London. These Saracenic and Mogul-style buildings were quite useful to receive Muslim diplomats and visiting state rulers and to project a positive image of the metropolis' policy towards its Muslim citizens and subjects. The project for the Paris Mosque, conceived in 1916 during the war, was an initiative of the French authorities. To finance and build this religious complex, the government had to circumvent the Law of 1901 on the separation between church and state. For that purpose, it used the *Société des Habous* [*Waqfs*], founded during the First World War, to take charge of the project, which was presented not as a "mosque" but as an "institute". As a matter of fact, the "Muslim Institute" comprised, beside a mosque, a conference hall, library, *hammam*, restaurant and guesthouse.[19] The Paris Mosque, inaugurated in 1926, became the showcase of Islam in France (or, for some, the "Islam of France"). To show the concern of France for its Muslims, the authorities also founded the *Hôpital franco-musulman* in the Paris suburb of Bobigny (in 1935) and, two years later, a Muslim cemetery (opened in 1937). Like the Paris Grand Mosque, the Bobigny hospital was dedicated to the memory of the Muslim soldiers who died for the "fatherland".[20] In fascist Italy, it was also the government which decided to establish the *Associazione Musulmana del Littorio*

[18] In the cemetery of Douaumont, a project to build a Mosque was prepared but finally abandoned for lack of funds in 1926. Thirty years later, a small stele was erected in memory of "Muslim soldiers who died for France" and, on 25 June 2006, a monument for Muslim soldiers of the First World War was inaugurated by the French president; B. Hopquin, "Verdun, lieu de mémoire musulman", *Le Monde* (22 February 2006), p. 3.

[19] Alain Boyer, *L'Institut Musulman de la Mosquée de Paris*, Paris: CHEAM, 1992; J. Sbaï, "La République et la Mosquée".

[20] Marie-Ange d'Adler, *Le cimetière musulman de Bobigny—Lieu de mémoire d'un siècle d'immigration*, Paris: Autrement, 2005, pp. 64–86.

(Muslim Association of the Lictors)[21] in Rome in 1937, as a direct consequence of the annexation of African territories by Mussolini's regime.[22]

State authorities were not the only ones concerned with the foundation of Muslim institutions; local politicians also showed an interest. This was notably the case in France, where the Muslim immigrant population was most numerous. In Marseilles, the question of building a mosque, raised in 1937, was used by the different political parties to attract the support of North Africans; but the project failed mainly because of the reluctance of the Imam of the Paris *Grande Mosquée* to see the establishment of an institution which might slip out of his own control.[23]

In a non-colonial context, Islam turned out to be a potential instrument for some Balkan countries against the development, or the fear of development, of alien nationalisms. This was possibly the case in Yugoslavia where Islam could be used against Turkish and Albanian nationalist influence in the Southern part of the country, but this issue has not really been studied. As for Bulgaria and Greece, the presence of important Turkish-speaking Muslim groups living in border regions with Turkey made the authorities particularly anxious about the development of Turkish nationalism. The government of the kingdom of Bulgaria tended to support religious groups within the Muslim community who were opposed to the Kemalists. Thus, the Bulgarian authorities supported the newspaper *Medeniyet* (Civilisation) and the *Din-i Islam Müdafileri Cemiyeti*, the "Association of the Defenders of Islam" established in 1931 to counter the pro-Kemalist organisation *Turan*, formed in

[21] The Lictor is the Fascist bundle of rods with the protruding axe blade, which was the symbol carried in ancient Rome by the Magistrates to demonstrate their power of life and death in the courts.

[22] This first Italian Muslim organisation was founded by Somali Muslim soldiers from the colonial territories. Among other activities, this association helped to organise the religious life of Muslims in Italy by providing chaplain-imams and *qadis* (Dimitri Buffa, "Breve storia del movimenti islamici in Italia", http://members.xoom.virgilio.it/amislam/opinione11.htm).

[23] Michel Renard, "Aperçu sur l'histoire de l'islam à Marseille, 1813–1962. Pratiques religieuses et encadrement des Nord-Africains", *Outre-Mers*, XC, 340–41 (2003), pp. 281–86.

1926.[24] The governmental strategy was to sustain religious activities in the hope that they would help to divide the Turks of Bulgaria from those of Turkey. As Kemalism mainly spread through the activities of certain schoolteachers, some administrators of Turkish language educational institutions even thought that it would be better to replace the secular liberal teachers by *hojas*.[25] However, Mila Mancheva has rightly pointed out that Bulgarian official policy concerning the Muslim minority, as formulated and implemented, was far from being homogeneous and consistent. For instance, the Bulgarian-speaking Pomaks were not treated in the same way as other Muslims, since they were supposed to have a "natural" place in the Bulgarian nation, unlike the Turks or the Gypsies. Furthermore, besides the political changes that brought new policies towards the Muslim minority, differences of opinion among deputies, ministers and civil servants had quite an impact on the way that official policy was conducted. In particular, from time to time local officials may have implemented a policy that was quite different from the one elaborated in the capital, Sofia.[26]

Yannis Bonos' chapter illustrates a similar phenomenon for neighbouring Greece. While the central political authorities remained apparently neutral on the highly sensitive alphabet issue in 1928–29, the local authorities took measures against the use of the Latin alphabet. They favoured Arabic script because the police suspected that the teaching of the new alphabet would promote Turkish nationalist propaganda. At that time, local officials had already appointed "conservative" anti-Kemalist political refugees as teachers and muftis and to various posts within the Islamic Community Commissions. However, these authorities were not necessarily successful in their strategies, as illustrated by the way that the "spelling issue" altered the local political balance in the context of an electoral period.

As far as these alliances are concerned, while it is often argued that the political authorities of these countries collaborated with

[24] W. Höpken, "From Religious Identity", p. 62.

[25] Mila Mancheva, "Image and Policy: the Case of Turks and Pomaks in Inter-war Bulgaria, 1918–44 (with Special Reference to Education)", *Islam and Christian-Muslim Relations*, XII, 3, July 2001, pp. 355–74.

[26] Ibid.

"conservative '*ulama*", it should be stressed that this was not always the case. Indeed, it seems that more often than not state authorities became allied with reformist '*ulama*, rather than with traditional religious leaders, as we can see in the Yugoslavian and Albanian cases (see the chapters by Muhamed Aruçi and Nathalie Clayer), and also in the case of Bulgaria where the main religious educational institution, the *Medrese-i nüvvab*, was led by Yuzuf Ziyaeddin Ezheri, who was greatly influenced by late-Ottoman and Egyptian reformists.[27]

The political authorities also viewed Islam quite differently when it was a domestic—metropolitan or colonial—question and when it was a matter of foreign policy. For example, France was more likely to accept on its territory the political activism of exiled pan-Islamists from the British Empire, for example Indians or Egyptians, than those political activists coming from her own colonies. Nevertheless, it was not in Paris, but in Geneva and Berlin that the most radical anti-colonial activists found a safe refuge. The most specific use of Islam for a foreign policy purpose is certainly that of Germany as studied by Wolfgang Schwanitz in this volume. During the First World War, while the French and British governments sought the support of '*ulama* and Sufi *shaikhs* from their colonies as they did with all colonial opinion leaders, the German government tried to bypass this "collaborationist establishment" by using the Islamic concept of *jihad* in a modern context. Berlin financially supported Muslim activists who tried to encourage uprisings among the populations of French, British and Russian colonies against the "Christian powers". This Holy War was masterminded by the archaeologist and diplomat, Max von Oppenheim. The German propaganda networks included targets in Europe such as Tatar prisoners as recalled in Sebastian Cwiklinski's chapter. Even if this first attempt had a limited success, during the inter-war period Germany became a country of asylum for Muslim nationalists and students. Numerous Muslim associations were created there, and the country became important in Muslim merchant

[27] See Ibrahim Hatiboğlu, "XX. Yüzyılın ilk yarısında Bulgaristan Müslümanları arasında dinî ıslâhat çabaları", *Balkanlar'da islâm medeniyeti milletlerarası sempozyumu tebliğleri*, Istanbul: Ircica, 2002, pp. 347–62.

networks. Furthermore, networks were woven between Berlin and the Muslim world, involving figures such as Shakib Arslan, who was close to Max von Oppenheim (see Raja Adal's chapter), and the Mufti of Jerusalem, Amin al-Husaini. With the advent of the Third Reich, these networks became more robust, in order to prepare a new *jihad* that could open new fronts in the colonial hinterlands of its enemies.

In Italy, the interest in Islam was asserted earlier on with the personal friendship that existed between Benito Mussolini and Shakib Arslan from 1921.[28] In the 1930s, Islam became a noticeable component of the foreign policy implemented by Mussolini towards the Arab world, despite the increase in the number of its colonies with a Muslim population (Libya, Eritrea, the Dodecanese, then Ethiopia and later on Albania). Among the various initiatives that were connected to this Oriental foreign policy, one should mention the *Fiera del Levante* (Fair of the Levant), an International Trade Exhibition organised to promote Italian products and technologies in the Balkans and the Mediterranean Area, established in Bari in 1929 and continuing to the present day. There were also two congresses of Asian students organised in Rome in 1933 and 1934, the year of the first broadcasts in Arabic launched on Radio Bari. Italian official propaganda included the publishing of books in Italian and Arabic which promoted the analogy between fascism and Islamic tenets, among other themes. Such ideas were also promoted

[28] In those early years of the fascist regime, Mussolini also met the young reformist king Amanullah during his visit to Rome in January 1923. Six years later, he gave political asylum in Italy to the deposed Afghan monarch. After the ruthless "pacification" of Cyrenaica in 1931, Mussolini sought to accommodate his Arab critics and from 1933 Arslan saw him as a partner with whom he could negotiate. This improvement led to an address by the Italian Orientalist Laura Veccia Vaglieri, at the European Muslim Congress of Geneva in 1935 where Arslan presided. She was the only non-Muslim allowed to attend the congress. See "Swiss Exile: The European Muslim Congress, 1935", chapter twelve of Martin Kramer's *Islam Assembled: The Advent of the Muslim Congresses*, New York: Columbia University Press, 1986, pp. 142–53; R. Adal, "Constructing Transnational Islam: the East-West Network of Shakib Arslan," pp. 176–210 in A.A. Dudoignon, K. Hisao and K. Yasushi (eds), *Intellectuals in the Modern Islamic World: Transmission, Transformation, Communication*, London and New York: Routledge, 2006.

in some Arab newspapers, as for example in 1937 when the picture of Mussolini being presented with the "sword of Islam" in Tripoli in Libya was extensively publicised.[29] In the same years, the isolated Franco regime in Spain adopted a friendly attitude toward Islam for diplomatic reasons, welcoming for instance the visit by Ahmadi-Qadiani missionaries.

With much moderate expectations, Poland also used Islam in its relations with the Muslim world. For example, in 1925, the Polish government sent a Polish Muslim to the International Geographic Congress in Cairo; and from 1930 onwards the Mufti of Poland took part in the overseas delegations that were organised by the Ministry of Interior in order to secure the loyalty of the Polish Muslim community and to promote new economic and diplomatic relations with some Muslim countries (see Sebastian Cwiklinski's chapter). With similar expectations, the advocates of recognition of Islam in Hungary and Czechoslovakia had been arguing that such an official gesture could attract merchants and tourists from the Muslim world, which could bring benefits at a time of economic crisis.[30]

In the case of Albania, it was not Islam as such which came to be used in the field of foreign policy, but the image of a reformed Islam that the state wanted to promote (see Nathalie Clayer's chapter). Such a modernist *parti pris* did not primarily target the Muslim world, but rather other European countries. This was particularly evident in the issue of the banning of the veil, which had a "diplomatic dimension" as the authorities wanted to signify to the "West" that the country was determined to turn towards Europe.

N.C.-E.G.

[29] Renzo De Felice, *Il fascismo e l'Oriente*, Bologna: il Mulino, 1988; Enrico Galoppini, *Il fascismo e l'Islam*, Parma: Edizioni all'insegna del Veltro, 2001.

[30] G. Lederer, "Sur l'islam à Budapest", p. 28 ; M. Mendel, "The Islamic Religious community", p. 129.

ISLAM IN THE SERVICE OF SOCIAL CONTROL: THE CASE OF ARAB SEAMEN IN BRITAIN DURING THE INTER-WAR YEARS

Richard Lawless

INTRODUCTION: THE ORIGINS AND EARLY SETTLEMENT OF ARAB SEAMEN IN EUROPE

By the end of the First World War several thousand Arab seamen had established themselves at a number of European ports, especially in Britain and France but also in the Netherlands, Belgium and Italy, just one example of the larger phenomenon of global maritime migration. By the second half of the nineteenth century the technological transformation of the merchant shipping industry, notably the introduction of the steamship, had resulted in the creation of a new rating with no sea-going tradition, the fireman, whose job of shovelling coal into the furnace was arduous, dirty and hot. It was a position shunned by many Europeans and increasingly occupied by "colonial labour", in particular Indians and Chinese, but also Arabs, Somalis, West Indians, West Africans, and Malays, who were quickly incorporated into the new industrial working class that appeared with the advent of steam power.

Arabs and Somalis were engaged as firemen and trimmers on European steamers calling at the British-held port of Aden in South-West Arabia from the middle of the nineteenth century, especially after the sharp increase in maritime traffic and the growing demand for maritime labour after the opening of the Suez Canal in 1869; by the end of the century their recruitment was well established.

By the early twentieth century Arab and Somali seamen were shipping out regularly from a number of European ports where they were able to take up temporary or permanent residence, unlike Indian seamen (generally known as "Lascars") and Chinese seamen who were engaged on ships under agreements which specified the obligation of shipowners and shipmasters to repatriate them to the country of origin after they were discharged at a European port. The vast majority of Arab seamen were transients or sojourners and only a few settled permanently at British ports.

The outbreak of the First World War marked a significant increase in the number of Arabs shipping from British ports as they filled vacancies created by the transfer of large numbers of British seamen from the merchant marine to the Royal Navy or to other branches of the armed forces. The rapid rise in seamen's wages during the war years must have proved a powerful attraction and encouraged an influx of Arabs to certain British ports. Cardiff emerged as the main centre of Arab seamen in Britain, together with other South Wales ports such as Barry and Newport, South Shields on the Tyne, Hull, Liverpool, and London. The Arabs, together with the Somalis and a few Malay and Indian seamen, formed the first significant Muslim communities in Britain and, until large-scale immigration from South Asia beginning in the 1950s, these seaports, notably Cardiff, remained the demographic, if not the spiritual and intellectual, centre of Islam in Britain.

At European ports Arab seamen almost always stated that they were born in Aden and were therefore British subjects. Few, however, could produce documentary evidence to prove their claims, except the entry of nationality in their seamen's continuous discharge books. The vast majority however were from the Southern highlands of Yemen, until 1918 a province of the Ottoman Empire, and therefore were nominally Turkish subjects. Following the outbreak of the First World War, the British authorities in Aden advised that Arabs from parts of Arabia outside British jurisdiction engaged as seamen at Aden should be treated as British Protected Persons to facilitate their departure from European ports such as Marseilles. The India Office approved this suggestion. In Britain Arab labour was needed for the war effort, especially in the critically important shipping industry, and the Board of Trade suggested to the Home Office that the claims of Arab seamen to British nationality should not be challenged as such action might result in strikes or other labour troubles among these men.[1]

THE INTER-WAR YEARS: GOVERNMENT EFFORTS TO CONTROL AND REGULATE ARAB SEAMEN IN BRITAIN

Once the exceptional demands of the First World War were over, however, Arab seamen at British ports found themselves unwelcome guests and faced mounting hostility. The post-war boom quickly collapsed with an almost immediate effect on the shipping industry: the coal-carrying tramp trades, precisely the ships that employed Arabs, were the worst affected. The onset of the economic depression of the inter-war years merely intensified competition for jobs between white seamen and Arabs in an overstocked labour market. Sexual jealousy and moral outrage at the marriage of some Arabs to white women and the appearance of "half caste" children also contributed to the tensions. In 1919 there were race riots involving Arab seamen at several British ports, and in Cardiff, where the most violent disturbances took place, three people were killed and a great deal of damage done to property. The police, immigration officers, Board of Trade officials and the National Sailor's and Firemen's Union (NSFU, renamed the National Union of Seamen, NUS, in 1926), among whom racist sentiments were widespread, called for the repatriation of Arab seamen domiciled at British ports and tough measures to prevent new arrivals in order to prevent further disturbances. Local officials in Cardiff went so far as to call for the construction of a concentration camp to house Arab seamen because they were "of excitable temperament and it only needs some malignant spark to make a blaze".[2]

[1] On the origins and early settlement of Arab seamen in Britain see Richard Lawless, *From Ta'izz to Tyneside: an Arab Community in the North-east of England during the Early Twentieth Century*, University of Exeter Press, 1995, especially Chapters 1 and 2; also Richard Lawless, "Recruitment and Regulation: Migration for Employment of 'Adenese' Seamen in the Late Nineteenth and Early Twentieth Centuries", *New Arabian Studies*, 11 (1994), pp. 75–102.

[2] Tony Lane, "The Political Imperatives of Bureaucracy and Empire: the Case of the Coloured Alien Seamen Order, 1925", in D. Frost (ed.), *Ethnic Labour and British Imperial Trade: a History of Ethnic Seafarers in the UK*, London: Frank Cass, 1995, p. 118.

In 1920 the Home Office issued an Aliens Order which instructed immigration officers to refuse coloured seamen permission to land in Britain unless they could prove that they were British subjects, or that they were living in Britain or had signed on in Britain for a round trip. This restrictive measure was directed primarily at Arab seamen who found that their claims to be British subjects were now consistently challenged. But the Order proved difficult to enforce, and police and Immigration officials felt that greater control over coloured seamen already in the country and more effective action to restrict the influx of new arrivals could be achieved by introducing a system of registration. Under the terms of the Special Restriction (Coloured Alien Seamen) Order of 1925, also directed primarily at the Arabs, every Arab seaman who could not prove by documentary evidence that he was a British subject was obliged to register with the police; this effectively reclassified most Arab seafarers as "coloured aliens" required to report regularly to the police.

The Governor of Aden, the India Office, the Office of the High Commissioner for India, and the Colonial Office, conscious of the political implications in South-West Arabia and among Muslims in the British Empire of the restrictive measures imposed on Arab seamen in Britain, expressed concern. The sensitivity of the subject is clear from a despatch from the Political Resident, Aden to the Colonial Office in February 1921, stating that he had received a complaint from the Amir of Dhala, one of the tribal rulers of the Aden Protectorate, that his subjects were being turned out of Shipping Offices (Mercantile Marine Offices) because they were "Mohamedans".[3] In fact all the available evidence indicates that Arab seamen at British ports faced prejudice because of their colour, not their religion. However, the India Office recognised that imperial imperatives should not be pushed too far in the face of strong objections on other grounds, and agreed to fund the repatriation of over a thousand unemployed Arab seamen, mainly in Cardiff and South Shields.

The range of restrictive measures failed to prevent a further influx of Arab seamen during the inter-war years. Despite mounting racial

[3] Ibid.

hostility and high rates of unemployment among Arab seamen at British ports, there appears to have been no shortage of new recruits to seafaring. The conditions for chain migration had been firmly established since the late nineteenth century. After working for several years and accumulating sufficient savings, many Arab seamen returned to their home villages in Yemen, passing on their seamen's papers to other young men from the same family or village so that they could travel to Europe in search of work. After the end of the First World War the journey to Europe became more difficult and more expensive, but through several highly organised transnational networks run by seamen's agents at Aden many new recruits to seafaring, and former seamen wishing to return to work, were able to enter Britain illegally throughout the inter-war years. Trafficking in seamen's discharge papers, which could be used by newcomers to establish their claim to previous service on British ships, and documents of nationality and identity was widespread. Through these transnational smuggling networks the circulatory pattern of migration established in the late nineteenth century, involving the regular rotation of single males, was able to continue in spite of official controls.[4] There seems little doubt that the number of Arabs who entered irregularly certainly equalled, and may even have exceeded, those departing.

By 1930 as the economic depression deepened the National Union of Seamen (NUS) stepped up its campaign against the Arabs. There were demands for stricter control over the Arabs, an end to the system of supplying Arab crews through the boarding house keepers and the deportation of Arabs who had entered the country illegally. But by this time the NUS leadership itself was being challenged by the rise of the Communist-led Seamen's Minority Movement which denounced the close cooperation between the NUS leadership and the shipowners and called for a new union that would fight for an increase in wages, shorter hours and better working conditions for seamen whatever their colour. In early 1930 the Seamen's Minority Movement took up the cause of

[4] See Richard Lawless, "The Role of Seamen's Agents in the Migration for Employment of Arab Seafarers in the Early Twentieth Century", in D. Frost (ed.), *Ethnic Labour*, pp. 35–58.

Arab and other coloured seamen, denouncing the NUS for stirring up racial feeling against the Arabs. The radical movement began to attract considerable support among the Arab community.

In July the NUS and shipowners announced the introduction of a Rota System for Arab seamen at Cardiff, South Shields and Hull under which Arabs at these ports were to be re-registered and then engaged in rotation, with those longest ashore having the first chance of employment. The Seamen's Minority Movement in South Shields immediately denounced the Rota System as a new form of control over the employment of Arab seamen. In August, during picketing by the Seamen's Minority Movement, violent disturbances broke out between Arabs and the police in South Shields over the implementation of the Rota System and a number of Arabs and several leaders of the Seamen's Minority Movement were arrested and charged with rioting and incitement to riot. Violent clashes also occurred in Cardiff between Arabs and the police, although it is unclear whether the Seamen's Minority Movement, which was very active in the Welsh ports, was actively involved in these incidents.

By late September resistance to the Rota System had collapsed at both Cardiff and South Shields, and by the end of the year most Arabs who were eligible had registered under the new scheme. But the rate at which Arab seamen on the register were being shipped was slow because of the continued slump in shipping. Despite these problems, Immigration officials stated that there appeared to be no decline in attempts by Arabs to enter Britain illegally, but that the influx was being successfully checked with the assistance of the police.

The British Shipping (Assistance) Act of 1935 further reduced the number of jobs available for Arab seamen. Pressure from the NUS and the Transport and General Workers Union had ensured that in order to enjoy the government subsidy on merchant shipping, shipowners had to agree to employ only British crews, a serious blow to the Arabs as most of them were registered as aliens. At the same time, on the instructions of the Home Office, new restrictions were imposed at Aden on Arab seamen wishing to travel to Britain in search of employment, which applied to British subjects and British Protected Persons. The British Resident at Aden thought them "unduly harsh" but they appear to have been strictly enforced. Early in 1936 certain Arabs in South Shields asked the mayor to write to the Aga Khan and the Nizam of Hyderabad about the plight of Arabs in the town as a result of unemployment, requesting financial assistance. There was no reply from the Nizam but in August the Aga Khan sent a cheque for £100 to be used for the relief of distressed Arabs in the town. During the Second World War many Arab seamen lost their lives serving in the Merchant Navy or in the British armed forces; wartime losses in the Merchant Navy were particularly high.[5]

RELIGIOUS BELIEFS AND OBSERVANCE AMONG ARAB SEAMEN

Despite increasing regulation and control, and mounting discrimination and prejudice at both official and popular levels, there is no evidence that hostility towards the Arabs was rooted specifically in prejudice against Islam or Muslims; also the Arabs appear to have encountered few obstacles from the local authorities in observing their religious obligations and rituals. A detailed review of letters to the editor of the leading daily newspaper in South Shields on the subject of the Arabs during the inter-war period revealed no derogatory comments about Islam or even references to the Arabs as Muslims. In popular opinion they were stigmatised primarily because they were perceived as "coloured aliens" who took jobs from "white seamen". It is worth remembering that at this time the Arabs, together with other "coloured" seamen, formed the first significant concentrations of non-white immigrants in Britain. Moreover the ordinary Arab seaman did not see himself primarily as a Muslim; religion was an integral part of the tribal cultures that they brought with them from their Yemeni homeland. Beyond the extended family, the Arabs identified themselves according to tribe/region because the concept of national identity was poorly developed at this time. The majority of Arab seamen at British ports

[5] For more details on official measures to control and regulate Arab seamen in Britain see Neil Evans, "Regulating the Reserve Army: Arabs, Blacks and the Local State in Cardiff, 1919–45", *Immigrants and Minorities*, IV, 2 (1985), pp. 68–115; and R. Lawless, *From Ta'izz to Tyneside*, especially chapters 4, 5 and 6.

lived in Arab boarding houses, and where possible they preferred to go to a boarding house run by a man from their own tribe and sought out the company of members of their own tribe. Most belonged to the Shafi'i school of Sunni Islam, although a few were of the Zaydi sect of Shi'a Islam. In their dealings with most British officials Arabs emphasised that they were loyal British subjects, and it is interesting to note that it was only when their leaders contacted the India Office or the Office of the Indian High Commissioner in London that they identified themselves as "brother Muslims", members of the *umma*.[6] Until the late 1930s religion for the Arabs was essentially a private affair practised behind closed doors in the Arab boarding houses and a few private homes. Islam was rarely visible in public space, which may help to explain why it was not deployed by those who sought to vilify the Arabs. In some of the Arab boarding houses a room was set aside for the five daily prayers, and until the first mosques appeared in the late 1930s Friday prayers also took place there. In the absence of a full-time imam or religious leader, these duties were carried out by one of the seamen. As most Arab seamen were unable to read or write in Arabic, few were able to read the Qur'an, but all could repeat from memory in Arabic the prayers and verses used in their rituals and all had some knowledge of the narratives and stories contained in the Qur'an. Special facilities were provided at the boarding houses for prayers during the month of Ramadan, and it was there that the major annual religious festivals were celebrated, the *'Id al-Fitr*, and the *'Id al-Adha*.

The Arab boarding houses also provided food that was lawful according to their religion. In South Shields, for example, an Arab general dealer was licensed by the local council to kill animals at the municipal abattoirs in accordance with Muslim rites for consumption by the Arab population, and until 1928 a few boarding house masters were granted permission to slaughter a sheep in the backyards of their premises each year for the celebration of the

[6] PRO CO 725/21/8 Letter from Ali Said to the Secretary of State for India dated 27 December 1929; PRO CO 725/21/9 Letter from Abdulla Ali, 1 Tiny Street, South Shields to the High Commissioner for India, India House, London, dated 3 September 1930.

'Id al-Adha. However, when it was discovered that other Arabs were doing the same thing without permission, the local authorities banned the practice for everyone, stating that the manner in which the animals were being killed in the backyards of houses constituted a menace to public health.

Sydney Collins, an anthropologist who carried out his doctoral research on Muslims in South Shields in the 1940s, concluded that the most assiduously observed features of religious life among the Arabs were the giving of alms, fasting and the daily and seasonal rituals.[7] In addition, we know that some of the Arab seamen also undertook the Hajj at least once in their lives. There are also examples of seamen giving instructions in their letters home that part of the money they sent back to their families in Yemen should be used to build, repair or refurbish a village mosque.

Until the late 1930s burial ceremonies for Arab seamen who died at British ports were among the few public manifestations of the Islamic faith. However, the local authorities insisted that the body had to be buried in a coffin to conform to British regulations and not in a shroud according to Islamic custom, as was the practice in the homeland.[8]

THE ROLE OF ISLAMIC ORGANISATIONS AND TRANSNATIONAL ISLAMIC NETWORKS

The Islamic Society

During the inter-war years a number of Islamic organisations with transnational connections, and several Sufi brotherhoods, notably the Algerian-based Alawi *tariqa*, became actively involved with the Arab communities established at British ports. The first organisation to take an interest in the Arab seafarers was the London-based Islamic Society, linked to the Woking Muslim Mission just outside London. Throughout this period the Mission, which was run by

[7] Sydney Collins, *Coloured Minorities in Britain: Studies in British Race Relations Based on African, West Indian and Asiatic Immigrants*, London: Lutterworth Press, 1957, p. 182.

[8] For more details on religious beliefs and observances see R. Lawless, *From Ta'izz to Tyneside*, pp. 207–15.

Muslims connected with the Lahore Ahmadiyya Movement and supported financially by Muslims in India, was very much the spiritual and intellectual centre of Islam in Britain, attracting a number of British converts to Islam, some of them from the aristocracy and upper middle classes. The Society's stated objective was "to promote the religious, moral, social and intellectual advancement of the Muslim world" and its patrons numbered several members of the British government. After violent clashes in South Shields between Arabs and white seamen in February 1919 the President of the Society, Dr Abdul Majid, a Cambridge-educated Indian barrister, visited Tyneside in March where he held a watching brief at the trial of the twelve Arab seamen charged at Durham Assizes with rioting.[9] After the trial, during discussions with local officials, he upheld the Arabs' claim that they were British subjects and emphasised that he wanted British people to understand that they were most loyal to the Crown. The Arabs, who had made great sacrifices during the war, did not want to take jobs away from British seamen but asked for fair competition as British subjects; after all they were British subjects on British soil. The British Empire should be run for everybody, regardless of their colour. During the visit Dr Majid announced the establishment of a branch of the Islamic Society in South Shields with a committee which included the Arab boarding house masters and representatives of Muslim seamen from different parts of the world, Arabs, Indians and Malays. Its primary aim, according to Dr Majid, was to look after the economic, moral and religious welfare of Muslims in the town. He hoped that the branch would receive the patronage of prominent citizens in the town and in this way bring about better understanding between the Arabs and other sections of the community. There is no evidence whether the branch became active or whether similar branches were formed at other ports. Nevertheless, during the 1920s and 1930s Dr Majid appears to have kept in touch with Muslim communities at British ports and to have been informed of the continuing problems confronting Muslim seamen.

[9] It is worth noting that in the courts in South Shields a copy of the Qur'an was available for use by Arabs who were called to take the oath before giving evidence: see R. Lawless, *From Ta'izz to Tyneside*, p. 284.

In early 1921 the Society adopted a more critical tone towards the authorities, accusing the India Office of acting with the Board of Trade and the NSFU in victimising Arab, Malay, Somali and Indian seamen. Later, in April 1925, shortly after the Home Office imposed the Special Restriction (Coloured Alien Seamen) Order, Dr Majid wrote to the Under Secretary of State at the India Office, complaining that the police in South Shields were compelling coloured seamen in the town to register as aliens, thus depriving them of their status of British Indian subjects. The Home Office commented that it was aware that Dr Majid was ready to take up the cause of coloured seamen "whether in general or in particular, whether on good cause shown or otherwise".[10]

Dr Majid appears again in Cardiff in May 1937 when Prince Seif al-Islam Hussein, who was representing his father, Imam Yahya of the Yemen, at the Coronation of King George VI, visited the city. As President of the Islamic Society Dr Majid read an address of loyalty and welcome to the prince from the Muslims of Cardiff. He told the local press that one of the reasons for the Prince's visit was to encourage the efforts the Muslims of the city were making to obtain a mosque.[11] It is unclear whether Dr Majid was invited to give the address by the local Arab community or was the choice of the British authorities. Earlier the Prince had visited South Shields at the invitation of one of the leading Arab boarding house masters in the town and had received a warm reception from Yemenis there. Throughout the inter-war years, Imam Yahya, although both a spiritual and a temporal ruler, showed little or no interest in either the religious or material welfare of his subjects living in Britain and did nothing to provide them with religious leadership or instruction. However, his subjects in Britain all had relatives in Yemen and most intended to return permanently to their homeland one day; consequently it was in their best interest to show proper respect for an autocratic, cruel and much feared ruler. In a society that still had

[10] PRO HO 45/12314 Letter from the Home Office to the Chief Constable, South Shields, 30 July 1926.

[11] "King of Yemen's son in Cardiff—support for mosque proposal", *Western Mail* (28 May 1937), p. 13.

a weakly developed sense of nationality, respect for the ruler was expressed in religious terms.

The Western Islamic Association

By early 1930 we find evidence of another London-based Islamic organisation with branches among the Arabs of Cardiff and South Shields, the Western Islamic Association. It was headed by Khalid Sheldrake, one of the British converts to Islam associated with the Woking Muslim Mission, who adopted the title of "Life President". He described the association as "a large body with branches and representatives throughout the whole of the civilized world" which had support from eminent Muslims in all parts of the world, "including several royal personages". Early in 1930 Sheldrake took up the cause of the Arab seamen, strongly criticising the NUS for its racist campaign against the Arabs at British ports. In a letter to the press that attracted some attention nationally, he deplored the action of the union in turning against its own members and seeking to deny them employment. He was sure that fair-minded people would agree that any organisation which deliberately tried to arouse racial hatred must be condemned. The main thrust of his argument was that this question should be seen from the point of view of the British Empire because the constant attacks made on Arabs in this country were bound to have repercussions in lands under the control of the Empire. He pointed out that the British Empire was the largest Islamic power in the world and that King George V had more Muslim subjects than Christians. He reiterated the point made a decade earlier by Dr Majid, that the Arabs had nobly played their part on behalf of the Empire and its allies on both land and sea. In his comments, however, Sheldrake was careful not to criticise the British government. He acknowledged that there was serious unemployment in the country and stressed that the present government was doing its best to grapple with this problem. Sheldrake's impassioned plea to think of Empire appears to have had absolutely no impact on either the well-publicised NUS campaign against the Arabs or the more covert activities of the police and port-based officials.

Sheldrake also addressed meetings of the local branches of the Western Islamic Association to express his support for the Arabs, and accompanied their representatives to the Home Office and the House of Commons to put the case of the Arab seamen. Addressing a meeting of some 170 Arabs in South Shields in March 1930, he called for unity among all Muslims and urged the Arabs to work together to fight their case. He also argued that with a Muslim population of over 1,000, the town urgently needed a mosque, a Muslim cemetery, and Islamic schools to ensure that the children were brought up in the faith. The press reported that the local branch of the Association had been strengthened as a result of Sheldrake's visit; several new members were enrolled at the meeting and a strong working committee appointed. The solicitor who acted for the local branch of the Association also addressed the meeting and announced that the Arabs were alive at this time to the question of organising themselves "industrially, socially and religiously".[12]

Not all the Arabs chose to join the local branches of the Western Islamic Association. Divisions among the Arab seamen at British ports were endemic and most often the result of rivalries between Arab boarding house masters, sometimes reflecting tribal differences. The ordinary seaman followed the instructions of his boarding house master. These divisions came to the surface in the summer of 1930 when the NUS and shipowners announced the introduction of a new Rota System for the registration of Arab seamen, which enjoyed government support. In South Shields, a leading boarding house master, Hassan Mohamed, the secretary of the local branch of the Association, led the faction that was prepared to accept the new scheme, whereas a rival boarding house master, Ali Said, led the faction bitterly opposed to it, and established a close alliance with the local leadership of the Communist-led Seamen's Minority Movement, although the relationship appears to have been tactical rather than ideological. When pickets from the Seamen's Minority Movement attempted to prevent other Arabs from signing on, the legal adviser to the local branch of the Association thanked the police for intervening and escorting one of the men to his ship.

Local officials of the association were in touch with the London-based leadership about the situation, but Sheldrake himself did not

[12] *Shields Daily Gazette* (25 March 1930), p. 5.

express any opinion publicly on the Rota System until after the violent disturbances between Arabs and the police in both South Shields and Cardiff in August 1930. In early September, in a letter to the local newspaper in South Shields, Sheldrake stated that he had spent many months in negotiation with several government departments on the question of the Rota System and had come to the conclusion that the Arabs should accept it or they would only suffer further distress. In talking to the Arabs in South Shields he found opinion divided on the Rota System; some, he stated, suspected a trick and feared that they would be driven out of the country; he assured them that these fears were "absolutely absurd". Again he warned of "implications for the Empire". In the article Sheldrake claimed that about 240 Arabs had already registered under the Rota System in Cardiff; the true figure was only 16 Arabs and two Somalis.

He also protested about the activities of those individuals who made collections among the Arabs to send men to London "for religious and other purposes", pointing out that such activities contravened the rules of the local branch of the Association. He stated that when the South Shields branch was formed the Arab boarding house masters in the town had agreed to regularise collections from the men (possibly *sadaqa*) and that money could only be withdrawn on four signatures. We know from later correspondence that these protests were clearly directed at the activities of Ali Said and another boarding house master, Ali Hamed Dheli. After the violent disturbances of August the local police accused both men of continuing to foster opposition to the Rota System by claiming that the India Office was going to give relief to all Arabs who refused to register under the new system. The India Office had given assurances to the police that there was no truth in the claims. In a letter to the Secretary of State for India in mid-September, Sheldrake stated that both Ali Said and Ali Hamed Dheli were well known to him as troublemakers and that their activities had aroused suspicion in the minds of "Arabs of repute" in the town who were officials of the local branch of the Association, and they had written to him on the subject.

Following the publication of Sheldrake's article, a number of Arabs in South Shields wrote to the newspaper accusing him of being in collaboration with the officials of the Shipping Federation and the NUS and of championing the Rota System on behalf of the shipowners. They declared that if anyone wanted to collect funds from the Arab seamen to send representatives to London they were free to do so without applying to the Western Islamic Association for permission. Peter O'Donnell, Chairman of the South Shields Seamen's Committee of Action, who claimed to speak on behalf of the 400 Arabs in South Shields who were members of the Seamen's Minority Movement, appealed to Sheldrake to give advice to the Arabs on religious matters but, where their bread and butter was concerned, to allow them to make up their own minds and continue to fight the Rota System.

The day before his article appeared in the local press, Khalid Sheldrake, together with Messrs Hassan Mohamed and Muir Smith, the legal adviser to the South Shields branch of the Association, announced that the Aga Khan, a patron of the Western Islamic Association, had handed over a cheque to purchase land for a mosque in South Shields and had promised a substantial sum for the actual building. A few weeks later, it was reported that the Aga Khan would visit South Shields the following year under the auspices of the Association to lay the foundation stone of the mosque. In fact, the mosque was never built and no more was heard of the proposed visit by the Aga Khan. Indeed, five years later, Sheldrake, who was then living in India, is reported to have sold the land purchased for the proposed mosque back to the South Shields Corporation without informing the local Arab leadership who knew nothing about the sale. It seems likely that the offer of financial assistance for the religious aims of the Arab community was used by Sheldrake and the Association as part of their efforts to defuse tensions, win acceptance of the government-backed Rota System and counter the activities of the Arab faction opposed to the new scheme. When this was achieved the project was quietly dropped.

After the departure of Sheldrake the local branches of the Association appear to have survived but to have declined in importance. In 1942 the Cardiff branch still owned three houses and had some money in a local bank, but the Muslim community had divided largely along ethnic lines. These divisions were avoided in South Shields. After Hassan Mohamed left for France in 1932 a Somali boarding house master, Yusuf Hersi Sulliman, succeeded him as local secretary of the Association, and in 1936 he became secretary of the newly-established branch of the "Zaouia Islamia Allawouia Religious Society" founded by a *muqaddam* (senior representative of the *tariqa*'s spiritual master) of the Algerian-based Alawi *tariqa*, Shaikh Abdullah Ali al-Hakimi.[13]

The Alawi tariqa

The Alawi *tariqa* was the most influential Sufi brotherhood active among the Arab seamen during the inter-war years. Founded in 1914 by Shaikh Ahmad ibn Mustafa al-Alawi, during the inter-war period the order rapidly expanded into a transnational movement with disciples across North Africa and also in the Middle East. Especially noted for its missionary work in Europe, by the 1920s the *tariqa* had established *zawiya*s in Paris and Marseilles where the emphasis was on raising the spiritual and intellectual level of North African immigrant workers. A number of Europeans, mainly artists and intellectuals, were converted to Islam through the activities of the *tariqa* while other converts attracted by Sufi Islam sought spiritual guidance from Shaikh al-Alawi. Eric Geoffroy states that Shaikh al-Alawi had many disciples among Yemeni seamen and that this was a key factor in the rapid diffusion of the *tariqa*'s particular brand of Islam among Muslims in key port cities in Europe.[14] For many of the seamen, the Islam of their home villages would have been strongly influenced by Sufism, and they probably brought with them to Europe certain rituals and practices that they had grown up with. As a result they would have been susceptible to the spiritual message transmitted by the "guides" of the Alawi *tariqa*. By the early 1930s we have evidence of Yemeni *fuqara* (initiates) of the Alawi *tariqa* in Marseilles and others at the channel ports of Rouen and Le Havre. These centres were important transit points for Arab

[13] On the activities of the Islamic Society and the Western Islamic Association see R. Lawless, *From Ta'izz to Tyneside*, especially chapters 4, 5 6 and 8; and R. Lawless, "Religion and Politics among Arab Seafarers in Britain in the Early Twentieth Century", *Islam and Christian-Muslim Relations*, V, 1 (1994), pp. 35–56.

[14] This French scholar states that the *tariqa* had 14 *zawiya*s in Britain during the 1930s (see www.religioperennis.org/Document/Geoffroy/Alawi.html). This figure probably includes the prayer rooms in Arab boarding houses.

seamen travelling to British ports, and it is therefore possible that the Alawi *tariqa* had adepts in Britain before a formal presence was established in 1936 with the arrival of one of Shaikh al-Alawi's pupils, Abdullah Ali al-Hakimi, and the foundation of the "Zaouia Islamia Allawouia Religious Society of the United Kingdom".

In contrast to the Islamic Society and the Western Islamic Association, which were London-based organisations led by professionals whose education and social class gave them access to senior levels of government, the Alawi *tariqa* became more firmly rooted among the Arab seafaring communities in Britain and its leadership was drawn from the same ethnic and tribal background as the seamen and lived among them. Under the influence of the *tariqa* the Arab seamen's religious sphere was reoriented away from the British Indian section of the *umma* towards French North Africa and the Arab world. During the period when he was based in Britain, Shaikh Abdullah Ali al-Hakimi for example travelled regularly to Paris, Marseilles and Algiers in order to maintain contact with other branches of the Alawi network, and during the Second World War he spent much of his time in the Middle East.

Shaikh Abdullah Ali al-Hakimi's origins are obscure but we know that he was from Dhubhan in the Imamate and was a merchant with business interests in Aden where he was well-connected within the city's Yemeni merchant community. He was clearly a well-educated man and published two books on religion and Sufism. He appears to have met his spiritual guide, Shaikh al-Alawi, in Morocco in the late 1920s, and was subsequently appointed a *muqaddam* or sectional leader within the *tariqa*. When he came to England he was in his mid-thirties and had previously lived and worked in Algeria, France and Holland. According to Sydney Collins, who interviewed al-Hakimi in the late 1940s during his doctoral research, the *shaikh* started his work in Britain on the authority of the head of the *tariqa* "to whom God had revealed his choice".[15] After arriving in England al-Hakimi divided his time mainly between the seafaring communities in Cardiff and South Shields, but *zawiya*s were also established in Hull and Liverpool. In the Cardiff community, by far the largest, he was assisted by his

[15] S. Collins, *Coloured Minorities*, p. 178, note 2.

deputy, Shaikh Hasan Ismail, who was from Shamir in the Imamate. Little is known about his background but he appears to have been a member of one of the prominent *sayyid* families of Yemen and may have studied with religious scholars in Cairo who were members of the Alawi *tariqa*.

The two leaders set about their work with great energy establishing *zawiyas*, schools and libraries in the years before the outbreak of the Second World War. Evening classes were organised in Qur'anic studies for the children of Arab seamen, and weekly classes in religious instruction were also provided for those European wives who had converted to Islam. Some of the young boys who showed special ability in the Qur'anic classes were sent for advanced study with the *tariqa* in Algeria or Egypt. Their activities resulted in the re-Islamisation of the Arab seafaring communities, a sort of spiritual renaissance, with the institutionalisation of several facets of religious life. New rituals and practices were introduced and for the first time Islam burst out into public space. Elaborate and colourful processions through the streets were organised to mark the major Muslim festivals of *'Id al-Adha* and *'Id al-Fitr* and a third annual festival was introduced to commemorate the death of Shaikh al-Alawi; this three-day festival (*al-Ihtifal*) became a feature of the religious life of all communities where the Alawi *tariqa* was active.[16] Groups of Arabs from one port city often travelled to another port to participate in these festivals alongside their fellow countrymen. These were occasions when members of the Arab community were able to make a strong public demonstration of their faith. On these occasions many of the seamen discarded their European clothing for Yemeni dress (*futa*) or the Arab dress (*djellaba* and *burnous*) of the Maghreb. Indeed Shaikh al-Alawi had emphasized the dangers of adopting European habits of thought and life and in particular had condemned Muslims who wore modern European dress. Green banners inscribed with the words *La ilaha illa'llah* (There is no God but Allah), together with a white crescent and stars, were always carried aloft at the head of the procession and those taking part

[16] In August 1937 Shaikh Abdullah Ali al-Hakimi invited the Imam of the Woking Mosque to attend this first festival; *Shields Daily Gazette* (16 August 1937), p. 2.

carried beautifully-worked prayer mats and chanted Alawi *nashids* (praises to God). Women and girls, always in long white dresses, regularly took part in these processions, which were often headed by a group of small children. In Cardiff and South Shields these processions attracted hundreds of curious onlookers from the host community, but there are no reports of any hostile reactions. These public displays of the Islamic faith were well received by local people and often reported in some detail, and illustrated with photographs, in the local press.

One of the religious rituals practised by the Alawi *tariqa*, the ceremony of *dhikr* (the "mentioning" of the name of Allah), remained however a strictly private affair.[17] It is unclear whether this ritual was introduced by the Alawi *tariqa* or whether it was already practised by Sufis before Shaikh al-Hakimi's arrival in Britain. The late Professor Serjeant, attending a *dhikr* in South Shields during the Second World War, observed that one of the English wives had learned to perform the ritual. One of Shaikh Abdullah Ali al-Hakimi's most outstanding achievement was the enthusiasm and devotion for Islam that he inspired in the English wives. One of these working class women told Sydney Collins: "Before the Shaikh came, we felt that we were only Arabs' wives, but after we felt better. We had our own religion and priest and we were proud of it".[18] Only men were eligible to join the "Zaouia Islamia Allawouia Religious Society"—the *tariqa*'s corporate form in Britain –, although some of the English wives who had converted to Islam took part in some of the society's activities.

Funds to support the *tariqa* in Britain and its local branches came from the weekly contributions made by members. Details are set out in a booklet outlining the aims and objectives of the "Zaouia Islamia Allawouia Religious Society" which was circulating among

[17] For a description of the performance of the *dhikr* in South Shields see R.B. Serjeant, "Yemeni Arabs in Britain", *The Geographical Magazine*, I, 3 (August 1944), p. 143.

[18] S. Collins, *Coloured Minorities*, p. 179. Collins points out that it was unusual for the white wives and partners of Arabs to attend funeral ceremonies; those who did travelled in a separate carriage to the cemetery, stood away from the grave, outside the group of men and took no active part in the rituals; ibid., pp. 211–12.

the Arab seamen during the 1940s.[19] It states that each member was required to pay a minimum of one shilling and a maximum of two shillings and six pence per week and anyone who, whilst ashore, failed to pay his subscriptions for three months would be expelled. These funds, administered by a local committee, were to be used to rent a *zawiya*, pay the expenses of a teacher to instruct the children in the Islamic faith and award scholarships to those with special ability so that they could continue their religious studies in the Middle East. It was compulsory for local branches to hold annual processions to celebrate the death of Shaikh al-Alawi and extra subscriptions could be levied to pay for the expenses involved. Funds could also be used for the repatriation of seamen who became ill or were too old to work, and for the funeral costs of any seaman who died destitute in Britain. The booklet also stated that the sole purpose of the Society was for "the propagating of the religion of Islam and no other interests will be allowed to intrude". Each member on joining automatically became a "brother" and "only good feelings towards each other will be tolerated". If quarrels occurred between members, the local committee was to act as arbitrator. However, if a member got into trouble of his own making, the Society would not take any part in the affair, unless there was evidence of a miscarriage of justice.

In Cardiff and South Shields Shaikh Abdullah and his deputy Shaikh Hasan carried out marriages according to Shari'a law; both men had been granted diplomas or licences from the leadership of the *tariqa* authorising them to conduct these ceremonies.[20] However, the local authorities in Britain insisted that couples should also go to the Civil Registrar to legalise the marriage under English law. When Shaikh Abdullah himself married a nineteen-year-old girl in

[19] The text of the booklet is quoted in S. Collins, *Coloured Minorities*, pp. 206–7. The influence of the *tariqa*'s English solicitors is clearly visible in this unique document, which represents one of the few pieces of literature from the Alawi *tariqa* in Britain that has come to the attention of researchers.

[20] An English translation of the text of the diploma granted to Shaikh Hasan Ismail by the Committee of the *Nahdat al-sufiyya al-'alawiyya* (Committee for the Promotion of the Alawiyya *tariqa*) in Egypt in 1941 can be found in PRO CO 876/26 Letter from J.L. Keith to Mr Clauson dated 3 February 1942.

South Shields in 1937 he refused to submit to a civil ceremony and declared that if he did so he would lose his licence as a "priest". Later, when Shaikh Abdullah was living in Cardiff, the police reported that they suspected he performed marriages according to Islamic law without sending the couple to the Civil Registrar, and that if this was the case then the Shaikh was liable to criminal prosecution. No action appears to have been taken against Shaikh Abdullah, and one suspects that the police had their own reasons for not pursuing the matter.

On the whole, the activities of the Alawi *tariqa* appear to have been welcomed by the local authorities at British ports and to have received their support. Shaikh Abdullah and Shaikh Hasan for their part diligently cultivated contacts with local officials in Cardiff and South Shields such as the mayor, leading councillors and the police. Al-Hakimi also enjoyed good relations with some senior British officials in Aden. At British ports the *tariqa*'s leadership was acknowledged as representing all the Muslims resident there, even though it won few adherents apart from the Arabs. Good relations with local officials quickly produced dividends. Early in 1937 strong support from a leading Tory councillor in South Shields ensured that Shaikh Abdullah's request that part of the local cemetery be set aside for exclusive use by the Muslim community was approved by the Town Council. Some local officials and senior police officers also lent their support to efforts by the *tariqa*'s leadership to secure funds for the construction of purpose-built mosques in Cardiff and South Shields. In Cardiff the six prayer rooms in Arab boarding houses were unable to accommodate an estimated 4,000 Muslims and soon after his arrival Shaikh al-Hakimi began negotiations with the local authorities to purchase land in the Docks district for a purpose-built mosque, modelled on the *Grande Mosquée de Paris* (opened in 1926), with accommodation for some 2,000 worshippers, a school and a library. Similar plans were prepared in South Shields where the Alawi *tariqa* had only two prayer rooms, one in a converted public house, and another in an Arab boarding house.

At both ports, the *tariqa* appears to have been able to secure land and planning permission from the local authorities for the construction of "Oriental-style" mosques close to the docks. In South

Shields a leading Tory councillor became "business adviser" to the mosque committee and his meetings in London with "Moslem potentates" attending the Coronation of King George VI attracted much interest in the local press but failed to produce the necessary financial support for the project. At the end of 1938 the *tariqa* turned to the British government for financial assistance for the proposed mosques in Cardiff and South Shields, pointing out that support would be appreciated by Muslims throughout the world. The Colonial Office noted the possible propaganda value of these projects, but in the end no government funds were forthcoming. In Cardiff the *tariqa* by its own efforts succeeded in converting three terraced houses in Peel Street into a temporary mosque, but the building was destroyed by enemy bombing during the early part of the Second World War.[21]

CONCLUSION

From the outset, the Home Office and the Board of Trade saw the Arabs as a "problem", a threat to public order. The prominent involvement of Arab seamen in the 1919 "race riots" in Cardiff and South Shields, even though the instigators were white ex-soldiers and sailors, provided justification for a policy of coercion and control. During the late 1920s a widely publicised and virulent campaign by the NUS against the Arabs only served to increase racial tensions at key British ports. Meanwhile the activities of the small but militant Communist Party in the coalfields of South Wales and Tyneside during the General Strike and miners' lockout of 1926, and the growing influence within the trade union movement of the Communist-inspired National Minority Movement, especially its Seamen's Section which by 1930 had taken up the Arab cause, must have set alarm bells ringing in official circles. In South Shields local leaders of the Seamen's Minority Movement began picketing as part of their campaign against the NUS and the imposition of the Rota System on Arab seamen. Many Arabs attended their meetings and took part in picketing, although claims by the Seamen's

[21] For further information on the Alawi *tariqa* in Britain see R. Lawless, *From Ta'izz to Tyneside*, pp. 218–36; and R. Lawless, "Religion and Politics", pp. 41–4.

Minority Movement leaders that they had the support of all the Arabs at the port were exaggerated. There were violent clashes between Arabs and police in Cardiff and South Shields in August 1930, and during the so-called "Arab riot" in South Shields several leaders of the Seamen's Minority Movement and the leader of the Arab faction closely associated with them were arrested.

The first Islamic organisations reached out to the Arab seafaring communities during periods of acute tension and unrest—the Islamic Society after the 1919 riots and the Western Islamic Association after the violent disturbances in 1930. The wealthy, well-educated, London-based leaders of these organisations had little in common with, or understanding of, the Arab seamen who were illiterate villagers recently incorporated into the industrial working class, and significantly there is little evidence of concern for the welfare of their co-religionists before the violent events of 1919 and 1930. When addressing the Arabs their language was often pompous, paternalistic and, in the case of Sheldrake, deliberately misleading. The Islamic Society called for reconciliation and understanding rather than resistance; the Western Islamic Association urged acceptance of the government-backed Rota System and its local officials sought to counter the activities of those Arabs who chose resistance and solidarity with the radical alternative provided by the Communist-led Seamen's Minority Movement. The creation of local branches of these organisations and offers of financial assistance for the religious aims of these poor and vulnerable communities were used to diffuse tension and win acceptance of government policies. Sheldrake's promises of funds to build a mosque in South Shields—, promises never fulfilled after tensions had subsided— represents a particularly blatant example of manipulation of religious aims for political purposes. The timing of these interventions leads one to suspect that they were encouraged, perhaps initiated/prompted, by certain government officials in the India Office or Colonial Office, but using the well-entrenched and pervasive "old boys' network" rather than formal committee structures. Those Arab boarding house masters who became the local officials of the Islamic Society and the Western Islamic Association were no doubt motivated by self-interest and used their involvement with these London-based organisations to bolster their influence within the faction-torn communities and gain advantage over their rivals.

The arrival of the Alawi *tariqa* in Britain, formalised as the "Zaouia Islamia Allawouia Religious Society of the United Kingdom" in 1936, appears to have been an initiative of the mother *zawiya* in Mostaganem in Algeria. Its leaders were not part of the "old boys' network" which linked key figures in the Islamic Society and the Western Islamic Association to senior government officials, but they succeeded in quickly ingratiating themselves with local councillors and senior police officers. Their efforts to re-Islamise these small seafaring communities, characterized by a dramatic "coming out" of popular Islam into public space for the first time in Britain, were not seen as threatening the status quo and appear to have been welcomed and supported by local officials. At a time of continuing high rates of unemployment among both white and coloured seamen, new restrictions on the employment of alien seamen, and widespread poverty and distress within the Arab communities, the potential for violence to erupt again was ever present; promoting self-control through Islam no doubt provided local authorities with a useful additional mechanism to enforce social control.[22]

[22] See N. Evans, "Regulating the Reserve Army", p. 102; on the use of Islam as a "social regulator" by the French authorities during the 1970s and 1980s to maintain order and defuse potential social conflicts among mainly North African immigrants see Gilles Kepel, *Les banlieues de l'islam: naissance d'une religion en France*, Paris: Seuil, 1987, pp. 127–74.

THE REFORM OF SHARI'A COURTS AND ISLAMIC LAW IN BOSNIA AND HERZEGOVINA 1918–1941

Fikret Karčić

This chapter attempts to highlight the reform of Shari'a courts in Bosnia and Herzegovina and substantive and procedural laws which they applied during the period between the two world wars. The discussion of this question is preceded by some introductory remarks on the application of Shari'a law in this province under non Muslim rule.

THE APPLICATION OF THE SHARI'A IN BOSNIA AND HERZEGOVINA

The Shari'a in Bosnia and Herzegovina under Habsburg rule (1878–1918)

In Bosnia and Herzegovina, together with other parts of interwar Yugoslavia with a considerable Muslim population, Islamic law continued to be administered by state Shari'a courts after the end of Ottoman rule. The Habsburg Empire, which occupied Bosnia and Herzegovina on the basis of article 25 of the Berlin Treaty of 1878, preserved the Shari'a courts as state courts with the same jurisdiction that they had exercised during the late Ottoman period. This was done by Austro-Hungary confirming the validity of the Ottoman Law on Shari'a courts of 16 *safar* 1276 (10 September 1859) in Bosnia and Herzegovina.[1] In this way, during the period

[1] "Gesetz Wirkungskreis der Scheriatsgerichte", in *Sammlung der für Bosnien und der Herzegowina erlassenen Gesetze, Verordnungen und Normalweisungen*, II, Vienna, 1880, pp. 476–81.

1878–1918, the Shari'a courts in Bosnia and Herzegovina continued to have jurisdiction over matters of Muslim personal status, family, inheritance and *waqf* affairs. It was during this period that the first steps towards the modernisation of the Shari'a courts took place.

The basic legal act of the Habsburg administration in Bosnia and Herzegovina pertaining to the Shari'a courts was the Ordinance on the Organisation and Jurisdiction of the Shari'a Courts n°7220/III issued by the provincial government on 30 October 1883.[2] This ordinance was followed by a number of similar acts which further elaborated the organisation and jurisdiction of the Shari'a courts. Extensive Habsburg normative intervention in this domain is illustrated by some 387 administrative acts published between 1878 and 1918 and related to the Muslim judiciary.[3]

The most important innovations introduced into the Shari'a judiciary during this period were:[4]

– firstly, Muslim acceptance that Shari'a courts could be a part of the judicial system of a non-Muslim state. There was no Muslim resistance to this solution since Muslim '*ulama* as well as political leaders insisted on keeping the Shari'a courts as state agencies. Muslim history and jurisprudence provided a sufficient number of precedents for the acceptance and validity of the appointment of *qadi*s by a non-Muslim ruler. For instance, Hanafi scholars such as Ibn al-Humam (d. 681 h./1282–83), Ibn Nujaym (d. 970 h./1562–63), and Ibn Abidin (d.1253 h./1837–38) took this position. Faced with the reality of the loss of Muslim territories in Spain and the Mongol conquest of the Abbasid Caliphate, Muslim jurists were ready to accept non-Muslim authority provided that Muslims in those territories continued to be under the jurisdiction of the Shari'a. That decision led the jurists to accept the appointment of *qadi*s by non-Muslim rulers. In the eyes of Muslim jurists what mattered was the law that was administered, not the

[2] *Zbornik zakona i naredaba za BiH*, Sarajevo: Zemaljska štamparija, 1883, pp. 538–42.

[3] Eugen Sladović, *Priručnik zakona i naredaba za upravnu službu u BiH*, Sarajevo, 1915, pp. 329–33.

[4] Fikret Karčić, *Šerijatski sudovi u Jugoslaviji 1918–1941*, Sarajevo: Islamski teološki fakultet, 1986, pp. 22–6.

appointing authority. In elaborating this view, Ibn al-Humam specifically mentioned places like Cordoba and Valencia, which Muslims lost—so that Muslims remaining there were in the position of a minority.[5] These developments forced Muslim jurists to take into consideration the lives of Muslims who stayed in lost territories, and slowly to develop what is today known as *fiqh al-aqalliyyat* (jurisprudence of Muslim minorities). Mustafa Hilmi Hadžiomerović, the Mufti of Sarajevo and the first *Reis ul-Ulema* (head of the '*ulama*) of Bosnia and Herzegovina, expressed this position in a *fatwa* given to the Habsburg government in order to legitimise the appointment of the *Reis ul-Ulema* by the Emperor of Austro-Hungary.[6]

– Secondly, the introduction of appellate jurisdiction into the Shari'a judiciary and the establishment of the Supreme Shari'a court in Sarajevo consisting of four judges, two of whom were *qadi*s and two civil judges (in 1913 civil judges were excluded from Shari'a courts, but the collegial structure of the Supreme Shari'a courts was preserved). The Supreme Shari'a court was authorised to issue circulars to subordinate Shari'a courts providing them with compulsory interpretation of particular Shari'a rules. In this way, the Supreme Shari'a court became an agent of reform of Shari'a law administered in Bosnia and Herzegovina. Similar developments were recorded in Turkey during the *Tanzimat* era, and in a number of Middle Eastern countries as well as in British India.[7]

– Thirdly, adoption of the Austrian-introduced Code of Civil Procedure for Bosnia and Herzegovina of 1883 for the Shari'a courts. This acceptance opened the way for an interesting combination of Shari'a substantive regulations and Austrian procedural rules.

[5] Ibn al-Humam, *Fath al-qadir*, VII, Beirut: Dar al-fikr, n.d., p. 294.

[6] Fikret Karčić, "The Office of Rais al-Ulama among the Bosniaks (Bosnian Muslims)", in *Intellectual Discourse* (Petaling Jaya, Malaysia), V, 2 (1997), pp. 114–17. For the text of this *fatwa* see *Istorijski razvoj institucije Rijaseta*, compiled by Omer Nakičević, Sarajevo: Rijaset Islamske zajednice u Republici Bosni i Hercegovini, 1996, pp. 90–91, 160–61.

[7] Noel J. Coulson, *A History of Islamic Law*, Edinburgh University Press, 1978, p. 163.

– And finally, the introduction of the Bosnian language (Serbo-Croat; in Habsburg terminology "*zemaljski jezik*", the language of the land) into the Shari'a courts. The use of Arabic and Turkish was limited to citations from Islamic law manuals.

Debates concerning the Shari'a under the Yugoslav monarchy (1918–1941)

During the period of the Yugoslav monarchy, Shari'a law continued to be applied to Muslims in Bosnia and Herzegovina. The application of Islamic personal law was the result of an international obligation, i.e., the St. Germain Agreement on the Protection of Minorities of 10 September 1919, under which the Yugoslav government accepted the obligation to allow Muslims to regulate their personal and family affairs according to "Muslim customs". According to some Bosnian historians (Muhamed Hadžijahić and Atif Purivatra), this clause was included in the Agreement on the Protection of Minorities on the initiative of the French government. According to this version, some Muslim dignitaries from Sarajevo, using as intermediary a journalist working for *Le Temps*, Charles Rivet, submitted a request to the French government to help them obtain protection for mosques, *waqf*s and other Muslim institutions, the appointment of a *Reis ul-Ulema* (head of the '*ulama*) as a religious leader, and the preservation of the Shari'a courts.[8] Consequently, the French government supported the inclusion of a special clause on Muslims in the Agreement on the Protection of Minorities. Thus, keeping the Shari'a courts as special courts for Muslims became an international obligation for the Yugoslav royal government, and consequently, a provision was included in the first Yugoslav constitution of 28 June 1921.

Debates in the Constitutional Assembly of the Kingdom of Serbs, Croats and Slovenes in 1921 indicate attitudes of Muslim and non-Muslim political representatives towards the Shari'a and its application for Muslims in the newly established state. Thus, for

[8] Atif Purivatra, *Jugoslovenska muslimanska organizacija u političkom životu Kraljevine Srba, Hrvata i Slovenaca*, Sarajevo: Svjetlost, 1977, p. 66, n.14. The author has relied on Muhamed Hadžijahić's private documents in giving this interpretation.

instance, Fehim Kurbegović, a delegate of the Yugoslav Muslim Organisation[9] in the Constitutional Assembly, said:

> . . . Besides, a very important question for us is that of the Shari'a courts. These courts are at present (in Bosnia) state courts and we ask that they remain as such. Mainly they are competent to deal with family matters, inheritance and public record of marriages.
>
> These matters are constituent parts of the Shari'a law and we cannot make any concession against the Shari'a law, since such an act will be an act against our own institutions. Therefore, we ask that these courts remain as state courts and that their competence remain within the area elaborated in our proposal . . .[10]

Similar views were expressed by Mehmedalija Mahmutović, a mufti from Sanjak. He was not a member of the Yugoslav Muslim Organisation, the main Muslim-based political party of Bosnia and Herzegovina, but with regard to the Shari'a courts he agreed with his Bosnian co-religionists. He proposed that the following article should be included in the Constitution:

> Muslim marital, family and inheritance matters are under the jurisdiction of state Shari'a spiritual courts which judge according to the rules of the Hanafi *madhhab*.
>
> These courts independently take care of the guardianship of Muslim orphans and keep records of births and deaths of Muslims, solemnisation and dissolution of their marriages. These books enjoy the status of public records.[11]

However, among non-Muslim representatives, there were voices against the constitutional guarantee for the existence of the Shari'a

[9] *Jugoslovenska muslimanska organizacija* (JMO) or the Yugoslav Muslim Organisation was the main political party of Muslims of Bosnia and Herzegovina and Sanjak in the period between the two world wars. Under the leadership of Dr Mehmed Spaho, it participated in most of the governments of the Kingdom of Serbs, Croats and Slovenes and later the Kingdom of Yugoslavia. Its leadership included members of the Bosniak middle class, some '*ulama* and nobility (*begs*). With regard to religion, the JMO stood for the preservation of Islam as a recognised religion and the application of the Shari'a for Muslims. See Atif Purivatra, *Jugoslovenska muslimanska organizacija*.

[10] See *Stenografske beleške. Rad ustavnog odbora Ustavotvorne skupštine Kraljevine SHS*, I, Beograd, 1921, p. 124.

[11] Ibid., III, pp. 4–5.

courts. Milosav Rajčević, from Montenegro, agreed with the proposal to keep the Shari'a courts with jurisdiction similar to that of Christian ecclesiastical courts (marital and family matters) but was against their proposed jurisdiction in inheritance matters. Delegate Vojislav Marinković was generally against the constitutional guarantee for the Shari'a courts and was of the opinion that this issue should be dealt by the introduction of new laws.

However, Muslim political parties—the Yugoslav Muslim Organisation of Bosnia and Herzegovina and the *Jemiyet (Yugoslavya'da Islam Muhafazayi Hukuk Cemiyeti)* of Kosovo and Macedonia—had a tacit agreement to ask for the constitutional guarantee for the existence and jurisdiction of the Shari'a courts. They wished these institutions to be preserved and, in their view, this objective would be best served by constitutional guarantees, since the state constitution was difficult to change and only by following a special procedure. Laws could be easily changed and, thus, the Shari'a courts could be abolished at any time.

Therefore, Muslim political parties asked that family and inheritance affairs of Muslims should be dealt with by the state Shari'a judges and made the inclusion of a "Shari'a clause" one of their conditions for voting for the Constitution. The government was in need of Muslim votes and finally in April 1921 an agreement was reached. The mutually accepted formulation of the relevant clause was: "Muslim family and inheritance matters are judged by state Shari'a judges". This clause was included in the state Constitution as clause n°109.

Non-Muslim delegates who supported the government offered a number of reasons as justification for the inclusion of the "Shari'a clause" in the Constitution. They included: it was a Muslim request and as such should be accepted; non-acceptance of the Muslim demand would mean that the Yugoslav state was more intolerant than the Ottoman which allowed Christians to retain their respective ecclesiastical courts; and the Shari'a courts should be accepted in order to keep the peace in the country and take into consideration Muslim attitudes and the like. Opposition delegates in the Constitutional Assembly did not share such views. Socialist delegate Milan Korun said that "the Shari'a clause" was "medieval currency for buying Muslim votes for the Constitution". Minister of Justice

Marko Djuričić was categorical, responding: "Gentlemen, I cannot say I am happy with the Shari'a courts, but they must stay. . .The Shari'a courts should be left to evolution".[12]

Apart from this debate in the Assembly, it is interesting to note that prior to the establishment of Socialist (Communist) rule in Bosnia and Herzegovina no significant Muslim intellectual or political group called for the abolition of the Shari'a. For instance, the Congress of Muslim intellectuals held in Sarajevo in 1928 to discuss the causes of Muslim backwardness called only for the elimination of misuse of Shari'a law at the expense of women's rights.[13] The journal *Reforma*, a short-lived organ of Muslim secular reformers in Bosnia and Herzegovina—the Organisation of Progressive Muslims—expressed views that the Shari'a was the most adequate family law for Muslims and that only the possibility of misuse of some of its institutions should be prevented.[14]

Non-Muslim authors regularly criticised the application of the Shari'a for Muslims in Bosnia and Herzegovina and called for the abolition of the Shari'a courts. For instance, Maksim Svara, a Sarajevo-based Serbian publicist, criticised Muslim intellectuals meeting at a Congress in Sarajevo for not demanding the abolition of "un-modern and un-civilised norms of the Shari'a", pointing primarily to polygamy and juvenile marriages.[15]

Muslim intellectuals regularly responded to this kind of criticism. The most probable reason for the pro-Shari'a stance of Bosnian Muslim intellectuals was that they were aware of the traditionalism of the Muslim population and believed that keeping the Shari'a as a regulator of Muslim personal affairs was the last line of defence of Muslim identity under constant threat from turbulent changes of regime, modernisation policies and an uncertain future. Thus, the issue of Shari'a law and Shari'a courts was left to Marxist revolutionaries to solve, in a radical way, as with many other issues.

[12] Ibid., I/44, p. 8.

[13] Ibrahim Kemura, "Kongres Muslimana intelektualaca u Sarajevu 1928", in *Prilozi Instituta za istoriju* (Sarajevo), XVII (1980), pp. 182–3.

[14] Hamid H. Efendić, "Šerijatsko bračno pravo", *Reforma* (30 March 1928).

[15] Maksim Svara, *Emancipacija muslimanke u svijetu i kod nas*, Sarajevo, 1932, p. 49.

THE REFORM OF THE SHARI'A COURTS

The functioning of the Shari'a courts

In terms of judicial organisation and procedure, the Shari'a courts in Yugoslavia were modernised following the model applied in Bosnia during Habsburg rule. Procedural law was considerably influenced by Austrian law through the Bosnian and Herzegovinian Civil Code of 1883. This project was carried out on the initiative of the Austro-Hungarian administration in Bosnia and Herzegovina, which was generally preoccupied with the idea of bringing order to Islamic institutions in this province. Since the new government preserved the Shari'a courts as a part of the state judicial system, the Habsburg project of modernisation was accepted by Muslims. Its acceptance was helped by the fact that Muslim legal scholars were of the opinion that the sovereign ruler of a particular Muslim country, even a non-Muslim, had the right to determine the jurisdiction and the organisation of the Shari'a courts there.[16] European influence on the procedure of the Shari'a courts in Bosnia and Herzegovina proved that it was possible to mix different substantive and procedural laws in order to create a more efficient system.

During the period 1918–1929 the administration of Islamic law in those Yugoslav regions inhabited by Muslims other than Bosnia and Herzegovina (i.e. Sanjak, Kosovo and Macedonia) continued according to the model inherited from earlier times. Islamic law was applied to Muslim family, inheritance and *waqf* matters through the jurisdiction of Muslim religious officials-muftis,[17] a model which exists today in Greece.

The provision embodied in article n°109 of the 1921 Constitution had significant consequences: the jurisdiction of the Shari'a courts was compulsory for all Muslims, Shari'a judges continued to be state officials, verdicts of the Shari'a courts were enforced by state authority, and the state was responsible for the organisation of Shari'a courts, their foundation and maintenance, the training of

[16] Fikret Karčić, *Društveno-pravni aspekt islamskog reformizma*, Sarajevo: Islamski teološki fakultet, 1990, p. 26.

[17] Mehmed Begovitch, *De l'Évolution du Droit Musulman en Yougoslavie*, PhD thesis, Algiers University, 1930.

personnel, etc. On the other hand, *qadi*s were appointed by the King and issued verdicts in his name. The head of the Muslim community (the *Reis ul-Ulema*) had the right to issue a letter of authority (*murasela*) to the Shari'a judges.[18]

During the period between 1918 and 1929 Shari'a courts in Yugoslavia continued to function in the way inherited from earlier states, Austro-Hungary in the case of Bosnia and the Kingdom of Serbia for Sanjak, Kosovo and Macedonia.[19] However, on 21 March 1929 the Kingdom of Yugoslavia passed a new law—the "Law on the Organisation of the Shari'a Courts and on the Shari'a Judges"—bringing uniformity to the organisation and functioning of these courts.[20] This was in line with the policy of the King Aleksandar Karadjordjević, who on 6 January 1929 dissolved Parliament and proclaimed his personal rule. In order to strengthen the concept of a common Yugoslav identity, his dictatorial regime banned all political parties and associations bearing ethnic or religious attributes and began to bring uniformity to the regulation of different aspects of life in Yugoslavia. For instance, the legal status of religious communities was regulated by state laws for the whole territory of the Kingdom. As a part of this policy, the two different systems for the application of Islamic law were abolished and uniformity, reflecting the Bosnia and Herzegovina model, was introduced into the Shari'a judiciary.

[18] F. Karčić, "The Office of *Rais al-Ulama*", pp. 109–20.

[19] In Serbia before the Balkan wars, Islam was given the status of "recognised religion" by virtue of article 77 of the Law on the Organisation of Liberated Territories of 3 January 1878. The Mufti of Niš had jurisdiction in personal matters of Muslims living there. After the Balkan wars, under the Administrative Order on the Organisation of Courts and on Courts' Procedure in Reunited Territories of the Old Serbia of 7 June 1914, muftis became responsible for the administration of Islamic law in personal matters for Muslims living in Sanjak, Kosovo and Macedonia. A similar situation prevailed in Montenegro. The basic difference between this system and that in Bosnia and Herzegovina was that the office of *qadi* was preserved only in Bosnia, while in other regions muftis, essentially jurisconsults, became Muslim judges. As far as substantial law is concerned, the same interpretation of Islamic law—that of the Hanafi *madhhab*—was administered.

[20] On the organisation and competence of the Shari'a courts according to this law see F. Karčić, *Šerijatski sudovi*, pp. 66–74.

After the passing of the Law on the Organisation of the Shari'a courts and on the Shari'a Judges in 1929, the Bosnian model for the organisation and jurisdiction of the Shari'a courts was extended to other parts of Yugoslavia. The very process of the establishment of Shari'a courts outside Bosnia and Herzegovina was subject to administrative decisions and was sometimes slow. However, this was one of the most important changes introduced in the administration of Islamic law in the Kingdom of Yugoslavia.

Courts were established at two levels: district Shari'a courts in areas in which at least 5,000 Muslims lived, and the Supreme Shari'a Courts in Sarajevo and Skopje. Administratively, the Shari'a courts were departments of their respective regular civil courts. In the district Shari'a courts, judicial power was exercised by individual judges, while the Supreme Shari'a courts consisted of at least three judges.

The Shari'a courts were authorised to deal with matters of family law, where both spouses were of the Islamic faith or where the marriage was solemnised before the Shari'a court; matters pertaining to the relations between parents and their children; matters pertaining to inheritance; matters pertaining to the custody and guardianship of Muslim persons; declaration of the death of Muslim persons; legalisation of the signature of Muslim persons; matters pertaining to Muslim endowments (*waqf*), provided that their status was not uncertain; and some religious-administrative questions such as proclamation of the beginning of a new month in the Muslim lunar calendar.

Shari'a judges had the status of civil servants, and were educated in state educational institutions. The Shari'a Law School in Sarajevo, established by the Habsburg authorities in 1887, which was elevated by the Yugoslav royal authorities to the rank of a faculty in 1937 and known as the High School of Islamic Theology and the Shari'a. In addition, from 1931, there was a department for Islamic law at the Belgrade University Law Faculty. This situation continued until the abolition of the Shari'a courts by a law adopted by the Assembly of the People's Republic of Bosnia and Herzegovina on 5 March 1946.[21]

[21] *Službeni list NR BiH*, 10 (6 March 1946).

A project for a reform of procedure

The law on the Shari'a Courts of 1929 paved the way for a move towards the further reform of procedure followed by the Shari'a courts. In the same year, the Minister of Justice received a draft of a Code for the Procedure before the Shari'a Courts from the Association of the Shari'a Judges[22] but the government hesitated to enact it. Attempts at the codification of Islamic procedural laws continued through the following decade and both Supreme Shari'a Courts—in Sarajevo and Skopje—supported this idea. However, the draft code was not promulgated as a law until the Kingdom of Yugoslavia collapsed in 1941. A possible reason why the Yugoslav government hesitated to codify Islamic procedural law was the strong tendency during the 1930s towards the unification of civil law across the whole country. Within that framework the very existence of the Shari'a courts was questioned by many civil lawyers. With such a tendency in legal circles, state-sponsored codification of Islamic procedural laws was highly unlikely.

Even without practical results, the very project for reform of the procedure of the Shari'a courts was important as an indicator of the understanding of Shari'a among Bosnian Muslim scholars and legal practitioners. It illustrated the idea of compatibility between Islamic law and the non-Islamic state and the possibility of combining different features of Islamic and European continental legal cultures. It is equally important that the idea of codification was supported by leading Shari'a judges and scholars in inter-war Bosnia and Herzegovina such as Abdulah Škaljić, Abdulah Bušatlić, Fehim Spaho, Mehmed Begović and others. The French scholar Georges-Henri Bousquet praised this draft.[23]

The most important changes proposed by this draft were:

(1) The Shari'a judge must examine the case and make a verdict on the first hearing;

[22] Abdulah Škaljić, "Osvrt na rad staleške organizacije šeriatskih sudaca", *El-Hidaje* (Sarajevo), 10–11 (1943), pp. 315–16.

[23] Georges-Henri Bousquet, "Nouvelles observations sur quelques réformes apportées au droit musulman en Yougoslavie", *Revue Algérienne, Tunisienne et Marocaine de Législation et de Jurisprudence* (Paris), XLVIII (1932), pp. 202–4.

(2) The Shari'a court could delegate inheritance cases to a civil court on the basis of the petition of an heir;
(3) The procedure for the appointment of a guardian was elaborated. The natural father of a child was among the persons authorised to initiate this procedure; traditionally an illegitimate child was legally bound only to his/her mother;
(4) The pronouncement of *talaq* was defined as an initiative to start divorce before the *qadi* and not a final termination of marriage.

However, these reforms of the Shari'a court procedure, described by Bousquet as a better solution than the introduction of the Swiss Civil Code in Turkey, were not enforced in Yugoslavia.

THE REFORM OF ISLAMIC LAW

Codification

The law administered by the Shari'a courts underwent reform comparable in content and methodology with the reform carried out in modernised Muslim countries at that time. Thus, traditional *fiqh* works were abandoned in favour of modern Egyptian and Turkish codifications of Islamic law. From Ottoman times, the Shari'a courts adhered to the *Majalla* (*Mejelle-i ahkjami adliyye*), a codification of Hanafi *fiqh* in the area of civil affairs (*mu'amalat*). Subsequently, the *Majalla* was translated into the Bosnian language and published in Sarajevo in 1906.[24] In addition, another codification of Islamic law—the Ottoman Family Law of 1917 (*Hukuk-i aile nizamnamesi*)—was referred to by the Shari'a courts, cited in their judgements, translated into Serbo-Croat and published.[25]

The Shari'a courts also referred to compilations of Islamic law by the Egyptian scholar Muhammad Qadri Pasha (1821–86), namely *al-Ahkam al-shari'iyya fi al-ahwal al-shakhsiyya* and *Ahkam al-awqaf*. The first compilation was later translated into Serbo-Croat by

[24] *Medžellei ahkjami šerijje (Otomanski gradjanski zakonik)*, Sarajevo: Nakladna knjižara Antona Kajona, 1906.
[25] Abdulah Škaljić, *Ženitbeni zakon "Hukuki aile kararnamesi"*, Sarajevo: El-Hidaje, 1945.

Hasib Muradbegović and prepared for publication in 1944. Owing to the war it was never published.[26]

Changes in Islamic family law and the failure of its codification

Apart from the change in the form of Islamic legal rules and the move towards codification, Islamic substantive laws were also subject to reform in Bosnia and Herzegovina and Yugoslavia in general. Changes in Islamic family law included:[27] obligatory registration of Muslim marriages solemnised by the Shari'a judges or imams delegated by them; obligatory presence of the bride during the ceremony of solemnisation of marriage before the Shari'a court; restriction of polygamy by a circular of the Supreme Shari'a Court in Sarajevo in 1916, whereby a Muslim man wishing to marry a second wife was asked to prove that he was financially capable of supporting a polygamous marriage; and granting a wife the right to initiate divorce proceeding in cases where the husband was a lunatic, ill of a contagious disease, or unable financially to maintain the family.

These changes in Islamic family law were introduced by the Shari'a Supreme Courts through circulars issued to subordinate courts instructing them how to decide particular cases. Since these reforms were introduced by authoritative Muslim judges and often by referring to similar practices in Egypt and Turkey before the abolition of the Shari'a in 1924, there was no resistance to them. The main method of reform was (1) selection (*takhayyur*), i.e. the choice of one of several possible interpretations within the four Sunni schools of law and (2) "policy in accordance with the Shari'a" (*al-siyasa al-shar'iyya*), i.e. the right of higher authorities to determine the jurisdiction and procedure for the administration of Islamic law. The other two methods of reform known in Middle

[26] Hasib Muradbegović, *Tumač šeriatskih propisa hanefijskog mezheba o ženitbi, obitelji i nasljedstvu s važnijim okružnicama Vrhovnog šeriatskog suda, Ulema medžlisa i Šireg savjeta reis-ul-uleme i s osvrtom na gradjansku i kanonsku ženitbu i obiteljske odnose*, Zagreb: Naklada Ministarstva pravosudja i bogoštovlja, 1944, p. 561.

[27] Fikret Karčić, *Društveno-pravni*, pp. 233–7; Ibrahim Džananović, *Primjena šerijatskog porodičnog prava kroz praksu Vrhovnog šerijatskog suda 1914–1946*, Sarajevo: Fakultet islamskih nauka, 2004.

Eastern countries—eclecticism (*talfiq*) and the new *ijtihad* (rational interpretation)—were not practised in Bosnia.

Apart from these partial interventions in the area of family law, the idea of a comprehensive codification of Shari'a substantive law of personal status was suggested. In 1928 Hafiz Abdulah Bušatlić proposed the preparation of the Code of Muslim Family and Inheritance Law which "will fit the spirit of the time and be within the framework of the fundamental precepts of the Shari'a, regardless of a particular *madhhab* and the divergent opinions of individual scholars. . ."[28] Among Yugoslav civil legal scholars, Bertold Eisner enthusiastically supported the idea of codification of the Shari'a family and inheritance law. He offered three reasons for this: (1) It was the right of the government to oversee the Shari'a courts as a part of the state judiciary and that could be done efficiently if an official codification of relevant Shari'a laws existed; (2) It was in the interest of Muslims themselves, who very often did not know relevant Shari'a rules, because codification would make the Shari'a law more accessible to them; (3) It was necessary to ensure uniformity of the Shari'a courts' practice. As a model, he suggested that relevant Egyptian and Turkish codifications should be followed.[29]

However, this idea, even though it was very popular among prominent Shari'a judges and civil lawyers, was not implemented for the same reason that the codification of Shari'a procedural laws was not carried out—that is, the strong will among lawyers to unify the civil law for all citizens.

The impossibility of reforming the management of waqfs

In addition to family affairs, management of *waqf*s (inalienable Islamic charitable endowments) considerably improved in Bosnia and Herzegovina. In 1931 in Sarajevo, centralisation of ninety-two independent public *waqf*s (*waqf khayri*)—endowments from which the income was allocated to the benefit of the general public—was carried out. However, this move provoked resistance from traditional '*ulama* and was revoked. Instead, the '*ulama* were in favour of preserv-

[28] Abdulah Bušatlić, "Šerijatski sudovi", *Gajret* (1928), p. 157.

[29] Bertold Eisner, "Nadležnost u porodičnim i nasljednim stvarima muslimana i primjena šerijatskog prava", *Arhiv za pravne i društvene nauke* (Beograd), XXII, 3 (1922), pp. 235–6.

ing each *waqf* endowment as an independent unit administered by a manager (*mutawalli*) appointed by the founder, operating according to conditions prescribed by him/her (*shart al-waqif*) and not subject to any centralised authority. In contrast, reformist scholars, such as Mehmed Džemaludin Čaušević, were of the opinion that individual *waqf*s should be put under the centralised supervision of the Waqf administration, and that in certain situations the Waqf administration could depart from the expressed will of the founders if *waqf* property could be better used in changed social conditions. Thus, in Bosnian Muslim circles there was a clash between two conceptions of the institution of *waqf*—one individualistic, supported by traditional '*ulama*, and the other centralistic, shared by reformist scholars and the Waqf administration. Those who supported the individualistic conception adhered to Islamic traditional law and were against the intervention of any modern organisation—state or institutionalised Muslim community—in the area of Muslim endowments.

Similarly, there was no change in the area of family *waqf*s (*waqf ahli*). These were *waqf*s for which the income of the endowed property was allocated, partially or in total, to the family members of the founder. In some Muslim countries, such as Egypt, these *waqf*s occupied large portions of arable land and their beneficiaries had no interest in improving the state of *waqf* property since their income was guaranteed. Therefore, modern Muslim states usually intervened in this area and subjected family *waqf*s to reform during the twentieth century.[30] Family *waqf*s were either abolished or, after some time, turned into public *waqf*s (*waqf khayri*). In Bosnia and Herzegovina, the opposition of the traditional '*ulama* to any institutional intervention in the area of *waqf* resulted in family endowments being left intact.

Debates on reforms in the area of social ethics

Apart from the area of positive Islamic law, reformist endeavours in Bosnia and Herzegovina focused on the area of social ethics as well. The most debated issue in this area was the "issue of Muslim women" (*muslimansko žensko pitanje*). The debate centred on the questions of veiling, education and the public role of Muslim

[30] Fikret Karčić, "Glavne tendencije u pravnom uredjenju vakufa u nekim muslimanskim zemljama 1850–1950", *Zbornik radova Islamskog teološkog fakulteta u Sarajevu*, (Sarajevo), 2 (1987), pp. 113–16.

women. Muslim public opinion became deeply polarised over these questions. Three positions were taken during the debate which lasted until the Kingdom of Yugoslavia collapsed in 1941. First, a group of "secular reformers" whose main representatives were Dževad-beg Sulejmanpašić and Edhem N. Bulbulović (1892–1953) called for the introduction of new attire for Muslims, including a hat (*šešir*) for men, unveiling of women and an active role for women in economic and social life.[31] They argued that the fez and the veil represented the main obstacle to the adaptation of Muslims to "new times" and a barrier to the advancement of the Muslims. The reforms of Mustafa Kemal were cited as a model to be emulated.

Second, there was the group of "religious reformers", including *Reis ul-Ulema* Mehmed Džemaludin Čaušević (1870–1938), Šukrija Alagić (1881–1936), Abdulah Bušatlić (1871–1946) and others. Referring to Islamic sources, they supported unveiling of Muslim women, their education and their participation in public life in accordance with the principles of Islamic social ethics.

Both these groups called for a change in the existing social situation of the Bosnian Muslims. The first group referred to modern times and Kemalist reforms as their frame of reference, while the second group, also sympathetic to Kemalist reforms, tried to justify reforms by emphasising more Islamic sources and the need for a new interpretation of Islam (*ijtihad*).

Third, there was the group of traditional Muslim *'ulama*, which included Ali Riza Karabeg (1873–1944), Ibrahim Hakki Čokić (?-1948), and Ali Riza Prohić (1867–1942). Voices of this group were the journals *El-Hidaje*, the organ of the Association of *'Ulama* in the Kingdom of Yugoslavia, and *Hikjmet*, a journal published in Tuzla.[32] An example of the position of this group is provided by a treatise on *hijab* by Ali Riza Karabeg (1873–1944) published in 1928.[33] The main points made by the author were: (1) traditional attire for Muslim women (*čaršaf, feredža*) was the basic symbol of

[31] They were centred around a short-lived paper *Reforma*, which appeared in Sarajevo between 23 March 1928 and 6 July 1928.

[32] For information about this journal see Adnan Jahić, *Hikjmet—riječ tradicionalne uleme u Bosni i Hercegovini*, Tuzla: BZK "Preporod", 2004, p. 206.

[33] Ali Riza Karabeg, *Rasprava o hidžabu (krivenju muslimanki)*, Sarajevo, 1928.

Islam; (2) no one could expect a new interpretation of Islam in Bosnia when such a thing was hard to find even in the Arab world; (3) the movement toward a new interpretation of Islam (the reformist views of the *Reis ul-Ulema* Čaušević) was an attempt to establish a "fifth [Kemalist] *madhhab* in Bosnia".

Hafiz Abdulah Bušatlić, a representative of the group of religious reformers, responded with a brochure entitled "About 'tasattur' and 'hijab'/covering of Muslim women. . .".[34] In this treatise, he defended modernist views on the role of Muslim women in contemporary society taken by *Reis ul-Ulema* Džemaluddin Čaušević and pleaded for a departure from traditional Muslim views if demanded by "the spirit of the time".

In a such polarised situation in Muslim public life in Bosnia there was no possibility for a negotiated solution of the "Muslim women's question". This question was radically solved in 1950 by the Socialist government which banned the practice of veiling of Muslim women, introduced compulsory elementary education for both girls and boys and opened job opportunities for women.

CONCLUSION

Ideas for reform of Islamic law, common in the modernising Muslim countries during the first half of the twentieth century, were echoed in Bosnia and Herzegovina in the inter-war period. Modernisation of the Shari'a courts and Islamic law followed the model applied in Bosnia during the Habsburg era and the path followed by Muslim Middle Eastern countries. They were conducted by reformist-minded Shari'a judges, and supported by the state authorities, and met no resistance among the Muslim population. Changes in social ethics, especially external symbols of Islamic identity, however, were limited owing to resistance from traditional circles and a large portion of the Muslim population.

It is interesting to note that during the debate on the reform of Islamic law and the Shari'a courts in Bosnia and Herzegovina, no

[34] Abdulah Bušatlić, "O 'teseturu' i 'hidžabu'/pokrivanju/kod muslimanki-osvrt na brošuru g. Čokića i g. Karabega i potkrepa tvrdnji iznešenih u mojoj brošuri", *Novi behar* (Sarajevo), II, from n°1 (15 May 1928) to n°7 (1 August 1928).

participant made reference to the notion of "European Islam" or "Bosnian Islam". They were aware that the Bosnian Muslims (Bosniaks) were a European Muslim nation, but they did not envisage any form of "European" or "Bosnian" Islam normatively different from Islam in general. Specific characteristics of Bosnian Muslim practices were described as "customs" (*običaji*) and the totality of those practices was subsumed by non-Muslim authors under the expression of "our Muslims" (*naši muslimani*). All Bosnian Muslim groups engaged in the debate about reform in Bosnia referred to the practice of a preferred foreign Muslim scholar, movement or state outside Bosnia in order to strengthen their own position—a practice not unusual for Muslim minorities. Secular reformers referred to Mustafa Kemal's reforms in Turkey, religious modernists to Muhammad Abduh in Egypt and traditionalists to the traditional authorities of the Ottoman-Islamic cultural zone. According to our research, the only instance when the expression "Bosnian Islam" was used in the inter-war period in Bosnia and Herzegovina was in the translation of an article written by the German historian Georg Stadtmüller, "Bosnian Islam-a bridge of Europe toward the Islamic world", published in *Glasnik Islamske vjerske zajednice*—an official journal of the Islamic Community in the "Independent State of Croatia"—in 1943.[35] It seems that the notion of "Bosnian Islam" did not attract the attention of Bosnian Muslim authors during that time. It was only after the war of 1992–95 that some Bosniak authors, reacting to *salafi* influences brought to their homeland by foreign humanitarian workers and local graduates of mainly Saudi universities, began to use the expression "Bosnian Islam" in order to describe the totality of interpretation and practice of Islam in Bosnia. At the same time, the expression "European Islam" found its way into Muslim discourse in this country.

However, even if the expression "European Islam" was not used in the inter-war period in Bosnia and Herzegovina, reforms in interpretation of Islamic norms and institutions, described in this chapter, indicate that they were carried out in order to help the Muslim community in Bosnia and Herzegovina preserve its Islamic identity in a European environment.

[35] *Glasnik Islamske vjerske zajednice*, XI, 7 (1943), pp. 174–9.

EURO-ISLAM BY '*JIHAD* MADE IN GERMANY'

Wolfgang G. Schwanitz

I discuss in this chapter the German "jihadisation" of Islam in the light of Berlin's Middle Eastern policy and the birth of a Euro-Islam during and between the two world wars. In this contribution, the term "Middle East" includes the Near East in its widest definition; altogether it refers to the area in Africa and Asia between and including Arab North Africa in the West, Iran, Afghanistan, and India in the East, the Fertile Crescent, Turkey, and Cyprus in the North, and the Arabian Peninsula in the South.

I argue that the concept of using Islam during mainly non-religious wars came from German and Ottoman advocates. Of course, a general concept of *jihad* had existed since the advent of Islam. Moreover, in history war alliances were occasionally formed between Muslims and non-Muslims.[1] But never before was there a concept which attempted to modernise and use *jihad* in a modern global coalition war among Western powers. This was the starting point for the development of a so-called Euro-Islam by a bellicose axis of non-Muslims and Muslims.

In peacetime Berlin respected the status quo in the Middle East, preventing also the further dismemberment of the Ottoman Empire. It had never wished for colonies and Muslim subjects there, and this was an outstanding feature of Germany's Middle Eastern policy. It was not only because Germany was a late comer to the concert of nations. Rather, mainstream politicians in Berlin

[1] Rudolph Peters, *Jihad in Classical and Modern Islam*, Princeton: Markus Wiener, 2005 (updated edition).

watched all the negative consequences for the metropolis of having colonial territories, notably for the British in India and Egypt, the French in Algeria and the Russians in the Caucasus and the Balkans. The first German Chancellor, Otto von Bismarck, in particular displayed a distaste for colonial acquisitions overseas, though of course he used the colonial lobby for his policy towards the European Great powers.

Consequently, Germans kept a critical eye on the colonial empires of their neighbours. Mainstream German politicians even favoured Muslim nationalists who tried to get rid of their British, French and Russian overlords. Thus, some Muslim leaders asked Berlin for help in their anti-colonial struggle. In Berlin Germans and Muslims developed a new brand of Islam, a Euro-Islam, first as a tool of war. But how did this *jihad* made in Germany come about? Before this subject is investigated, three features of German policy toward this region will be discussed.

THE GERMAN CRADLE OF A NEW BRAND OF POLITICAL ISLAM

Berlin's Middle Eastern policy

First, it should be noted that there was not much territory left in North Africa and West Asia to be claimed by the newly established German Reich after 1871. Large parts of what later became known as the Middle East had already been distributed among Germany's neighbours. Thus, keeping the status quo in the region was most likely to serve Germany's national interests.[2] Trade, commerce, and peaceful penetration, especially in open-door areas, were cornerstones of Berlin's Middle Eastern policy. This was also true during the *Deutsche Orient-Gründerjahre,* the "German Orient founding years" which started in 1884 and lasted for three decades.[3] It was also a time during which Germany explored new regions in Africa

[2] For the Prussian tradition of keeping the status quo overseas see Ulrich van der Heyden, *Rote Adler an Afrikas Küste. Die brandenburgisch-preußische Kolonie Großfriedrichsburg in Westafrika*, Berlin: Selignow, 2001, pp. 14–15.

[3] For an overview of the German Orient founding years 1884–1914 see: August Bebel, *Die Muhammedanisch-Arabische Kulturperiode*, Berlin: Edition Ost, 1999 [1889], pp. 173–83.

and Asia. Berlin established colonies in West and East Africa, becoming a small colonial power.[4] But during that era the Germans intensified their economic, cultural, and military relations with the Middle East with its lands under Ottoman rule, as well as with Egypt and Morocco. The first feature of Berlin's Middle Eastern policy in peacetime was respecting the status quo and avoiding any colonial ambition.[5]

Second, the Eastern Question—who would get which part of the declining Ottoman Empire—had already caused many conflicts. Chancellor Otto von Bismarck, until 1890 the main German foreign policy maker[6] who disliked colonial acquisitions, regarded the Eastern Question above all as part of his policy towards neighbouring European colonial powers. He was of the opinion that Germany's policy towards Europe and America came first and its Middle Eastern policy had to serve that primary policy. Thus, the second feature of Berlin's Middle Eastern policy was that it was always subordinate to a primary policy towards Europe and America.[7]

Third, the Middle East did not offer enough potential to warrant a great design of German policy. Otto von Bismarck used to put it this way: "The Eastern Question is not worth the bones of a single Pomeranian grenadier". For example, at that time German policy toward Egypt was considered a question not of relations between Berlin and Cairo, but between Berlin and London. In the Chancellor's eyes there was not much to be gained from direct relations with Egypt. But Egypt made an effective "stick"[8] to be used against

[4] Horst Gründer, *Geschichte der deutschen Kolonien*, Paderborn: F. Schöningh, 1995; David Birmingham, Muriel Chamberlain and Chantal Metzger, *L'Europe et L'Afrique de 1914 à 1970*, Paris: SEDES, 1994.

[5] For German colonial pressure groups see: Axel Fichtner, *Die völker- und staatsrechtliche Stellung der deutschen Kolonialgesellschaften des 19. Jahrhunderts*, Frankfurt/Main: Peter Lang, 2002.

[6] Konrad Canis, *Bismarcks Außenpolitik 1870–1890. Aufstieg und Gefährdung*, Paderborn: Ferdinand Schöningh, 2004.

[7] Diktat Bismarcks, Kissingen, 15 June 1877, in Heinz Wolter, *Otto von Bismarck. Dokumente seines Lebens*, Leipzig: Philipp Reclam, 1986, pp. 320–1.

[8] Martin Kröger, '*Le bâton égyptien'—Der ägyptische Knüppel. Die Rolle der 'ägyptischen Frage' in der deutschen Außenpolitik von 1875/76 bis zur 'Entente Cordiale'*, Frankfurt/Main: Peter Lang, 1991.

London to undermine alliances between Germany's neighbours. He used this *bâton égyptien* diplomatically. Since Berlin had no colonies in the region, Germany slipped into the role of a key mediator in European conflicts over the East. The third feature of Berlin's Middle Eastern policy was therefore a diplomacy of mediation, during a series of conferences on African frontiers and Asian topics from the 1880s.[9]

Berlin's Middle Eastern policy in peacetime and during the course of the three decades of the "German Orient founding years" until 1914 emphasised maintaining the status quo, pursuing a secondary policy with peaceful penetration of the region, and mediating in Oriental conflicts. For reasons that cannot be discussed here, the always-feared "Sarajevo effect" dragged Europe and the world into a war starting in the peripheral Balkans.

Jihad *as war ideology*

After the outbreak of the First World War in mid-1914 Berlin switched to a primary wartime policy in the colonial territories of its enemies. It very secretly instigated *jihad* in British and Russian Asia and in French Africa, creating fifth columns, revolts and trouble there to take pressure off main European battle fronts. Six months later, a public dispute erupted between two founding fathers of Islamic studies in Europe. Did the Germans push the Turks to proclaim a *jihad* after the Ottoman Empire entered the First World War I against the British, the Russians, and the French? The leading Dutch Arabist C. Snouck Hurgronje maintained that they did and blamed his German colleagues—among them Carl Heinrich Becker—for having supported this "fever of *jihad*". Hurgronje insisted that this *jihad* was an intellectual weapon "made in Germany". In response, Becker stated that supposing this were true, had not Berlin and Istanbul every right to do so? Hurgronje insisted that they did not because this hurt humanism and religious peace. Becker replied that "there is no taboo for religion".[10]

[9] Imre Josef Demhardt, *Deutsche Kolonialgrenzen in Afrika*, Hildesheim: Olms, 1997.

[10] "The Holy War 'Made in Germany', 1915" in C. Snouck Hurgronje, *Verspreide Geschriften*, III, Bonn/Leipzig: E.J. Brill, 1923, pp. 257–8; "Die Kriegsdiskussion über den Heiligen Krieg", in Carl Heinrich Becker, *Islamstudien*, Hildesheim: Olms, 1969, pp. 281–304.

Indeed, if we consider Berlin's switch to a wartime policy against the British, French and Russian Muslim territories, there is a unique feature: *jihad* made in Germany.[11] Eye-witnesses, such as one of Britain's finest writers, made the whole German-Ottoman *jihad* plot public in October 1916. In his classic espionage thriller *Greenmantle*, John Buchan told a worldwide audience the story of how the Kaiser and his agents pushed the Ottoman Turks to proclaim a Holy War against the British throughout the Muslim lands.[12] Buchan's main character was partly modelled on T.E. Lawrence, and the book recounts how London launched a counter action led by "Lawrence of Arabia". Others, such as the US ambassador to Turkey in Istanbul, Henry I. Morgenthau, also used the expression "*jihad* that was made in Germany".[13]

It is not clear whether Hurgronje used the term "made in Germany" in a pejorative or a positive sense. At that time this trade mark had lost his early connotation of cheap products (stemming from the British Merchandise Marks Act of 1887). On the contrary, "made in Germany" then denoted products of high quality, and trust in science and progress. Indeed, in the present case humanities played a big role, the new field of Islamic studies. Were Hurgronje, Buchan and Morgenthau aware of this, and were they indeed right?

The idea of *jihad* developed as a concerted German-Ottoman action. It consisted of five parts: Max von Oppenheim's design to provoke revolts in enemy colonial territories; promoting *jihad* through the Berlin-based Oriental News Department; the Ottoman *fatwa*; Shaikh Salih's commentary on the *fatwa*; and the realisation of the *jihad*. It was used as a weapon to globalise the war, but it was a slap in the face to the Enlightenment.[14] Although Hurgronje's criticism hit the mark, Becker held to a chauvinistic

[11] Wolfgang G. Schwanitz, "Djihad 'made in Germany': Der Streit um den Heiligen Krieg (1914–1915)", *Sozial Geschichte*, XVIII, 2 (2003), pp. 7–34.

[12] John Buchan, *Greenmantle*, New York: Oxford University Press, 1999.

[13] Henry I. Morgenthau, *Ambassador Morgenthau's Story*, New York: Doubleday, Page & Co., 1918, Chapter XIV.

[14] Gertrude Himmelfarb, *The Roads To Modernity. The British, French, and American Enlightenments*, New York: Knopf, 2004.

approach. To understand this approach, it is worthwhile examining the five elements of the *jihad* according to the German design.

Origins of the modern pan-Islamic jihad

Max von Oppenheim served as an archaeologist and diplomat in the Middle East for two decades, and the Kaiser was used to his reports about Pan-Islam and *jihad*.[15] From his view point there were only two possibilities to deal with Germany's enemies: directly at the main fronts in Europe or indirectly by creating a new ideology for Muslims and organising political opposition, even revolts, in their colonial territories.

After the war began, Max von Oppenheim became responsible in the German Foreign Ministry for dealing with the Middle East and the Islamic regions.[16] On 2 August 1914, the Ottoman-German pact was signed with a clear intention of using the Ottomans for the proposed concept of *jihad*. General Hellmuth von Moltke wanted the Ottoman War Minister Enver Pasha to weaken their enemies from within. The Kaiser also asked Enver to enter the war right away: the Ottoman Sultan-Caliph ought to call for *jihad* in Africa and Asia in order to get Muslims to fight for the Caliphate. Even academics in Berlin, such as the University Professor for Turkish History, Ernst Jäckh, expected "Islamic fanatics fighting for Germany".[17]

This *jihad* was mainly Oppenheim's idea. He had presented its basic elements to the Kaiser in his report about pan-Islamic movements in 1898.[18] The Kaiser was about to visit the Ottoman Sultan, and two months before his trip to Istanbul Oppenheim wrote that Islam was still a vital force. Since European colonial policy cared more and more for Christianity and the Western culture, an Islamic counter movement was on the rise aimed at breaking the Christian grip on the Islamic regions. This movement could count on

[15] Martin Kröger, "Max von Oppenheim—mit Eifer ein Fremder im Auswärtigen Dienst", in G. Teichmann and G. Völger (eds), *Faszination Orient. Max von Oppenheim, Forscher, Sammler, Diplomat*, Cologne: Dumont, 2001, pp. 106–39.

[16] Fritz Fischer, *Griff nach der Weltmacht*, Düsseldorf: Droste, 1961, p. 134.

[17] Ernst Jäckh, *Der aufsteigende Halbmond*, Stuttgart: Deutsche Verlags Anstalt, 1916.

[18] Political Archive, Foreign Office (ParchAA), R14556, An Reichskanzler Fürst Hohenlohe-Schillingsfürst, Bericht 48, Die Panislamische Bewegung, Cairo, 5 July 1898, gez. Max von Oppenheim.

pan-Islamic solidarity that was nurtured by the pilgrimage, the inner religiosity of Muslims and their feeling of unity. Moreover, there were anti-European Sufi brotherhoods at work such as the Sanusiyya of Northern Africa and Arabia. In addition, messianic movements such as that of the Mahdi in Sudan were spreading so that even tribes indifferent to religion "were suddenly inflamed by a fanaticism that borders on madness".

Furthermore, Oppenheim reported to the Kaiser that *jihad* would be a mighty weapon with unforeseeable consequences if Muslims could actually be prepared for holy war. Although the Islamic regions had ceased to be a unified state, the pan-Islamic idea was very much alive. Oppenheim emphasised that if *jihad* was proclaimed volunteers and money from all over the Islamic world would arrive for the Sultan, as was the case in his 1877–78 war against Russia. According to him, the pan-Islamic movement had started some decades ago in Istanbul where Islamic scholars gathered, translated the Qur'an into many other languages[19] and founded religious schools. More than ever, Oppenheim explained, the Sultan was considered to be the greatest Islamic ruler and protector of the Holy Places of Mecca and Medina. As a direct enemy he might be of little importance for a Great Power. But as an ally he was valuable because he ruled over many Muslim subjects. Germany was considered by Muslims to be their best friend among the Christian nations. The message to the Kaiser was clear: prepare the field and use the Sultan for *jihad* in the colonial territories of potential enemies. Berlin might very well need the pan-Islamic fanaticism and anti-European brotherhoods.[20]

[19] Oppenheim wrote: "In Constantinople a Pan-Islamic movement started a couple of decades ago. The current Sultan took it over very skilfully and with great energy. He delegated envoys to the far most regions of the Islamic world. And he attracted Islamic scholars to Constantinople through the translation of the Qur'an in all possible languages, of course in keeping the Arabic script, and through the inauguration of *madrasas* in South Africa etc.". Probably Oppenheim had also in mind the "Arabo-afrikaans" case. See also Eric Germain, "L'Afrique du Sud dans la politique 'panislamique' de l'Empire ottoman", in *Turcica*, 31 (1999), pp. 109–48.

[20] For the delicate relationship of Pan-Turkism and Pan-Islam see "Pan-Islam and Pan-Turkism during the final years of the Ottoman Empire: some considerations" in Jacob M. Landau, *Exploring Ottoman and Turkish History*, London: Hurst, 2004, pp. 25–9.

The mastermind

Oppenheim was an expert on the Middle East with insider knowledge, but not a scholar of Islam. Thereafter he became the German "Abu Jihad", that is "father of the Islamic Holy War". He represented a large circle of mainstream politicians, officers and academics and designed his master plan before the Ottomans entered the war on the side of the Central Powers. His top secret 136 page report for the Kaiser was entitled: "Fomenting rebellion in the Islamic territories of our enemies".[21] The Kaiser, who was familiar with this idea, accepted Oppenheim's proposal to incite Muslims to *jihad* under the leadership of the Ottoman Sultan-Caliph as part of a larger scheme of destabilising Germany's enemies.

Under the plan the Sultan would proclaim a *jihad* against the British, the French, and the Russians, and Berlin would deliver money, experts, and material. The targets were Muslims in British India, French North Africa and Russian Asia. The call to fight would go out in several languages using psychological techniques, and for this aim Berlin created an Oriental News Department in the Foreign Ministry in 1914. Encouraging the Muslims in India to revolt was the key to victory. Expeditions were to be sent to Afghanistan to trigger an uprising from there. The Germans would provide intelligence to the Muslims, while the Turks would encourage them to revolt against their foreign masters. Islam, concluded Oppenheim, would be Germany's "deadly strike" against the British.[22]

Oppenheim became the head of the Oriental News Department in Berlin in 1914 and was later succeeded by Karl E. Schabinger and Eugen Mittwoch. He employed a dozen German academics—among them the Orientalists and professors Sebastian Beck, Martin Hartmann, Helmuth von Glasenapp, Oskar Mann, Wilhelm Spatz and other regional specialists like Edgar Pröbster, Curt Prüfer and Heinrich Jacoby—and two dozens foreign Muslims, among them the Islamic scholar Abd al-Aziz Shawish of Egypt, Shaikh Salih al-Sharif al-Tunisi of Tunisia, Mamun Abu al-Fadl from the Hejaz

[21] Archive Sal. Oppenheim jr. & Co., Oppenheim 25/10, Max Freiherr von Oppenheim, *Denkschrift betreffend Die Revolutionierung der islamischen Gebiete unserer Feinde*, Berlin, 1914.

[22] Ibid., p. 136.

in the Arabian peninsula, and the Tatars Said Effendijev, Shamil Safarov and Muhammad Kazakov. The three Tatars were central figures who wanted support for the creation of a national home for their people.[23]

Some called Oppenheim's strategy of *jihad* "a war by revolution".[24] But it was far more: it was an asymmetrical war waged by written and oral incitement to *jihad* and by instigating "anti-imperial" uprisings. The aim was a double strategy between the European front and the colonial territories, supporting fighting on the European fronts by tying up Allied troops in the wide lands of Islam.

Euro-Islamic tools

In 1915, Oppenheim also became the head of the News Department within the German Embassy in Istanbul,[25] and later the News Department moved to a house of its own at Pera in Istanbul. From there he developed two action centres for key figures of this new brand of Islam, advocated by the non-Muslim German circles in cooperation with their Muslim Ottoman counterparts who reached—if we regard Turkey as partially European—to European Muslims too.

Thus we see the birth of Euro-Islam as an ideology for a globalised religious war. On the one hand Oppenheim created guidelines for *jihad* which he planned to spread by establishing a network of seventy reading halls and their chapters within the Ottoman Empire. They were located in the most populated centres where they were easy of access for a wide audience. German consuls often acted as supervisors. The reading halls also opened during special hours for Muslim women only.

[23] Eva Maria Auch, *Muslim-Untertan-Bürger. Identitätswandel in muslimischen Ostprovinzen Südkaukasiens (Ende 18. - Anfang 20. Jh.)*, Wiesbaden: Reichert, 2004.

[24] Donald McKale, *War by Revolution. Germany and Great Britain in the Middle East in the Era of World War I*, Kent: Kent State University Press, 1998.

[25] Since March 1915 "Nachrichtenstelle der Kaiserlich-Deutschen Botschaft" and since April 1st 1917 only "Nachrichtenstelle" that is News Department; see Max von Oppenheim, *Die Nachrichtensaal-Organisation und die wirtschaftliche Propaganda in der Türkei, ihre Übernahme durch den Deutschen Überseedienst*, Berlin, 1917, p. 12.

The German jihadists propagated their war news and insurgency ideas in a dozen leaflets (usually produced in 10,000 copies), depending on the topic in at least seven languages: Turkish, Tartar, Urdu, Persian, Arabic, French and Greek. Sometimes they translated the propaganda into Portuguese, Hindi, Italian and Chinese as well. The Germans produced more than a dozen booklets (typically 10,000 to 25,000 copies) with topics such as *The British Rule in India* or *L'islam dans l'armée française.* They planned to use still and moving pictures. Oppenheim's service delivered news within the Empire in two days. He used war maps and pictures to communicate with a mostly illiterate audience. He founded during the autumn of 1916 Balkan-Orient-Movie Inc. which produced news reels and other short movies for his war propaganda. In May 1917 it was taken over by the German Picture Society. In the same year he intended to develop the News Department's network into an organisation that would promote German investment and commerce within the Ottoman Empire. In a sense, it was a fairly modern marketing strategy in Africa and Asia, using advanced techniques and advertisements. In 1917 Oppenheim succeeded in getting the News Department taken over by the German Overseas Service responsible for economic affairs.[26]

Oppenheim's second centre in Berlin had the task of supervising prisoner of war camps for Muslims. By general policy Muslim prisoners were fairly well treated. Exceptions occurred, though. A testimony from an Arab seamen interned in a prisoner of war camp in Germany paints a very different picture. Held in Ruhleben, he stated that coloured men were singled out for harsh treatment and when he refused to carry out tasks assigned to him that were against his religion he was thrown into a prison cage for 72 hours. Born in Yemen, a province of the Ottoman Empire until the end of the First World War, he was technically an Ottoman subject.[27]

[26] Max von Oppenheim, *Die Nachrichtensaal-Organisation*, p. 21.; see an earlier manuscript of Max von Oppenheim, *Die türkische Nachrichtensaal-Organisation der Nachrichtensteller der Kaiserlichen Botschaft in Konstantinopel im Dienst deutscher Wertarbeit im Orient*, 15 pp. (produced by the Deutscher Wirtschaftsdienst).

[27] I thank Richard Lawless for this testimony from an Arab seamen.

In Wünsdorf near Berlin, prisoners were provided with their own camp newspaper and mosque and were persuaded either to join the Central Powers as soldiers or to promote the anti-colonial cause after returning to their home lands. The Oriental News Department edited the weekly journal *al-Jihad* in Arabic, in other languages of the Islamic world and in Russian at the beginning of March 1915. In this connection the Germans also built in the Muslim prisoner of war camp at Wünsdorf the first mosque of the Berlin area, inaugurated by the Ottoman envoy, Ibrahim Hakki Pasha, in 1915.[28]

A young lieutenant, Fritz Grobba, who later became an outstanding German envoy to the Middle East, led a battalion composed of 1,000 French-Arab prisoners of war from Wünsdorf to Istanbul in March 1916. However, the War Minister Enver Pasha distrusted them, and they were assigned to work on road construction.[29]

Nevertheless, all this raised some basic questions that must have troubled the minds of ordinary Muslims all over the Islamic lands. Was the Ottoman Sultan the accepted Caliph for all of them? Were they permitted to fight with infidels against other infidels and their Muslim allies? As Oppenheim had suggested, a *fatwa* provided the answer.

The Ottoman jihad fatwa *and Shaikh Salih's commentary*

The Ottoman *Shaikh al-Islam* affirmed five points in a *fatwa* issued on 11 November 1914.[30] They may be summarised as follows: Because the enemy of Islam has attacked the Islamic world, His Majesty the Padishah of Islam orders a *jihad* as a general mobilisation and individual duty for all Muslims in all parts of the world according to the Qur'an. Since Russia, England, and France are now hostile to the Islamic Caliphate, it is also incumbent upon all Muslims ruled by these governments to proclaim *jihad* against them and

[28] Gerhard Höpp, *Muslime in der Mark. Als Kriegsgefangene und Internierte in Wünsdorf und Zossen, 1914–1924*, Berlin: Verlag Das Arabische Buch, 1997.

[29] Fritz Grobba, 'German Exploitation of Arab Nationalist Movements in World War II'. Manuscript for the United States Army (MS P-207), Stuttgart, 1956, p. 16.

[30] "The Ottoman *Jihad Fatwa* of 11 November 1914", quoted in Rudolph Peters, *Jihad in Classical and Modern Islam*, Princeton: Markus Wiener, 1996, pp. 55–7.

actually to attack them. The defence of the Ottoman Empire depends on all Muslims hastening to take part in the *jihad*; if some refrain from doing so, it is a horrible sin and they deserve divine wrath. For Muslims of the named enemy countries it is absolutely forbidden to fight against the troops of Islamic lands even if the enemies force them to do so, otherwise they deserve hell fire for murder. It is a great sin for Muslims under the rule of England, France, Russia, Serbia, Montenegro, and their allies to fight against Germany and Austria, which are the allies of the Supreme Islamic Government.

According to this *fatwa* the Sultan-Caliph was the sovereign over all Muslims, so it was permitted for them to fight with infidels against other infidels and their Muslim allies. The latter had no right to fight back and also had to turn against their foreign overlords. Shaikh Salih al-Sharif al-Tunisi, a Tunisian mufti and confidant of the Ottoman War Minister Enver Pasha, confirmed this new doctrine of *jihad* in support of the Central Powers in a booklet.

Enver Pasha had asked Shaikh Salih to travel to Berlin to popularise the *jihad* among the Germans and it was for this purpose that he wrote a commentary *Haqiqat al-jihad* or "The Truth of *Jihad*", published at the beginning of 1915 by the German Society for the Study of Islam. It was also translated into Italian and French. Martin Hartmann of the Seminar of Oriental Languages in Berlin wrote a friendly foreword and the dragoman (official interpreter) Karl E. Schabinger added some remarks.

Both recommended the booklet as a development of *jihad*. What did it mean? A "partial *jihad*" was possible: on the side of allied infidels and just against certain enemy infidels. This *jihad* was an individual duty for all Muslims. Peace between the world of Islam and Europe would be possible if all foreign occupation of Islamic lands was ended.[31]

Realization of jihad

Oppenheim and the Ottoman War Minister Enver Pasha influenced public opinion within the Ottoman Empire in favour of the

[31] Shaikh Salih al-Sharif At-Tunisi, *Haqiqat al-Jihad*, Berlin: Verlag Dietrich Reimer (Ernst Vohsen), 1915 [translated from Arabic by Karl E. Schabinger, foreword by Martin Hartmann].

Central Powers. The American Ambassador Morgenthau watched the changes in the Ottoman Empire shortly before the war began. According to him, Oppenheim succeeded in controlling a large part of the Turkish press, in a country where the British and the French had been much more popular than the Germans. Morgenthau's German colleague, Hans von Wangenheim, started a press campaign to win over the public, and it was reported that he paid for a lot of newspaper articles. *Iqdam*, the biggest Turkish daily, and the *Ottoman Lloyd* came under German influence. Behind it all lay the power of Berlin's money.[32]

Morgenthau also maintained that the declaration of war made by Sultan Mehmed Reshad V on 14 November 1914 was a result of German efforts to wage *jihad* against selected infidels. The ambassador reported secret *jihad* instructions. An Arabic pamphlet (10,000 words in its English translation)[33] was distributed in India, Egypt, Morocco, Syria and other lands of Islam. It appealed to racial and religious hatred, and basically called for the systematic assassination and extermination of Christian neighbours within Islamic lands and for war against Christian countries on the edges of Islamic regions. Some extracts include: "O Muslims, enemies of the true religion, the English, the Russian, and the French, have oppressed Islam. Muslims work, infidels eat. Muslims are hungry, infidels gorge themselves in luxury. Muslims are enslaved, infidels are the great rulers". The pamphlet explained that this was all because Muslims had abandoned the plan set in forth in the Qur'an: "But the time has come for *jihad*. The lands of Islam shall be forever free. Who kills even one infidel, secretly or openly, shall be rewarded by God. Let us rise up as one man, in one hand a sword, in the other a gun. Let us fight the war of hearts, the war of speeches and the true war by killing the infidels. Organise bands, train armies, make campaigns."[34]

32 H. I. Morgenthau, *Ambassador*, Chapter VIII: "A classic instance of German propaganda".

33 Most likely Enver Pasha, who could read and speak German, knew Oppenheim's secret plan presented to the Kaiser. Maybe he was behind the secret Arabic document that Morgenthau described. It was certainly not the work of a religious person because there was some confusion about *jihad* concepts.

34 H. Morgenthau, *Ambassador*, Chapter XIV.

When Ambassador Morgenthau discussed the *jihad* with Talaat Pasha, one of the members of the Ottoman ruling circle, he stated that he had given orders to kill three Christians for every dead Muslim.[35] As the American diplomat discussed the *jihad* with his German counterpart, Hans von Wangenheim pointed out that the concept of the Islamic Holy War was the quickest way to make England sue for peace. This *jihad* would be nothing else than a great peace offensive.[36]

At the beginning, most Germans expected the war to be very short. From this point of view we can easily understand that the original approach was to use *jihad* more as a political threat to blackmail the other Great Powers than as a real military factor in the balance of power; in modern military terms there was not to much to be expected from the Ottoman side. Nevertheless, this German-Ottoman step to *jihad* had a greater impact the longer the war endured.

The 'jihadisation' of Islam

Direct and indirect results of the incitement to *jihad* are not easy to identify. First, the pan-Islamic propaganda did not lead to a major rebellion in Egypt or India as expected. The majority of Muslims ignored the *jihad,* even though Berlin spent a lot of money on expeditions—such as the one headed by Otto Werner von Hentig and Oskar Ritter von Niedermayer to Kabul in Afghanistan.[37]

In addition Berlin financed secret missions. The dragoman Edgar Pröbster for example, head of the German Consulate in the Moroccan city of Fez before the war, carried out two such missions. During the first expedition in November 1915 he tried to convince the Shaikh of the Sanusiyya in the Cyrenaica to enter the war on the side of the Central Powers against the Allies. Dr Pröbster went by German submarine from Cattaro to the Libyan coast. He also used

[35] Ibid., Chapter XII.

[36] Ibid., Chapter XIV.

[37] Thomas L. Hughes, "The German Mission to Afghanistan, 1915–1916", in W.G. Schwanitz (ed.), *Germany and the Middle East, 1871–1945*, Princeton, Markus Wiener, 2004, pp. 25–64.

a submarine to get to Morocco for his second mission among the tribes endangering the French positions there.[38]

In the end, especially after the loss of Baghdad, Mecca and Jerusalem, the *jihad* was disappointing for its masterminds who of course kept people in the dark most of the time and tried not to reveal their real intentions. But Schabinger, Oppenheim's deputy, concluded that "the seeds of an Islamic uprising had been planted all over the Islamic world". There will be a silent growth, he concluded, and one day the Muslims will turn against their foreign rulers.[39]

Why did Muslims not follow the call to arms by the Ottoman Sultan? Firstly, the majority lived outside of the Ottoman Empire. Secondly, he was not recognized as the Caliph of all of them; thus, he had no authority to call for a *jihad* in Africa and Asia at the beginning of the First World War. Thirdly, he was himself allied with the infidel Germans and their non-Muslim partners.

Indeed, this *jihad* was a concerted German-Ottoman action, planned to export an Islamic uprising or revolution into the enemy's colonial territories, and the idea was truly made in Germany. Unfortunately, renowned German Oriental experts like Carl Heinrich Becker, Martin Hartmann, Ernst Jäckh, and Max von Oppenheim unleashed the old genie of pure religious hatred.

Other Oriental experts such as Snouck Hurgronje remained firmly against this concept and defended basic values of humanism and enlightenment. The most distinctive features of Berlin's Middle Eastern policy during the First World War were not the 30,000 German troops fighting as part of the Ottoman army, the two attempts to capture the Suez Canal, or General Hans von Seeckt's role as the last Ottoman Chief of Staff. Of course, from a Middle Eastern viewpoint, the foremost element was that the Ottomans sided with the Germans. What was unique, after the switch from a secondary peace policy to a primary war policy, was the "*jihad*

[38] I am very grateful to my first teacher of Islamic history, Professor Dr Holger Preißler (1943–2006) of Leipzig, for Dr Edgar Pröbster's (1879–1942) biography.

[39] Karl Emil Schabinger (ed.), *Weltgeschichtliche Mosaiksplitter. Erlebnisse und Erinnerungen eines kaiserlichen Dragomans*, Baden-Baden, 1967.

made in Germany". Consequently, the field of Islamic studies lost its innocence not long after its birth.[40]

Friedrich Rosen, who was briefly to become Foreign Minister, said the instigation to *jihad* was "a crazy idea *à la* Karl May" (referring to the famous German novelist who had great influence over the German public with his fictional Oriental stories). The German General Staff drew an even more unfavourable conclusion, arguing that it was an illusion that the *jihad* would decide the war.[41] As for the Allies, according to some writers the French declared their own *jihad* in 1915 when all Muslims in French territories were called on to fight for France against the infidel Germans.[42] In mid-1916 a French source on the Sultan's call for *jihad* concluded that the opposition movements had generally been in the name of Islam, and although they failed, they caused no end of trouble for the Allied Powers.[43] On the other hand Thomas E. Lawrence of Arabia did not use *jihad*.

Nevertheless, an idea was born, advocated and globalised in a concerted action by Europeans, the most powerful of them being non-Muslims, while some were Muslims. It was to politicise, jihadise and globalise Islam as an ideology and instrument of war and hatred.

FROM WAR TO WAR

The Weimar Republic returns to a secondary Middle Eastern policy

The Germans lost the war and overthrew their Emperor with his "world policy". The German Reich was no longer a monarchy but became the Weimar Republic and as such, now one-third of its former size lost, Germany was forced to meet the victors' demands. Reconstruction and reform were the order of the day. Berlin returned to its secondary Middle Eastern peace policy. Under the terms of the Treaty of Versailles Germany lost its African colonies. The new German republic was now free to concentrate on trade, commerce, and

[40] Efraim Karsh and Inari Karsh, *Empires of the Sand. The Struggle for the Mastery in the Middle East 1789–1923*, Cambridge, MA: Harvard University Press, 1999.

[41] Werner Steuber (ed.), *"Jildirim". Deutsche Streiter auf heiligem Boden*, Oldenburg: G. Stalling, 1925, p. 65.

[42] Kate MacDonald, introduction to John Buchan's *Greenmantle*, p. XI.

[43] Secret French Report, 1 June 1916, in Jacob M. Landau, *The Politics of Pan-Islam. Ideology and Organisation*, Oxford: Clarendon, 1994, p. 102.

culture, re-establishing two of the pre-war pillars of its Middle Eastern policy: respecting the status quo and not claiming any territories. The third pillar, mediating in Oriental disputes, was excluded since Germany was not permitted any role in international relations, and that encouraged thoughts about vengeance in Berlin.

The German Foreign Ministry broke with some traditions by introducing reforms at the beginning of the 1920s. The traditional profile of a diplomat of noble descent, trained in jurisprudence, faded away. The dragoman, who knew Oriental languages and judicial matters, was joined by colleagues trained in a wider range of disciplines. Thus, it was possible for Berlin quickly to regain most of its lost positions.

Once again Germany became the Middle East's third most important foreign trade partner. One question that was often discussed in Berlin was whether or not to assist with industrialisation in the region. Finally, the argument prevailed that if Germany did not provide support its competitors would take over these lucrative business opportunities. The Germans were attractive partners, especially for Middle Eastern nationalists who looked for alternative suppliers to newly emerging countries, such as Saudi-Arabia and Iraq. Students who studied in Germany after 1920 returned to their homelands and, rising to positions of responsibilities there, favoured Germany in a climate that became hostile to the British and French Mandatory powers.[44]

At the same time a larger Muslim community became established in many German towns with dining clubs, student organisations and other institutions of mutual support on foreign soil. More stable structures such as chambers of commerce and friendship societies also played their role. What had begun as a Euro-Islamic war ideology served as a starting point for pan-Islamic organisations and developments, especially after the abolition of the Ottoman Sultanate and Caliphate in 1922 and 1924. Many new ideas started in the Muslim diaspora.

The Lebanese politician Shakib Arslan founded the "Orient Club" in Berlin during 1921. As its president, he established a network of relations throughout Europe. He participated in the Syrian-

[44] Wolfgang G. Schwanitz (ed.), *Araber, Juden, Deutsche*, Berlin: Dietz, 1994.

Palestinian Congress and headed the Syrian-Palestinian delegation to the Peoples' League in Geneva. After living in Turkey and Germany, he settled down in 1925 in Switzerland, from which he maintained excellent relations with the Muslim community in Germany. From Geneva and Lausanne Shakib Arslan cosponsored the establishment of the "Islam Institute" in December 1927, located in the Alexander von Humboldt-Building in Berlin. Supported by the Arabist Georg Kampffmeyer, head of the "German Society of Islamic Research" established in 1912, the Institute was intended to be a spiritual centre for all Muslim students. Moreover, Shakib Arslan founded the journal *La Nation Arabe* in 1930 in Geneva and became the chairman of the Congress of European Muslims in 1935. He attracted to Germany the Grand Mufti of Jerusalem, Amin al-Husaini, and welcomed the uprisings in Palestine from 1936 to 1939 under the Mufti's leadership. Later he had no trouble with the Nazis when they came to power, and they paid him a monthly stipend for his pro-German propaganda in the press. A group of about 125 to 150 Arab students in France also ended up on the Nazi payroll and it was Amin al-Husaini who distributed the money to them.[45]

The Palestinian Amin al-Husaini had served as an officer in the Ottoman army with German military advisers. He also most likely met bankers from the German Orient Bank who managed parts of the Islamic *waqf* funds in the Ottoman Empire. Amin al-Husaini became responsible for those funds in Turkey and Palestine in 1922 in his capacity as Grand Mufti of Jerusalem. He favoured the Germans among all the foreigners in the Middle East, and fifteen years later he proposed a far reaching deal to them: in return for Berlin's support for the elimination of a Jewish homeland in Palestine and the recognition of an independent union of Arab states, he would spread the Nazi's ideology, promote German culture and trade, and fight the British, Jews and the Communists in the Islamic regions.[46]

[45] Office of Chief of Counsel for War Crimes, document no. NG-5461, Affidavit by Carl Rekowski, Bremen, 5 October 1947, p. 10.

[46] Documents On German Foreign Policy, Series D, vol. V, pp. 655–6; see also the official Nazi view on the Grand Mufti in Kurt Fischer-Weth, *Amin al-Husseini, Großmufti von Jerusalem*, Berlin: Titz Verlag, 1943. See also Abd al-Karim Al-Umar, *Muzakkirat Haj Amin al-Husaini* (The Memoirs of Haj Amin al-Husaini), Damascus: Al-Ahali Lil-Tibaa wa an-Nashr wa al-Tauzia, 1999.

The case of the Grand Mufti shows that there was a tradition of common ground between Germans and Muslims stemming from the First World War, continuing in the Weimar Republic and culminating in the Third Reich. During the First World War Oppenheim had established connections with Indian Muslims. In his plan to the Kaiser in 1914 he stressed that they belonged to the Caliphate and that Sultan Abdulhamid had influenced them with his pan-Islamic and anti-British movement. He stated: "I founded here [Berlin] and in Switzerland a secret committee of 18 Indian members. They are by our standards highly educated and trained people of high intelligence. They have skills in organisation, they are patriots (. . .). Some of them are chemists for revolutionary purposes, willing to die and kill the traitors".[47]

A member of the Indian Independence Committee, Chempakaraman Pillai, had founded the Swiss Pro Indian Committee in 1912. Others in this circle, which enjoyed the support of the German missionary Ferdinand Graetsch and the expert on India Helmuth von Glasenapp, included Taraknath Das, Bhupendranath Dutta, Heramba Lal Gupta, Har Dayal, Tarachand Roy, Dhirendra Sarkar, Jod Singh, Sardar Umrao Singh, and Indian Muslims such as Muhammad Barakatullah and the brothers Abdul Jabbar Khairi and Abdul Sattar Khairi. They founded the "Writers' Club" at the end of February 1918 in Berlin, where the influential German-Persian Society was also established in the same year. In April 1922, Abdul Jabbar Khairi founded the Islamic Community of Berlin, but it was another group that built a mosque in Wilmersdorf on the edge of the city. The Indian Maulana Sadr ud-Din from the *Ahmadiyya Anjuman-i-Isha'at-i-Islam* of Lahore served as imam of the mosque which was inaugurated in April of 1925 and enlarged in 1927. As Muhammad S. Abdullah rightly emphasised, from this time we see a really organised Islamic community in Germany. In 1930 Berlin's mosque community was renamed the German Muslim Society.[48]

[47] Max von Oppenheim, *Denkschrift betreffend Die Revolutionierung der Islamischen Gebiete unserer Feinde*, Berlin, 1914, p. 91.

[48] Muhammad S. Abdullah, *Geschichte des Islams in Deutschland*, Graz/Köln: Styria, 1981, pp. 28–29.

On the other hand, an outstanding figure like the poet and politician Muhammad Iqbal was influenced by German humanities, having completed his PhD at the University of Munich. Serving as president of the All India Muslim League in 1930, he discovered that the desire for statehood posed a great danger for Islam since it would split the entire *umma* into a mosaic of nation states. But unlike other Indian Muslims in Germany he gained a deep understanding of the Western democracy and did not get involved in the Nazis' plans.[49]

As in the Jerusalem Mufti's case and in contrast to the life of Muhammad Iqbal, there was a clear continuity into the following decades. In mid-1933 the Indian nationalist Subhas Chandra Bose contacted the German Foreign Ministry and also met the racial ideologue Alfred Rosenberg. Bose tried to combine Socialism and Nazism as models for an independent India. He adopted Oppenheim's plan for an insurgency in India to be promoted by the Germans and the Italians. At the beginning of April 1941 Bose visited Berlin again and two years later travelled by a German and then a Japanese submarine to South Asia and Tokyo to implement his ideas.[50]

The Weimar Republic provided good conditions for the Muslim community in Germany. During the 1920s we see a rapid expansion in the number of daily newspapers and journals published by Muslims from India, Egypt, Syria, Turkey and other Islamic lands. Nationalists, often as students, circulated such publications as *Liwa' al-Islam*, *Der Islamische Student* and the *Moslemische Revue* in major German towns. Berlin became the centre of their activism and it was there that the Egyptian Union of Students was founded in 1922, the *al-Islamiyya* open to all Muslim students in 1924 and a year later the *al-Arabiyya* especially for Arab students in Germany. They and their main figure, the Syrian Muhammad Nashi Shalabi,

[49] Muhammad Iqbal, *Die Wiederbelebung des religiösen Denkens im Islam*, Berlin: Hans Schiler, 2004. See also Bettina Robotka, "Iqbal und Deutschland", in G. Höpp (ed.), *Fremde Erfahrungen. Asiaten und Afrikaner in Deutschland, Österreich und in der Schweiz bis 1945*, Berlin: Das Arabische Buch, 1996, pp. 347–58.

[50] Jan Kuhlmann, *Subhas Chandra Bose und die Indienpolitik der Achsenmächte*, Berlin: Hans Schiler, 2003.

published their papers either in German, in German and Arabic or completely in Arabic.[51]

A similar development occurred in business. Muslim entrepreneurs visited Germany quite frequently during the 1920s and 1930s. Industrialists and bankers such as Tal'at Harb, founder of the first national Bank Misr in 1920, looked for new ventures and methods to industrialise their countries with German assistance and capital goods. They promoted mutual chambers of commerce. Among them was Aziz Cotta Bey who founded in mid-1934 the Egyptian Trade Chamber for Germany in Berlin which had close connections to its Egyptian counterpart founded in Cairo in November 1928. A bridge between these organisations was the Society of Egyptian Alumni of Germany that traces its origins back to Egypt and Germany at the beginning of the Weimar Republic. Abd al-Magid Amir, one of the society's leading figures after the Second World War, said they regarded Berlin as a "Mecca for young Egyptians" and Arabs. On the other hand, some of the Arab visitors to Germany were deeply offended by the rising anti-Semitism there. The businessman Sayyid al-Lauzi of Egypt broke all relations between his companies and their German counterparts because of the growing racist tide that he had experienced at first hand in Berlin. So the overall picture of the development of the Muslim community and its advocates in Germany was mixed.

Turning to foreign policy, in general, the Weimar Republic applied a secondary Middle Eastern peace policy, cautiously avoiding trouble with London and Paris. Nevertheless, the Germans remained critical of the role of declining colonial empires in the region.[52] They supported Arab nationalists in their desire to rid themselves of foreign masters. In this light there was a natural basis for cooperation between the Germans on the one hand and the Arabs, Turks, and Persians on the other. It was not difficult for the old guard of diplomats like Dr Fritz Grobba to exploit all the feelings that were nurtured by the experience of having fought and lost on the same side in the

[51] Gerhard Höpp, *Arabische und islamische Periodika in Berlin und Brandenburg*, Berlin: Das Arabische Buch, 1994.

[52] L. Carl Brown (ed.), *Imperial "Legacy": The Ottoman Imprint on the Balkans and the Middle East*, New York: Columbia University Press, 1996.

war.[53] After the Treaty of Versailles, Germany possessed neither a navy nor any major military forces. Consequently the Middle East was not of great importance to Berlin apart from economic and cultural relations, and Germany returned to playing a marginal role.

London, on the other hand, had decided to support a Jewish homeland in Palestine. As the waves of new Jewish immigrants (*olim chadashim*) arrived there, Palestine became a focal point of British foreign policy. Berlin tried not to get involved in this project and kept its distance. Nevertheless, anti-Semitism was on the rise in Germany[54] and some politicians in Berlin saw the emigration of Jews to Palestine as a solution to problems in Central Europe.

But the most dangerous trend was that the advanced Jewish assimilation in Germany was in jeopardy and with it some of the most important results of the European enlightenment. Throughout the 1920s the inhumane nature of German racism became obvious. What appeared in the following decade was no surprise. Even founding fathers of Islamic studies such as Carl Heinrich Becker showed a racist tendency that divided mankind into "higher" and "lower" races. Some Muslims living in Germany were mistaken for Jews in the streets and felt this racism too.

Nazi efforts and Max von Oppenheim again

After Adolf Hitler established his dictatorship he was content to leave the Middle East to Britain, Italy and Soviet Russia until the Second World War.[55] As part of his racism, he promoted a hatred for "coloured people". He built the Berlin-Rome Axis with a role for Italy in the Middle East. Arab nationalists like the Grand Mufti of Jerusalem, Amin al-Husaini, were more interested in him than vice versa. Shortly before Hitler started the war he told the chief commanders and commanding generals at his residence on the Obersalzberg: "We shall continue to create disturbances in the Far

[53] Wilhelm Doegen, *Unter fremden Völkern*, Berlin: Otto Stollberg Verlag, 1925.

[54] Peter G.J. Pulzer, *Die Entstehung des politischen Antisemitismus in Deutschland und Österreich 1867–1914*, Göttingen: Vandenhoeck und Ruprecht, 2004.

[55] Heinz Tillmann, *Deutschlands Araberpolitik im Zweiten Weltkrieg*, East Berlin: Verlag der Wissenschaften, 1965; Lukasz Hirscowicz, *The Third Reich and the Arab East*, London: Routledge & Kegan Paul, 1966.

East and in Arabia. Let us think as 'gentlemen' and let us see in these peoples at best lacquered half maniacs who are anxious to experience the whip".[56]

Thus the idea of instigating revolts in the colonial territories of the Allies was a fixed point in Hitler's plans. But as the *Blitzkriege* failed, the Middle East became more important, and with it, the *jihad* made in Germany. There were two factions in the Foreign Ministry: one led by Foreign Minister Joachim von Ribbentrop which worked for *jihad* and revolts, and the other led by State Secretary Ernst von Weizsäcker which worked against this policy.[57]

Just at that moment Oppenheim came up with his old concept and forwarded it in a much shorter version to the Foreign Ministry. But the circumstances had changed. Turkey had no Caliphate any more and was not at war, France was neutralised and had opened its Middle Eastern territories to the Nazis, and the Soviets had not yet entered the war. So Oppenheim concentrated his plan against the British: it consisted of an uprising in Greater Syria, to be enlarged to Iraq and Saudi Arabia, the Suez Canal was to be blocked, and India was to be mobilised against the British. He advised cooperation with the Palestinian leader, Amin al-Husaini, and with Shakib Arslan. Fritz Grobba in Syria and Franz von Papen in Ankara were to act as coordinators. There should be a new government under Amin al-Husaini in Palestine, and among the Jews of Palestine only those who had lived there before the war should be allowed to stay.[58]

[56] "No 314: Contents of the Speech by the Führer to the Chief Commanders and Commanding Generals on the Obersalzberg, August 22, 1939" in *Documents on British Foreign Policy 1919–1939*, vol. VII (1939), London, 1954, p. 259. The German version: "Wir werden weiterhin die Unruhe in Fernost und in Arabien schüren. Denken wir als Herren und sehen wir in diesen Völkern bestenfalls lackierte Halbaffen, die die Knute spüren wollen", in *Akten zur Auswärtigen Politik 1918–1945. Aus dem Archiv des Auswärtigen Amtes*, Baden-Baden, Imprimerie Nationale, 1961, p. 172.

[57] For a detailed description of both groups see my article "Der Geist aus der Lampe: Fritz Grobba und Berlins Politik im Nahen und Mittleren Orient", *Comparativ*, XIV, 1 (2004), pp. 126–50, see pp. 135–6.

[58] PArchAA, Nachlass Otto Werner von Hentig, vol. 84, Memorandum Max von Oppenheims, 25 July 1940, 7 pp.; see also my article "Max von Oppenheim und der Heilige Krieg. Zwei Denkschriften zur Revolutionierung islamischer Gebiete 1914 und 1940", *Sozial.Geschichte*, XIX, 3 (2004), pp. 28–59.

Description of German war propaganda by the Allies

Dr Fritz Grobba, who over a period of 25 years had served as German envoy to Afghanistan, Iraq and Saudi Arabia, used Islam in inflammatory Arabic broadcasts in order to promote Germany's aims. Whether or not they had an impact on the Allies can be gauged from two American documents. The first one entitled "Axis propaganda in the Moslem World" came from the US Coordinator of Information, a secret service that was a forerunner of the Office of Strategic Services (OSS). The agency watched the German-Arabic broadcasts of "Radio Zeesen", named after a village near Berlin.[59] As mentioned, Grobba's Arab Committee of the Foreign Ministry promoted broadcasts in Arabic and Grobba, as its head, was responsible for the contents.

The US Coordinator of Information drew this general conclusion about German propaganda in the Muslim world at the end of 1941:

> The Arabs are united on one general purpose, to free their world from the domination of French and British masters. Some Arabs are blinded to Italian imperialism and to German domination of Europe by their anxiety to get rid of the foreign control. This arises not only from a desire to play all European powers off against each other but from a naiveté which assumes that anyone who is against their masters is a friend of the Muslims. They fail to realize that, in case of a British defeat, there would be a substitution of Axis for the British or the French domination.

Regarding the targets of the propaganda, the Americans identified the sentiments and feelings on which the Germans relied. The anti-British sentiment had two causes: the British support for Jews in Palestine and other minorities for the apparent purpose of dividing and ruling the Arab states; and the reluctance of Britain to grant independence to mandated territories. This made it easy for Axis

[59] Radio Zeesen was the German short wave broadcasting station near Berlin-Königswusterhausen. The Propaganda Ministry supervised the station from April 1933; in September 1939 it came under the direction of a department of the Foreign Ministry headed by Ernst Wilhelm Bohle. It had several transmitters in Athens and Tunis from 1940 to 1942. Among the Arabic speakers employed was also Habib Bourguiba, the leader of the Tunisian nationalist movement and later President of the Tunisian Republic. See also Herbert Schröder, *Ein Sender erobert die Herzen der Welt*, Essen: Essener Verlaganstalt, 1940.

propaganda to stir up Arab nationalist sentiments. On the other hand, the anti-American sentiment resulted from the expressed sympathies of American officials for political Zionism in Palestine and America's increasingly close alliance with Britain. All these factors, the Americans concluded, were fully exploited by Radio Zeesen in broadcasts to the Near East and India.

According to the American Coordinator, anti-Semitism had an important effect on the Arabs. There can be no doubt that the situation created by the Zionist programme in Palestine caused the position of Jews to deteriorate throughout the Arab world. There were said to be too many Jews in Palestine and abroad who, according to William B. Ziff,[60] had the attitude: "The Jews are entering Palestine by divine right and intend to make the Arabs go back to the desert where they came from". Radio Zeesen had recently been broadcasting anti-Jewish passages from the Qur'an, emphasising that the Jews were the enemies of Islam.

The American analysis of the German-Arabic propaganda also elaborated on anti-French and anti-Bolshevik feelings. All this, it concluded, appealed to conservative Muslims from Morocco to India. The fact that Iraq and Egypt had won their independence only after years of rebellion convinced the Arabs that force was the only means by which they could extract from the British what they regard as their rights. An illustration of the strength of this attitude was the Arab population's support for the Mufti Amin al-Husaini, the apostle of force against the British.

What success the Axis powers had in playing to this state of mind could be judged from the fact that the Mufti was now in Berlin. The report continued that recently Radio Zeesen had been playing up the alleged suppression of Muslim minorities in Soviet Russia (Britain's ally at the time); another curious anti-British blast from Zeesen accused the British of being pagans like pre-Islamic Arabs and thus the natural enemies of Islam. The announcement that Britain was stripping Arab countries and India of food was often repeated by Zeesen, which added that Britain meant to sacrifice millions of Indian and Arab lives in a vain attempt to resist the Axis.

[60] This text mentions: William B. Ziff, *The Rape of Palestine*, New York: Argus Books, 1938.

All in all, we can see here that Fritz Grobba's Arab Committee had a direct impact, especially through the German-Arabic broadcasts to the Muslim world.[61]

Temptation for an Allied jihad

The second document that illustrates the impact of German Islamic propaganda activities on the Allies was a secret communication circulated within the OSS (Office of Strategic Services). It reflects the indirect impact of Grobba's propaganda and the Allies' reaction. The most critical time for the Middle East was between mid-1940 and mid-1942. After British troops capitulated at Tobruk in Libya and General Erwin Rommel advanced with his German-Italian troops into Egypt, the (Anglo-American) Joint Psychological Warfare Committee discussed the problem of how to use Islam and its leading figures for warfare in North Africa.

One member of the Joint Psychological Warfare Committee suggested enlisting the legendary leaders Abd al-Karim of Morocco and Idris as-Sanusi of Libya. He reminded the members of the Warfare Committee that in the First World War German propaganda was "not totally unsuccessful", at least as far as stirring up trouble among the Muslim Berber tribes who resisted Spanish and French penetration was concerned. According to the document, the Committee concluded: "Under the tutelage of the United Nations, and more especially that of the United States, these two [Arab leaders, Abd al-Karim and Idris as-Sanusi] can make the Mediterranean safe for the Allies. Equally important is the influence that such a move will have throughout the Muslim world. From India to the Atlantic, Allah will be praised, and the Allies will receive the plaudits and the support of the faithful".[62]

[61] For an American analysis of the content of the German Arabic broadcasts guided by Grobba see US National Archives II (USArchII), RG 165, Box 3061, Coordinator of Information, Washington, DC, 23 December 1941, "Axis Propaganda in the Muslim World", 6 pp.

[62] USArchII, RG 218, Box 59, Joint Psychological Warfare Committee, Abd al-Karim of the Rif, JPWC 21st meeting, 3 August 1942, secret note from Secretary A.H. Othank, 1 August 1942, discussions, memoranda to Generals Handy and Smith, and investigation request to OSS, The Joint Chiefs of Staff, secret, Washington, DC, 4 August 1942.

The head of the OSS, William J. Donovan, approved further investigation into this project, whereas General Kroner pointed out the potential repercussions, especially the possibility of a Christian-Muslim war. Thus, General Wedemeyer, Chief of the Strategy and Policy Group of the War Department, was very reluctant to submit the proposal for using the two Arab leaders to General Dwight D. Eisenhower who was preparing the first landing of American troops in North Africa.

It was only when intelligence about Amin al-Husaini's service to the Axis became known that the OSS looked for a counterpart to the Mufti on the Allied side. But this was not an easy task, since not every Arab leader could claim to be a direct descendant of Prophet Muhammad as the Mufti did. Moreover, in mid-May 1941 the former American Military Attaché to Cairo considered the Mufti to be a religious authority and the "greatest leader of the Arab peoples alive". General Bonner F. Fellers, who was also an adviser to the OSS, evaluated the consequences if the Mufti declared a Holy War for the Axis. He stated that it would be an anti-Semitic, not a religious war, and concluded that Amin al-Husaini was a religious turned political figure.[63]

But the discussion within the OSS and the choice of Abd al-Karim as a potential asset for the Allies brought up a really big question: "Will he be of use to the war effort, or will his release be like that of a Jinnee out of the magic bottle?"[64] The German Islamic policy and Fritz Grobba's propaganda apparently pushed the Allies towards a matching policy, defining a non-religious war not only in religious terms, but adopting a concept similar to that of "war by proxy".

[63] USArchII, RG 165, Box 3055, To Secretary of War, State Department, "Amin el Husseiny and a Muslim Holy War" by Bonner F. Fellers, confidential, Cairo, 19 May 1941. Compare it with the description of the Grand Mufti for Hitler: USArchII, T120, roll 63, serial 71, frames 50682 ff., "Der Großmufti von Jerusalem", Berlin, 28 November 1941, signed Grobba, 4 pp.

[64] USArchII, RG 218, Box 59, Joint Psychological Warfare Committee, Abd al-Karim of the Rif, JPWC 21st meeting, 3 August 1942, secret note from Secretary A.H. Othank, 1 August 1942, discussions, memoranda to Generals Handy and Smith, and investigation request to OSS, The Joint Chiefs of Staff, secret, Washington, DC, 4 August 1942.

Fortunately, it did not come to that, nor did such a policy determine the Allies' actions. Oppenheim's *jihad* concept, born in the First World War and promoted by him again in 1940, was further developed by Fritz Grobba for using Islam for political aims. At least until 1945, it remained a concept made in Germany.

Impact on the war in the Middle East

Many of Oppenheim's ideas were realised. Adolf Hitler's orders on the Middle East included inciting revolts and cooperation with Arab nationalists or Muslim insurgents. Egypt became a battleground with Erwin Rommel's advancement and the help of Egyptians. The Grand Mufti proclaimed jihad against the British and Jews in his Berlin-based broadcasts to the Middle East. A German presence was established in Syria, and Iraq rebelled under Rashid Ali al-Kailani. His circle had widespread connections via former Iraqi students in Germany who had established clubs and societies in Baghdad and throughout Iraq.

After two Turkish generals, Emir Hüsnü Erkilet and Fuat Erden, visited Germany in October 1941 Hitler agreed to their proposal for *jihad* in Russian Asia and for the establishment of Muslim legions recruited from the large mass of prisoners of war.[65] Moreover, he ordered plans to destabilise the British Empire and to

[65] Camilla Dawletschin-Linder, "Die turko-tatarischen sowjetischen Kriegsgefangenen im Zweiten Weltkrieg im Dreiecksverhältnis zwischen deutscher Politik, turanistischen Aspirationen und türkischer Außenpolitik", *Der Islam*, 80 (2003), pp. 1–29. A personal letter written shortly after the Second World War II states: "But at last two Turkish generals, Erkilet and Erden, who in October 1941 visited Germany, convinced Hitler that he should allow Muslim prisoners of war from the Soviet Union to begin a sort of holy war against the godless regime they had come from. And because it was the wish of the Turkish generals, Hitler, with great reluctance, consented to the formation of legions. Thanks to this episode and to that holy war thousands and ten thousands of people were later condemned as collaborators". Letter to Mr Thomas written by Erich von Mende's wife shortly after the Second World War, p. 3 (I am grateful to Dr Stefan Meining of Munich for locating this letter). For the meeting between the Turkish generals and Hitler see also Sebastian Cwiklinski, "Die Panturkismus-Politik der SS: Angehörige sowjetischer Turkvölker als Objekte und Subjekte der SS-Politik", in G. Höpp and B. Reinwald (eds), *Fremdeinsätze. Afrikaner und Asiaten in europäischen Kriegen, 1914–1945*, Berlin: Das Arabische Buch, 2000, p. 149.

inflict an "uncompromising war against the Jews". Furthermore, he told the Grand Mufti that he actively opposed a Jewish home in Palestine. His battle against the "Judeo-Communist Empire in Europe" would also decide the fate of the Arabs. He hoped to force open the Caucasian gate to the Middle East. Luckily this failed at Stalingrad and Alamein, in Morocco and Algeria, and in Normandy. This spared Jews in the Middle East from the Holocaust and the region as a whole from a terrible experience.

Many Middle Easterners, like many Germans, did not recognise the true nature of Nazi Germany. But some leading thinkers, among them the Egyptian poet Taufiq al-Hakim had a clearer understanding.[66] On the other hand, young Egyptian officers like Nasser and Anwar as-Sadat pinned their hopes on the Germans.[67] It was not German racism or anti-Semitism that attracted them, for this was a concept alien to the Islamic tradition. But they were fascinated by the rapid modernisation of Germany under the Nazi dictatorship. And there was still another group of Arab leaders like the Palestinian Amin al-Husaini and the Iraqi Rashid Ali al-Kailani. They obtained in Berlin a clear knowledge of the ongoing Holocaust. Nevertheless, they supported the Nazis actively regardless of this murderous policy.

Thus, the German Middle Eastern policy and *jihad* plans found a wider echo within radical Arab nationalism even though this policy was planned, organised, and executed in Berlin and Istanbul in a selfish and inhuman manner. As Middle Easterners including the much smaller Muslim diaspora in Germany became aware of this approach, their disappointment deepened and a new anti-Westernism with a hatred of modernity and democracy began to grow in strength.

66 Israel Gershoni, "Egyptian Liberalism in an age of "Crisis of Orientation": Al-Risâla's Reaction to Fascism and Nazism, 1933–1939", *International Journal of Middle East Studies*, 31 (1999), pp. 551–76; Israel Gershoni, "Confronting Nazism in Egypt—Tawfiq al-Hakim's Anti-Totalitarianism 1938–1945", *Tel Aviver Jahrbuch für deutsche Geschichte*, XXVI (1997), pp. 121–50.

67 Anwar El-Sadat, "Rommel at El-Alamain: An Egyptian view (1942)", in B. Lewis (ed.), *A Middle East Mosaic*, New York: Random House, 2000, pp. 314–16.

CONCLUSION ON *JIHAD* AS A PRODUCT OF EURO-ISLAM

Germans and their Muslim counterparts in and outside Europe politicised Islam during and between the two world wars. They used *jihad* doctrine in non-religious European disputes, and as a result invented in Europe a brand of Euro-Islam for the non-European Islamic lands which was officially sponsored in Berlin by non-Muslims and adapted by Muslims against the Judeo-Christian tradition partially, later globally. It served as tool of war: as an ideology to globalise a partial *jihad* coalition. On three occasions Max von Oppenheim served as the mastermind of this jihadisation of Islam.

For a long time, the mainstream of European thinkers were of the opinion that a social revolution in Islamic lands was impossible: Muslims could only organise coups d'Etat or revolts in their palaces but not deep-rooted revolutions resulting in structural changes. Oppenheim foresaw the German "jihadisation of Islam" as early as 1898. He merged both Islam and revolution in his secret plans, the first time in a German-Ottoman project in 1914 and again in 1940 in a German-Arab plan. Both were directed against the Great Powers with their formal and informal colonial empires.

Berlin had no Muslim subjects in the Middle East, and its foreign policy could therefore feel free to be critical of the colonialism of Germany's European neighbours. The mainstream of German politicians and academics was sympathetic towards anti-imperialist movements and their nationalistic Islamic expressions. Muslim leaders turned to Berlin for help to get rid of their foreign masters. In this way the *jihad* made in Germany was of a limited mutual benefit for two reasons. First, the Germans injected a deadly racism into this potion, and for this aim, they used the Arab-Jewish conflict both before and during the Second World War; the Iraqi Rashid Ali al-Kailani and the Palestinian Amin al-Husaini served as devil's advocate. The Jerusalem Grand Mufti's motivations can be seen most clearly in his letter to Adolf Hitler in 1941.

Second, with *jihad* against one Judeo-Christian tradition, in this case against the British, the French and Russians, Berlin legitimised *jihad* as an end in itself. Whereas this "Abu Jihad" advocated an anti-enlightenment policy, his Muslim partners promoted it as an

Islamic "anti-imperial and anti-colonial liberation struggle". It would be interesting to know whether or not there were similar concepts of *jihad* made in France and later, during the Cold War, in America. As we have shown, the British and Americans resisted some of these temptations, at least during the two world wars.

The Muslims' disappointment with Europe grew after the Second World War. Radicalism and Muslim anti-Semitism in all kinds and shapes emerged. After regionalisation of the idea of an Islamic rebellion and the unusual alliances of the Cold War, the time had come to reappropriate *jihad*, to purify it without any alliance with infidels. Islamists like Usama Bin Laden took up this politicisation and jihadisation of Islam, bringing *jihad* into the enemy's heartlands. Thus, we see that Oppenheim initiated the creation of a global political Islam made in Europe by non-Muslims, exported to, adapted in and globalised beyond the Muslim lands.

Part IV. MINORITIES BETWEEN ACCULTURATION AND IDENTITY CLAIMS

During the inter-war period, Islam in Europe was a minority religion demographically as well as politically. Even in Albania, the only exception, Islam was no longer the state religion. How did Muslims and their religious and political leaders cope with such a situation? There were of course various responses to this situation according to the social class and the general characteristics of each group or individual. In the Balkans, Muslims experienced this position after having enjoyed for many years the status of first class citizens within the Ottoman Empire. This marginal status resulted from a very different context for Muslims of the European colonies who had migrated to the metropolis to find jobs, and for European converts.

To present a general overview of all the possible responses, from acculturation to the revival of Muslim identity, one might use part of the typology drawn up by Olivier Roy who compared the alternatives for Muslims in Western Europe at the end of the twentieth century with those of Muslims of Spain after the *Reconquista*: i.e. exodus, re-conquest through *jihad*, conversion—real or nominal—, Islamisation of Christian society, theological justification for life in a non-Muslim environment and some "ethno-religious communitarianism".[1] Those categories are useful, although the situation in inter-war Europe differed both from the situation of medieval Spain and from that of present-day Europe.

[1] Olivier Roy, *Vers un islam européen*, Paris: Editions Esprit, 1999, pp. 74–84.

EXODUS

As we have already seen in the main introduction, the choice of exodus (labelled with the Qur'anic reference *hijra*) to Turkey was a common feature for Muslims living in the Balkan countries during the inter-war period. Economic factors could have driven some Muslims to leave their homes, especially during the depression of the 1930s, but emigration most often resulted from a rather complex mixture of factors. They included the humiliation of being treated as second class citizens, a feeling that living under a non-Muslim regime was impossible in the long term, and various kinds of more or less subtle economic pressure. For example, in the Romanian province of Dobrudja, the government tended to confiscate lands and give them to ethnic Romanian settlers.[2] Whereas emigration from Bosnia-Herzegovina and Albania was essentially on an individual basis, it was a large-scale phenomenon from the Southern regions of Yugoslavia (Kosovo and Macedonia), Bulgaria, Greek Thrace and Romania; the latter even concluded an agreement on this matter with Turkey in 1936.[3]

RECONQUEST THROUGH *JIHAD*

The idea of re-conquest through holy war (*jihad*) was not seen as realistic among Balkan Muslims, who emigrated to Turkey or remained in South-Eastern Europe. In the Kemalist republic, the nation-building process rejected the Ottoman past. Only among some Muslim circles in the Balkans did one find people striving to preserve the Ottoman legacy, with even the hope of one day returning to rule from Istanbul.

[2] György Lederer, "Islam in Romania", *Central Asian Survey,* XV, 3–4 (1996), pp. 352–3. In the North-Eastern Bulgarian region of Deli-Orman, an organisation called *Rodna Zaštita* (The Defence of the Mother Country), composed of former military personnel, worked for the seizing of lands belonging to Muslims and their distribution to Bulgarians (Alexandre Popovic, *L'islam balkanique*, Berlin-Wiesbaden: Otto Harrassowitz, 1986, pp. 82–3).

[3] Turkey also concluded emigration agreements with Yugoslavia and Bulgaria (Wolfgang Höpken, "From Religious Identity to Ethnic Mobilisation: the Turks of Bulgaria before, under and since Communism", in H. Poulton and S. Taji-Farouki (eds), *Muslim Identity and the Balkan state*, London: Hurst, 1997, p. 63).

As an alternative to the rather unlikely reestablishment of the Ottoman Empire, the idea of a "Greater Albania", including not only Albania but also Kosovo and a part of Macedonia, spread especially among Muslims from these last two Yugoslavian regions, as shown in Muhammed Aruçi's chapter. It was imagined that such a state would secure a Muslim homeland in the Balkans, although the religious policy of the Kingdom of Albania towards Islam was far from making Albania a "Muslim state".

In Greek Thrace, a region bordering Turkey, some people advocated the total exchange of minorities between Greece and Turkey, while others thought that the region, which contained an important Muslim minority, could be liberated by Mustafa Kemal (see Yannis Bonos' chapter).

However, armed rebellion was not envisaged as a response to the difficulties arising from the minority position of Muslims in the Balkans. The last one occurred in 1914–15 in central Albania, when Muslims led by the Mufti of Tirana rose up to oppose the decision made by the Great Powers to offer the crown of the newly independent country to the German prince Wilhelm von Wied. The rebellion, which endeavoured to achieve a return to Ottoman sovereignty, was unsuccessful.

CONVERSION TO CHRISTIANITY AND DISSIMULATION

Conversion to Christianity—real or nominal—as another possible response was the exception among Muslims in inter-war Europe. It seems that some Muslim Gypsies adopted Protestantism in Bulgaria as the result of missionary work that specifically targeted this population.[4] There was also the case of Muslims in Hungary, mostly Turkish and Bosnian men who married Hungarian women and whose children were brought up as Christians. As a result, the tiny Muslim community of Hungary vanished soon after the Second World War.[5] On the whole, the phenomenon of conversions was rather marginal.

[4] On Christian proselytism in Bulgaria at that time, see A. Popovic, *L'islam balkanique*, p. 83.

[5] György Lederer, "Islam in Hungary", *Central Asian Survey*, XI, 1 (1992), p. 16.

"Secret Islam" that existed in medieval Spain also represented a very limited response. There was hardly any clandestine practice of Islam since there were no forced conversions, as occurred during the First World War in places such as Bulgaria and Montenegro. However, the phenomenon of nominal conversions may have existed in Bulgaria from the end of the 1930s onwards, when the patriotic "Rodina Fraternity" organisation launched a campaign among the Pomaks (Bulgarian-speaking Muslims) promoting the Christian faith. It encouraged changing of Islamic names to Bulgarian ones, and demanded the abolition of the *fereje* (the traditional long coat worn by women) in order to liberate women and the replacement of the Turkish Islamic clergy with Rodina members.[6]

In Western Europe, because of the predominantly negative image of Islam among public opinion, some "neo-Sufi" leaders tried to distance themselves from Islam, and sometimes advocated that their followers adopt the secretive attitude of the crypto-Muslim. In his chapter, Mark Sedgwick highlights the fact that Frithjof Schuon, the Swiss spiritual master, gave dispensations from fasting during Ramadan, and allowed his followers to drink beer in public.

As for the Muslim migrants in Western and central Europe, they did not adopt an attitude of dissimulation, but for them Islam remained a private affair, with only a limited expression within the public sphere. Besides, the host society perceived them more as "coloured people", "Arabs" or "Africans", rather than distinctively as Muslims, as in the case of seamen living in the major European ports (see Richard Lawless' chapter). Many migrant labourers were not seen by the host society as Muslims because there was nothing in public space that would indicate their religious affiliation. In France, Muslim religious practice also seems to have remained in the private domain. In Marseilles in 1938, an Algerian living in the city asked to be appointed imam by the local officials, claiming that he had been performing Muslim funeral rituals for the past twenty years.[7] In

[6] Mila Mancheva, *State-minority Relations and the Education of Turks and Pomaks in Inter-war Bulgaria*, 1918–1944, unpublished PhD thesis, Central European University (Budapest), 2003, pp. 86–7.

[7] Michel Renard, "Aperçu sur l'histoire de l'islam à Marseille, 1813–1962. Pratiques religieuses et encadrement des Nord-Africains", *Outre-Mers*, XC, 340–41 (2003), p. 281.

Paris, in 1930, young men from Kabylia (Algeria) were reported to have rapidly adopted "European" clothing, food and wine consumption.[8]

It was only during the 1930s, and mainly through the activity of the Alawi Sufi brotherhood, that seamen in British ports began to assert more openly their religion, which also became more institutionalised. On the occasions of public demonstration of their faith, as Richard Lawless points out, many of the seamen discarded their European clothing and affirmed a specific identity by wearing traditional Yemeni or Maghrebian dress in public. It was also at this time that the few hundred Muslims of Czechoslovakia decided to create an Islamic Community, as we have seen in the introduction to the previous part, in order to foster their religious identity and organise rituals and practices.[9]

In the case of the Polish Tatars, Muslim identity emerged even earlier and was more strongly expressed in order to counter their acculturation into mainstream Christian society. Since the seventeenth century, they were already linguistically assimilated into Polish society, and they were politically well integrated thanks to the fact that some of them rose to the senior ranks of the army. The attempt to "re-Tatarise" the community through the promotion of Russian Tatar folklore turned out to be unsuccessful. Sebastian Cwiklinski's chapter shows how Islam, so closely linked to Tatar national identity, appeared to be the only way to assert a specific identity within Polish society.

THE ATTEMPT TO ISLAMISE CHRISTIAN SOCIETY

Another type of response present in Olivier Roy's typology, the "attempt to Islamise Christian society"—or, at least, the use of religious polemic to present Islam as the most accomplished religion —, was chosen by a few Muslims in Europe during the inter-war period. As Eric Germain explains in his chapter, the Lahori-Ahmadi

[8] L.M. [Louis Milliot], "Carte de répartition des Kabyles dans la région parisienne", *Revue des Études Islamiques*, IV (1930), p. 167.

[9] See Miloš Mendel, "The Islamic Religious Community in Bohemia and Moravia (1934–1945)", *Archív Orientální*, 66 (1998), pp. 127–41.

missions in particular attempted not only to counter Christian propaganda aimed at converting Muslims, but also to present Islam as more compatible with modern thought and less dogmatic than the various Christian denominations. The publications of the Woking and Berlin Muslim Missions continuously emphasised the qualities of Islam, by pointing out how this "Oriental" religion could meet the spiritual challenge of "Western" scientific modernity as well as social issues raised by the political ideologies of the time.[10] Not only did the zealous Indian missionaries refute the accusation of the backwardness of Islam, but they audaciously presented it as the only religion able to face the social, material and spiritual challenges of the new century. In order to improve the self-esteem of Muslims in Europe—and all over the world thanks to the large diffusion of Ahmadi reviews and booklets—the Woking Mosque Trust introduced a new style of publication. This gave a large place to compilations of the positive comments on Islam by "famous authors" including scholars (T. Arnold, W. Muir and R. Bosworth Smith), writers (Goethe, Renan and Bernard Shaw) and, of course, by converts. The conversion of Europeans to Islam was particularly promoted in such publications, the aim being not so much the scale but rather the high social status of the individuals who converted, such as professional people and especially members of the aristocracy—for example Lord Headley, Sir Archibald Hamilton and Lady Evelyn Zeinab Cobbold in Britain and Baron Rolf Omar von Ehrenfels in Austria, to name the most publicised examples. Some of these European converts became very zealous in their eagerness to spread Islam in Europe, such as the Czech Alois Bohdan Brikcius alias Mohammed Abdullah (1903–59), who adopted Islam in Djibouti in the 1920s.[11] However, the prospect of a large-scale Islamisation of the continent was a mere rhetorical incentive used mostly in religious polemics with Christian missionaries.

[10] Maulvi F.K. Khan Durrani, head of the Berlin Mission, wrote in 1925 a booklet entitled "Islam and Socialism"; in the Mosque library were books such as the English translation from Russian of Mikhail Kefeli's *Theory of High Cost of Living* (Berlin: Emil Ebering, 1923).

[11] M. Mendel, "The Islamic Religious community", pp. 136–9. His adherence to Islam seems to have had a strong political component, against British and French colonialism, leading him to support Germany.

As for theological justifications concerning the life and practice of Islam in a non-Muslim environment, they are certainly to be found in texts and discourses produced by *'ulama* in Europe at that time, but the subject needs further research. Fikret Karčić's chapter on Yugoslavia gives us an example of Muslim judges collaborating with their non-Muslim counterparts in order to integrate Shari'a law into a non-Muslim judicial system. Yugoslav muftis accepted the appointment of Muslim judges by a non-Muslim political authority, justifying their position by previous *fatwa*s given by *'ulama* concerning the jurisprudence applied to Muslims living as minorities.

'ETHNO-RELIGIOUS COMMUNITARIANISM'

For the majority of inter-war European Muslims the response to the minority situation was found in some kind of "ethno-religious communitarianism". Indeed, in South-Eastern Europe, where the most compact groups of Muslims were living, it was the most frequent answer to their position in the period considered here. Such a communitarianism response was legally rooted in the special rights conferred on Muslim communities by international treaties and national constitutions and laws. As we have seen in the previous part, Muslim communities in South-Eastern Europe generally enjoyed religious and cultural autonomy, with various degrees of state control and intervention, through their Shari'a courts, their religious and non-religious schools and their pious foundations (*waqf*). They also had their own newspapers, and sometimes launched their own political parties. In fact, political mobilisation was effective only in Yugoslavia and most particularly in Bosnia-Herzegovina where several parties were founded in 1919–20. In addition, in Southern Yugoslavia, Muslim notables gathered around an "Organisation for the Defence of the Rights of the Muslims" that existed between 1919 and 1925.[12]

[12] On these political parties, see Alexandre Popovic, "La création des premiers partis politiques musulmans dans les Balkans: le cas de la Yougoslavie", in A. Popovic, *Les musulmans des Balkans à l'époque post-ottomane. Histoire et politique,* Istanbul: Isis, 1994, pp. 267–80; and A. Popovic, "Le parti politique 'Džemijet' (Cemiyet) de Skoplje/Üsküp (1919–1925) et ses organes *Hak* (1920–1924), *Hak Yolu* (1925) et *Mudžahede/Mücahede* (1925)", in ibid., pp. 281–93. In Southern Yugoslavia, there were also short-lived branches of two Yugoslav parties.

In Bulgaria, a group of pro-Kemalist Turks made several failed attempts, between 1925 and 1934, to organise their political representation.[13] In Greece, Muslims did not found their own parties, despite the creation of a separate electoral college for the Muslims of Western Thrace.[14]

However, as Yannis Bonos points out, the case of Greece illustrates how such an "ethno-religious communitarian" framework certainly did not imply a single homogeneous attitude. Debates and confrontation were common among the Muslims of Western Thrace on various issues ranging from internal Greek politics to education, dress code, the position of women in society, the adoption of the Latin script, etc. In the same way, the studies by Xavier Bougarel and Fikret Karčić show that in Bosnia and Herzegovina the reform of Shari'a law and courts was less debated than the highly sensitive issues about the management of *waqfs,* or the position of woman and the dress code. The question of education was also a matter of debate, as we can see in Muhammed Aruçi's analysis of the situation in Macedonia.

The debates among Muslims during these years have often been described in terms of "traditionalists" versus "modernists". In fact, it is necessary to distinguish at least three categories of discourse: "revivalist" or "traditionalist" (Islam being the core-reference), "reformist" (accommodating religion to Western technical and scientific developments) and "Westernist" or "secular reformist" (asserting the superiority of the "Western" secular approach to that of religious dogma). Xavier Bougarel and Muhammed Aruçi show how such categories could be drawn from the way that groups positioned themselves in relation to different reference frameworks. These categories were linked to ideological developments in the Muslim world, and particularly in Kemalist Turkey and Egypt, as well as to political contexts in the "West". However Bougarel and Aruçi also point out how such categories were drawn from positioning vis-à-vis the main local issues. In Macedonia, as we can read

[13] See M. Mancheva, *State-minority relations*, pp. 48–51.

[14] In Albania, there were no proper political parties during the inter-war years and the two "parties" formed in the parliament at the beginning of the 1920s had no religious basis.

in Muhammed Aruçi's chapter, the dispute between the leaders of the community on the subject of education not only reflected different religious and cultural convictions. It was also linked to more political considerations such as the acceptance of minority status. Other factors can also be seen beyond the different claims: the power struggle among '*ulama*, rivalries between old and new elites, regional tensions opposing Muslims from Bosnia-Herzegovina and those from Southern Yugoslavia, etc. In Bosnia-Herzegovina, as Xavier Bougarel explains, what was at stake behind the debate about "Islamic" dress, the status of women and the reform of religious institutions was the best way to ensure the long-term survival of the Bosnian Muslim community in a non-Muslim European state. Consequently, the inter-war period can be considered a time of adaptation to the European nation-state model, as well as a period which saw the birth of Bosnian Muslim nationalism.

However, Yannis Bonos' contribution shows that, in the case of Greek Thrace at least, local Muslim notables, who wanted first to assert their position as intermediaries between the local Greek authorities and the "Muslim" population, could not always adopt a clear stance on the main debated issues, because they had to take into account different conflicting political, social and economic interests. Yet our knowledge of the life of these Balkan Muslims and their relations with the surrounding non-Muslim society still lacks sufficient depth fully to understand this whole interplay between the social, economic, political and religious spheres.

In some areas, the building of a national identity also began to be the driving force that competed with religion or gave it a slightly different place as a reference, but only for small groups of generally young educated men (often working as school teachers). The question of education and the spread of printed matter, as well as the changes in Kemalist Turkey and the development of non-Muslim nationalisms in the different Balkan countries, encouraged some Muslims to take into account a "national dimension". Whereas in Bosnia-Herzegovina, some Muslims were influenced by Serb and Croat nationalisms, in Greece, Turkey, Romania, Macedonia and Kosovo it was Turkish nationalism that some groups of Muslims adapted to their own needs. In Albania, and to a lesser extent in Macedonia, Kosovo and Greece (in the Çamëria region), Albanian nationalism also began to spread. Among some Muslims in Western Europe, Arab nationalism was also spreading, as highlighted in the chapter devoted to Shakib Arslan.[15]

It is worth mentioning that, apart from the development of national consciousness, geographical, cultural and linguistic differences proved to be important factors emphasising differences among Muslims in Europe. We have already mentioned the division of Muslims in Hungary into two separate "Bosnian" and "Turkish" groups, each with its own leader: Huszein Hilmi Durics for the Bosnians and Abdul Latif for the Turks.[16] In France, most of the *zawiyas* of the original Alawi brotherhood were frequented only by Arabs, whereas those of the Alawi brotherhood founded by Schuon, as Mark Sedgwick points out in his chapter, were attended exclusively by European converts. In Berlin, Muslims were also organised along national lines, and Eric Germain in his chapter suggests that the "neutral" Indian nationality of Ahmadi missionaries might have been helpful in creating a bridge between the various Tatar, Arab and Persian associations. However, even within a single "national group" there were divisions since these groups were socially, economically, and politically heterogeneous, and power relations existed among them, as exposed by Richard Lawless in his study of Arab seamen in British ports. Personal enmities and egotism also played a not insignificant role in some controversies such as the one that occurred among Indians in Germany, between the association led by the Khairi brothers and the Lahori missionaries, over the construction and control of the first mosque in Berlin.[17]

During the inter-war period, ethno-religious communitarianism was the most widespread response to the Muslims' minority position, but there was also a considerable number of European Muslims who were becoming increasingly assertive in ranking their faith first. They

15 For France, see Benjamin Stora, *Les sources du nationalisme algérien. Parcours idéologiques. Origines des acteurs*, Paris: L'Harmattan, 1989.

16 Huszein Hilmi Durics (1887–1940); Abdul Latif (d. 1946) (see G. Lederer, "Islam in Hungary").

17 Nasir Ahmad, *A Brief History of the Berlin Muslim Mission (1922–1988)*, 2004, on www.aaiil.org/text/articles/others/briefhistoryberlinmuslimmissiongermany.shtml).

were becoming aware that acculturation was not inevitable and that Muslims in Europe possessed several assets that they could deploy to claim and secure their religious identity. In the Balkans, international treaties and national laws gave special rights to Muslim minorities, rights which were constantly renegotiated according to internal and external political factors. In Western Europe, it was colonial interests that were pragmatically taken into account by Muslim leaders to negotiate fair treatment for Islam in the metropolis. They understood perfectly well the governments' fear of political unrest in their Muslim colonies and consciously used this threat to demand that all religions should be treated equally. This argument was not only effective in countries with Muslim colonies, such as France and the United Kingdom, but also in Germany which, although it did not have colonies, nevertheless had a very active foreign policy towards Muslim countries. On the European continent as a whole, the advance of secularist ideas was also seen by some Muslim leaders as a favourable factor in establishing a permanent place for Islam in societies with a Christian majority.

N.C.-E.G.

FAREWELL TO THE OTTOMAN LEGACY? ISLAMIC REFORMISM AND REVIVALISM IN INTER-WAR BOSNIA-HERZEGOVINA

Xavier Bougarel

Many works dealing with the history of the Bosnian Muslim community tend to present the late Ottoman period (1804–1878), the Austro-Hungarian period (1878–1918) and the early Communist period (1945–1953) as a clash between conservative local elites and modernising external actors. Such an approach to Bosnian history can be misleading, owing to the categories on which it is based ("tradition" versus "modernity") and the role it attributes to internal and external actors. As far as the inter-war period (1918–41) is concerned, it plays a secondary part in this approach, and is mainly dealt with by historians interested in the inter-ethnic tensions that contributed to the collapse of the first Yugoslav state in 1941.[1]

Bosnian society, however, experienced deep transformations within the Kingdom of Serbs, Croats and Slovenes, renamed the Kingdom of Yugoslavia in 1929. While the Austro-Hungarian authorities had left the agrarian structures inherited from the Ottoman period untouched, the agrarian reform of 1920 dismantled them completely, hastening the economic decline of Muslim *agas* and *begs* (landowners), and transforming the relationship

[1] Ivo Banac, *The National Question in Yugoslavia: Origins, History, Politics*, Ithaca, NY: Cornell University Press, 1984; Aleksa Djilas, *The Contested Country: Yugoslav Unity and Communist Revolution 1919–1953*, Cambridge: Harvard University Press, 1991.

between peasants, local political elites and the state bureaucracy.[2] Party politics, which had started to develop in the last years of the Austro-Hungarian period, resumed in the 1920s, before King Alexander's dictatorship (1929–34) put serious limitations on political and associative life. Finally, educational and cultural institutions continued to develop, and ethno-religious identities also continued to evolve, as illustrated by the activities of Muslim cultural societies such as *Gajret* ("Effort", founded in 1903 and showing an increasingly "pro-Serbian" orientation) and *Narodna uzdanica* ("Popular Hope", founded in 1924 with a "pro-Croatian" orientation).[3]

The importance of the inter-war period in the overall history of Bosnia-Herzegovina is confirmed by the fact that, in the 1960s and 1970s, the increasing assertiveness of the Socialist Republic of Bosnia-Herzegovina and the recognition of Bosnian Muslims as the sixth constitutive nation within the Yugoslav federation went together with the publication of several major works on this period. They included Atif Purivatra's book on the Yugoslav Muslim Organisation (*Jugoslovenska muslimanska organizacija*, JMO)[4] and Dana Begić's papers on the Movement for the Autonomy of Bosnia-Herzegovina.[5] The same holds true at the religious level, and the revival of the Islamic Community (*Islamska zajednica*) from the 1960s onwards was accompanied by a return to the religious debates of the inter-war period, as illustrated by Fikret Karčić's works on the reform of Shari'a courts and the development of

[2] Milivoje Erić, *Agrarna reforma u Jugoslaviji 1918–1941,* Sarajevo: Veselin Masleša, 1958; Jozo Tomasevich, *Peasants, Politics and Economic Change in Yugoslavia*, Stanford University Press, 1955.

[3] Ibrahim Kemura, *Uloga "Gajreta" u društvenom životu Muslimana 1903–1941*, Sarajevo: Veselin Masleša, 1986; Ibrahim Kemura, *Značaj i uloga "Narodne uzdanice" u društvenom životu Bošnjaka 1923–1945*, Sarajevo: Bošnjački institut / Institut za istoriju, 2002.

[4] Atif Purivatra, *Jugoslovenska muslimanska organizacija u političkom životu Kraljevine Srba, Hrvata i Slovenaca*, Sarajevo: Svjetlost, 1974.

[5] Dana Begić, "Akcije muslimanskih građanskih političara poslije skupštinskih izbora 1935. godine", *Godišnjak društva istoričara Bosne i Hercegovine*, XVI (1965), pp. 173–89; Dana Begić, "Pokret za autonomiju Bosne i Hercegovine u uslovima sporazuma Cvetković-Maček", *Prilozi instituta za historiju radničkog pokreta*, IV, 4 (1968), pp. 177–91.

Islamic reformism in inter-war Bosnia-Herzegovina.[6] Additional works were published after the collapse of Communist Yugoslavia in 1991, and booklets and collections of articles dating back to the inter-war period were reprinted in the 1990s.[7] This recent literature, of course, is not devoid of ideological bias, but it provides a lot of useful data and analyses. It represents the main source used in writing the present chapter, since the press and archives of the inter-war period were not consulted.

UNDERSTANDING THE INTERNAL PLURALISM OF ISLAM IN INTER-WAR BOSNIA-HERZEGOVINA

The origins of Islamic reformism in Bosnia-Herzegovina

The first attempts at reforming the local military and administrative structures in Bosnia-Herzegovina date back to the early nineteenth century, with the creation of a professional Ottoman army in 1826 and the promulgation of the *Hatt-i-sherif* of Gülhane in 1839, the latter symbolising the beginning of the *Tanzimat* (reforms) period in Ottoman history. Despite the fierce resistance of Bosnian *kapetans* (a specific type of military leaders settled on the frontier with the Austro-Hungarian Empire) and *ayans* (local political strongmen), the late Ottoman period was thus characterised by reinforcement of state authority and far-reaching administrative reforms. Some of these reforms, such as the secularisation of the judiciary in 1856 (limiting the competence of Shari'a courts to family issues) and the opening of *ruždijas* (from Turkish *rüşdiye;* non-confessional primary

[6] Fikret Karčić, *Šeriatski sudovi u Jugoslaviji 1918–1941*, Sarajevo: Islamska zajednica, 1986; Fikret Karčić, *Društveno-pravni aspekti islamskog reformizma*, Sarajevo: Islamski teološki fakultet, 1990.

[7] Udruženje Uleme "el-Hidaje"/Rijaset Islamske zajednice, *Islamska misao H. Mehmeda Handžića*, Sarajevo: Oko, 1994; Udruženje Uleme "el-Hidaje", *Zbornik radova sa znanstvenih skupova o Hadži Mehmedu Handžiću*, Sarajevo: Oko, 1996; Esad Duraković (ed.), *Mehmed Handžić: izabrana djela* (six volumes), Sarajevo: Ogledalo, 1999; Enes Karić and Mujo Demirović (eds), *Džemaludin Čaušević, prosvjetitelj i reformator* (two volumes), Sarajevo: NIPP Ljiljan, 2002; Enes Karić (ed.), *Bosanske mulimanske rasprave* (seven booklets), Sarajevo: Sedam, 2003; Adnan Jahić, *Hikjmet. Riječ tradicionalne uleme u Bosni i Hercegovini*, Tuzla: BZK "Preporod", 2004; Enes Karić, *Prilozi za povijest islamskog mišljenja u Bosni i Hercegovini 20. stoljeća-knjiga I*, Sarajevo: el-Kalem, 2004.

schools) in 1869, infringed on the jurisdiction of religious elites. But Bosnian *'ulama* (religious scholars) never reacted in a coherent way to the reforms of the *Tanzimat* period.[8]

In 1878, in the wake of the Russo-Ottoman war (1877–78), the Congress of Berlin placed Bosnia-Herzegovina under Austro-Hungarian military occupation. On the ground, the advance of Austro-Hungarian troops first met armed resistance by the local Muslim population. Four years later, the introduction of compulsory military service by Austro-Hungary resulted in a joint Serb-Muslim uprising in Eastern Herzegovina and in the following decades tens of thousands of *muhajirs* (refugees) fled to Ottoman territories.[9] Most Bosnian *'ulama*, however, quickly gave their allegiance to the Austro-Hungarian authorities. Moreover, they opposed statements by their Ottoman counterparts which insisted that Bosnian Muslims had a duty to perform *hijra* (emigration to Muslim-controlled territories), and in 1882 the Mufti of Sarajevo, Mustafa Hilmi Hadžiomerović, issued a *fatwa* (opinion on legal issues) encouraging Muslims to serve in the Austro-Hungarian army.[10] This behaviour was probably tactical, linked to the hope that the Austro-Hungarian occupation would not last for long or, on the contrary, to the fear that Muslims could be expelled from Bosnia-Herzegovina, as they had been from Slavonia and Dalmatia (in today's Croatia) at the end of the seventeenth century. But the allegiance of Bosnian *'ulama* to the Austro-Hungarian authorities can also be seen as a continuation of their subordination to the state, and as part of a wider tendency to reproduce and adapt some features of the Ottoman "*millet* system"[11] to new circumstances.

[8] Fikret Karčić, *The Bosniaks and the Challenge of Modernity–Late Ottoman and Hapsburg Times*, Sarajevo: el-Kalem, 1999, pp. 35–71.

[9] Justin McCarthy, *Death and Exile. The Ethnic Cleansing of Ottoman Muslims 1821–1922*, Princeton University Press, 1996.

[10] F. Karčić, *The Bosniaks*, pp. 109–23; Muhamed Mufaku al-Arnaut, "Islam and Muslims in Bosnia 1878–1918: Two Hijras and Two Fatwas", *Journal of Islamic Studies*, V, 2 (1994), pp. 242–53.

[11] Within the framework of the "*millet* system", the non-Muslim minorities of the Ottoman Empire enjoyed a large autonomy in religious, educational and judicial matters. The specific contours of the "*millet* system" depended both on time and place, and it was only fully institutionalized in the nineteenth century. See Benjamin Braude and Bernard Lewis (eds), *Christians and Jews in the Ottoman Empire: The Functioning of a Plural Society*, New York: Holmes and Meier, 1982.

In an effort to separate Bosnian Muslims from the Ottoman Empire, in 1882 the Governor of Bosnia-Herzegovina, Benjamin Kallay, appointed Mustafa Hilmi Hadžiomerović as the first Bosnian *Reis ul-Ulema* (Chief of the '*ulama*), assisted by an *Ulema medžlis* (Council of the '*Ulama*) and, later on, a *Vakf-mearif sabor* (*Waqf* Assembly). The creation of these new provincial bodies facilitated the bureaucratisation of the *waqfs* (religious foundations), *madrasa*s (secondary religious schools) and Shari'a courts.[12] At the beginning of the twentieth century, representatives of the traditional elites demanded the right to elect the *Reis ul-Ulema,* the *Ulema medžlis* and the *Vakf-mearif sabor.* This first political mobilisation of the Bosnian Muslim community resulted in the creation of the Muslim Popular Organisation (*Muslimanska narodna organizacija*, MNO) in 1906, and the promulgation by the Austro-Hungarian authorities of a "Status for the Autonomous Administration of Islamic Religious and Educational Affairs" in 1909.[13] Contrary to what happened around the same period with the Orthodox (Serb) community,[14] however, this movement did not encourage the emergence of a modern national identity but withdrawal into an autonomous but non-sovereign confessional community, i.e. a kind of "neo-*millet*", as illustrated by the generalisation of the term "Muslim". Consequently, the movement for religious and educational autonomy was of a highly paradoxical nature. Although it was led by the traditional Muslim elites, it resulted in the creation of the first modern political party in Bosnia-Herzegovina, and while it aimed at obtaining the autonomy of religious institutions created or bureaucratised by the state, it was unable—or unwilling—to develop a modernisation project of its own. As a result, the origins of Islamic reformism in Bosnia-Herzegovina are not to be found in this movement but on the contrary among its

[12] F. Karčić, *The Bosniaks*, pp. 123–39; Alexandre Popovic, *L'islam balkanique. Les musulmans du sud-est européen dans la période post-ottomane,* Wiesbaden: Harrassowitz, 1986, pp. 273–8.

[13] Robert Donia, *Islam under the Double Eagle. The Muslims of Bosnia and Hercegovina 1878–1914,* New York: Columbia University Press, 1981; Nusret Šehić, *Autonomni pokret Muslimana za vrijeme austrougarske uprave u Bosni i Hercegovini,* Sarajevo: Svjetlost, 1980.

[14] Božo Madžar, *Pokret Srba Bosne i Hercegovine za vjersko-prosvjetnu autonomiju,* Sarajevo: Veselin Masleša, 1982.

foremost critics: the representatives of a nascent Bosnian Muslim intelligentsia.

The creation of provincial religious institutions by Benjamin Kallay was part of a larger programme to bring about the complete "Europeanisation" of Bosnia-Herzegovina and the promotion of an all-embracing Bosniak identity (*bošnjaštvo*) able to counter Serbian and Croatian nationalist claims.[15] This idea of *bošnjaštvo* had already been advanced in the last decades of Ottoman rule, after the military defeat of Bosnian *ayan*s by Omer Pasha Latas in 1851 and the promulgation of the *Hatt-i hümayun* in 1856. It is therefore not surprising that Kallay's project was embraced by former Ottoman civil servants such as Mehmed-beg Kapetanović Ljubušak (1839–1902), editor of the newspaper *Bošnjak* (1891–1910). The idea of *bošnjaštvo*, however, was not supported by the traditional Muslim elites, and was abandoned by the Austro-Hungarian authorities after Kallay's departure in 1903. Around the same period, a first generation of Muslim intellectuals educated in Austro-Hungarian *gimnazija*s (secondary schools) and universities played a key part in the emergence of a modern Muslim press and literature, and the creation of the cultural society *Gajret*.[16]

The names most frequently associated with this cultural awakening are Edhem Mulabdić (1862–1954), Osman Nuri Hadžić (1869–1937), Safvet-beg Bašagić (1870–1934) and Musa Ćazim Ćatić (1878–1915). In the newspapers they established, such as *Behar* ("Blossom", 1900–11), *Gajret* (1906–8) and *Biser* ("Pearl", 1912–14), the use of Turkish was abandoned in favour of the Bosnian/Serbo-Croat language,[17] Western European forms of literary

[15] Tomislav Kraljačić, *Kallajev režim u Bosni i Hercegovini (1882–1903)*, Sarajevo: Veselin Masleša, 1987.

[16] Muhsin Rizvić, *Književno stvaranje muslimanskih pisaca u Bosni i Hercegovini u doba austrougarske vladavine*, Sarajevo: Veselin Masleša, 1985; Ibrahim Kemura, *Uloga "Gajreta"*; Alexandre Popovic, *Cultures musulmanes balkaniques*, Istanbul: Isis, 1994.

[17] Until the end of the nineteenth century, the newspapers close to the traditional Muslim elites used the Turkish language, whereas *Bošnjak* already used the vernacular language (called the Bosnian language until 1907, and the Serbo-Croatian language later on) written in the Latin alphabet. In the late Austro-Hungarian period, reformist '*ulama* such as Džemaludin Čaušević failed in their attempt to promote the use of the Serbo-Croatian language written in a modified Arabic alphabet (so-called *arebica*) in the Bosnian Muslim newspapers.

expression were promoted, and the commitment to progressive values and modern national identities—most often the Croatian one—was constantly emphasised. At the same time, traditional elites were criticised for their hidden nostalgia for the Ottoman Empire, their inability to adapt to new economic and cultural circumstances, and their tactical alliance with representatives of the Serb community.[18] In the same newspapers, reformist writers of the Ottoman Empire (Mehmed Akif Ersoy, Sait Halim Paşa), Egypt (Muhammad Abduh, Abd al-Aziz Shawish), India (Sayyid Ahmad Khan) and Russia (Ismail Gasprinski) were used in order to denounce the conservatism of local *'ulama*. At that time, reformist discourse focused on the need to reform the main Islamic religious institutions, beginning with the curriculum of *madrasa*s and the administration of *waqf*s, and to lift some religious bans concerning in particular banking activities (notably the question of interest) and women's education. Although these first debates were limited to narrow intellectual circles, there is no doubt that they opened a new chapter in the history of Islamic thought and life in Bosnia-Herzegovina.

The main religious debates of the inter-war period

After the First World War and the creation of the Kingdom of Serbs, Croats and Slovenes in 1918, the debates about Islamic reformism experienced profound changes in Bosnia-Herzegovina. On the one hand, issues such as the duty to perform *hijra* and the use of the Turkish language became obsolete, while the need to fight the "backwardness" *(zaostalost)* of the Bosnian Muslim community and to adapt to the "spirit of the time" *(duh vrijemena)* was unanimously

[18] In the early 1900s, the Muslim Popular Organisation and the Serb Popular Organisation (*Srpska narodna organizacija*, SNO, founded in 1907) were both fighting for the religious and educational autonomy of their respective communities, and entered into a tactical alliance. Bosnian Muslim intellectuals, on the contrary, felt closer to the Croatian national project. In 1908, they created the Muslim Progressive Party (*Muslimanska napredna stranka*, MNS), whose influence remained marginal. In 1911, the agrarian question led to the breakdown of the Muslim-Serb coalition, and the MNO and the MNS merged into the Unified Muslim Organisation (*Ujedinjena muslimanska organizacija*, UMO). See Martha Čupić-Amrein, *Die Opposition gegen die österreichisch-ungarische Herrschaft in Bosnien-Hercegovina 1878–1914*, Frankfurt/Main: Peter Lang, 1986; R. Donia, *Islam*.

acknowledged, at least in principle. On the other hand, socio-cultural issues such as the adoption of Western dress codes and the role of Muslim women in public life became new bones of contention between the advocates and adversaries of reformist ideas, and new divisions began to appear among the reformists themselves.

In his work on Islamic reformism, Fikret Karčić establishes for example a distinction between the "secular modernists" (Dževad-beg Sulejmanpašić, Edhem Bulbulović, Šukrija Kurtović, etc.), who gathered in 1928 in the association *Reforma*,[19] and the "religious modernists" (Džemaludin Čaušević, Fehim Spaho, Abdulah Ajni Bušatlić, etc.), who launched the newspaper *Novi Behar* (New Blossom) in 1927. The former favoured the suppression of Shari'a courts and permission for Muslim women to be completely unveiled,[20] and encouraged Muslim men to wear a hat instead of the fez. The latter, on the other hand, only wanted to modernise the interpretation of Shari'a and the administration of *waqfs*, and maintained that Muslim women did not have a duty to hide their faces, especially if this was an obstacle to their education and to their participation in economic life.[21] Both "secular" and "religious" reformists denounced the conservatism of the *ahmedijaši* ("turbaned people", a derogatory term for the '*ulama*) and the ignorance of the rural *hojas* (local imams). However, the "secular reformists" were members of the intelligentsia, favoured the "nationalisation" (national assimilation) of the Bosnian Muslims, and sometimes had sympathies for the Yugoslav Communist Party.[22] "Religious reformists", for their part, quite often

[19] On the *Reforma* association, see Sabina Ferhadbegović, "Fes oder Hut? Der Islam in Bosnien zwischen den Weltkriegen", *Wiener Zeitschrift zur Geschichte der Neuzeit*, V, 2 (2005), pp. 69–85.

[20] Before 1950, most Bosnian Muslim women wore a long shawl called *zar* or *feredža* covering body and hair, as well as a veil called *peča* or *jašmak* covering the face. This traditional Muslim dress code was banned by the Communist authorities in 1950 (see Senija Milišić, "O pitanju emancipacije muslimanske žene u Bosni i Hercegovini", *Prilozi instituta za istoriju*, 28 (1999), pp. 225–41).

[21] In the 1920s, out of conviction or for tactical reasons, religious reformists only required that a women's face should be uncovered, that is, they called for abolition of the *peča/jašmak* (see note 20).

[22] Edhem Bulbulović, for example, was elected in 1921 to the Constituent Assembly of the Kingdom of Serbs, Croats and Slovenes as a representative of the Communist Party. In the 1930s, Communist influence was also perceptible in

belonged to the *ilmiyya* (class of the *'ulama*), and shared the tactical "Yugoslavism" of the JMO's leaders.[23]

The growing influence of reformist ideas within Islamic religious institutions is in fact one of the most striking features of the inter-war period. Džemaludin Čaušević (1870–1938), the main figure of Bosnian Islamic reformism, was elected *Reis ul-Ulema* in 1913, a few months before the breakout of the First World War, and occupied this position until his resignation in 1930. A former student of the famous *Mekteb-i hukuk* (Faculty of Law) in Istanbul, Čaušević had been a member of the *Ulema medžlis* since 1905, in charge of educational issues. Appalled by the poor state of Islamic educational institutions, he had encouraged the introduction of non-religious subjects into the curricula of *madrasa*s and the printing of schoolbooks in the vernacular language.[24] He had also been the main initiator of the Association of Imams and Religious Teachers (*Udruženje imama i muallima*) created in 1909 and of the Association of *'Ulama (Udruženje Ilmijje Bosne i Hercegovine*) founded in 1912. Finally, he had played a very active part in the development of the Bosnian Muslim press, as shown by his contributions to the newspaper *Behar* and his role in the publication of bilingual religious newspapers (in Turkish and Serbo-Croat, written most often in *arebica*[25]): *Tarik* ("The Path", 1908–10), *Muallim* ("The Teacher", 1910–13), and *Misbah* ("The Torch", 1912–14).

Čaušević's election as *Reis ul-ulema* was the logical consequence of his own activism as well as a reflection of the growing influence of Islamic reformism in Bosnia-Herzegovina. But hostility to reformist ideas remained strong within Islamic religious institutions,

---

the *Gajret* cultural association and in the Gazi Husrev-beg *madrasa* (see I. Kemura, *Uloga "Gajreta"*, pp. 215–41; Dubravka Škarica, "Napredna srednjoškolska omladina Bosne i Hercegovine u revolucionarno-demokratskom pokretu 1937–1941. god.", *Prilozi instituta za historiju radničkog pokreta*, IV, 4 (1968), pp. 593–617).

[23] A. Purivatra, *Jugoslovenska muslimanska organizacija*; Xavier Bougarel, "Bosnian Muslims and the Yugoslav Idea" in Dejan Djokic (ed.), *Yugoslavism. Histories of a Failed Idea 1918–1992*, London: Hurst, 2003, pp. 100–14.

[24] E. Karić and M. Demirović (eds), *Džemaludin Čaušević*, especially vol. I, pp. 17–53 and vol. II, pp. 235–65.

[25] See note 17.

as shown by the attacks against Čaušević in the 1920s and 1930s. On 6 December 1927, during a conference hosted by the cultural society *Gajret*, Čaušević declared that Islam did not prohibit women from unveiling or men from wearing a hat, and invited intellectuals who wore the hat to go to the mosque more often, "so that I can preach to them, and they also get the opportunity to speak from the *minbar* (pulpit from which the imam holds his sermon on Friday)".[26] He added that it was possible to modify the initial purpose of a *waqf* and to destroy old graveyards if this could promote the economic and cultural advancement of the Muslim community. These typically reformist statements triggered fierce reactions from the executive board of the *Vakf-mearif sabor* (Waqf Assembly), the Sarajevan *džematski medžlis* (local religious council) and some leading *'ulama* such as Ali Riza Karabeg (1872–1944), who accused Čaušević of promoting a "fifth Kemalist *madhhab*".[27] In the following months, Bosnian Muslim *'ulama* and intellectuals became involved in a heated debate about the veiling of women and, beyond this symbolic issue, about the place of *ijtihad* (rational interpretation) in *fiqh* (Islamic jurisprudence). Čaušević's adversaries went so far as to declare him a *kafir* (infidel) and a *murtad* (renegade), while Čaušević responded that they were *munafiks* (religious hypocrites).

On 10 July 1928, the *Islamska izborna kurija* (Islamic Electoral Curia), the body in charge of electing the *Reis ul-Ulema*, issued a *taqrir* (statement) insisting on the need to conform to the Hanafi *madhhab*,[28] restricting the right to issue *fatwas* to the muftis and conceding that women could unveil their faces under certain conditions, but condemning the wearing of the hat and rejecting any possibility of circumventing a *vakufname* (the founding act of a *waqf*,

[26] Quoted in Smail Balić, *Das unbekannte Bosnien. Europas Brücke zur islamischen Welt*, Cologne: Bohlau Verlag, 1992, p. 341.

[27] Ali Riza Karabeg, *Rasprava o hidžabu (krivenju muslimanki)*, Mostar: Hrvatska tiskara, 1928; reprinted in E. Karić (ed.), *Bosanske muslimanske rasprave*, booklet III, pp. 61–92, here p. 79. Between the seventh and the ninth century, four distinct *madhhabs* (legal schools) appeared within Sunni Islam. Bosnian Muslims are affiliated to the Hanafi *madhhab* (from the name of its founder, Abu Hanifa, 699–767), which was the official *madhhab* of the Ottoman Empire.

[28] See note 27.

mentioning the purpose chosen by its founder).[29] A few months later, on 7 September 1928, a Congress of Muslim Intellectuals (held in Sarajevo) summoned by the *Gajret* society adopted a conciliatory resolution insisting on the education of Muslim women rather than their unveiling, and on the depoliticisation of the way the *mutawalli* (a *waqf*'s administrator) was elected, rather than the rationalisation of the way the *waqfs* themselves were administered.[30] As for Čaušević, he complied with the *taqrir*, but stressed that the "Curia" had not rejected the principle of the unveiling of women.[31]

In the 1930s, the debate about Islamic reformism experienced new transformations. While the influence of reformist ideas was declining, revivalist circles hostile to *reformaštvo* (a derogatory term for "reformism") started to agitate for a strict implementation of Shari'a rules, especially with regard to the dress code and other markers of Muslim identity.[32] Bosnian revivalists gathered around the newspapers *Hikjmet* ("Wisdom", 1929–36), published in Tuzla, and *el-Hidaje* ("The Right Path", 1936–45), published in Sarajevo. Their leading figure was Mehmed Handžić (1906–44), a young *'alim* (scholar) who, after studying at the Islamic University of al-Azhar in Cairo (1926–31), became a professor at the Gazi Husrev-beg *madrasa* in Sarajevo and, from 1939 onwards, at the *Viša islamska šerijatsko-teološka škola* (Higher Islamic Sharī'a-Theological School).

[29] Islamska izborna kurija, *Takrir*, Sarajevo: H.M. Merhemić, 1928; translated in S. Balić, *Das unbekannte Bosnien*, pp. 343–4. On the *waqfs* in inter-war Bosnia-Herzegozina, see e.g. Abduselam Balagija, *Uloga vakufa u verskom i svetovnom prosvećivanju naših muslimana,* Belgrade: Štamparija D. Gregorić, 1933; Hajrudin Mulalić, *Institucija vakufa u Bosni i Hercegovini*, Sarajevo: Svjetlost, 2001.

[30] I. Kemura, *Uloga "Gajreta"*, pp. 172–81.

[31] S. Balić, *Das unbekannte Bosnien*, p. 344.

[32] Islamic revivalists are defined in recent literature as "traditionalists" (Fikret Karčić) or "traditional '*ulama*" (Adnan Jahić). Such a definition, however, can be misleading, since revivalists did not always belong to the traditional Bosnian Muslim elites, and were critical of some religious traditions inherited from the Ottoman period. On the notions of traditionalism, reformism and revivalism, see Antony Smith, "La 'légitimation dualiste', matrice du nationalisme ethnique", in G. Delannoi and P.-A. Taguieff (eds), *Théories du nationalisme: nation, nationalité, ethnicité*, Paris: Kimé, 1991, pp. 256–83.

The rise of Islamic revivalism in Bosnia-Herzegovina has a clear international dimension and reflects in particular the influence of authors such as Shakib Arslan (1869–1946), who visited Yugoslavia in 1932.[33] For their part, in the 1930s Islamic reformists started to cultivate regular contacts with the Lahori Ahmadiyya movement,[34] as illustrated by the fact that the imam of the Ahmadiyya mosque in Berlin, Shaikh Muhammad Abdullah, visited Yugoslavia in 1936, meeting representatives of Islamic religious institutions and the former *Reis ul-Ulema* Džemaludin Čaušević.[35] These contacts with the Ahmadiyya gave rise to new attacks against Čaušević. In 1937, two translations of the Qur'an, one by Ali Riza Karabeg and the other by Džemaludin Čaušević and Muhamed Pandža, were published in Bosnia-Herzegovina. Despite the hostility of the newspaper *Hikjmet*, the principle of such a translation was no longer a central issue at that time. In his review of Karabeg's translation, Handžić himself wrote that "we need such a translation and commentary [of the Qur'an], although we hold that a translation can never be used for the same purposes as the original, that is the foundation of religious rules".[36] But, as shown by Enes Karić, revivalists rejected the

[33] Shakib Arslan, a publicist and political activist born in Lebanon, was a leading figure of the pan-Islamic movement in the inter-war period, and one of the organisers of the Muslim Congress held in Geneva (1935). Several papers by Shakib Arslan were published in *Hikjmet* and *el-Hidaje*, and his famous brochure *Our Decline, Its Causes and Remedies* was translated into Serbo-Croat in 1934. See Martin Kramer, *Islam Assembled. The Advent of the Muslim Congresses*, New York: Columbia University Press, 1986; E. Karić and Rešid Hafizović, "Aktuelnost djela Emira Šekiba Arslana", in Emir Šekib Arslan, *Zašto su muslimani zaostali, a drugi napredovali*, Sarajevo: NIPP Ljiljan, 1994, pp. 75–81; and Raja Adal's chapter in the present volume.

[34] On the Lahori Ahmadiyya, see Eric Germain's chapter in this volume.

[35] Dr S.M. Abdullah, "Der Islam in Jugoslawien", *Moslemische Revue*, XIII, 1 (April 1937), pp. 15–19. In a paper published in 1970, Husein Đozo writes that Muhammad Abdullah was a "personal friend" of Džemaludin Čaušević, and that "it is possible that Čaušević did not have a clear idea [*nije bio na čistu*] concerning the Qadiani movement" (Husein Đozo, "Kur'an časni", *Glasnik IVZ*, XXX, 1–2 (1970), pp. 3–7; reprinted in E. Karić and M. Demirović (eds), *Džemaludin Čaušević*, I, pp. 260–4, here p. 261.

[36] Mehmed Handžić, "Prijevod Kur'ana od Hadži Ali Riza Karabega", *el-Hidaje*, II, 9 (1938–1939), pp. 141–42; reprinted in E. Duraković (ed.), *Mehmed Handžić*, I, pp. 758–61, here p. 760.

rationalist bias of Čaušević's and Pandža's comments, and blamed them for having used translations by Omer Riza (in Turkish) and Muhammad Ali (in English), two other religious figures linked to the Ahmadiyya. Ten years after having been accused of introducing a "Kemalist *madhhab*" into Bosnia-Herzegovina, Čaušević was thus denounced as a representative of the "Qadianist *madhhab*".[37]

The growing influence of Islamic revivalism, however, was also related to the Yugoslav political and cultural context. The influence of both international and local factors on the debates of the inter-war period is best demonstrated by a comparison of the educational background and public commitments of Džemaludin Čaušević and Mehmed Handžić, the leading figures of Islamic reformism and revivalism in Bosnia-Herzegovina during this period.

Čaušević and Handžić: Two Generations of 'ulama?

Džemaludin Čaušević was born in 1870, while Bosnia-Herzegovina was still part of the Ottoman Empire. After frequenting the *madrasa* of Bihać, he left in 1887 for Istanbul, where he studied at the *Mekteb-i nüvvab* (Training School for *Qadis*) and the *Mekteb-i hukuk* (Law Faculty). While in the Ottoman capital, he became acquainted with some of the Young Turks and with reformist-minded *'ulama* such as Ismail Hakki Manastirli (1846–1912). In 1901 and 1902, he travelled to the Hejaz and to Yemen as correspondent of the Istanbul newspapers *Tasvir-i efkar* (The Description of Thoughts) and *Tercüman-i hakikat* (The Interpreter of the Truth), and spent some time in Cairo, where he attended classes given by Muhammad Abduh (1849–1905), the Mufti of Egypt and a leading figure of nineteenth-century Islamic reformism. Thus, Čaušević's educational background was mainly an Ottoman one, and he had direct contacts with the first generation of reformist *'ulama*. During the inter-war period, Cairo replaced Istanbul as the main centre of higher education

[37] Muhamed Pašić, "U čemu se sastoje greške, podvale i potvore Glavnog odbora 'el-Hidaje' u prikazu djela 'Kur'an časni'", *el-Hidaje*, I, 1 (1937–1938), pp. 9–13; quoted in E. Karić and M. Demirović (eds), *Džemaludin Čaušević*, I, p. 115. Here the Lahori branch of the Ahmadiyya was confused by Čausevic's opponents with the other branch, the Qadiani Ahmadiyya, broadly condemned in the 1930s as "outside the pale of Islam".

for Bosnian *'ulama*. But the University of al-Azhar that Mehmed Handžić entered in 1926 was quite different from the one Čaušević had known at the time of Abduh. Moreover, Handžić's five-year stay in Egypt provided an opportunity for him to discover the Islamist ideology of the Muslim Brotherhood, a movement founded in 1928 by Hasan al-Banna (1906–49).

Čaušević's and Handžić's educational backgrounds reflect the political and religious changes taking place in the Muslim world. In contrast, a comparison of their official positions during the inter-war period reveals the importance of local political circumstances. As already mentioned, Čaušević was elected *Reis ul-Ulema* on 27 October 1913, shortly before the First World War broke out. Living in such a troubled time, he could not avoid getting involved in politics.[38] At the end of the war, Čaušević rallied to the Yugoslav project, allegedly stating that he was tired of both "the Turkish and the German power",[39] and tried—along with other political and religious leaders—to give his support to the Kingdom of Serbs, Croats and Slovenes in exchange for the preservation of Bosnia-Herzegovina as a distinct administrative unit and of the 1909 Status of Autonomy for Islamic Religious Institutions. In the following years, however, he clashed regularly with the state authorities over the fate of the Bosnian Muslims in the new kingdom and, more specifically, over the government's attempts to limit the autonomy of Islamic religious institutions. In 1919 and 1920, Čaušević denounced the murders and pillaging by Serb veterans and irregulars in Eastern Bosnia-Herzegovina and in the Sanjak region (between Bosnia-Herzegovina and Kosovo), as well as the expropriation of *waqf*s and the transformation of mosques into military warehouses. In 1921, he demanded from the new state authorities that all religious communities should enjoy the same rights, that family matters should remain within the jurisdiction of religious

[38] On the political activities of Džemaludin Čaušević, see e.g. Enes Durmišević, "Džemaludin Čaušević i pravni položaj Reis-ul-Uleme od 1918 do 1930", in E. Karić and M. Demirović (eds), *Džemaludin Čaušević*, pp. 124–45; Mustafa Imamović, "O političkoj aktivnosti reis-ul-uleme Čauševića", *Glasnik IZ*, LIV, 1 (1991), pp. 26–34.

[39] Quoted in A. Purivatra, *Jugoslovenska muslimanska organizacija*, p. 18.

institutions, that any form of proselytism should be forbidden and that no religious symbols or holidays should be introduced in state institutions.[40] While the Radical Party in power and the JMO were fighting for control of the *waqfs*, an important channel for clientelism, Čaušević was above all opposed to the introduction of the cult of Saint Sava (the patron saint of the Serbian Orthodox Church) in elementary and secondary schools, which he defined as "temples of education" (*hramovi prosvjete*). His definition of public education was therefore a strictly secular one: "The best is that all that is religious belongs to the mosques, to the churches and to the books on religious instruction of each confession, and that in our public schools, which are intended for all citizens, nation and science are cleansed of all that belongs to places of worship and to religious books".[41]

Already in the mid-1920s, Čaušević was attacked as one of the main obstacles to the "nationalisation" of Bosnian Muslims. The newspaper *Politika* wrote that "there are in Bosnia nationally-oriented people and one should not prevent Čaušević from playing the Turk as much as he wants [*da i dalje turkuje do mile volje*]. Pension him off, and let him go wherever he wants: either to Istanbul, or to Ankara".[42] But the final clash between Čaušević and the Yugoslav state took place in 1930, after King Alexander had established a centralised dictatorship on 6 January 1929 and passed a new law on Islamic religious institutions on 31 January 1930. This law abolished the 1909 Status of Autonomy and created a Yugoslav-wide *Islamska vjerska zajednica* (Islamic religious community) whose main bodies were appointed by the King. Čaušević protested against this law, rejected his appointment as Yugoslav *Reis ul-Ulema* on 26 February, and was pensioned off on 6 June 1930. He was replaced by Ibrahim Maglajlić (1861–1936), the Mufti of Tuzla and an '*alim* close to the revivalist newspaper *Hikjmet*.

[40] Džemaludin Čaušević, "Odnošaj islama prema državi i drugim konfesijama (Beograd, 22. novembra 1921. god.)", reprinted in E. Karić and M. Demirović (eds), *Džemaludin Čaušević*, I, pp. 274–79.

[41] Džemaludin Čaušević, "Nacija i vjera", *Novi Behar*, IX, 1–3 (1935–1936), pp. 1–2; reprinted in ibid., II, pp. 377–80, here p. 380.

[42] *Politika* (13 February 1925); quoted in ibid., I, p. 138.

Mehmed Handžić, for his part, became politically active when Čaušević had already withdrawn from public life and interethnic tensions were increasing in the Kingdom of Yugoslavia. In 1935, at a time when political freedoms were restricted, most JMO leaders agreed to join the Yugoslav Radical Community (*Jugoslovenska radikalna zajednica*, JRZ) in power, and Fehim Spaho (1877–1942) was appointed as the new *Reis ul-Ulema*.[43] In the following year, Handžić took part in the creation of the Association of *'ulama el-Hidaje* (The Right Path) which published a journal under the same name. Its aim was to "raise the authority of the class of the *'ulama* as the spiritual leadership of the Muslims"[44] and, beyond that, to provide new moral and political guidelines to a disoriented Bosnian Muslim population. Shortly after its creation, the *el-Hidaje* Association protested against the amendment of the law on Islamic religious institutions and, especially, against the suppression of the office of mufti. According to Mahmud Traljić, "Mehmed Handžić was a candidate on the opposition list in parliamentary elections [in 1938]".[45] On 26 August 1939, Prime Minister Dragiša Cvetković and Croatian political leader Vlatko Maček agreed to divide Bosnia-Herzegovina between Serbia and the new autonomous *banovina* (province) of Croatia, in a last attempt to calm down growing Serb-Croat tensions. As the recently elected president of the *el-Hidaje* Association, Handžić participated in several meetings of the main Muslim cultural and religious associations which led to the creation of the Movement for the Autonomy of Bosnia-Herzegovina (*Pokret za autonomiju Bosne i Hercegovine*) on 30 December 1939.[46]

[43] Fehim Spaho was the brother of Mehmed Spaho, the main leader of the JMO until his death in 1939.

[44] The programme of the *el-Hidaje* Association is extensively quoted in Enes Karić, "Časopis 'el-Hidaje'", in E. Karić, *Prilozi*, pp. 421–58, here p. 423.

[45] Hafiz Mahmud Traljić, "Handžić kao društveni i javni radnik", in Udruženje Uleme "el-Hidaje", *Zbornik radova*, pp. 45–50, here p. 49. Traljić does not provide more details about Handžić's candidature. However, the list in question is probably the one led by the Croatian Peasant Party (*Hrvatska seljačka stranka*, HSS) and its Bosnian Muslim branch, the Muslim Organisation (*Muslimanska organizacija, MO*), created in 1936 by pro-Croatian intellectuals and JMO dissidents (see D. Begić, "Akcije muslimanskih građanskih političara", esp. pp. 178–80).

[46] D. Begić, "Pokret", esp. pp. 180–5.

ISLAMIC REFORMISM AND REVIVALISM IN BOSNIA-HERZEGOVINA: WHAT WAS REALLY AT STAKE?

Two antagonistic trends with a common intellectual origin

Čaušević's and Handžić's biographies show that the religious debates of the inter-war period have to be considered within their historical context. A closer examination of the writings of the main reformist and revivalist authors also demonstrates that, in Bosnia-Herzegovina as elsewhere, the relationship between Islamic reformism and revivalism is not one of outright opposition, but one of contradictory evolution from a shared intellectual legacy: the ideas of early reformist *'ulama*, and above all of the Egyptian scholar Muhammad Abduh.[47] Both reformists and revivalists, for example, condemned the heterodox practices of popular Islam. While Dževad-beg Sulejmanpašić made fun of the rural *hojas*' belief in the power of written amulets,[48] Handžić considered that "it is shameful and unfortunate that, at a time when medicine is experiencing progress and when we have medical specialists for every disease, we turn for remedy to dead people who are unable to help themselves, let alone to cure us".[49] Reformists and revivalists alike stressed that Islam was compatible with "sound reason" *(zdrav razum)*, and that it strongly encouraged learning and work. Within this background, Čaušević and Handžić also agreed on the need to preach on worldly topics in the vernacular language and to promote the diffusion of religious newspapers and brochures among the Bosnian Muslim masses.

Common ground between reformists and revivalists, however, stopped when it came to more sensitive issues such as reform of the *waqfs* and the reinterpretation of the Shari'a. Reformists insisted on

[47] Elie Keddourie, *Afghani and Abduh*, London: Frank Cass, 1966; Aziz al-Azmeh, *Islams and Modernities*, London: Verso, 1993; Armando Salvatore, *Islam and the Political Discourse of Modernity*, Reading: Ithaca Press, 1999.

[48] Dževad-beg Sulejmanpašić, *Zelen čovjek. Komedija u jednom činu iz muslimanskog seoskog života*, Sarajevo: Gajretova mala pozornica, 1932; quoted in S. Ferhadbegović, "Fes oder Hut?", pp. 76–77.

[49] Mehmed Handžić, "Islam zabranjuje traženje pomoći od mrtvih i u tom cilju posjećivanje turbeta i crkvi (a ovo naročito osuđuje)", *Glasnik IVZ*, I, 8 (1933), pp. 13–17; reprinted in E. Duraković (ed.), *Mehmed Handžić*, III, pp. 355–62, here p. 362.

the need for *ijtihad* (rational interpretation), in order to take into account "what exists, what will exist and what should exist".[50] At the end of his life Čaušević went so far in this direction that he seemed to deny any value to the accumulated legal corpus of *fiqh* and to promote instead an individual relationship with the Qur'an and the *hadiths* (Muhammad's deeds and sayings). In 1928, in response to those who accused him of not conforming to the Hanafi *madhhab*, he wrote: "My answers on the veiling of women conform to what God is ordering in the Qur'an, and even if I know what Shari'a lawyers and commentators have said, I prefer to conform to the precepts of the Qur'an, since it is here forever and for all times. I am required to do this by the Qur'an, since it orders me to ponder, to learn and to investigate".[51] Of course, many *'ulama* disagreed with such statements and instead set strict limitations on *ijtihad*. In its *taqrir*, the "Curia" warned, for example, that "each individual Muslim has a duty to follow those prescriptions which are in accordance with the opinions of our religious authorities. Any individual interpretation of the Shari'a which is not confirmed by the Tradition (*Sunna*) has no value from the point of view of the Shari'a, and has therefore no binding effect".[52] Similarly, in 1939, after *Reis ul-Ulema* Fehim Spaho had suggested that "together with the time in which we are living, Shari'a jurisprudence, which is based on custom (*'urf* and *'ada*), has to be changed",[53] Handžić replied that, "every question which deals with belief, religious rituals or legal issues is, in terms of the Shari'a, a 'religious' one", and no mufti could issue a *fatwa* without basing it on a quotation from the Qur'an or a legitimate *hadith*. He therefore rejected Spaho's justification of usury in post-Ottoman Bosnia-Herzegovina, as well as his

50 Džemaludin Čaušević, "Naša kulturna pitanja", *Novi Behar*, II, 17 (1928–1929), pp. 257–9; quoted in F. Karčić, *Društveno-pravni aspekti*, pp. 217.

51 Džemaludin Čaušević, "Sarajevskom vafufsko-mearifskom džematskom medžlisu putem kotorskog vakufsko-mearifskog povjerenstva u Sarajevu (Sarajevo, 27. januara 1928)", reprinted in E. Karić and M. Demirović (eds), *Džemaludin Čaušević*, I, pp. 298–307, here p. 298.

52 Islamska izborna kurija, *Takrir*, p. 343 (translated from the German version).

53 Fehim Spaho, "Tumačenje šeriatsko-pravnih pitanja kod nas", *Kalendar Narodne uzdanice*, VII (1939), pp. 21–25; translated in S. Balić, *Das unbekannte Bosnien*, pp. 346–8, here p. 346.

suggestion that modern astronomy should be used in calculating lunar months.[54]

This conflict about the scope of *ijtihad* was linked to another issue, the relationship between the *ilmiyya* (class of the *'ulama*) and the intelligentsia. Both secular and religious reformists accused the *'ulama* of being one of the main causes of the decline of their community and, in particular, of having encouraged rejection of the Austro-Hungarian educational system (*švabska škola*: "German school") and the Latin and Cyrillic alphabets (*vlaški alfabet*: "Vlach alphabet"). In Abdulah Bušatlić's eyes, for example, "the *hoja*s are the first culprits for our backwardness since, during all our long history, they were not up to the hard task of educating their people in a contemporary way. Nobody taught them how to work with the people, how to facilitate their moral and material advancement and progress".[55] As a religious reformist, however, he also complained that "instead of being exemplary in its conduct and behaviour, [the Westernised intelligentsia] has behaved provocatively and has prompted in the masses the feeling that Western science corrupts instead of ennobling".[56] For their part, revivalists admitted that the Muslims of Yugoslavia represented "a mighty religious community which lags behind in many domains, and which needs to dedicate all its might to its religious, cultural and economic renaissance".[57] But they wanted to put this process under the leadership of the *ilmiyya*, especially in a period "when, as a consequence of the First World War, the level of morality has begun to decline, when perversion has started to spread rapidly among men and women, when Islam is publicly insulted and attacked in newspapers, reviews, in various books and even in schoolbooks, and when some would-be Muslims

[54] Mehmed Handžić, *Tumačenje šeriatsko-pravnih pitanja kod nas—odgovor na istoimeni članak g. F. Spahe*, Sarajevo: Štamparija J. Karić, 1939; reprinted in E. Duraković (ed.), *Mehmed Handžić*, III, pp. 191–235. The Yugoslav authorities banned this brochure.

[55] Abdulah Ajni Bušatlić, *Pitanje muslimanskog napredka u Bosni i Hercegovini*, Sarajevo: Islamska dionička štamparija, 1928; reprinted in E. Karić (ed.), *Bosanske muslimanske rasprave,* booklet V, pp. 85–120, here p. 94.

[56] Ibid., p. 96.

[57] "Uvodnik", *el-Hidaje,* I, 1 (1937–1938), pp. 2–3; quoted in E. Karić, "Časopis 'el-Hidaje'", p. 426.

undermine the basic tenets of the true Islam with their articles and books".[58] More generally, revivalist *'ulama* maintained that the *ilmiyya* "is closest to its people . . . and has grown with it".[59] They also insisted that the secular intellectuals did not have the right "to rummage around in Islamic upbringing and religious education",[60] and criticised them for trying "to introduce into [Islam] some Western points of view which they like, allegedly in order to reconcile Islam with the so-called sound legacy of the West".[61]

This last quotation reveals that, in Bosnia-Herzegovina as elsewhere in the Muslim world, what was finally at stake was the definition of the relationship between "Islam" and the "West", perceived as two distinct and homogeneous civilisations.[62] Reformists were eager to "connect the treasury of Islam with the material treasury of the Western school, which represents knowledge and technique", in order "to reach a happy life in both worlds".[63] They warned that:

> The world is going ahead, and if we do not conform to the spirit of the time, we will be run over. We often lay dormant in the past, and we have now to stop doing that. While we were seeking help from *turbets* [tombs of holy men], from dead people, while we were expecting that the Caliphs and the Caliphate would protect our faith, others . . . dug the mountains, entered into the earth's core, extracted ore, exploited the forests and got rich.[64]

To support such arguments, authors like Čaušević not only referred to Japan and Turkey as examples of the successful appropriation of Western science and culture, but were sometimes tempted to

[58] Mehmed Handžić, "Uloga uleme u narodu (govor održan na skupštini 'el-Hidaje')", *el-Hidaje*, I, 2 (1937–1938), pp. 20–23; reprinted in E. Duraković (ed.), *Mehmed Handžić*, pp. 46–53, here pp. 49–50.

[59] "Uvodnik", *el-Hidaje*, I, 1 (1937–1938).

[60] [Ibrahim Hakki Čokić], "Na rabotu reformaša", *Hikjmet*, III, 25 (1931), p. 29; quoted in A. Jahić, *Hikjmet*, p. 124

[61] [Ibrahim Hakki Čokić] "Na namjerno uvredljive izraze", *Hikjmet*, III, 23–24 (1931), pp. 374–7; quoted in ibid., p. 128.

[62] A. Salvatore, *Islam*, esp. pp. 67–96.

[63] Džemaludin Čaušević *et al.*, "Braćo Muslimani!", *Novi Behar*, I, 1 (1927–1928), pp. 1–2; reprinted in E. Karić and M. Demirović (eds), *Džemaludin Čaušević*, II, pp. 166–9, here p. 168.

[64] Džemaludin Čaušević, "Kur'an i Muslimani", *Novi Behar*, VIII, 11–14 (1933–1934), pp. 161–2; reprinted in ibid., II, pp. 194–6, here p. 195.

depict Westerners as "better Muslims" than the Muslims themselves: "The Qur'an says: 'Obey, learn and see how the past nations ended'. English, German and other people conform to this commandment. And what about us? We Muslims are learning the Qur'an, we are listening to the Qur'an, we are doing good deeds (*sevap*) and are praying for the dead, but we do not care about its commandments, especially not about those which require sacrifice, effort and work".[65]

Admittedly, Čaušević himself was aware that "the hate which has been fed in the Middle Ages against Islam and Muslims has not yet completely disappeared".[66] However, he considered that the Crusades belonged to the past, that the biggest threat for Muslims was not Western science or dress code, but their own passivity and ignorance, and that "it is due to the Qur'an, as a great divine miracle (*mu'džiza*), that Muslims have today their mosques in London, in Paris, in Berlin and in other places".[67]

Revivalists, on the contrary, insisted much more on the differences or even the incompatibility between Islamic and Western civilisations, the latter perceived as "materialistic" and "corrupt". Handžić, for example, deplored the ongoing "Westernisation" of Bosnian society:

> Under the influence of the West and of corrupt times, [men and women] have started to go together to the cinema, to the theatre, to the cafés and to other places, to take part in various excursions far away from the cities and, in some perverted cases, to have intimate intercourse which they do not consider as an evil since they will get engaged and married later on. . . . Even in the decent and useful gatherings which have a religious character, the consumption of alcoholic drinks is becoming more and more frequent.[68]

65 Džemaludin Čaušević, "Vjera", in *Gajretova predavanja*, Sarajevo: Gajret, n.d.; reprinted in ibid., II, pp. 313–20, here p. 319. The editors do not provide original page numbers.

66 Džemaludin Čaušević, "Božje svjetlo ne može nitko ugasiti", *Kalendar Narodne uzdanice*, II (1934), pp. 17–21; reprinted in ibid., II, pp. 209–13, here p. 211.

67 Džemaludin Čaušević, "Džamija (Džamiun)", *Kalendar Narodne uzdanice*, V (1937), pp. 113–19; reprinted in ibid., II, pp. 214–19, here p. 218.

68 Mehmed Handžić, "Ružni običaji u vezi s ženidbom", in Glavni odbor 'el-Hidaje', *Islamski obiteljski život*, Sarajevo: el-Hidaje, 1942, pp. 23–5; reprinted in E. Duraković (ed.), *Mehmed Handžić*, III, pp. 244–5.

Handžić also stressed the superiority of the Islamic classical age over the "twentieth century, the century of tolerance, as Europeans call it",[69] and criticised Western Europe for its lasting hostility toward Islam: "When the Turks slaughter the Armenians, all European newspapers write about Turkish savagery, barbarity and crimes. But when the Balkan Christians massacre Muslims in Rumelia [the European part of the Ottoman Empire], the same newspapers call this heroism, bravery and liberation".[70]

Bosnian Muslim elites and the challenge of being Muslim in Europe

The debates taking place within the Bosnian Muslim community were reminiscent of those in the Muslim world in general, but took place in the particular context of the post-Ottoman Balkans. Already in 1893 Mehmed-beg Kapetanović Ljubušak contrasted the benevolent attitude of Austro-Hungary towards Bosnian Muslims with that of the new Balkan states and the European colonial powers:

> Until now it had never happened that more than half a million Muslims were living with full freedom under the protection of a Christian ruler, as we are doing happily in our dear homeland. . . Austro-Hungary did not proceed [as Serbia, Bulgaria and Montenegro did in 1878] and it will never do that, provided that we remain loyal and devoted to it, but it behaved as a cultured and powerful state. Soon after crossing the Sava [river], it bestowed . . . on all of us the equality of rights, it granted a complete civic and religious freedom which the followers of all confessions are still enjoying today.[71]

Considering *hijra* as unnecessary and harmful, Kapetanović reminded his fellow citizens that "we are living in the nineteenth century in the middle of Europe",[72] and that "it is better to learn in the *gimnazija* than to go to Asia" ("*bolje učiti u gimnaziju nego ići u Aziju*").[73]

[69] Mehmed Handžić, "Položaj nemuslimana u muslimanskoj državi (s upoređenjem sa nekim današnjim prilikama)", *el-Hidaje*, IV, 9–11 (1940–1941), pp. 234–49; reprinted in ibid., pp. 265–91, here p. 268.

[70] Ibid., pp. 273–4.

[71] Mehmed-beg Kapetanović Ljubušak, *Budućnost ili napredak muhamedovaca u Bosni i Hercegovini*, Sarajevo: Tiskara Spindlera i Löschnera, 1893; reprinted in E. Karić (ed.), *Bosanske muslimanske rasprave*, booklet I, pp. 83–107, here pp. 86–7.

[72] Ibid., p. 93.

[73] Ibid., p. 98.

The awareness of living in Europe, and in a regional environment that was potentially hostile to the very presence of Islam, was also manifest in the inter-war period. In an interview in 1919 with the French journalist Charles Rivet, Čaušević deplored that "the hidden hostility of our Orthodox neighbours has turned into open hate, unfortunately with the approval of the [Serb] occupation authorities".[74] Fourteen years later, he mentioned that "we Muslims of the Kingdom of Yugoslavia have people on the right side and on the left side [i.e., Serbs and Croats] who should perceive us as their brothers, but it is unfortunately not the case".[75] This situation explains why the Bosnian Muslim elites reproduced the "neo-*millet*" strategy set up during the Austro-Hungarian period, bargaining their allegiance to the Yugoslav state for physical security and religious freedom. With the exception of some intellectuals, their support for the Yugoslav idea was mainly a tactical one. The insistence on a South-Slav background shared with Serbs and Croats was a way of distancing oneself from the Ottoman past, of avoiding an exclusive identification with the Serb or Croat national identity and of playing a leading role within the Yugoslav *Islamska vjerska zajednica*. The public statements of the Bosnian *'ulama* were also part of this strategy. In 1919, for example, Čaušević said: "We can still bear the injustice that [the Serbs] govern without us but, for God's sake, they have at least to respect our lives, our honour and our goods".[76] Similarly, on the eve of the Second World War, in a resolution protesting against the turning of mosques into Orthodox churches in Southern Serbia (Kosovo and Macedonia), the *el-Hidaje* Association reminded the state authorities that Yugoslav Muslims "have never endangered the religious peace or the state and national interests. They are fulfilling their civic duties without reservation and have always done so".[77]

[74] Interview published in *Le Temps* (1 April 1919), and reprinted in E. Karić and M. Demirović (eds), *Džemaludin Čaušević*, I, pp. 271–3, here p. 272.

[75] Džemaludin Čaušević, "Neka nam je Kur'an vodič!", *Islamski svijet*, II, 31 (1933), p. 9; reprinted in ibid., II, p. 225.

[76] Interview published in *Le Temps* (1 April 1919), p. 273.

[77] The resolution was quoted extensively in M. Handžić, "Položaj", pp. 288–91, here p. 288.

Moreover, the geopolitical situation of Bosnia-Herzegovina influenced the attitude of Bosnian Muslim elites toward the issue of the Caliphate. In the Austro-Hungarian period, some reformists such as Osman Nuri Hadžić, Džemaludin Čaušević and Fehim Spaho perceived pan-Islamism as a way to free Islam from its Ottoman distortions and to reopen the "gates of *ijtihad*". After the abolition of the Ottoman Caliphate by Mustafa Kemal in 1924—a move welcomed by some intellectuals but deplored by the '*ulama*—, the JMO and the Islamic religious institutions supported the project of a Caliphate exercising purely religious functions, and thus not infringing on the sovereignty of the Yugoslav state.[78] Yugoslav Muslims were not allowed to participate in the General Islamic Congress for the Caliphate in Cairo (1926), but a delegation of Muslim politicians and '*ulama* did attend the General Islamic Congress in Jerusalem (1931) and the European Muslim Congress in Geneva (1935). In the meantime, however, the hope of restoring the Caliphate had vanished, and the Muslim Congresses had turned into anti-colonial and anti-reformist forums.[79] In the absence of a legitimate religious authority for the whole *umma* (community of the Faithful), reformists and revivalists were once again opposed to each other over the possibility of resorting to *ijtihad* in Bosnia-Herzegovina. Ali Riza Karabeg, for example, considered that "one cannot expect '*ijtihad*' from other nations [than the Arabs], and especially not from us in Bosnia", since "the minimal conditions for this are, among others, a perfect and active knowledge of the Arabic language and a comprehensive knowledge of the Qur'an and the *hadiths*, and it is clear that this does not exist among us".[80] Fehim Spaho, on the contrary, opposed Mehmed Handžić's rejection of usury in the following terms:

> The same Shari'a rule can be implemented differently in different places, depending on the customs existing in these places. . . . Was it necessary and

[78] In its programme, the JMO demanded that "our link with the Caliphate is granted and that it is organised in such a way that we have the same free links as the Catholics have with the Holy See" (see "Program JMO", reprinted in A. Purivatra, *Jugoslovenska muslimanska organizacija*, pp. 418–20, here p. 418).

[79] M. Kramer, *Islam Assembled*; F. Karčić, *Društveno-pravni aspekti*, pp. 228.

[80] A.R. Karabeg, *Rasprava*, p. 74.

timely, precisely here at the periphery of Islam, where we are fighting for our economic survival, was it appropriate to raise this question [of usury] which time has solved for so long? Can the discussion of such outdated questions bring anything else but trouble?[81]

The inter-war period and the origins of Bosniak nationalism

Enes Karić, one of the leading intellectual figures of the *Islamska zajedmica*, rightly notes that "as numerous treatises and debates by Muslim intellectuals during the first half of the twentieth century show, all that remained for them was the issues of dress, old graveyards, *waqf*s and the decline of the Caliphate", and that "those Muslim intellectuals who did discuss questions relating to state and nation were few and far between".[82] But his statement that "[instead] there should have been debates about the state as an institution of security"[83] is an *a posteriori* reconstruction and hinders a proper understanding of the links existing between the religious debates of the inter-war period, the impact of political and cultural Westernisation on Bosnian society and the crystallisation of a modern national identity among Bosnian Muslims.

As Karić himself acknowledges, "the debate about dress was . . . in a sense a debate about the community's security and survival".[84] This means that the clashes between Islamic reformists and revivalists about the adoption of Western dress codes, the role of women in public life and the reform of religious institutions also reflected deeper disagreements on the best way to ensure the long-term survival of the Bosnian Muslim community. Čaušević, for example, encouraged Bosnian Muslims to emulate their non-Muslim fellow citizens: "The Catholics, the Orthodox and the Jews take care—and this very aptly—of the education of their youth, of assistance to their poor, but we Muslims stay motionless, as we would sleep in the Arabian Peninsula, and not find ourselves in this corner of

81 F. Spaho, "Tumačenje", p. 348.

82 Enes Karić, "Islamic Thought in Bosnia-Herzegovina in the 20th Century: Debates on Revival and Reform", *Islamic Studies*, XLI, 3 (2002), pp. 391–444, here p. 393.

83 Ibid.

84 Ibid.

Europe".[85] In his eyes, "if the Islamic community wants the continuing existence [*opstanak*] of Islam in this region, it has to take care of the education of the future [generations of] Muslims"[86] and, more generally, to acquire "all that the other communities have to ensure their conditions of existence".[87] Revivalists, for their part, put a much stronger emphasis on the preservation of Islamic values and symbols, claiming that "we do not want to disappear as Muslims, we do not want to get assimilated into others and the like",[88] and suggesting for example that Muslim female workers be employed in separate workshops in which they could "be employed in the best possible moral and material conditions".[89] While reformists stressed the necessity of keeping pace with the other ethno-religious communities of Bosnia-Herzegovina, revivalists were preoccupied with the maintenance of ethno-religious boundaries.

This difference between reformists and revivalists, which was neither clear-cut nor stable, reflected in part their attitude toward the issue of the "nationalisation" of Bosnian Muslims. As already stated, many intellectuals identified themselves as Croats or Serbs and therefore perceived the veil and the *fes* (fez) as obstacles to the "nationalisation" of the Muslim masses. Dževad-beg Sulejmanpašić, for example, wrote: "The *fes* is one of the social dividing lines between us and our national brothers of another confession. Wearing the *fes* as a compulsory religious uniform constantly emphasises our social isolation, and represents a permanent obstacle to the reinforcement of our national consciousness".[90] Some '*ulama* took

[85] Dž. Čaušević, "Božje svjetlo", p. 213.

[86] Džemaludin Čaušević, "Iman, Islam", *Novi Behar,* VI, 19–20 (1932–1933), pp. 253–4; reprinted in E. Karić and M. Demirović (eds), *Džemaludin Čaušević,* II, pp. 188–90, here p. 190.

[87] Dž. Čaušević, "Kur'an i Muslimani", pp. 194–5.

[88] Ibrahim Hakki Čokić, *O teset-turu (pokrivanju muslimanki)*, Tuzla: Štamparija Petrović, 1928, p. 31; quoted in A. Jahić, *Hikjmet*, p. 31.

[89] Programme of the Association *"el-Hidaje"*, p. 423.

[90] Dževad-beg Sulejmanpašić, "Za šešir i protiv fesa", *Jugoslovenski list* (October 1925); quoted in Dževad-beg Sulejmanpašić, *Slobodna misao i hikmetovština. Dva gledanja na naše muslimanske verske i socijalne probleme*, Zagreb: Štamparija Gaj, 1933, p. 96; reprinted in A. Isaković (ed.), *O "nacionaliziranju" Muslimana*, pp. 80–3, here p. 80.

a similar stance. In his brochure defending the unveiling of women, for example, Abdulah Bušatlić encouraged "the nationalisation of our people [*naš svijet*] as an indigenous element in these provinces, with the aim of introducing it into the circle of civilised people dedicated to their own wellbeing and progress in their national fatherland".[91] Most '*ulama*, however, agreed that "the purity of our language is a proof of which nation and community we belong to", and that "we are pure Yugoslavs by our blood".[92] But they were anxious to preserve the symbolic boundaries of their community. Consequently, in its *taqrir*, the "Curia" condemned any attempt at adopting non-Islamic dress codes for the sake of "fashion, custom or even the wish for unification with our brothers by blood and language".[93]

Once again, historical circumstances played an important role in the evolution of this debate on the "nationalisation" of Bosnian Muslims. The 1930s were not only marked by increasing inter-ethnic tensions at the political level but also—paradoxically enough—by the disappearance of some ethno-religious boundaries in everyday life. Against this background, revivalist '*ulama* insisted more and more on "the importance of external symbols"[94] and condemned syncretic practices as well as attendance at non-Muslim ceremonies (weddings, burials, etc.). In addition, both reformist and revivalist '*ulama* condemned materialistic ideologies such as Communism and new cultural trends such as the spread of Western fashion and mixed marriages in urban centres. In 1939, the *Ulema medžlis* denounced Muslim women who uncovered and dressed their hair,[95] and Mehmed Handžić and Fehim Spaho agreed that mixed marriages should be forbidden for both Muslim men and women in Bosnia-Herzegovina (whereas the Shari'a allows the

[91] A.A. Bušatlić, *Pitanje*, p. 99.

[92] Chameran [Ibrahim Hakki Čokić], "Hamiš 'Odgovoru Ilmije'", *Hikjmet*, IV, 46 (1933), pp. 309–10; quoted in A. Jahić, *Hikjmet*, p. 94.

[93] Islamska izborna kurija, *Takrir*, p. 344 (translated from the German version).

[94] Mehmed Handžić, "Važnost vanjskih znakova sa šerijatskog gledišta", *el-Hidaje*, III, 6–7 (1939–1940), pp. 80–2; reprinted in E. Duraković (ed.), *Mehmed Handžić*, V, pp. 249–55.

[95] Muhamed Pašić, "Tražena fetva", *el-Hidaje*, III, 10–11 (1939–1940), pp. 133–4; quoted in F. Karčić, *Društveno-pravni aspekti*, p. 223.

marriage of a Muslim man with a non-Muslim woman). Handžić stated that "one has to differentiate between Muslims living in an Islamic state and Muslims living in an environment where non-Muslims are in a majority",[96] while Spaho considered that "in this exposed place, where we are living with so many other faiths and where the use of Shari'a rules is too limited, mixed marriages are a threat which endangers our family life and thus our complete future as followers of Islam".[97]

Finally, the influence of historical circumstances is obvious in the attitude of the intellectuals and *'ulama* towards the issue of nationalism. At the end of the nineteenth and the beginning of the twentieth century, both Serb and Croat nationalisms were able to embody the hopes of the Bosnian Muslim intelligentsia, and this explains why, in 1914, intellectuals such as Šerif Arnautović or Šukrija Kurtović supported Serbia against the Austro-Hungarian Empire. Similarly, in the 1920s, "Yugoslavism" represented a framework within which the Bosnian Muslim elites could reproduce their "neo-*millet*" strategy, while remaining ambiguous about their national affiliation. Čaušević's attitude toward patriotism and nationalism is characteristic of this period. On the one hand, he combined religious with linguistic solidarity in order to legitimise a specific feeling of togetherness among Bosnian Muslims:

> God tells us that Muslims are only brothers and that, as such, they have to work together for the good of their religious community. . . . But there is also a brotherhood by homeland and language. Whoever is living with us in our homeland and is speaking our language is our brother, even if he is not a Muslim. But in any case the links are stronger with the Muslims who are together with us in our homeland.[98]

[96] Mehmed Handžić, "Mišljenja islamskih učenjaka koji su bili protiv mješovitih brakova", *Novi Behar*, XII, 1–4 (1938–1939), pp. 14–17 and XII, 5–6 (1938–1939), pp. 55–8; reprinted in Rijaset Islamske zajednice, *Mješoviti brakovi*, Sarajevo: Biblioteka glasnika IZ, 1996, pp. 23–44, here p. 23.

[97] Fehim Spaho, "Mješoviti brakovi", *Glasnik IVZ*, VI, 1 (1938), pp. 1–10; reprinted in Rijaset Islamske zajednice, *Mješoviti brakovi*, pp. 7–22, here p. 8. It is interesting to note that, in this peculiar case, Handžić agreed with Spaho on the need to adapt the Shari'a to specific local circumstances.

[98] Džemaludin Čaušević, "Međusobno se potpomažite u dobrim i pobožnim djelima", *Novi Behar*, VIII, 1–2 (1933–1934), pp. 1–2; reprinted in E. Karić and M. Demirović (eds), *Džemaludin Čaušević*, II, pp. 191–3, here p. 192.

On the other hand, he was anxious to ensure the religious neutrality of the state, to distinguish religious from national identity and to preserve his own neutrality with regard to the national question:

> There are in our state Croats and Serbs who are closely following their Islamic faith, and this has to be taken into account. I am firmly convinced that the most accurate solution is that neither the Catholics nor the Orthodox link their Croat or Serb identity with their religious feelings, since it causes a great confusion among those Croats who are not Catholics and those Serbs who are not Orthodox.[99]

This attitude, however, became less and less tenable in the political context of the 1930s. It is thus not surprising that Mehmed Handžić, the leading figure of Islamic revivalism in Bosnia-Herzegovina, was also the one who laid the foundations of contemporary Bosniak (Bosnian Muslim) nationalism.[100] On the one hand, he borrowed from works written during the Austro-Hungarian period by authors such as Franjo Rački (1828–94), Ćiro Truhelka (1865–1942) and Safvet-beg Bašagić (1870–1934) the idea that the Islamisation of Bosnia-Herzegovina resulted from a massive conversion of Bosnian Bogomils[101] and that the literature published in Oriental languages during the Ottoman period represented a first manifestation of Bosnian cultural identity.[102] On

[99] Džemaludin Čaušević, "Nacija i vjera", *Novi Behar*, IX, 1–3 (1935–1936), pp. 1–2; reprinted in ibid., pp. 377–80, here p. 379.

[100] On the link between revivalism and nationalism, see Antony Smith, "La 'légitimation dualiste'".

[101] Mehmed Handžić, *Islamizacija Bosne i Hercegovine i porijeklo bosanskohercegovačkih Muslimana*, Sarajevo: el-Hidaje, 1940; reprinted in E. Duraković (ed.), *Mehmed Handžić*, I, pp. 7–46. Bogomilism was a Christian heresy present in the medieval Balkans. The Croatian historian Franjo Rački was the first to state that the Bosnian Church (*bosanska crkva*) which existed in medieval Bosnia was linked to Bogomilism, and that its repression by the Orthodox and Catholic Churches explained the massive conversion of Bosnians to Islam. This thesis has been refuted by more recent academic works on the Bosnian Church and the Islamisation process in Bosnia-Herzegovina (see e.g. John Fine, *The Bosnian Church: A New Interpretation*, New York: Columbia University Press, 1975).

[102] Mehmed Handžić, *Rad bosanskohercegovačkih Muslimana na književnom polju*, *Glasnik IVZ*, I, 1 (1933), pp. 15–22; I, 2, pp. 22–27; I, 3, pp. 22–29; I, 6, pp. 20–25; I, 7, pp. 11–16; I, 8, pp. 19–26; I, 9, pp. 25–32; I, 10, pp. 16–20; I, 11, pp. 10–18; I, 12, pp. 14–18; reprinted in ibid., II, pp. 308–451.

the other hand, he stated that Islam was compatible with nationalism, promoted a definition of nation (*narod*) close to the German definition of *Volk* and, more specifically, introduced a new notion of *bošnjaštvo* which applied solely to the Bosnian Muslim community. In a speech given in 1940, shortly after the Cvetković-Maček agreement (i.e. the division of Yugoslavia into several provinces in August 1939), he claimed that:

> Islam has reinforced the innate patriotism of the Bosniaks [*Bošnjaci*] and they have become in this way the most patriotic element of this country and almost the only element which sincerely perceives Bosnia-Herzegovina as his native soil. Almost nobody perceives Bosnia-Herzegovina as his homeland in the same way as the Muslims of Bosnia-Herzegovina do, and this is the reason why, when it comes to the interests of our homeland, almost nobody strives [to defend them] but the Muslims of Bosnia-Herzegovina.[103]

In December 1939, the creation of the Movement for the Autonomy of Bosnia-Herzegovina was the specific manifestation of this nascent Bosniak nationalism, just as the movement for religious and educational autonomy had been the first collective expression of the "neo-*millet*" strategy during the Austro-Hungarian period.[104] One could argue that, while playing a leading role in the autonomy movement, Handžić was also supporting the pan-Islamist organisation *Mladi Muslimani* (Young Muslims), which dreamed of "a great Islamic state which would count more than 400 million inhabitants belonging to the most diverse races and nations".[105] But,

103 Mehmed Handžić, "Patriotizam, narodnost i nacionalizam sa islamskog gledišta", *el-Hidaje*, V, 1 (1941–1942), pp. 7–16; reprinted in ibid., III, pp. 323–39, here p. 331.

104 On the autonomy movement during the Second World War, see Enver Redžić, *Muslimansko automaštvo i 13. SS divizija. Autonomija Bosne i Hercegovine i Hitlerov Treći Rajh*, Sarajevo: Svjetlost, 1987; Rasim Hurem, "Pokušaj nekih građanskih muslimanskih političara da Bosnu i Hercegovinu izdvoje iz okvira Nezavisne Države Hrvatske", *Godišnjak društva istoričara Bosne i Hercegovine*, XVI (1965), pp. 191–221; Rasim Hurem, "Koncepcije nekih muslimanskih građanskih političara o položaju Bosne i Hercegovine u vremenu od sredine 1943. do kraja 1944. godine", *Prilozi instituta za historiju radničkog pokreta*, IV, 4 (1968), pp. 533–48. On Mehmed Handžić's political activities during the same period, see Udruženje Uleme "el-Hidaje", *Zbornik radova*.

105 Mladi Musliman, medicine student [Tarik Muftić], "Kompromisni islam i kompromisni Muslimani", *el-Hidaje*, VI, 4 (1942), pp. 91–96, here p. 92.

in Bosnia-Herzegovina as elsewhere, political pan-Islamism was nothing but a form of proto-nationalism,[106] as illustrated by the hostility of the "Young Muslims" to the "Yugoslav" idea during and after the Second World War, their interest in the creation of Pakistan and—last but not least—their role in the founding of the Party of Democratic Action (*Stranka demokratske akcije*, SDA) and the renewal of Bosniak nationalism in the 1990s.[107]

Bosnian Muslims had been separated from the Ottoman Empire in 1878, a few decades earlier than the Muslims of Sanjak, Kosovo, Macedonia and Albania. It is therefore logical that, in Bosnia-Herzegovina, the rise of Islamic reformism occurred before the First World War. Nevertheless, for the Bosnian Muslims the inter-war period represents not only a period of rupture and crisis, with the demise of the Ottoman Empire and its replacement by Kemalist Turkey, but also the incorporation of Bosnia-Herzegovina within the Kingdom of Serbs, Croats and Slovenes. Against this background, it is clear that, although apparently limited to the issues of dress, graveyards, *waqf*s and the Caliphate, the religious debates of the inter-war period played a key role in the way Bosnian Muslim elites have positioned themselves towards European political modernity, which means, first of all, towards the nation-state.

106 Nikki Keddie, "Pan-islam as Proto-Nationalism", *Journal of Modern History*, XLI, 1 (1969), pp. 17–28.

107 Xavier Bougarel, "From Young Muslims to Party of Democratic Action: The Emergence of a Pan-Islamist Trend in Bosnia-Herzegovina", *Islamic Studies*, XXXVI, 2–3 (1997), pp. 533–49.

THE MUSLIM MINORITY IN MACEDONIA AND ITS EDUCATIONAL INSTITUTIONS DURING THE INTER-WAR PERIOD

Muhammed Aruçi

After the First World War when the Kingdom of Yugoslavia (Kingdom of Serbs, Croats and Slovenes, Kraljevina SHS) was founded, many Muslims living in that part of Macedonia which became incorporated into this new state emigrated to Turkey: especially the Turkish speaking population of Eastern Macedonia, but also an important proportion of the Turkish and Albanian speaking Muslims of Western Macedonia. Muslims in Macedonia, Kosovo, Sanjak and a part of Montenegro experienced profound and rapid political and administrative transformations when these former Ottoman lands were integrated first into Serbia (1912–13), then into the new kingdom (1918), later renamed the Kingdom of Yugoslavia. The first name of the new state—Kingdom of Serbs, Croats and Slovenes—shows clearly that sovereignty belonged to its non-Muslim populations. Moreover, in the new state Muslims were often considered as a "remnant" of the Ottoman Empire which had been sovereign for centuries in these regions, and they were regarded as an "enemy within". Having been first class citizens in the Ottoman Empire, they were now reduced to the status of a second class minority.[1]

In this chapter, we concentrate on the trends of thought present among the Muslim minorities in Macedonia in this new context, with particular reference to Skopje, the main city. We will focus on

[1] Muhammed Aruçi, "Eski Yugoslavya II", *Günümüz Dünyasında Müslüman Azınlıklar—III. Kutlu Doğum İlmî Toplantısı*, Istanbul: Türkiye Diyanet Vakfi—İslâm Araştırmaları Merkezi, 1998, pp. 175–6.

the question of education as one of the fields that best illustrate the different positions taken by leaders of the Muslim minority facing the new situation created by the collapse of the Ottoman Empire. Indeed, three different Muslim educational institutions were created in Skopje during the inter-war period; two of them were founded from the top and the third from the bottom.

THE TWO *MADRASAS* FOUNDED FROM THE TOP

During the inter-war period two schools were founded by the authorities in Skopje to educate Muslims. The first one—the Madrasa of King Alexander—was founded in 1924 by the Yugoslav political authorities. The second one was opened twelve years later by the Islamic religious authorities, mainly because the first institution was not considered appropriate for the training of religious officials.

The King Aleksander Madrasa or Great Madrasa (Velika Medresa)

With the end of Ottoman rule and the creation of the Kingdom of Yugoslavia, the new political authorities saw the need to open a "modern" and "advanced" school for the Muslims of Macedonia, Kosovo, Sanjak and Montenegro, which would be strongly linked to the state, as shown by its name of King Alexander Madrasa. Since the building was burnt down during the Second World War with all its archives, we have very little information about this institution. However, the work of Mustafa Memić provides an important reference on the subject.[2]

On 17 December 1921, an important Muslim Congress was organised in Skopje, which ended with the creation of a political party named *Jemiyet* (the "Society" or the "Assembly"), under the leadership of Ferhat Bey Draga, in order to defend the rights of the Muslim population of Southern Yugoslavia as a distinctive group. This new organisation was supported by Nikola Pašić, the head of the Serbian Radicals, and in the elections of 1920 the two parties campaigned together. In September 1923, a different group led by Hasan Rebac, Dr Ahmed Mehmedbašić and Derviš Tafro began to demand the opening of a "modern" *madrasa*. They operated totally outside the

[2] Mustafa Memić, *Velika Medresa i njeni učenici u revolucionarnom pokretu*, Skopje: IPZRO "Fonografika" Skopje, 1984.

framework of the principles adopted by *Jemiyet*, and they tried, with little success, to make Muslim public opinion accept, among other ideas, that Muslims were an inseparable part of Yugoslavia.[3]

As the Director of the Department of Religious Affairs, Hasan Rebac was in a position to facilitate the establishment of such a school. According to Dr Ahmed Mehmedbašić, who was chosen as the school's Director, the Muslims of Southern Yugoslavia were without proper education, and forced to rely on the classical *madrasa* system that, in his opinion, kept the Muslims of the region in a state of ignorance. So it is clear that one of the main objectives of the founders of this new school was to challenge the traditionalist *'ulama*. We know that the founders were also in conflict with the *Jugoslovenska muslimanska organizacija* (JMO), the Muslim political party of Bosnia and Herzegovina, about the political activity that this party should undertake in Southern Yugoslavia.

Following a decision by a commission of experts composed of Dr Vladimir Ćorović, the future rector of Belgrade University, Osman Nuri Hadžić and Abdulhafiz Džumhur, the curriculum was accepted and the school recognised as having the status of a secondary school. The authorisation for its opening was given by the King himself, on 28 April 1924, and in this document, the school is referred to as "the Great Madrasa of King Alexander the First in Skopje" (*Velika Medresa Kralja Aleksandra I u Skoplju*).[4] Although it was decided from the outset that the language of instruction in the school would be Turkish (as in all official Muslim schools during the Ottoman period), in practice the lessons were always given in Serbo-Croat (the official language of Yugoslavia). The King Alexander Madrasa was a boarding school, and the majority of the students had scholarships from the Yugoslav Ministry of National Education. Most of the teachers were Serbs.[5]

The aim of the "Great Madrasa" was to train religious officials for Southern Yugoslavia and provide the possibility for some of its

[3] Ibid., p. 15.

[4] Ibid., p. 21; *Službene Novine,* 148 (2 July 1924); Dragan Novaković, *Školstvo Islamske Zajednice: Školski sistem Islamske Zajednice na jugoslovenskim prostorima od 1878–1991 godine*, Niš: JUNIR, 2004, pp. 36–8.

[5] The teachers who taught at the *Velika Medresa* from the outset were Dr Pero Slijepčević, Svetomir Lazarević, Edo Štefan, Miloš Rakić, Vido Latković and Nasuf Gadžović.

graduates to continue their studies in various universities, like students of other secondary schools. The curriculum, which had been prepared to fulfil these objectives, was composed of three groups of courses. The first group comprised religious courses: Qur'an, Law (*fiqh*), Islamic dogma (*akaid*), introduction to Islamic sciences, Islamic inheritance Law (*faraiz*), Qur'an Commentary (*tafsir*), Tradition (*hadith*), and the history of Islam. However, these courses were to be taught only during two years of an eight-years programme, and they represented barely 11.5 per cent of the whole curriculum. The second group was composed of language courses (Serbo-Croat, French, Arabic, Turkish, German and Latin), but with more time allocated to Serbo-Croat courses than all other language courses together. The various language courses represented some 40 per cent of the curriculum. The third group was made up of courses that were found in the programmes of secular secondary schools (i.e. mathematics, history, geography, physical education, natural sciences, drawing, physics, chemistry, philosophy, hygiene, music), in addition to calligraphy, civil law and criminal law. These courses represented another 48.5 per cent of the whole curriculum.

The structure and content of the *madrasa*'s curriculum were totally different from those of the classical *madrasas*. According to its promoters, it aimed to train religious officials for a modern society according to a new educational system. On several occasions, the director explained this and stressed that religious officials trained by classical methods would not meet the needs of the new society.[6] However, because many teachers in the school were non-Muslims and because the Communist Party succeeded in attracting some of its students, the local population was suspicious of the new institution. Furthermore, the ratio of students from Macedonia—Turks or Albanians—was rather low and most of the students came from the Serbo-Croat speaking Muslim communities of Sanjak and Montenegro. Between 1925 and 1941, 187 students received their diplomas from the King Alexander Madrasa.[7]

[6] M. Memić, *Velika Medresa*, pp. 23–7; D. Novaković, *Školstvo Islamske zajednice*, pp. 36–8.

[7] Kasim Hadžić, "Velika Medresa i njeni učenici u Revolucionarnom Pokretu", *Takvim*, Sarajevo (1985), pp. 229–34; D. Novaković, *Školstvo Islamske zajednice*, p. 38.

The Isa Bey Madrasa

The Isa Bey Madrasa, which was named after one of the most ancient Ottoman *madrasas* in Skopje,[8] was very probably opened because the "Great Madrasa" fell short of the expectations of the Directorate of *Waqfs* (*Vakufska Direkcija*) and the Council of '*Ulama* (*Ulema Medžlis*), the two local bodies of the Islamic religious Community. There had been conflicts between the *Velika Medresa* and these two bodies whose members had come to realise that the graduates of the *Velika Medresa* were not suitable for them to employ as religious officials. Consequently, from 1932 onwards, a movement for the opening of a new *madrasa* began under the leadership of some reformists, and on 2 October 1936 the school officially opened, with Hamid Hadžibegić (a Bosnian Muslim born in Sarajevo in 1898, a teacher of Islamic Law at the *Velika Medresa*) as Director. During the opening ceremony, some representatives of the religious authorities from Sarajevo stood side by side with General Dr Hočivar, the King's representative.[9]

This school was also a boarding school. Its students had to perform the five daily prayers in the Gazi Isa Bey Mosque, next to the *madrasa*, and only the Friday prayer (*juma*) was performed in one of the other mosques in Skopje. Most of the students came from Sanjak, Kosovo and Montenegro, with only a few from Macedonia. In fact, the school was conceived as a religious school with the status of a secondary school. Its objective was to train a staff of religious officials for the region and some of its graduates were expected to continue their training in some religious universities in Yugoslavia or abroad.

The curriculum was constructed to achieve these aims and reflected the reformists' agenda. As in the *Velika Medresa* there were three groups of courses, but they differed because of the greater importance given to religious courses. The curriculum included Qur'an Commentary (*tafsir*), Tradition (*hadith*), Sources of Islamic Law (*usul al-fiqh*), Islamic Law (*fiqh*), Islamic Dogma (*aqaid*), Ethics (*ahlak*), History of Islam, calligraphy, Arabic and Turkish courses.

[8] Gliša Elezović, *Turski spomenici u Skoplju, Glasnik Skopskog Naučnog Društva*, I, Skopje, 1925, p. 135 and elsewhere.

[9] "Proslava otvaranja Gazi Isabegove centralne reformisane medrese i Vakufske Biblioteke u Skoplju", *Glasnik VIS*, 1 (1937), pp. 9–39.

Great importance was also given to the teaching of Serbo-Croat, the official language of the state. In addition, courses taught in secular secondary schools were also included in the curriculum: history, geography, mathematics, physics, chemistry, logic, psychology and pedagogy. French and German were the Western foreign languages taught.[10]

This curriculum did not provoke a negative reaction from the traditional '*ulama*, since it did not deviate from the classical type of Islamic education. Consequently, there was also no hostility from the Muslim population. Nevertheless, the Isa Bey Madrasa was short-lived. It was closed after the bombing of Skopje in April 1941 and throughout the Bulgarian occupation. It did not reopen until 1984, in the last years of the Communist regime.[11]

A *MADRASA* FOUNDED FROM THE BOTTOM

As well as the *Velika Medresa* and the *Isa Bey Medresa*, another *madrasa* functioned in Skopje during the inter-war period, but it is rarely mentioned. It was called the *Meddah Medresa*, because its founders revived a *madrasa* of the same name that had existed in Skopje during the Ottoman period.[12] It had a totally different character from the other two *madrasas*, because it was not created by a decision from the top and had a classical Islamic-Ottoman curriculum.

There are few documentary sources on the history of the *Meddah Medresa* during the inter-war period, and it is only through personal testimonies and the books and poems of former students that we can try to shed more light on this institution.

[10] Ibid., p. 31; Bahri Aliu, "Isa Begova medresa nekad i danas", *Islam u zapadnom svijetu*, Zagreb: Zagrebačka džamija/Islamski, 1997, pp. 55–65. Among the professors were Hacı Bedri Hamid, Hajri Šećeragić, Fettah Sulejmanpašić, Hafiz Ćamil Ibrahimović, Aški Sulejman, Hafiz Muzafer Sulejmanović, Nihat Adžemović, Nijaz Resulović, Sulejman Mašović.

[11] For more details, see Bahri Aliu, "Isa Begova medresa".

[12] On this Ottoman *madrasa*, see Gliša Elezović, *Turski spomenici*, pp. 136, 140; Salim Asim, *Üsküp tarihi ve civarı*, Skopje, 1932, pp. 9, 21; Ekrem Hakkı Ayverdi, *Avrupa'da Osmanlı mimârî eserleri—Yugoslavya*, III/3, Istanbul: Fetih Cemiyeti, 1981, pp. 247, 290, 291.

The Meddah Medresa

According to the testimony of students who are still alive, the *Meddah Medresa* was revived in 1923 or 1924, after the collapse of the Ottoman Empire.[13] Bekir Sadak, who belonged to the third intake of students to the *Meddah Medresa*, describes this institution as an "Islamic secondary school", and during the Bulgarian occupation (1941–44) it was defined in the same way. According to Sadak, the school was divided into three sections (primary, medium and high), Turkish was the language of instruction, and the curriculum was similar to the one found in the *madrasas* of Fatih, in Istanbul, with some additions.[14] According to Kemal Aruçi, also from the third intake of students, who enrolled at the *Meddah Medresa* in 1931 and received his diploma (*ijazet/ijaza*) in 1944, it took from twelve to thirteen years for a student to complete his studies at the school.[15] After the Second World War the diploma of the *Meddah Medresa* was recognised by the religious authorities as the equivalent of a secondary school diploma.[16]

We do not know exactly which subjects were taught in this school. In the classical way, the first classes of the programme included the study of different books, such as *Emsile*, *Binâ*, *Maksud*, *Merah*, *İzzî*, *Avâmil*, *Emâlî*, *Halebî-i Sagîr*, *Multekâ* and *Molla Jâmî* for Arabic grammar and Islamic Law (*fiqh*). In addition, there were many courses in logic (*mantık*), and parts of other books such as *Şemsiye* and *Fenârî*, the *Tasavvurat* and the *Tasdikat* for Law (*fiqh*) and logic (*mantık*) were studied.[17] The precise curriculum and the progression from one book to another was exclusively defined by the head teacher.[18]

The entrance qualification and the system of classes do not seem to have been constant. It is generally thought that there were about

[13] Aliriza Selmani-Hafiz Avni Aliu, *Myderriz Haki Efendiu 1914–1948*, Prishtina: Lidhja e Historianeve të Kosovës "Ali Hadri", 2005, pp. 37–42.

[14] Bekir Sadak, "Biz oralarda kalmalıydık", *el-Hilâl*, Skopje, IV, 22 (1990), p. 15.

[15] Muhammed Aruçi, *Kemal Efendi Aruçi—şiirlerim*, Skopje: Logos-A, 1999, pp. 30–1 and 60.

[16] *Starešinstvo na Islamska Verska zaednice vo NRM*, broj 287/66 , Skopje, 8 October 1966 (signed by the president, Hacı Bedri Hamid).

[17] Bekir Sadak, "Biz oralarda kalmalıydık", *el-Hilâl*, IV, 23 (1991), p. 15.

[18] Ibid.

"five intakes of students". From the first intake there were seven boys, one of whom quickly left in order to study at Al-Azhar University in Cairo.[19] The remaining six students, including Abdulfettah Rauf who became the assistant to the *madrasa*'s head teacher, graduated in 1933, and began to serve as religious officials in different places in Macedonia and Kosovo. Commenting on the graduation ceremony, Sadak wrote:

When I was in the second class, I was learning the Qur'an by heart, and in 1933, in seven months I had finished learning it. This same year, the *madrasa* produced its first graduates. The ceremony was to take place in the Mosque of Sultan Murad in Skopje. Already two days before, the streets filled up with '*ulama*, *shaikh*s and other guests coming from elsewhere. There was an atmosphere of feasting that had not been seen for many years. For the Muslims who were cut off from Ottoman rule and had been living under foreign rule since 1918, and even since 1914, this ceremony was very important. The ceremony began on *juma* (Friday) and a thousand persons had lunch and dinner in certain houses during three days. No one could remember such a wonderful ceremony in Skopje.[20]

There were nine students from the second intake, but we have no information about the date when they graduated. The six students of the third intake began their studies in the *madrasa* around 1931 and graduated in 1944.[21] There were also two other groups: the fourth one began its studies in 1938 and the fifth one year later, but we do not have further information about them. Some of the students left Skopje during the bombing of the city in 1944 and went to the village of the head teacher, twelve kilometres from Skopje, where the lessons continued for a short period. After the Second World War, the *madrasa* continued to function until

[19] This student was Şuayp Aziz. He was later one of the founders of the illegal organisation "Yücel" established in the years 1941–45, which fought for the religious and national freedom of the Turks of Macedonia. He was the cousin of Abdulfettah Rauf. Despite this, we were unable to find any information about whether or not there was a link between the *Meddah Medresa* and this organisation. See Mehmed Ardıcı, *Yücelciler 1947*, Istanbul, 1991; Muhammed Aruçi, "Fettah Efendi", *TDV İslam Ansiklopedisi*, XII, Istanbul, 1995, pp. 483–4.

[20] Bekir Sadak, "Biz oralarda kalmalıydık", *el-Hilâl*, IV, 22 (1990), p. 15.

[21] Bekir Sadak, "Biz oralarda kalmalıydık", *el-Hilâl*, IV, 23 (1991), p. 15.

the Yugoslav Communist authorities closed it down in April 1947.[22]

Most of the staff of the *madrasa* was generated by the school itself. As Bekir Sadak explains: "The *Meddah Medresa* had its own rules. Some of the senior students taught in the primary classes. [. . .] Before I got my diploma, I was in charge of preparation time and gave certain courses".[23] Even some of the graduates (Abdulfettah Rauf, Hafiz Shaban Efendi, Hafiz Nejati Efendi, Mehmet Efendi, Bekir Sadak and Kemal Aruçi) joined the staff of the *madrasa*, and it appears that no teachers were appointed from outside. The head teacher of the *madrasa* was Ataullah Kurtish.

Ataullah Kurtish

As we have already pointed out, the *Meddah Medresa* did not result from a decision taken from the top. The initiative to open such an institution in inter-war Skopje came from two *'ulama* who had been trained during the last years of Ottoman rule and who wanted to protect and preserve Ottoman culture and civilisation. The founders and leading figures of the *Meddah Medresa* were Ataullah Kurtish (also known under of the name of Atâ Efendi), who was the head teacher of the establishment (*başmüderris*), and his assistant and successor from 1938 onwards, Abdulfettah Rauf (or Fettah Efendi).[24]

Ataullah Kurtish was born in the village of Studeniçan, not far from Skopje, and studied in Istanbul. When the Ottoman Empire was abolished and the Republic of Turkey created, he came back to Skopje and revived the *Meddah Medresa* situated near the mausoleum of Yiğit Pasha. In Skopje and its surroundings he was known as Atâ Efendi or Atâ Hoja, while the students of the *madrasa* were called "*Atâ Hojalılar*" ("those of Atâ Hoja"), which had some conservative political connotations. In fact, we do not know much about his life (even his date of birth) or his education. In the

[22] The main personalities of the *madrasa* were tried and condemned (see "Fettah Rauf ve onun grupuna dahil Balistlerin yargılanması", *Birlik*, Skopje (1 October 1947), p. 4; B. Sadak, "Biz oralarda kalmalıydık", *el-Hilâl*, IV, 23 (1991), p. 15.

[23] Ibid.

[24] Bekir Sadak, "Biz oralarda kalmalıydık", *el-Hilâl,* IV, 26 (1991), p. 17.

madrasa he was the head teacher and taught Islamic Tradition (*hadith*) as well as Arabic.
The testimony of Bekir Sadak describes the man as follows:

> He was a reader, but not a writer. When he had to write, if he had a problem, he would call his student Fettah Efendi, explain the topic to him, draw the main outlines and even mention the sources and then give him the task of writing it. I had many occasions to be with him for a long time. We witnessed his dignity, and we tried to follow the example of his great humility towards people.[25]

He added:

> From him I learned only a part of *Buhârî*, and prosody and rhyme lessons as well. I easily understood the lessons, because his way of explaining was very clear and concise. He always dedicated the last minutes of the lesson to observations by the teacher. This was a way of bringing up the young men which involved education and training at the same time. The goal was to connect the knowledge he was giving to current events. His student Fettah Efendi had the same characteristics, but Atâ Efendi, as a typical dialectical combatant (*erkân-i harb*), tackled the problems at a general level and was more able to identify the main lines of attack and defence. In contrast, Fettah Efendi had a tendency to go into details. Atâ Efendi also had the ability to take the correct decisions during a crisis, without becoming involved in disputes.[26]

In 1936, because of a political conflict with the person administering the *waqf* (*mutawalli*), Ataullah Efendi was dismissed as head teacher. However, in 1938, he was appointed to the *Ulema Medžlis* (Council of '*Ulama*) in Skopje. His former student, Fettah Efendi, was then in charge of the *madrasa*. We know very little about the rest of his life, only that he died on the day of feasts (*bayram*) in 1948.

The Meddah Medresa*: a civil movement*

The *Meddah Medresa* was a private school which did not enjoy very harmonious relations with the state authorities. Above all, because of its classical method of teaching, the *madrasa* has been considered as a firm protector of the Ottoman tradition. After events such as

[25] Ibid.
[26] Ibid.

the end of the Ottoman rule in the Balkans and the suppression of the Caliphate, the *madrasa* represented a bastion of the Ottoman Islamic trend of thought in the region. In some Muslim circles, it was considered that the fight to preserve the Ottoman legacy had to be continued. In this respect, the *madrasa* was not only an educational institution, but also a stronghold of the Ottoman Islamic trend of thought.

The way of thinking that existed in this establishment and in the circles linked to it did not correspond to the ideology promoted by the local official Islamic authorities, i.e. the Council of '*Ulama* (the official leadership of the Muslim Community) and the Directorate of *Waqfs*, and this provoked tensions.[27] The Director of *Waqfs*, Hasan Rebac, who was one of the strong figures in the Belgrade government at that time (and whose wife was Dr Anica Savić, a Serb), played an important role. An intense dialogue took place between Ataullah Efendi, the founder of the *Meddah Medresa*, and Hasan Rebac which turned into a dispute and was reflected in newspapers such as *Naš Dom*.[28] The creation of the *madrasa* also provoked tensions between Ferhat Draga, the leader of the *Jemiyet* party, and Ataullah Kurtish.[29] Furthermore, the students of the "Great Madrasa" of King Alexander suspected Ataullah Efendi of being an opponent of the Republic of Turkey and its founder Mustafa Kemal Ataturk.[30]

At that time, under the terms of the Law for Religious Autonomy of 1930, all *waqfs* had to be supervised by the Directorate of *Waqfs*. However, the *Meddah Medresa*, the mosque and the *waqf* to which it was bound remained under the administration of an independent *mutawalli* (administrator). Because of a political misunderstanding between the head teacher and the *mutawalli*, the latter used his influence to dismiss Ataullah Efendi in 1936, as we have already seen. For a short period, the students left the *madrasa* to follow their teacher who rented a building in which he continued to teach them.[31]

[27] Bekir Sadak, "Biz oralarda kalmalıydık", *el-Hilâl*, IV, 22 (1990), p. 15.
[28] "Odgovor g. Ataullah Kurtiša g. Hasanu Rebcu", *Naš Dom*, Skopje, II, 15 (1939), pp. 1–2.
[29] M. Memić, *Velika Medresa,* p. 18.
[30] Ibid., p. 28.
[31] Bekir Sadak, "Biz oralarda kalmalıydık", *el-Hilâl*, IV, 23 (1991), p. 15. According to a poem written by Kemal Aruçi in September 1936, we understand that this event occurred in 1936 (M. Aruçi, *Kemal Efendi Aruçi*, pp. 86–7).

The official authorities were suspicious of the leaders of the *madrasa*. They believed that their teaching was opposed to the policies of the state. Indeed the ideal of the group linked to the *madrasa* was a return to Ottoman times. However, since the end of Ottoman rule and the abolition of the Caliphate, other solutions had been put forward. During the Second World War, when Hitler's Germany and Mussolini's Italy created a "Greater Albania",[32] people linked to the *Meddah Medresa* believed that it would offer an opportunity to return to the values of the Ottoman period. This belief that a "Greater Albania" could somehow replace Ottoman rule was widespread.[33] With the end of Yugoslav hegemony, many Muslims preferred to be placed under the sovereignty of a state with a Muslim majority. Because the Bulgarian occupation forces knew that the staff of the *Meddah Medresa* held such views, students of the *madrasa*, like Haki Efendi Hogoshti and Hafiz Suleyman Efendi Şehabi from Kalkandelen, were sent on visits to Italy or Germany, but we do not know what the Fascists promised them.[34] After 1945, when Tito came to power in Yugoslavia, these former students were arrested and executed, the *madrasa* was closed down and Ataullah Efendi and his students were harshly treated, some of them remaining in prison for many years.[35]

We can find evidence of the ideological orientation of the *Meddah Medresa* in poems written by some of its former students. '*Ulama* such as Abdulfettah Rauf and Kemal Aruçi composed verses expressing the sadness of the local Muslim population and its longing for the heritage of the Ottoman past and the lost fatherland. They tried to evoke with emotion themes such as the realisation of the "dreams of the Ottoman Caliphate" or "Great Albania", "salvation from slavery

[32] This "Greater Albania" included Albania, most of Kosovo and the Western part of Macedonia (Skopje being included in the Bulgarian occupation zone).

[33] Muhammed Aruçi, *Kemal Efendi Aruçi*, p. 225.

[34] Bekir Sadak, "Biz oralarda kalmalıydık", *el-Hilâl*, IV, 26 (1991), p. 17; "Shqiptarët duhet t'i kthehen vlerave të tyre shpirtërore", *Dituria Islame*, Prishtina, X, 61 (1994), p. 12.

[35] Later, some of the former students became scholars in Macedonia (Abdulfettah Rauf and Kemal Aruçi, because of their knowledge of Oriental languages, were employed in the National Historical Institute and in the Archives) or in Turkey (Bekir Sadak). See Muhammed Aruçi, "Fettah Efendi", *TDV İslam Ansiklopedisi*, XII, Istanbul, 1995, pp. 483–4; and the same, *Kemal Efendi Aruçi*.

under the Orthodox Panslavists" and "recovering the freedom which they had under Ottoman rule".[36]

The traditionalist movement, which was supported by the *Meddah Medresa* group, can also be seen as part of a broader Islamic movement found throughout the Muslim world, although it has to be analysed first at the local level. We know that Ataullah Efendi and Abdulfettah Rauf supported Mustafa Sabri Efendi, former Ottoman *Shaikh al-Islam*, who during his exile in Greece and later Egypt became one of the strongest opponents of Mustafa Kemal's Turkey. According to a personal testimony, when the latter had to leave Istanbul he came first to Skopje and was the guest of Ataullah Efendi in the *Meddah Medresa*.[37] Afterwards, Ataullah Efendi remained close to Mustafa Sabri and, with his students, he very carefully followed the dispute between Mustafa Sabri and the school of thought of Muhammad Abduh and Rashid Rida. One may see the dispute between the traditionalists and the modernists in Skopje as a kind of local continuation of the Egyptian debate. Moreover, on some religious topics, particularly the question of the hat, Ataullah Efendi asked Mustafa Sabri to issue a *fatwa* in order to defend the fez as Islamic headdress.[38]

We also know that the traditionalist '*ulama* were quite well informed about the *Ikhwan al-Muslimīn* (Muslim Brothers) and were filled with admiration for the movement. The Cairo journal *al-Fath* arrived in Skopje on a regular basis and was red by staff and students of the *Meddah Medresa*. However, because of the lack of sources, it is not possible to say exactly what kind of relations the *madrasa* had with the Egyptian movement. I personally witnessed how the '*ulama* of the *Meddah Medresa* nourished a great admiration of the Muslim Brothers, particularly of the ideas of Sayyid Qutb, but there is no evidence of an organic link between this group in Skopje and the Egyptian movement.

[36] Ibid.

[37] This information was confirmed to me by Mustafa Sabri's son, Ibrahim Sabri Bey, in Alexandria (Egypt) in 1977.

[38] This *fatwa* was written in Arabic. It was later translated into Turkish, but was never published. This topic was also the subject of a written debate between Ataullah Kurtish and Abdulhamit Efendi from Kičevo, a member of the *Ulema Medžlis*. The manuscript, 92 pages long, is in my own library.

WESTERNISATION AND REFORM VERSUS TRADITION

Focusing on the educational issues in the main city of Yugoslav Macedonia, Skopje, we have seen that three main trends of thought appeared among the local Muslims during the inter-war period: the "Westernist", the "reformist" and the "traditionalist". Each one supported its own *madrasa*, with its own teaching methods and curriculum. These ideological trends already existed before the collapse of the Ottoman Empire; however, the balance of forces was quite different in the inter-war period. From the perspective of the Westernist and reformist movements, the main difference between the post-war period and the pre-war years was that after the First World War their demands for Westernisation and reform were finally taken into account, since radical changes were introduced by the victors of the war and particularly by the leaders of the newly created Yugoslav Kingdom. Their demand for "Westernisation" and "reform" (*islah*) can be understood as an effort to transmit to the Muslim communities, totally or partially, the vision and ideals which were perceived as the dominant values of the main European countries. On the other side, a section of the intellectuals tried to maintain continuity with the Ottoman world view, and they had the support of the majority of the population.

Accepting or reacting to the new order

The end of Ottoman rule in Macedonia occurred in 1913, after the Balkan Wars. The Muslim population, however, including the '*ulama*, still considered themselves as part of the Ottoman state and found it very difficult to accept the new Kingdom of Yugoslavia and the new order it introduced. Muslims, who had enjoyed the status of first class citizens in the region, were now exposed to rapid changes under Serb, and then Yugoslav rule. Like Muslims elsewhere, the Muslims of Macedonia experienced important transformations from the end of the nineteenth century.

In such a context, the traditionalists of the region believed that the Ottoman state could recover and rule the Balkans again. It was only with the abolition of the Caliphate in 1924 that such political expectations were blighted, and the main goal shifted to the preservation of their way of life and their national-religious identity. This was particularly clear in the field of education. Ataullah Kurtish, one of the leaders of the traditionalists, founded the *Meddah Medresa* in order to ensure the continuation of the Ottoman system of education and in reaction to the establishment of the Madrasa of King Alexander, which he saw as reflecting Serbian hegemony in the Kingdom of Yugoslavia and the promotion of Western ideas. Whether this was actually the case or not, with the creation of the *Velika Medresa* the Yugoslav regime wanted to abolish the Ottoman system of religious education and, through its control over the new institution, ensure that it trained religious officials who would be loyal to the Kingdom.

As for the reformists, they were people who were at the point of intersection of two cultures. They were aware of the classical approach because they shared the same training as the traditionalists, but they did not despise the Western approach. Because of this openness, they tried to combine the two tendencies. Many were not absolute opponents of the West nor, in this particular case, of Yugoslav rule. Among the teaching staff of the *Isa Bey Medresa*, the main representatives of this school of thought inspired by the Islamists (*İslâmcılar*) of Turkey and the reformists of Egypt were Hamid Hadžibegić, Tajjib Okić and Bedri Hamid. Their *madrasa* was founded for the "training of *'ulama* capable of answering the needs of the modern era". Consequently, there was a thin line of demarcation between the demands of the Westernists for a "religion in harmony with the new life" and the attempt of the reformists to argue that it was possible to take many elements from the West while acting in accordance with Islamic prescriptions.

The questions debated, their social and political impact

The confrontation between these different trends was unavoidable. However, many persons involved in the debates generally did not take up their pens to make their point, and as a result most of the debates remained personal and verbal. However, occasionally journals published in Skopje, such as *Vardar* and *Naš Dom*, echoed the polemics, discussing at a scholarly level the position of the different actors involved.[39] It is especially difficult to follow the traditionalist

[39] The best example of this is the debate between Hasan Rebac and Ataullah Kurtish published in the journal *Naš Dom* ("Odgovor").

trend as these people were led by a large group of '*ulama* who were reluctant to participate in the debates in the periodical press. Consequently, we do not find much information about their ideas in the context of Westernisation, because there are few examples of their writings. The traditionalist tendency was represented by people who wanted to have a "classical" Islam as religious reference, and the traditional usages and customs of the Muslim population as social reference.

So far as we know, just as in the Muslim world as a whole, there were different topics of controversy, such as education, of course, but also religious duties, clothing and the veiling of women.

For instance, as already pointed out, there were disputes between the three trends concerning the *madrasa*s opened in Skopje and their curricula. The curriculum of the *Velika Medresa* provoked a big protest from the Council of '*Ulama* (*Ulema Medžlis*), where both the traditionalist and the reformist trends were represented. For some twenty years, the Ministry of National Education in Belgrade faced such objections. At the beginning, the curriculum of the school headed by Hasan Rebac was defended by the official authorities and was retained unchanged, but when Fehim Spaho, an important Muslim notable from Sarajevo, became Minister, the curriculum was changed in accordance with the wish of the reformists. On the other hand, as we have seen, Ataullah Kurtish opened the *Meddah Medresa* because of his opposition to the original curriculum of the *Velika Medresa*. However, even one of the founders of the *Velika Medresa*, Abdullah Hafiz Hacı Hüsman, is supposed to have publicly criticised the original curriculum of this institution, protesting that music and piano lessons had become more important than the religious courses.[40] The reformists, in fact, were found among those who decided to open the *Isa Bey Medresa*. They thought that the curriculum of the *Velika Medresa* could remain virtually unchanged, except that the religious courses had to be given greater prominence. Some years later, the curriculum of the *Isa Bey Medresa* was formulated according to these ideas. As for the traditionalists, they decided to go on in their own way, with the classical Ottoman curriculum of the *Meddah Medresa*.

[40] M. Memić, *Velika Medresa*, pp. 27–33.

Among the contentious subjects raised by the traditionalists were questions relating to the uniform worn by students of the *Velika Medresa*, their life style, their religious duties, and particularly their way of performing prayers (*namaz*). The fact that the students wore a cap or a hat instead of the fez was criticised both by reformists and traditionalists who, from time to time, even spoke of blasphemy. There were also protests because the students were not obliged to perform the five daily prayers, as the school authorities had not even allocated time for these prayers in the timetable, and because two classes were dedicated to music courses. The students of the *Velika Medresa* only performed the Friday prayer together, at the Gazi Isa Bey Mosque. Because of their criticisms, the traditionalists, with Ataullah Kurtish at their head, were accused of being the enemies of Turkey and opposed to the new Turkish Republic.[41] As for the reformists, they adopted the fez as part of the school uniform of their *madrasa*, the *Isa Bey Medresa*, and insisted that the students perform all the prayers together in the Gazi Isa Bey Mosque.

As in other parts of the Muslim world, the question of the emancipation of women was also hotly debated. Most of the teachers of the *Velika Medresa* were Serbs (and so Orthodox Christians), including Dr Anica Savić, Hasan Rebac's wife. The fact that the administrators and professors of this institution adopted a liberal position on the question of the veil was one of the reasons why they lost support among the local population. In contrast, the traditionalist '*ulama* obstinately defended the veil, even during the first years of the Communist regime after the Second World War, which led to some of them being imprisoned.[42]

CONCLUSION

The establishment of three educational institutions during the inter-war period, and the debates that took place between the different groups, reveal the different positions adopted by Muslim leaders with regard to the state and society.

[41] Ibid., pp. 27–8.

[42] *Makedonyada ferece ve peçenin izalesile ilgili faaliyetler çerçevesinde İslam camiasının yüksek din makamlarının karar, beyanat ve tamimleri*, Skopje: Makedonya Halk Cumhuriyeti Ulema Meclisi, 1951.

If we consider the relationship between the traditionalists and the reformists, we can see exactly the same difference of opinion that existed throughout the Muslim world. However, the views of the reformists, who often had strong connections with intellectual circles in Sarajevo, kept them apart from the local population of Macedonia and their religious leaders. Being mainly Muslims from Bosnia and Herzegovina, the reformists, who were the promoters of the *Isa Bey Medresa*, did not succeed in gaining much support in Macedonia during the inter-war period. The traditionalist '*ulama* were much closer to the people. Another reason for the failure of the reformists was the question of language. In their school and press they used Serbo-Croat, a language which was not adopted by most Muslims in Macedonia, whereas the traditionalists used Ottoman Turkish in their school and publications, a language which retained great social prestige among local Muslims during the inter-war period. However, the success of the traditionalists was mainly due to their grassroots action in the various mosques throughout Southern Yugoslavia.

Indeed, the "traditionalists" gave more importance to religious and emotional poetry, held regular religious discussions and gave sermons to the population in local mosques. They remained very close to large sections of the Muslim minority, far beyond the framework of the *Meddah Medresa* which was their main institution in the new educational field.[43] The impact of the *Velika Medresa* was quite different. It was not so important for Macedonia or Kosovo, since most of the students came from Sanjak and Montenegro. But for the Muslims of Yugoslavia in general, it played an important role in their future integration into Tito's Yugoslavia, since many of the students became senior figures in the Communist Party. After Tito's death one of them, Sinan Hasani (from Kosovo), even became head of the Council of the Yugoslav state Presidency. As for the reformist trend, its impact seems to have been less important among the Muslim population as its school institution was founded very late. Most of the teachers involved were Muslims from Bosnia-Herzegovina, and they went back to Bosnia at the beginning of the 1940s.

[43] This trend also played an important role in the Islamic revival in Macedonia in the 1980s.

THE TURKISH SPELLING MISTAKES EPISODE IN GREEK THRACE, JUNE 1929: BEYOND MODERNISTS VERSUS CONSERVATIVES*

Yannis Bonos

In the aftermath of the First World War, Europe was divided into a greater number of nation-states than before and, facing the rise of Communism and Fascism, was deeply troubled about the future of liberalism. On the other hand, a new Middle East was brought into being after the collapse of the Ottoman Empire and the abolition of the Caliphate. This region, composed of mandates, protectorates and independent states, was experiencing a number of attempts at modernisation and Islamic reformism.

Between these two areas, Greece and Turkey were trying to manage their Ottoman heritage and to go on with the process of nation-state building. First, the voluntary, but indirectly forced, migrations contributed to a certain extent to create homogenised populations in terms of religion and language. Then, the first compulsory population exchange marked a climax of the respective projects of Greece and Turkey, although some resistance occurred.

The issue of minorities, which arose during the war, was to be given special treatment by the European states during the inter-war period. Amidst the triumph of the principle of nationalities, the age of minorities was inaugurated by the newly-established League of Nations which sponsored the protection of minorities by a series of treaties.

* I am most grateful to Nathalie Clayer, for her helpful comments on drafts of this chapter.

In this sense, the case of "the Moslem inhabitants of Western Thrace"[1] was unique. Among all the minorities recognised by an international treaty at the end of the war, it was the only one whose status was defined by its own specific law (the Shari'a) and its own separate institutional organisation based on Islam within a state with an Orthodox Christian majority ruled by Roman law. At that time, an estimated 100,000 Muslims in Greek Thrace were living alongside "183,000 Orthodox Greek, 3,000 Orthodox Armenian speakers and 2,880 Spanish speaking Jews",[2] and next to Bulgaria and the "New Turkey" of Mustafa Kemal. Most of these Muslims spoke Turkish, but there was a small group of Pomaks speaking a Bulgarian dialect, and a tiny group of Gypsies speaking Roma.[3] Bilingualism was not uncommon but, of all these languages, only Turkish was written and taught together with Arabic. Meanwhile, Greek had been added to the curricula of some schools. The Lausanne Treaty (1923) gave the state the right to introduce the official language in minority schools while guaranteeing members of the minority the use of their mother tongue in every sector of public life such as press, justice, and education.

The aim of this chapter is to examine the emergence of the Turkish alphabet issue within this minority, in particular how the long-established use of Arabic script came to be challenged by the idea of

[1] According to the term used in the Art. 2 of the Convention Concerning the Exchange of Greek-Turkish Populations. However, the phrasing of Article 45 of the Section III, "Protection of Minorities", of Part I of the Lausanne Treaty is rather different. The latter stipulated that "the rights conferred by the provisions of the present Section to the non-Moslem minorities of Turkey will be similarly conferred by Greece on the Moslem minority in her territory". For a full text of the Convention and a reprint of the minority clauses, see Harry J. Psomiadis, *The Eastern Question: the Last Phase*, Salonica: Institut for Balkans Studies, 1968. Finally, the Greek translation of this article refers to the "Muslim minorities found in her territory", see *Praxeis pou ypografikan sti Lozanni stis 30 Ianouariou kai 24 Iouliou 1923*, Ypourgeio Exoterikon, Athens: Ethniko Typografeio, 1992, p. 21.

[2] According to the terms used in *Résultats statistiques du recensement de la population de la Grèce du 15–16 mai 1928*, Athens: Imprimerie Nationale, 1932, p. 254.

[3] According to the 1928 Greek census of population, in Thrace 84,585 Muslims spoke Turkish, 16,740 Bulgarian and only 845 Roma, see *Résultats statistiques*, p. 254. At that time, six hundred Roma-speaking people declared themselves Orthodox Christians.

replacing it with the Latin alphabet. By 1928, when the new Turkish alphabet was proclaimed in Ankara, new questions emerged within the minority in Greece about its spoken, written and taught languages. However, the "letters revolution" affected more the existing balances among the prominent people of the Muslim minority than the use of the Arabic script itself. As with most of the socio-cultural changes experienced in Turkey, the reform reached the minority but its formal rejection or application, as far as its leaders were concerned, depended on the complex local context and specific circumstances. The dominant view about this minority and its leaders during the inter-war period generally considers that the minority was divided into two main groups: the modernists (or progressives) and the conservatives (or traditionalists). This chapter is about the limitations of this view, and attempts to overcome it and achieve a better understanding of the discourses and acts of these notables.

In a way that owes much to an interview with Michel Foucault,[4] I will try to present a new interpretation of the arguments used by the two sides of the conflict and of the answers that were given by the minority authorities concerning the new Turkish alphabet issue.[5] More precisely, I will focus first on the polemic between two major minority newspapers on the issue, in order to re-examine the differences in the way of thinking of two editorialists representing two different camps. In parallel, I will examine how the Turkish alphabet issue turned into a political problem by considering the conditions that prevailed particularly during its emergence (the period August 1928—August 1929). Finally, I will concentrate on the key elements that constituted the solution provided by the minority leaders, without taking for granted the view that this minority's place was decided once and for all during the Lausanne negotiations. However, it is necessary at the outset to give some information concerning the minority institutions.

[4] "Polemics, Politics and Problematisations. An Interview with Michel Foucault", in Paul Rabinow (ed.), *The Foucault Reader*, New York: Pantheon, 1984, pp. 381–90.

[5] For a previous study of the question, see Kosti Tsioumi, "I stasi tis ellinikis kuvernisis sto zitima tis didaskalias tis latinikis grafis sta mousoulmanika skholeia kata tin teleftaia kuvernitiki thiteia tou Venizelou (1928–1932)", *Thrakiki Epetirida*, Komotini, X (1995–98), pp. 111–17.

MINORITY POLITICS: THE INSTITUTIONAL FRAMEWORK

At the end of the Greek-Turkish war, the Lausanne Treaty stipulated the exchange of populations between Turkey and Greece as well as the exemption of two groups: the Greek Orthodox of Istanbul and the Muslims of Western Thrace, who were considered as "established" (that is as non-exchangeable populations). For both of these groups, the Lausanne framework of protection was partially set up on the Ottoman "*millet* system", the pattern of social and political organisation for the Ottoman Empire's religious-linguistic communities. This communitarian religion-based model that was favoured contained special rights for the preservation of the social status and practices of minorities within the national majorities.

In the case of Muslims, it assured a certain kind of autonomy vis-à-vis the Christian majority and the policies of the Greek state.[6] Muslims were not only free to practice their religion, but also free to treat community affairs—such as education, and judicial questions relating mainly to family matters—through the organs of the minority's self-administration. The Greek laws that implemented the Lausanne stipulations created three posts of mufti (in Turkish *müftü*) and an equal number of "Muslim Communities" or "Islamic Community Commissions" (*Jemaat-i Islamiyye*) for their "autonomy" in Greek Thrace. These were to be found in the three major towns of the region, Komotini (or Gümülcine in Turkish), Xanthi (Iskeçe) and Didymoteikho (Dimetoka).[7]

Nevertheless, if the "*millet* system" survived within a nation-state, it was slightly altered since the mufti had acquired certain legal functions. Under Ottoman rule, the power to judge on the basis of Islamic laws belonged to the *kadi* (or *qadi* in Arabic), but this post was abolished in Greece after the annexation of Thessaly to Greece

[6] On the nineteenth century precedents for this state of affairs in Greece, see Malcolm D. Evans, *Religious Liberty and International Law in Europe*, Cambridge University Press, 1997, pp. 64–7.

[7] The mufti's office in Didymoteikho was created in 1927 following its transfer from Alexandroupolis (Dedeağaç), see Konstantinos Al. Tsioumis, 'I mousoulmaniki meionotita tis Dytikis Thrakis kai oi Ellinotourkikes skheseis (1923–1940)', PhD thesis, Aristotle University of Salonica, 1994, p. 147 and Symeon A. Soltaridis, *I istoria ton moufteion tis Dytikis Thrakis*, Athens: Nea Synora-A.A. Livani, 1997, p. 92.

(1881), because as an institution it contravened the Greek Constitution, which outlawed the existence of extraordinary courts.[8] However, the Greek law ΑΛΗ'of 1882 on the functioning of religious institutions in the regions annexed in 1881 gave the mufti the right in certain legal cases to put forward his opinion (*fatwa*, in Turkish *fetva*) that would be recognised as binding in Greek courts.[9] Until 1913, the number of the cases treated under the mufti's authority was very limited.[10] However, when Greece annexed large parts of Epirus and Macedonia, the religious freedom and communitarian autonomy of their compact Muslim populations were ensured by a new law. Law 2345 of 1920, which put in force the provisions of Article 11 of the Athens Peace Treaty (1913), provided regulations for the formation and function of religious courts. Thus the mufti, who was recognised implicitly by the Greek authorities as the authentic interpreter of Qur'anic rules, acquired the former prerogatives of the *qadi*. Lastly, while the Lausanne Treaty did not refer explicitly to any judicial authority, it included the obligation for Greece to take all the necessary measures vis-à-vis its Muslims in order to ensure that questions relating to their personal and family status were treated according to their customs.[11]

Beside each mufti's office and Shari'a court, Law 2345 of 1920 brought about the establishment of "Islamic Community Commissions", composed of six to twelve members who were normally elected for three years. Charged with auditing budget plans of

[8] N.P. Eleftheriadou, *Oi mousoulmanoi en Elladi*, Athens: P.A. Petrakou, 1913, p. 19. On minority protection in Greece from 1880 to 1920 see Lena Divani, *Ellada kai meionotites. To systima tis diethnous prostasias tis Koinonias ton Ethnon*, Athens: Kastaniotis, 6th ed., pp. 52–63.

[9] G.A. Rodopoulou, *Peri thriskeftikis anexartisias ton Mousoulmanon kai peri dioikiseos kai diakheiriseos ton othomanikon vakoufion en Elladi*, Athens: D.G. Efstratiou-D. Deli, 1913, p. 29.

[10] N.P. Eleftheriadou, *Oi mousoulmanoi*, p. 21.

[11] This involved the mufti's competency to judge, of course, not at will, but on the basis of the Shari'a law, and only on questions of marriage, divorce, guardianship and emancipation of minors, Islamic inheritance and appointment of a new administrator (*mutevelli/mutawalli*) of a community property (*vakıf/waqf*). On all of the mufti's rights and obligations, see Konstantinos Tsitselikis, "I thesi tou moufti stin elliniki ennomi taxi", in D. Khristopoulos (ed.), *Nomika zitimata thriskeftikis eterotitas stin Ellada*, Athens: Kritiki, 1999, pp. 271–330.

income and expenditure, they were responsible for the management of state grants and administration of the community property (*vakıf/waqf*). They were also accountable for the educational matters of their communities such as the hiring, payment and dismissal of teachers, school buildings, curricula and textbooks. Finally, the muftis, along with their judicial prerogatives, were to supervise all these activities.[12]

For the Muslims of Greek Thrace, the minority protection framework resulting from the Lausanne Treaty and previous Greek laws led to the institutionalisation of Islam, as norm and as practice. Moreover, at a time when Turkey and Albania were about to abolish the Shari'a courts and, in the case of Turkey, also the religious schools, this was reinforced by the requirements of the Greek electoral law.

The League of Nations' liberal model for the protection of minorities enforced the attribution of Greek citizenship to the Muslims of Greek Thrace. Among other things, this meant that they had the right to elect members of all local and national political institutions—municipalities, trade unions, cooperatives, Parliament and Senate—and to stand as candidates. Yet the bitter disappointment for the Venizelist Party[13] in the results of the parliamentary elections of 1915 and 1920 led the pro-Venizelist army officers who came to power in 1922 to create separate electoral colleges for the Jews of Salonica and the Muslims of Western Thrace.[14] According to the official justification, the electoral segregation aimed to protect the minorities. However, the main reason for its introduction in the elections to Parliament and Senate in 1928, 1929, 1932 and 1933 was essentially partisan. As for its key results, it ensured the Muslims' representation in Athens and institutionalised their religious difference vis-à-vis the majority in the electoral process, as well as in both Parliament and the Senate.

In consequence, a series of laws and treaties provided Muslims inhabiting Greek Thrace with a complex political system that

[12] K.Al. Tsioumis, *I mousoulmaniki meionotita*, p. 149.

[13] That is the Liberal Party, led by Eleftherios Venizelos.

[14] George Th. Mavrogordatos, *Stillborn Republic. Social Coalitions and Party Strategies in Greece, 1922–1936*, Berkeley: University of California Press, 1983, pp. 236–42.

consisted of at least four deputies, a senator, three muftis, members of "Islamic Community Commissions" and members of city and village councils and trade unions. The whole system would not be complete without mentioning the General Administration of Thrace,[15] a Turkish Consulate, and the local bureau of the Mixed Commission of Population Exchange (MCE), all based in Komotini. Thus, it becomes evident that the role of each element in this complex system interfered in so many ways with the others that it was necessary for the different solutions to a problem, such as the Turkish alphabet issue, to pass through Athens and Ankara, via Istanbul and Komotini.

THE EMERGENCE OF THE ALPHABET ISSUE

When the news of the new Turkish alphabet reached Greek Thrace,[16] Greece was holding its most important election since the traumatic events of September 1922 when the victory of Kemalist troops put an end to the presence of Greek-Orthodox communities in Asia Minor and the idea of a "Greece of five seas and two continents". After six years of government instability, the former advocate of "Greater Greece" and leader of the Liberal Party, Eleftherios Venizelos, was about to make a resounding comeback in the country's political scene. But in Thrace, the parliamentary race of 19 August 1928 was being considered by some protagonists as a chance to test the strength of "two proper nations (*millet*): the Muslim Turks and the Atheist Turks".[17]

The day after the elections revealed that "the bastions of the old mentality" had won the war against "the followers of the new

[15] This was the highest hierarchical division of the Greek provincial civil service. The General Administrator's rank was equal to a government minister.

[16] Until the first days of September 1928, the declarations of Mustafa Kemal (Atatürk) on the "letters revolution" multiplied, see Utkan Kocaturk, *Atatürk ve Türkiye Cumhuriyeti tarihi kronolojisi, 1918–1938*, Ankara: Türk Tarih Kurumu, 1988 (2nd ed.), pp. 482–3. Similarly, the Istanbul newspapers gave increasing importance to the question.

[17] "İslam mebus müntehiblerine-En doğru nasihat", *Yarın*, 27 (15 August 1928/29; Safer 1347), p. 1. The content of the *Yarın* newspaper will be discussed below.

ideas".[18] A week later, the "old mentality" deputies met with the rest of the region's deputies, mayors and other representatives in the "Congress of Thrace and East Macedonia" convened by the Governor General, Th. Theofylaktos. On this occasion, the Governor General gave an interview to the newspaper *Yarın* in which he declared atheism to be the most important factor responsible for the troubles encountered by Christianity and Islam, adding that he respected pious people (*dindar*), and particularly the "old-mentality Muslims".[19]

The Turkish alphabet issue emerged shortly afterwards, at first as a debate between newspapers published by members of the minority. Their chief columnists engaged in a polemic where they confronted each other not as partners in the search for the truth, but as adversaries, enemies who were wrong and dangerous and whose very existence constituted a threat. However, the invectives and the rebukes that they articulated against each other, and the victories and defeats they announced, were nothing but theatre orchestrated according to political models and religious practices.

The first polemic

The debate started with an article by a local teacher,[20] who had been preaching the Kemalist reforms among members of the minority since 1926 when he edited the newspaper *Yeni Yol* (The New Road) in Xanthi. Mehmed Hilmi (1903–31)[21] had studied in the Teachers' Academy of Edirne during the years of the Greek campaign in Asia Minor (1919–22), and since his return to the Greek Thrace he had emerged as a leading journalist of the minority's "enlightened" (*münevver*) and "young people" (*gençlik*), as he described the partisans of the "new ideas". By the end of September 1926 he was editing *Yeni Adım* (The New Step), which

[18] The other newspaper that will be mentioned below, *Yeni Adım*, described these groups by the expressions "eski zihniyet sahipleri" and "yeni fikirlerin muakkibleri", see "İntıhabatın neticesinin neticesi", *Yeni Adım*, 146 (25 August 1928), p. 1.

[19] "Vali Hazretleriyle mülâkat", *Yarın*, 28 (31 August 1928; 15 Rebiülevvel 1347), p. 4.

[20] "Geri kalmamak lazim değil midir?", *Yeni Adım*, 149 (8 September 1928), p. 1.

[21] Ahmet Öztürk, "Mehmet Hilmi ve Batı Trakya'ya hizmet edenler anıldı", *Batı Trakya Dergisi*, Istanbul, XX, 231 (15 July 1986), pp. 11–20.

happened to be backed by the Turkish consulate in Komotini.[22] In presenting the plans of this circle, which included the "Hearth of Turkish Youth" (*Türk Gençler Yurdu*),[23] he put forward a vast modernisation project with direct political implications.[24]

Later, explaining the reasons for the Turkish alphabet reform, he coupled his positivist views with "the subject of the language [which] occupies a very important place within the civilized world's theories of development. The nations that possess languages that are easy to learn and that are appropriate to progress and development save themselves from very heavy burdens. Language has many basic functions within development".[25]

However, when he first welcomed the alphabet reform, he lamented the disastrous state of the Islamic Community Commissions and the education system in Greek Thrace: "If people who know their job were in the *Jemaat*s and education, if there were no fugitives and *hoja*, this year would start by an instruction in the new Turkish letters".[26] In that phase of the polemic, Mehmed Hilmi defined an alliance that consisted, on one side, of "the owners of the old mentalities", the minority's *hoja*s (religious teachers) and *aga*s (landowners) who were deputies and members of Islamic Community Commissions, and on the other of ex-Ottoman political

[22] According to a report, dated 22 May 1927, by the Governor General submitted to the Ministry of Foreign Affairs, see K.Al. Tsioumis, *I mousoulmaniki meionotita*, p. 141.

[23] Among its aims was to bring together the young people of this minority and "in a close and sincere contact with the rest of the citizens' young men. The non-Muslim young citizens are already preserving their existence in this country spiritually and bodily. [. . .] Except that, we are all Greeks (*Yunanlı*) and learning Greek (*rumca*) is the way to take advantage of our right under the laws of this country [. . .] One of the most important desires is to find ways to facilitate the practice and instruction of both Turkish and Greek languages among Turkish young men. [. . .] Of course, we will also follow very closely things of present-day needs like music and sports;" see "Gençlerimizle hasbıhal", *Yeni Adım*, 39 (24 April 1927), p. 2.

[24] In the first anniversary editorial of the newspaper, he defined the aims of this project as "making the Turks of Thrace attain a material and spiritual progress and catch-up with the living standards of the rest of the citizens"; see "Sene-i devrinin münasebetiyle", *Yeni Adım*, 70 (30 September 1927), p. 1–2.

[25] "Yeni Türk yazısı niçin alıyoruz?", *Yeni Adım*, 156 (3 October 1928), p. 1.

[26] "Geri kalmamak lazim değil midir?", *Yeni Adım*, 149 (8 September 1928), p. 1.

refugees who were occupying posts in the muftis' offices, Islamic Community Commissions and minority schools.

The most distinguished among these refugees was Mustafa Sabri (1869–1955),[27] the chief essayist of *Yarın* (Tomorrow), an Islamic tendency newspaper of Komotini. Born in Tokat, a city near Ankara, he was an *'alim* and, after the Young Turks came to power, had become a well-known intellectual of Istanbul. At the beginning of the Greek campaign in Asia Minor he was given a place within the cabinet of the last Ottoman Sultan as *Shaikh al-Islam* (*Şeyh-ül Islam*). As head of the religious hierarchy in the Ottoman Empire, he was strongly opposed to the movement of Mustafa Kemal. After the victory of the "National Forces", he felt obliged to escape from Turkey. By the mid-1920s, he was living in Komotini,[28] and from July 1927 he wrote articles together with his son, Ibrahim,[29] and one of their friends, Hasan Fehmi, the publisher of *Yarın*.

Some days after the teacher's article, Mustafa Sabri answered, declaring that the true reason for the adoption of Latin characters was the hostility "of the new Turk" against "the Arab", which was nothing less than hostility towards religion.[30] Having ended his first editorial on the alphabet issue by an accusation of heresy and a prophecy,[31] the former *Shaikh al-Islam* proceeded to a standard religious practice: the issuing of a *fatwa*.[32] Since several people were asking if "the Latin letters" resulted in any harm to the Islamic religion, in his *fatwa* the former *Shaikh al-Islam* tried to address two

[27] İsmail Kara, *Türkiye'de İslamcılık düşüncesi. Metinler/Kişiler II*, ilaveli 3 baskı, 1997, pp. 383–5.

[28] It was the birthplace of the *hoja* Ahmed Asim Efendi (1836–1911), who was his tutor in the famous *madrasa* of the Fatih Mosque. Later on, Mustafa Sabri married his daughter, Ulviye Hanım.

[29] For a biography of Ibrahim Sabri Rüşdi, born in 1897, see Mahmut Kemal İnal Ibnülemin, *Son asır Türk şairleri*, I, İstanbul: Dergâh Yay, 1988, pp. 2178–82.

[30] "Yeni harflar", *Yarın*, 29 (September 1928; 15 Rebiülahir 1347), p. 1.

[31] "Where are you going, you infidels (*kafir*) of good fortune and of truth? If you want to try a serious reform, given the writings of those who want to be saved from the Arabs, why don't you want to reject Arabic [language]? In this case you will see that neither the *Gazi* (Victorious), nor the *Reis-i Cumhur* (President of the Republic), even more Mustafa Kemal will remain!"

[32] "Latin harflarının dine zararı var mı?", *Yarın*, 31 (26 October 1928; 12 Cumadiyül'evvel 1347), pp. 1, 4.

points related to the alphabet issue. According to his opinion, the advocates of the new Turkish alphabet limited their arguments to the impossibility of writing the Qur'an in the new letters and the value of a Qur'an in the Turkish language. The first was something commonly known thanks to the newspapers that had published the report of the Turkish Language Committee (*Dil Enjümeni*) and some declarations of Mustafa Kemal. Since the Latin letters could not render Arabic words, it was impossible to transcribe the Qur'an in Latin characters. But if Mustafa Sabri agreed that its translation into Turkish was possible, he insisted that such a translation could not be called the "Qur'an". "Because the Qur'anic prescriptions could not be applied to it; the prayer could not be read; [. . .]; and somebody who denies that it was God's word could not be accused of being an infidel. Since it was no longer God's word; and in that case, it is not a Qur'an".

Indeed, from the religious point of view, it was not possible to consider a translation of the holy book into Turkish, or into any other language, as the true Qur'an. This had to do with an intangible point of Islamic dogma, and that was what the former *Shaikh al-Islam* was determined to defend. As a polemicist, Mustafa Sabri was telling the truth in the form of his judgement and by virtue of the authority he had conferred on himself. His *fatwa* made more actors enter the game, and from that moment the issue entered a totally new phase.

The treatment of the issue by the authorities

The muftis and presidents of Islamic Community Commissions of the region published a joint condemnation of *Yeni Adım* and *Zaman*[33] in which they declared that on this subject only *Yarın*, the newspaper which issued the *fatwa* of the former *Shaikh*

[33] "They wanted to replace the ten centuries old script of the Turks in the Muslim schools of Thrace by the Latin characters that have recently entered into use in New Turkey"; see "Latin harfları ve müslüman efkâr-i "umumiyyesi", *Yarın*, 32 (9 November 1928; 26 Cumadiyül'evvel 1347), p. 1. *Zaman* (Time) was a newspaper started by an influential notable of Xanthi, Kâtib Hüseyinoğlu Hamdi Efendi, just before the parliamentary elections. Its contributors included a wealthy merchant of the town, Ayaz-zade Tahsin bey, and an ex-Ottoman political refugee, Sakallı Rifki, see "Yeni bir gazete", *Yeni Adım*, 139 (1 August 1928), p. 2.

al-Islam, conformed to Muslim public opinion. Furthermore, they acknowledged that having an alphabet by which Muslim children could read the Qur'an was an irreversible duty of the Islamic Community Commissions and Muslim parents. As a matter of fact, the Islamic Community Commission of Komotini had appointed as Director of Muslim Schools Ibrahim Sabri, the son of the former *Shaikh al-Islam*, and as teacher of mathematics and the Turkish language Hasan Fehmi, the owner of the newspaper *Yarın*.[34]

Later on, they sent a memorandum to the Governor General of Thrace in which they asked the Greek government to stop the actions of those people "who were attacking in various ways our religion and serving foreign interests".[35] On 29 November 1928 the Mufti of Komotini sent it to the Prime Minister, Venizelos, and to the Ministers of Foreign Affairs, the Interior, and Education and Cults.[36] As for *Yarın*, it published the memorandum adding the following preface:[37]

As everywhere, unfortunately in Western Thrace also, there is a small group of people hostile to the religion of Islam and humanism who strive for a single aim: making the local Muslim population emigrate and destroying its tranquillity [. . .] Unfortunately, we have heard of certain persons who, although members of this population and citizens of the Greek government,[38] invested themselves with the duty to destroy the education or the good manners (*terbiye*) and the tranquillity of the local Muslim population by advertising the revolutionary actions of the new Turkey; and they took this matter up with the government, and they harassed certain *Jemaat* Commissions in order to achieve the teaching of the new letters in the schools [. . .]".

[34] "Tayyinler", *Yarın*, 31 (26 October 1928; 12 Cumadiyül'evvel 1347), p. 4.

[35] K. Tsioumi, "I stasi tis ellinikis kuvernisis".

[36] Ibid.

[37] "Müslümanlar oyuncak değil!", *Yarın*, 34 (7 December 1928; 25 Cumadiyül'ahir 1347), p. 1.

[38] Nevertheless, a document of the German Foreign Affairs Ministry refers to the effort of the Turkish representative of the Mixed Commission of Exchange to shift the focus of the investigation from economic matters to issues like the hat and the alphabet during the delegation's visit to the region in November 1928 (see K. Al. Tsioumis, *I mousoulmaniki meionotita*, pp. 92–4).

Consequently, the Minister of Education and Cults asked the Ministry of Foreign Affairs if international treaties gave the Greek state the right to interfere in this issue raised by the Muslims of Thrace about preventing the use of Latin characters in the Muslim schools of the region. On New Year's Eve, the Ministry of Foreign Affairs replied that the state was not interested at all in what alphabet they used. Instead of any interference, it recommended neutrality since any intervention in support of one group would without doubt provoke the justified protests of the other.[39]

Nevertheless, the local Greek authorities did not follow the instructions from Athens to the letter. At that time, the new alphabet was only taught in a few schools in the countryside, outside the *Jemaat*'s control. Police reports mentioned that, in most of the cases, this teaching was accompanied by wider nationalist propaganda.[40] Therefore, the provincial authorities took measures against the teaching of the new alphabet and its teachers. However, after an intervention by the Prime Minister in February 1929, this ban was lifted, and the General Administration was ordered to permit the teaching of the new alphabet.[41] Even though this order had not been communicated to the towns and the villages of the region until the middle of March, the Inspector of Public Education had already called the suppliers of schoolbooks[42] to a meeting in Komotini in order to inform them about the order and approve drafts of new books. The inspector told the teachers, who were also invited to this meeting, that they were free to teach the new letters and use the approved schoolbooks.[43]

But the issue had not been resolved because the muftis and the presidents of the Islamic Community Commissions still disagreed. However, what was equally important was the difficult position that *Yarın*, Mustafa Sabri's mouthpiece, faced in its polemic with Mehmed Hilmi's *Yeni Adım*.

[39] K. Tsioumi, "I stasi tis ellinikis kuvernitis".

[40] K. Al. Tsioumis, *I mousoulmaniki meionotita*, p. 174.

[41] "Yeni harflara müsaade edilmiştir", *Yeni Adım*, 184 (21 February 1929), p. 2.

[42] They were owners of bookshops in the major towns of the region who provided the local population with newspapers and books, mostly imported from Turkey.

[43] "Emr verildi", *Yeni Adım*, 187 (19 March 1929), p. 2.

The second polemic

Before professing its innocence by stating that *Yeni Adım* did not exist to cause trouble for the government, but for its benefit as well as for the good of the nation, Mehmed Hilmi was pleased to proclaim that continuation of education in the new letters was the duty of every Turkish school and teacher. He urged everybody to start learning the new letters to the best of their ability and said the new alphabet should be taught to the children immediately.[44]

In response Mustafa Sabri pointed out that the authorisation of the Greek government would not be sufficient. But what is surprising is that the very same authorisation led him to put forward a totally new argument against the use of the new Turkish alphabet, an argument never used before during the previous debates in the minority newspapers. Indeed, the former *Shaikh al-Islam* abandoned his polemic on the issue based on Islamic principles to seek a solution in the mountains, near the Greek-Bulgarian frontier:

> *Yeni Adım* continuously refers to the question of nationality . . . Even if the Latin letters could be the national (*millî*) script of Turks, it cannot be the national script of the Muslims of Thrace, because half of them are Pomaks. In consequence, the Latin script is not really the national script either of the Turks or the Islamic peoples (*akvam-i islamiyye*); if the Turks of Western Thrace, by submitting to the apostate and absolutist climate created by the separatist government of Ankara, adopt the Latin script of the Turks as their own, without seeing the harm to religion, how are Pomaks to take part in this business?
>
> The national script of Pomaks is Bulgarian and, by religion (*diyanet*) or nationality (*milliyet*), they have absolutely nothing to do with Ankara that has renounced religion . . . Now, how is the poor Pomak boy supposed to learn so many kinds of script? And to which community of the Prophet (*ümmet*) will he consider himself a member? Will he study the Latin script? Or the script of the Muslim religion to which he is attached? Or the script of the Greek government of which he is a citizen?[45]

[44] Ibid.

[45] "Latin Harflarının kabul etmenin manası", *Yarın*, 41 (22 March 1929; 10 Şevval 1347), pp. 1, 4.

The Prime Minister's decision had reactivated the political model of the polemic that the former *Shaikh al-Islam* fostered, thanks to new territory entered. Through the Pomaks and their vernacular language, Mustafa Sabri was touching upon a sensitive issue of linguistic families, religious alliances and political loyalties that he had never used before in his religious rhetoric. Manifestly the rhetoric he had used since September 1928 did not have the desired results, since the Greek government, which was modernist in essence, had given its permission for the use of the new letters. However, by abandoning arguments such as the incompatibility of the Latin characters to religious needs or the harm caused to the Islamic religion because of the obstacle they presented to the reading of the Qur'an, his polemic had shifted from a religious model to a political one. But what was equally significant was the total redistribution of models that followed.

The editor of *Yeni Adım* interpreted the former *Shaikh al-Islam*'s argument as if it implied that the Pomaks were Bulgarians.[46] Given the Bulgarian policy regarding the Pomaks since the Balkan wars, Mehmed Hilmi was able to exploit this "error". After having rejected it by insisting that the Pomaks were Turks without any difference, the teacher added that it was not right to call the Pomaks "Bulgarians". And he continued: "Today, our Turkish brothers called Pomaks are looking for a way to be delivered from the Bulgarian language". He then closed his article, as Mustafa Sabri had previously done, with a prophecy: "Those who call Mustafa Sabri a Muslim will be exposed to God's wrath". Relying on a legitimacy that his adversary was by definition denied, the teacher pushed the Pomak issue further and finally arrived at a revision of the justification for the "Latin letters":

> If God has sent his Book, his orders, his exhortations, he sent them for the people. So, if we do not understand what he says, how can the value of his orders and the truth of his exhortations be revealed? In this case, we have to translate God's orders and exhortations into our own language in order to understand and apply them in the right way.[47]

By highlighting this fundamental task of the believer, the teacher pointed to an essential principle that he believed had been neglected

[46] "Bulgar diyor . . .", *Yeni Adım,* 191 (1 April 1929), pp. 1–2.
[47] "Yeni Harflar ve Hocalar", *Yeni Adım*, 192 (6 April 1928), p. 1.

by his enemy. The new letters would not just promote the Muslim minority's progress and its struggle to catch up with the rest of the civilised world or the Greek nation; they would be more appropriate to its religious needs. Now it was Mehmed Hilmi who had abandoned his argument based on a political model, to adopt a religious rhetoric.

In response, Mustafa Sabri tried to show the "Muslim trick" (*müslümanlık oyunu*) of the "enemy of religion", but in vain.[48] His assumptions on their language and its script had unleashed a torrent of attacks on the part of the Pomaks of Bulgaria and Greek Thrace who denounced the former *Shaikh al-Islam* and refuted his interpretation of Muslim religion by letters addressed to Mehmed Hilmi's *Yeni Adım*.[49] This situation continued at least until June 1929 when "faithful" Pomaks sent a letter to *Yarın* that was signed by the Mufti of Komotini, as well as by preachers and religious teachers, contesting *Yeni Adım*'s discourse.[50]

Nevertheless, the essential point regarding the introduction of the new letters in the minority's schools was rather different. Almost four months had passed since the Greek government's decision in February to allow the teaching of the new alphabet, and the stance of the deputies and senator was not yet clear. Furthermore, as the owner of *Yarın*, Hasan Fehmi, first noted in a letter addressed to the Governor General of Thrace,[51] the position of muftis and members of the Islamic Community Commissions vis-à-vis both the government and the people, after the petition they had signed against the use of the "infidel letters" in mid-November 1928, was particularly uneasy.

48 "Acem kılıcıyla acemi hamlesi", *Yarın*, 42 (9 April 1929; 28 Şevval 1347), pp. 2–3.

49 "Bulgaristan mektubu: Mustafa Sabri Müslüman da değildir", *Yeni Adım*, 197 (24 April 1929), p. 2 and "Yeni Adım gazetesi müdüriyetine", *Yeni Adım*, 199 (4 May 1929), p. 2.

50 "Mukabil açık mektub", *Yarın*, 45 (14 June 1929; 7 Muharrem 1348), pp. 2–3. Another letter was sent by *Yarın*'s readers in the Balkans, see "Kar'ilerimizin mektupları: Kemalcı Pomaklar'a açık mektub", *Yarın*, 46 (28 June 1929), p. 4.

51 "Açık Mektub: Trakya Vali Umumisi Teofilaktos efendi hazretlerine", *Yarın*, 42 (9 April 1929; 28 Şevval 1347), p. 1.

The spelling mistakes

On Tuesday 11 June 1929, "a strange and farcical event" took place.[52] The school in the Şehre küstü quarter of Komotini was holding final exams, and *Yarın*'s staff members, Ibrahim Sabri, Director of Muslim Schools, and Hasan Fehmi, who was himself a teacher, visited the school in order to attend the exams in spelling.[53] At that time, the new letters were not of course in use in that school, but the Director of Muslim Schools discovered that the students were writing Turkish words of Arabic etymology as they pronounced them, and not necessarily as they were written in Arabic. On seeing the spelling mistakes, the son of the former *Shaikh al-Islam* asked the teacher of the school, Mehmed Pastira, why he had not corrected these words. The dialogue they had, as reproduced by *Yarın*, presents the terms of the dispute and reveals the annoyance provoked by the alphabet issue:

Schoolteacher – We are Turks. We are not attached to the old Arabic spelling. That is how the new Turkish spelling is !

Director of Muslim Schools – This is an ignorant idea. Do you teach ignorance at school? Are you trying to simulate words like « ma'r-i-fet » [معرفت, education] to a spelling based on the Latin alphabet like « ma'rifet »[معريفت]? I will not permit this kind of audacity.

Schoolteacher – It is you who is the ignorant one! We are Turks! It does not matter how; one day we will adopt the Latin script. Tiring children with Arabic spelling does not make any sense. I have abolished the Arabic spelling here. I do not recognise you; I am the chief of this school!

Director – You are being rude.

Schoolteacher – It is you who is the rude one![54]

The schoolteacher's answer resulted in a row that degenerated into a fistfight. It was evident that a difficult and defining moment had come for the partisans of both the old and the new letters, as well as for the Islamic Community Commission of Komotini that was responsible for the appointment of both the schoolteacher and the Director of Schools.

52 "Maşa'llah terbiyecilere. . .", *Yeni Adım*, 206 (15 June 1929), p. 3.

53 "Şayan-i dikkat bir hadise", *Yarın*, 45 (14 June 1929; 7 Muharrem 1348), p. 3.

54 Ibid.

The next day, the son of the former *Shaikh al-Islam* submitted a report to the president of the *Jemaat* Commission, in which he explained that he would not cooperate with teachers who were trying to spread atheist ideas. Therefore, Ibrahim Sabri asserted, it would be necessary to dismiss either the schoolteacher, Mehmed Pastira, or himself. A day after, his collaborator, Hasan Fehmi, asked the mufti to intervene, since the *Jemaat* was placed under his supervision in accordance with the law. From the columns of his newspaper, he requested the mufti to exert his authority and asked how it was possible for "servants of the ideals of atheism", like Mehmed Pastira, to be preachers in the largest mosque of Komotini.[55] On the other hand, this teacher and preacher had already addressed the deputy Hafiz Ali Galip, one of those "owners of the old mentality" who had been elected in August 1928, in order to obtain the dismissal of the Director of Muslim Schools.[56] According to *Yeni Adım*, the question had spread throughout Komotini.

Finally, the problem was raised for minority politicians in a way that they could no longer ignore. A series of acts, practices and thoughts had transformed the issue of the correct use of the Arabic alphabet into a question about the adoption of the new Turkish alphabet. But the elements of the problem that the different solutions were attempting to respond to arose from a whole web of social, economic and political processes.

To be or not to be?

At the end of the Turkish-Greek war (1920–22), the Lausanne Treaty was supposed to be the basis on which Greece and Turkey could settle the questions that rose from the exchange of populations. Nevertheless, the large-scale colonisation of Thrace, and Northern Greece in general, jeopardised the application of the treaty's clauses. The massive arrival of Greek Orthodox refugees from Anatolia and Turkish Thrace presented Greek officials with the solution to the so-called problem of national homogenisation,

[55] Ibid.

[56] "Maşa'llah terbiyecilere. . .", *Yeni Adım*, 206 (15 June 1929), p. 3.

which was acute at that time in the Northern provinces. But this project did not allow Muslims in Greek Thrace fully to enjoy their civil rights, specifically the free disposal of their property. At the same time, the Ankara government's Turkification programme of the economy and of other domains of public life was posing serious problems for the Greek Orthodox minority of Istanbul.

When Turkish-Greek talks started in July 1924, two sensitive matters were high on the agenda: Turkish permission for the Greek Orthodox inhabitants of Istanbul to return home[57] and the return of properties seized by the Greek authorities from Muslims of Thrace. The Greek authorities were already settling their refugees in these properties while the Turkish authorities were giving a new, stricter, definition to the term "established", referring to the Greek-Orthodox inhabitants of Istanbul who were exempt from the population exchange.[58] By that time, the Greeks started to suspect that the Turks were using the *établis* question in order to achieve a total exchange of populations.[59] A first accord signed in Ankara on 26 June 1925 could not be applied, and in January 1926 the Turkish Ministry of Foreign Affairs declared itself in favour of a complete exchange of minorities. In other words they advocated an exchange of those who were considered until that time as exempt from the exchange, the Muslims of Greek Thrace and the Greek Orthodox inhabitants of Istanbul.[60] Although some Greek officials also recommended this solution, Greece preferred to avoid a new exodus involving the Greek Orthodox inhabitants of Istanbul because it would result in a new economic catastrophe.

Subsequently, negotiations between Greek and Turkish delegates did not really make progress, and some advocates of the proposed exchange of minorities appeared in Greek Thrace where there

[57] i.e., those who had fled from the city during the Turkish war of independence.

[58] Iphigeneia Anastasiadou, *O Venizelos kai to ellinotourkiko symfono filias tou 1930*, Athens: Philippoti, 1982, p. 12.

[59] Alexis Alexandris, *The Greek Minority of Istanbul and Greek-Turkish Relations, 1918–1974*, Athens: Centre for Asia Minor Studies, 1983, pp. 113–15.

[60] K.Al. Tsioumis, *I mousoulmaniki meionotita*, p. 67.

were even some rumours concerning the future liberation of the region by Mustafa Kemal.[61] The Inspector of Minorities,[62] K. Stylianopoulos, who visited Thrace a few days before the episode of the spelling mistakes at the school in Komotini, gave an accurate account of the origins of the rumours concerning a total exchange of minorities and the liberation of Thrace. Although his reports may be considered as a perfect example of Greek Orientalism of that period,[63] his remarks on the main partisan groups and Greek policy towards them help us to understand the way Greek-Turkish relations were reflected in the alphabet issue, even if nothing was mentioned about the school incident.

According to his reports, the activities of the modernists grouped around the newspaper *Yeni Adım* and the "Turkish Youth Associations" went beyond organising football matches, theatre performances or the teaching of the new alphabet. Not only were they promoting the Kemalist reforms, the inspector argued, they were unjustly blaming the Greek authorities and encouraging rumours, such as rumours of the takeover of Greek Thrace by Mustafa Kemal or the exchange of minorities. In fact, these modernists were part of a well-organised propaganda campaign masterminded by the Turkish Consul in Komotini.[64] They were proceeding systematically and had gained ground, mainly among

[61] This was an older scenario current at least since October 1922, even in Egypt, where Kemal was compared to Muslim heroes like Khalid ibn al-Walid or Saladin and was expected to follow his successes in Anatolia by first reconquering Thrace, then liberating Syria from the French and, at last, entering Egypt, see Israel Gershoni and James P. Jankowski, *Egypt, Islam and the Arabs: the Search for Egyptian Nationhood, 1900–1930*, New York: OUP, 1986, p. 47.

[62] On this special bureau established on 4 April 1929 within the Prime Minister's Office, see Konstantinos A. Tsioumis, "I thesmothestisi epitheorisis 'Ethnikon, thriskeftikon i glossikon meiopsifion' apo ton El. Venizelo kai i mousoulmaniki meionotita", *Valkanika Symmeikta Thessalonica*, 7 (1997), pp. 185–98.

[63] For example, he described the minority as "a tradition-bound people; a fact responsible for its backwardness on matters of social modernisation. They devoutly practise their religion; they are very attached to the Islamic principles and their religious organisation is in a good state". See K. Al. Tsioumis, *I mousoulmaniki meionotita*, p. 147.

[64] Ibid., pp. 251–2.

the "most" educated young people of Xanthi, Komotini and Didymoteikho.[65]

Consequently, the modernists had fallen into disfavour with the Governor General and some civil servants who expressed their support for the conservatives.[66] This was clearly seen in their education policy since they imposed the appointment of anti-Kemalist political refugees to teaching posts. However, this proved to be an unsuccessful policy for it provoked a fierce reaction from many families, many of whom removed their children from the schools. The "fugitives" were considered as auxiliaries and agents of the Greek administration because they had collaborated with the Greek army during the occupation of Anatolia (1919–22).[67]

However, the Inspector of Minorities found the reaction of the local Greek authorities excessive in comparison to the Greek state's non-interventionist policy regarding the disputes between modernists and conservatives.[68] In the case of the new alphabet, they had prohibited its teaching despite the directive of the Ministry of Foreign Affairs, but later this measure too was revoked after the Prime Minister's intervention. Such ill-fated decisions and actions had created a feeling among the minority population that the modernists were being harassed. As a result, the modernists improved their standing in the eyes of the minority population and their work began to acquire a moral and national value.[69]

On the other hand, according to articles in the minority newspapers, the local Greek authorities had appointed both anti-Kemalist political refugees and the conservative notables of each town to the offices of mufti and to posts in the Islamic Community Commissions, the key institutions of the minority "self-administration". The members of these Commissions were not elected by the Muslim population as stipulated by Greek law, but appointed after complex

[65] By "most", the inspector meant a small group of young people who had received an education in the *rüşdiye* and *idadiye* schools, outside the *madrasa* education system which was dominant in Greek Thrace until that time.

[66] Konstantinos Al. Tsioumis, *I mousoulmaniki meionotita*, p. 132.

[67] Ibid., p. 162.

[68] Ibid., p. 163.

[69] Ibid., p. 133.

negotiations between the Muslim notables and intricate consultations with the General Administration. Although the details of such negotiations between Greek state officials and prominent people of the minority are not very clear at this time, it is manifest that these prominent people had concentrated real power in their hands thanks to the legitimacy they enjoyed within the minority and the majority population. The most outstanding among them were the deputy for the region in the Greek Assembly, Hafiz Ali Galip, and the senator Hafiz Salih who was succeeded in the presidency of the Komotini *Jemaat* by his son-in-law, Hafiz Hasan.

Apart from their declaration against the use of Latin characters in November 1928, these notables did not really undertake any initiative to support or discourage either of the scripts throughout 1928 and 1929. But when the school incident happened, a whole set of difficulties was unexpectedly transformed into a general problem. More precisely, the president of the *Jemaat* and the deputy Hafiz Ali Galip had to address several dilemmas because of the alphabet issue; should they support the Director of Muslim Schools, Ibrahim Sabri, or the schoolteacher Pastira? This meant a choice between, on one side, the son of the former *Shaikh al-Islam* and the political refugees, and on the other, the *Yeni Adım* circle and the Turkish consulate; a choice between the unsuccessful measures of the local Greek authorities, and, on the other side, the solution involving the exchange of minorities and the painful liberation of Thrace, which was unpopular for the Greek authorities and the Greek people.

At a time of polarisation and with the addition of the Pomak issue, the strongest faction of Komotini notables found themselves trapped between two diametrically opposed forces—Islamism *à la* Sabri vs. modernisation *à la Yeni Adım*—which for different reasons were either appealing or repugnant to the minority people and the local authorities. Consequently, at the end of June 1929, with the municipal elections of 4 August fast approaching, the most popular deputy for Thrace, Hafiz Galip, and the Senator for the Muslims, Hafiz Salih, faced two options that embodied at the same time several problems to which they had to respond. In the end they chose to dismiss both the Director of Muslim Schools and the schoolteacher.

Of course, it was neither a just nor a definitive solution, but a response necessarily rooted in the soil that had nourished these problems. Obviously, the *Jemaat* Commission that was in place did not enjoy sufficient legitimacy to announce such a twofold decision at the same time. The schoolteacher's dismissal was announced first, before the municipal elections. As in the parliamentary elections a year before, *Yeni Adım* faced two currents of thought in Komotini: the "young" and the "old mentality people".[70] However, it was not the same for *Yarın*. The delay in the announcement of the decision concerning Ibrahim Sabri[71] was proof that the *Jemaat* Commission was more like a business association under the influence of the deputy Galip than an institution under the supervision of the mufti.[72] In fact, gossip about the dismissal of the Director of Muslim Schools was circulating before the elections, but no decision could have been announced officially before the appointment of a new Islamic Community Commission.[73] Finally, the Commission was formed at the end of August and the dismissal of the son of the former *Shaikh al-Islam* was announced the following day.[74]

By the end of the elections, *Yarın* had already added a new "nation" to the "nations" composing the local "Muslim community". According to an editorial on the anniversary of its second year, between the "overt enemies" and the "true Muslims" there were the "secret enemies" or "the hypocrites".[75] For his part, the modernist teacher, Mehmed Hilmi, continued to observe the growing rift between Mustafa Sabri, one of the Turkish "fugitives", and Hafiz Ali Galip, the leader of "the Komotini fanatics".[76] Conversely, the October 1929 Report of the Inspector of Minorities

[70] "Gümülcine'de belediye intihabatı", *Yeni Adım*, 213 (3 August 1929), p. 3.

[71] "Ödünü patlatmış", *Yeni Adım*, 207 (22 June 1929), p. 1.

[72] "Ma'rif meselesi", *Yarın*, 47 (12 July 1929; 5 Safer 1348), pp. 1, 4. "Hile-i Şeriye", *Yarın*, 48 (26 July 1929; 19 Safer 1348), p. 3.

[73] "Cemaat ne halde", *Yarın*, 49 (12 August 1929; 7 Rebiülevvel 1348), pp. 3, 4.

[74] "Cehlin dinsizliğe hizmeti", *Yarın*, 51 (16 September 1929; 13 Rebiülahir 1348), pp. 2, 4.

[75] "Üçüncü sene", *Yarın*, 49 (12 August 1929; 7 Rebiülahir 1348), p. 1. Probably, the former *Shaikh al-Islam* had in mind the fourth Sura of the Qur'an when he described the followers of the deputy senator group as hypocrites (*münafık*). See 4: 142–3, Sura "An Nisaa".

[76] "Mustafa Sabri ve Ali Galip", *Yeni Adım*, 215 (24 August 1929), p. 3.

referred to the formation of a third group composed of modernists who were on friendly terms with the Greek administration and in conflict with the Turkish Consulate and Mehmed Hilmi because of their policies.[77]

CONCLUSION

This case study illustrates the countdown to the use of the new Turkish alphabet among the Muslims of Greek Thrace through a patchwork of discourses, acts and events. In the domain of discourse, as has been shown, none of the polemicists such as the essayists of *Yeni Adım* and *Yarın* necessarily used the same type of arguments all the time. On the resumption of their debate, the essayist of *Yeni Adım* for instance, who called himself a modernist, had no difficulty adopting a religious justification for the new letters. This might be the case for the rest of the subjects debated (without any reference to Europe, Europeanisation or European Islam), such as the hat, the position of women and the role of the family. However, this "paradox" suggests that the use of familiar and persistent dualisms centred on notions of progress and tradition has to be made with caution when authors, or social actors in general, are portrayed on the basis of their writings and choices according to the currents of thought they expressed in their times.

In the same spirit, the case of the teacher who, although from a religious background, was not interested either in changing the Arabic spelling or in obeying the authority of both a mufti and a former *Shaikh al-Islam* is equally evocative. More than that, however, the midway solution to the problem of education personnel given by the prominent people of Komotini, the Galip-Salih group, makes it clearer that hard concepts like modernism and conservatism are of limited value for a thorough examination of the particularly dynamic interactions between the authorities, religious, civil, political or intellectual, and people—whether in a minority or a majority, peasants, workers or merchants—in Greek Thrace during the inter-war period.

[77] K.Al. Tsioumis, *I mousoulmaniki meionotita,* p. 134.

To put it more simply, what was at stake behind the debates on the Kemalist reforms or Islamic values, for those "Muslim" notables who had not migrated to Turkey during the previous years, was far more complex and thus difficult to solve. If their ultimate goal was to assert their position as intermediaries between the local Greek authorities and the "Muslim" population, the establishment of social networks was an essential part of their task. However, this proved to be insufficient within the uncertain climate created mainly by rumours about the exchange of minorities, until the Turkish-Greek friendship of the 1930s. Each one of the groupings they formed had to proceed to delicate manoeuvres by taking into account different conflicting political, social and economic interests; these perhaps prevented them from holding open attitudes and clear stances with regard to questions of general interest such as the reform of education and the alphabet, or local issues such as the settlement of the exchanged population or the political refugees.

Therefore, the extent to which comparisons can be made between the Muslims of Greek Thrace and the Middle Eastern or European Muslims for the period that started immediately after the First World War is limited. And any attempt to relegate all their disagreements, more common of course to those Muslims in the Balkans or Turkey, to a simple clash between modernists (or Kemalists) and conservatives (Islamists, reformists or not) is more likely to fail.

INDEX